Derek Partridge

The Seductive Computer

Why IT Systems Always Fail

 Springer

Derek Partridge
University of Exeter
Emeritus Professor of Computer Science
Exeter EX4 4QF
United Kingdom
D.Partridge@exeter.ac.uk

ISBN 978-1-84996-497-5   e-ISBN 978-1-84996-498-2
DOI 10.1007/978-1-84996-498-2
Springer London Dordrecht Heidelberg New York

British Library Cataloguing in Publication Data
A catalogue record for this book is available from the British Library

Library of Congress Control Number: 2010937104

Printed on acid-free paper

Springer is part of Springer Science+Business Media (www.springer.com)

For Azzie and Ethan, the bookends of my life.

Dogs get mange. Horses get the staggers. Soldiers of fortune get malaria and computer programs get errors. Without doubt, error is a disease endemic to software — and a congenital one at that. The infection sets in before the first page of code is written. No computer system has ever been born without it; it's the automaton's answer to original sin. Phil Bertoni, 1983[1]

---

[1]Quoted by D. Lubar in *It's Not a Bug; It's a Feature* (Addison-Wesley, 1995) p. 202.

Acknowledgments

With more than two decades of on-and-off manuscript development to recall, I should start by apologizing to all those who have helped me in one way or another over the years but do not figure explicitly below. Sorry.

It was an invitation in the summer of 2009 from Regenia Gagnier to speak at the Exeter Interdisciplinary Institute Workshop on Emergence that re-ignited my enthusiasm, and I finished the manuscript. The spark was a realization that the programmer is grappling in high-precision mode with intractable emergent complexity.

In 1991 Margaret Boden sent me a very encouraging letter after reading an early speculative draft. So I persisted, and a few years later Celia James kindly read and commented extensively on an initial complete draft. Very usefully, she detailed the extent of my inability to communicate technical matters to non-technical persons. In modern times, Antony Galton has given me extensive feedback on a later version of the manuscript. Ken Paap wrote the original basis for Chapter 12, and I thank him for his permission to use it. Jacqui Christmas, Richard Everson, Chris Fields, Bob Malcolm and Yorick Wilks have all taken the time to read and comment on various chapters. Long discussions with Alasdair Forbes, the other constant gardener, opened my eyes to the possibility of worlds beyond the reach of empirical science. So soul and psyche may have roles in compulsive programming, but not in this book. Finally, a host of useful comments on the complete manuscript were provided by Tim Denvir. With all this help, I have managed to correct many errors, fill gaps and eliminate inconsistencies. However, a correct or perfect manuscript is almost as unlikely as a similarly faultless IT system, which (as you'll know if you read this book) is a human impossibility, so maybe blame for the remaining imperfections can be left hanging.

Preface

On the 12th of March 2009, the UK government announced that an Information Technology (IT) system for tracking prisoners from sentence to release, NOMIS, had been abandoned. Why? Because the National Audit Office had determined that the IT system's main aim of supporting end-to-end offender management would not be fulfilled. In addition, this unfinished IT system was two years behind schedule. Yet, the original £234 million estimate had blossomed to £690m of which the taxpayer had already put in £155 million.

Sadly, this was not a one-off, expensive, IT-system disaster. It was just the latest in a long line as the London Ambulance Service, the International Stock Exchange, the Performing Rights Society and the Child Support Agency (to name but a few) have all learned to their great cost – millions of pounds spent, years wasted and no usable IT system. Why does this keep happening?

Reports on the NOMIS debacle variously blame sloppy project management, overoptimistic planning, unclear financial responsibility and underestimation of technical complexity. The Editor of the technical magazine *Computing* was quoted as laying the blame squarely on this last issue – the proposed IT system was too complex.

Technical complexity, I shall argue, is at the heart of the problem of large IT-system development (and usage), but complexity can come in many forms, and, in this case, compounds to unavoidable unmanageability. The precise nature of this inevitable complexity is analysed and explained in this book. Conventional IT-system technology lures all parties – the technical developers, the system designers, the project managers, and the clients – into grappling with the unmanageable system behaviours that emerge. The inevitability of the consequent emergent chaos is the focus of this book – primarily its technical basis, but also its knock-on effects for project management, cost estimation and client satisfaction.

In 2005, the British Computer Society (BCS) produced a report on the problem of IT-system failure. After noting significant cost overruns on conventional engineering projects (Concorde, the Channel Tunnel and the Scottish Parliament building – none of which was abandoned, incidentally), they explicitly blame IT-system failures on management reasons, not technical reasons. The cynic might be tempted to observe that the BCS would say this wouldn't they. In the further elaboration of their argument the BCS did, however, adduce management's ignorance of the technology, and inability to reduce program complexity as two of the main reasons behind the problem.

The fundamental nature of the underlying technology – programming – is the single main reason behind all of the acknowledged difficulties. Its detrimental effect derives from a pernicious melding of factors from various sources: psychological and sociological problems coupled with unfulfilled mathematical promise and an excessive demand for mastery of fine detail. It is the inevitable escalation of the resultant complexity that will be exposed.

Further evidence that technological difficulties are at the root of the problem comes from the observation that in the USA, where management practices are somewhat different but the technology is exactly the same, the situation is no better. Annual costs of IT-system error avoidance and mitigation are estimated, by the US Department of Commerce, to range from $22.2 to $59.5 billion, and this is, of course, primarily for the IT systems that do get operational. A doubling, it is said, would probably cover world-wide costs, and a further doubling is anticipated in the next decade.

It is difficult to view our computerised society as anything but an ever-growing phenomenon – both reaching out to embrace new aspects of our lives, and simply expanding current activities to provide a more comprehensive coverage. This, I'm sure, you know already. What you are unlikely to know is that all these computer systems are, and will always be, imperfect, which is a polite way to say that they contain errors and will thus go wrong – sometimes irretrievably so. All IT systems will sometimes fail. Over half of the huge cost of IT-system error avoidance and mitigation in the USA is borne by the IT-system users – they are grappling with the failures of the system. Not all IT systems are abandoned as total failures, far from it, but all IT systems are failures to some extent.

As consumers (if that's the word) of this burgeoning technology, we really ought to know what we are getting into. One of my basic claims is that an understanding of how computer systems work (and, more importantly, don't work) is not way beyond anyone, and that possession of a "logical mind" (whatever that may be) is largely irrelevant. This book offers an explanation of modern computer technology that is readily comprehensible to anyone who is also prepared to devote a little effort to the endeavour.

This means that I have to delve into details. How much detail, and what detail?

First, what detail? I shall find no need to bring in bits, bytes, binary arithmetic, formal logic, AND gates, or any other of the similarly irksome objects that are traditionally part of the initiation rights for the computationally naïve. A sufficiently detailed understanding of computer technology is necessary, but it can be gained much less painfully, I believe. I am not hoping to turn you all into programmers, but I shall co-opt you into a small program-development exercise in order to provide the necessary depth in a simple and straightforward explanation of this technology.

How much programming detail? Some programming, involving just seven precise instructions for controlling a machine, is necessary. We gloss over this level of detail at our peril, I believe. Let me illustrate this.

The generally excellent book *Emergence* (Penguin, 2001), by Steven Johnson, is weakest when the author switches from ants and cities to the achievements and future implications of computer technology. Johnson makes much of a neat example of a non-traditional approach to sorting lists of numbers into ascending order. For Hillis, his sorting algorithm was a small boost to the case for his invention of a massively parallel computer. As a technologist, Hillis knew that he had done no more than apply a well-known technology (adaptive hill-climbing en masse, aka simulated evolution) to a special case of number sorting using an innovative procedure to avoid dead-ends. Johnson, a non-technologist, unacquainted with the long history of (and well-known problems associated with) adaptive hill-climbing procedures, misses the details and jumps to the conclusion that Hillis' demonstration has opened a new route to the stars. Hillis, however, was under no such illusion; he knew that if his little demonstration had pushed away from the earth-bound morass of conventional programming, it had only shown how to climb one very small and very specific type of tree. It is technical details that lay bare the non-technologist's misconception.

But exactly how much detail do you need to avoid such pitfalls? Whatever level I aim for, it will be too much for some readers, and too little for others. So, I have introduced a variety of strategies for making this a variable level-of-detail book.

Firstly, I have picked up on the advice that Mack of Palace Flophouse fame gave John Steinbeck about how best to make *Sweet Thursday* an improvement on *Cannery Row*.

> I ain't never been satisfied with that book *Cannery Row*. I would of went about it different ... Sometimes I want a book to break loose with a bunch of hooptedoodle ... But I wish it was set aside so I don't have to read it ... Then I can skip it if I want to, or maybe go back to it after I know how the story come out.

So, in the chapters where I feel compelled to break loose with a bunch of hooptedoodle (although Mack and I attach somewhat different meanings to this word), I've set them aside. These diversionary excursions can then be skipped, without real loss, pain or guilt, by the reader who feels so inclined. There is not even a need to return to them when you know "how the story come out", but feel free to do so, if you wish.

Secondly, each chapter concludes with a bullet-point list of the specific technical points that it has championed. The reader thus has various options with respect to every chapter: to accept the bullet-points on trust and forego the preceding technical arguments (with the opportunity to go back at some later stage if so motivated); to accept the bullet points as well-known and so just skip or skim the chapter; to accept the bullet points as foci of particular importance, interest or error, and read the associated chapter closely.

Thirdly, the book's penultimate chapter is explicitly structured to permit the browsing of detail at whatever depth the reader feels comfortable with, or feels is necessary. This is explained below. Lastly, each chapter is associated with detailed endnotes that, once more, can be selectively read, if so motivated, or totally ignored by Salinger's "amateur reader who just reads and runs". In addition, the endnotes often provide a hook into the published sources where the interested reader can find even more detail.

The book is divided into four parts: Part I is designed to be a relatively painless but sufficiently-detailed attempt to provide the non-computer literate reader with the necessary basics of modern computer technology. The computer literate might also skim it with profit, because it provides the basis for many subsequent examples. This is not a 'How to program' book; it delves into the essential nature of programming just as far as is necessary to properly appreciate both the opportunities and difficulties involved. Becoming a programmer and appreciating the difficulties (as well as the attractions) of the craft are two different things. It is this latter competence I am aiming to convey.

Part II addresses the consequent system-level problems. It begins by examining computer addiction, or less dramatically, computer dependency which is a widely acknowledged syndrome within the community of computer enthusiasts. Investigations of this phenomenon have tended to concentrate on the detrimental effects it has on the dependents themselves, or on their nearest and dearest. These relatively few and extreme cases are the tip of an iceberg, the vast bulk of which (as is the way with these chill leviathans) is largely invisible, yet capable of causing great damage. Importantly, this damage is not so much to the enthusiasts or technologists themselves, but to the rest of us – the IT-system-dependent society. So, as more properly befits my expertise, I shall be probing in a new direction. I shall direct your attention away from the adverse effects on computer people. Instead we will look towards the repercussions for IT-system development and so to the consequences for IT-system users – consequences that we must all endure.

Part III adds a more positive line of argument: innovative approaches to tackling the problems are described. The first three are potential patches for current practice; the last two are more speculative, but hold some hope for major renovation of current technological practice. Neither is a reiteration of the popular suggestion that from bottom-up rule-driven anarchy something wonderful will emerge. This is the fast (and easy) track to emergent chaos. Biological systems, which provide a framework for one innovation, are both complex and reliable. How is it done – incremental growth and redundancy? The Internet is an (accidental) example of the 'organic growth' approach to IT-systems development. It may be that the organic world is hiding a completely new framework that computer technologists might usefully adopt, adapt, and exploit. The second innovative technology might be termed a digital revolution, but a reversal of the ongoing revolution in UK TV broadcasting – the proposal offered is to abandon total reliance on digital and move to admit some analogue.

In Part IV, the main chapter provides an overall summary but one that is designed to provide an alternative entry point into the book for the eclectic reader. Each of the earlier chapters concludes with a bullet-point list summarizing its contribution to the overall case I am making. This penultimate chapter repeats these summary lists, and further summarizes them. My idea is that an efficient read (indeed a strategy for deciding what to read in detail) is to look at this chapter and see how "the story come[s] out." This super summary, which is linked back to the individual chapter summaries, should quickly clarify where what I have to say fits in your personal spectrum of interest, from thought-provoking and unexpected to simple and obvious. Then from this personal positioning, it should be possible to decide which chapters might be read with profit and which might be skimmed or even skipped (due to either a pre-existent competence, or a reluctance to engage fully with technical detail on a first read). The final chapter presents the totality of my case in soundbites whose justification is all of the foregoing.

All IT systems harbour errors that nobody knows about. IT systems control much of your life (and it's only going to increase). Now you should feel suitably motivated to read this book in order to learn why this highly disturbing state of affairs exists.

Contents

Chapter 1
Introduction

Anytime an engineer puts his arm around you and tells you not to worry because something can't possibly happen, then that's the time to be really scared[1]

Coasting into Heathrow Airport after a smooth night crossing of the Atlantic Ocean is typically a peaceful experience in a modern jetliner despite the unwelcome intrusion of several bad meals, out-of-focus film shows and the duty-frees presentation. The ease, speed and comfort of this major translocation are all down to advances in technology – aerodynamics, electronics, materials science and computer software technology, i.e. Information Technology (IT), which is mostly programming. But when the air-traffic controller's IT system hiccups and falters, that is the point where an appreciation of the supreme benefits suddenly evaporates, to be replaced instantaneously with a concern for the imperfections in this wondrous technology (to put it mildly).

On October 14, 1989, at 9.46 a.m., in the middle of the morning rush hour of flights in and out of Dallas Ft-Worth Airport (the centre of the second most-crowded airspace in the USA), the airport's air-traffic control (ATC) computer system crashed – i.e. ceased working.

It was also the day of the football match between Texas and Oklahoma, locally a very big event that thousands fly in to attend. It was this incoming volume of flights (many small and unscheduled) in addition to the rush hour loading that was overstretching the capacity of the ATC system. The controllers realised this, and authorisation was given for a new extension (recently acquired specifically to accommodate this sort of temporary overload) to be added to the system. On one of the many terminals within the local ATC network the necessary instructions were given correctly for the new extension to be added to the overstretched system.

Unfortunately, however, the particular terminal from which the instructions were given did not possess the proper authority for initiating such a significant change to the ATC system. It became confused and faltered for just a few milliseconds.

All of the screens displaying full details of each and every aircraft in a given sector of the airspace went blank, but only momentarily. As the screen images re-emerged and the phosphor dots settled, the ATC personnel were appalled to see

D. Partridge, *The Seductive Computer: Why IT Systems Always Fail*,
DOI 10.1007/978-1-84996-498-2_1, © Springer-Verlag London Limited 2011

that the displays had become jumbled and that certain information being displayed was clearly wrong – hence none of it could be trusted.

It was not until 30 minutes later, after a total shutdown and reinitialisation of the complete ATC system, that proper computer-aided management of the local airspace was restored. In the frantic intervening half hour, no collisions or crashes occurred, but only because all take-offs were halted, all new incoming flights were diverted elsewhere, the ATC personnel, working from memory with pencils and paper, applied their considerable technical skills, and finally the necessary luck was available. It could all have ended tragically differently.[2]

The natural response to such a story is relief (that it all happened to someone else), relief tinged with some appreciation of the horror of the situation for those concerned.

Any lesser response would be foolish. Or perhaps the more cautious reader will think that the real foolishness is to place one's life at the mercy of modern technology in the first place.

So, you don't fly in aeroplanes, or do any dangerous modern things (such as bungee jumping, joy riding, and you're not going to volunteer to be an astronaut)? Anyway experiences such as those sketched out in the above story are (mercifully) few and far between. However, for you who lead such a cautious life, the high dramatic peaks may be avoided, but actually the worst problems are to be found in the cosy valleys of everyday life. In fact, if you are capable of reading this book at all, then you're involved – modern computer technology shapes your life, and if you don't think that's true, it's even more important to read on.

In 1992, the London Ambulance Service took delivery of a new IT system, a computer-aided despatch (CAD) system. As expected for a large IT system, it cost millions of pounds to develop over a period of years. In October of that year it was abandoned as useless, indeed, worse than useless. It was positively dangerous. After commissioning the CAD system, the entire despatching structure quickly descended into chaos: ambulances arriving hours after patients had either died or had made their own way to hospital.[3]

In the same decades, the TAURUS IT Project for the International Stock Exchange was soon cut down to TAURUS II with estimated minimum development costs of about £14.5 million, but projected to save some £30 million a year. After further millions of pounds were spent, the Project was finally abandoned.[4]

In the first decade of the new millennium, a new £456 million IT system for the Child Support Agency (CSA) was meant to sort out many of the problems of tracing a non-paying parent and extracting financial support for the child. But in January 2006, the BBC News reported that not long after the system was installed in March 2003, it became apparent that claims were being processed so slowly that a backlog was building up. A backlog of 30,000 cases was building up each month, with an estimated 170,000 waiting to be processed. A new simpler system for calculating maintenance payments was introduced in March 2003 for new cases – but this could not be extended to the older cases because of problems with the computer system.

Department of Work and Pensions research suggested most CSA staff were overwhelmingly negative about the new computer system and unhappy with the level of training they had received. Staff told researchers that difficult cases were sometimes deleted and others stockpiled and never dealt with. Some staff knowingly entered incorrect details into the system to get it to move cases on, while others devised ways of avoiding talking to clients over the phone. The IT system was axed.

And so it goes on. In the Spring of 2009, we hear from the BBC in London that a multi-million pound IT system designed to track offenders from sentence to release has failed. In 2004 the National Offender Management Information System (NOMIS) was planned with an estimated cost of £234 million. But by July 2007, it was 2 years behind schedule, estimated costs had soared to £690 million, and it failed to do what was required. In 2009 the original system was officially abandoned; five separate smaller IT projects are now planned, and a snip at a mere £513 million (est.). Watch this space.

Perhaps the UK is particularly bad at IT-system development? Not so. A similar list of failures and cost (and time) overruns in the USA suggest this is not the case. In the late 1990s, a survey[5] of $250 billion worth of IT-system development by US companies found that 31% of the 175,000 projects were cancelled before completion. Indeed, a US survey by their Department of Commerce[6] states that "the annual costs of an inadequate infrastructure for software testing", i.e. IT-system problems, "is estimated to range from $22.2 to $59.5 billion." Software testing as will be introduced below (and dealt with in detail subsequently) is the badly flawed reality of IT-system validation.

> We have a perfect record on software schedules – we've never made one yet (a US General)[7]

How can this happen? How do hundreds of millions of pounds, and years of time, get eaten up unexpectedly just programming a computer? And then how can the resultant IT system behave so badly that it is abandoned? Surely the technologists can check that their IT systems are working correctly before they are allowed to go operational?

Let's suppose that your native adventurousness makes you rash enough to open a bank account. In all likelihood you will regularly receive comprehensive summaries of your personal banking activities – a monthly bank statement. An IT system is crucially involved with making this slick and accurate service possible, and it can extend the service to provide, for example, a virtually instantaneous statement of financial solvency on demand. But does the bank's IT system always get it right? If you doubt this, you can always do the sums yourself as a check. But can you? What would such a hand-calculation really show?

There are two possible outcomes (assuming that you succeed in completing the required calculations): the two balances, yours and the computer's, agree or disagree.

Suppose you end up with the situation of agreement. Does that confirm that the computer is computing correctly? It might do, but it might not. It could be that there is a mistake in both calculations, but nevertheless, quite by chance, the two final balances agree. This is clearly possible, but perhaps unlikely.

So, excluding this admittedly unlikely possibility, can we now say that we've checked it, and the bank's IT system is computing correctly? Not at all. What we can claim is that it computed the current balance correctly, but this is far from a determination that it always has, and always will, compute your balance correctly. So what do you do? Recalculate by hand to check every statement? Maybe you do, this is a real possibility. But for many applications of computer technology this option is not physically possible (quite apart from constituting a total undermining of the reason for having an IT system in the first place).

A modern IT system operates in terms of millions of computations per second. A mentally agile specimen of *Homo sapiens* with a hand calculator at his or her disposal will clock up less than one calculation per second when all is going well. The total population of the British Isles could thus be gainfully employed hand-checking the work of the IT system that processes personal accounts at the NatWest Branch in Bovey Tracey.

This doesn't seem to be a very sensible idea for a number of reasons. One of which is that successfully duplicating a calculation by hand or any other method, does not in fact tell us much at all. Curiously, it's the failure to duplicate results that provides real information. So, let's consider this other outcome.

After trying for an hour or two with pencil, paper and calculator, the balance you end up with does not agree with the one the bank has sent you. Now, you really do know something for sure: at least one of the calculations is definitely wrong (and maybe both of them). But which is it? Did you make a mistake? Is there a slip in your hand calculation, or did the computer not calculate your balance correctly? Even in this simple example, the correct placement of blame with a high degree of certainty is not possible. Here's a summary of the problem:

Your computation of your bank balance and the computer's	
Agree	Disagree
Both right	One wrong
or	or
Both wrong	Both wrong

Notice that nowhere do we have the option "the computer is right". So what do we do? Typically, the strategy would be to repeat the hand calculation – get someone else to do it, or do it differently, etc. Then, if several such independent recalculations all agree with each other but differ from the bank's computed balance, you would feel justified in getting on the 'phone to your local bank manager (or more likely, the bank's call centre halfway around the world) to register a complaint.

However, it is still quite possible that all your repetitions of the calculation will suffer from the same fault (perhaps a basic misconception about how some aspect of the computation should be done, e.g. how interest is computed and when it's added in). So actually the bank's computer system might have been correct all along. The point is that, even with this simplest of examples of computer technology, determination of whether the IT system is computing correctly is both time consuming and not guaranteed to provide a clear answer; it can never provide a guarantee that the computer will compute your future balances correctly, not even next month's.

You may get to the point where you're pretty confident that the bank's IT system computed your current balance correctly, but this falls far short of a sound justification for believing that this IT system is, in general, correct (even with respect to only account-balance calculations).

An important safeguard in this particular situation is that you will probably know approximately what your balance ought to be, and so a very wrong calculation will immediately be apparent as a problem to be sorted out. For many applications of IT systems this important safeguard is missing[8]

Why do we have to worry about errors in IT systems? Okay, small slips in large and complex systems can never be avoided, but a professionally designed and constructed system should not fail to compute what it was designed to compute, should it? Other large engineering projects such as office blocks and bridges, with a few glaring exceptions, may not always be perfect, but they can be generally relied upon to do whatever they were designed to do. IT systems, considered as large engineering projects, would seem to have a couple of significant advantages:

1. They are formal, mathematics-based systems, not systems reliant upon the approximations of real-world physics such as the interplay between gravity and materials science that will determine the precise curvature of a huge, non-vertical sheet of glass in a building, for example.
2. They are discrete rather than analogue systems, and so promise the possibility of exact precision in place of approximation: your bank balance is a precise number, all other numbers are wrong. By contrast, the curvature of the glass in a building can only be calculated approximately in advance, and the actual curvature must be accommodated once it is observed in the building.

These two points suggest that IT systems really ought to be totally correct. Indeed, for many – curiously, both the computationally naïve who know that computing is akin to mathematics, and many hard-core computer scientists – this is the implication. The catalogue of IT-systems disasters tells us different, for, as will be revealed, both points end up as negative contributions. Poor system design, implemented by programmers, rather than properly trained software engineers, under management that has little appreciation of technical detail: these all certainly contribute to a worsening of the problem. These, however, are all subsidiary aggravations: it is the technology itself that is at the root of the IT-system problem. In order to appreciate this we need first to establish a basic distinction: 'discrete' or 'digital' versus 'analogue' or 'continuous'. The former refers to information in indivisible chunks, and the latter represents information as an unbroken continuum.

So a clock with sweep hands offers a analogue representation of time, the observer can either accept this analogue time (such as, 'it's about 3 minutes to 10') or impose a digital interpretation ('it's 3 and a half minutes to 10'). A digital clock gives you a discrete time, but can tell you nothing more precisely than its most-precise digit. So if it only gave hours and minutes, then you would get '3 minutes to 10' followed by '2 minutes to 10'. For this digital clock, '2 and a half minutes to 10' is a time that does not exist.

A further example that UK residents will recognize is that a good digital signal can give a sharper TV picture than a good analogue signal. But as soon as the signal quality degrades the fundamental difference between digital and analogue is obvious: the digital picture freezes or becomes badly pixilated while the analogue picture carries on smoothly and simply getting generally fuzzier. In the digital case the erratic switching between an excellent picture and a frozen or pixilated one makes coherent watching impossible. In the analogue case, the generally poorer picture is still a watchable show, although a less satisfying experience.

Donald Norman in his book *The Invisible Computer*[9] shares this basic concern about the discrete/digital nature of computer technology, although he focuses on the need for "human-centered design" to make IT systems easier to use – to make them effectively 'invisible' to the user. He makes the point that 'analogue' (or 'analog' as they write it across the water) is derived from 'analogous', and an analogue representation is not necessarily continuous; "an analog device is one in which the representation of information corresponds to its physical structure … If the real world event is discrete, so too will be the analog one."(pp. 138–139). The distinction we will use is between discrete (sometimes digital) and continuous (always analogue).

In order to make this important distinction clear, Fig. 1.1 illustrates a variety of representations of two sorts of numbers: the *integers*, whole, numbers, like – 1, 2, 3, 33, 999; and the *real numbers* in which we use a decimal point to permit whatever value we wish, like – 1.15, 2.01023, 3.0, etc.

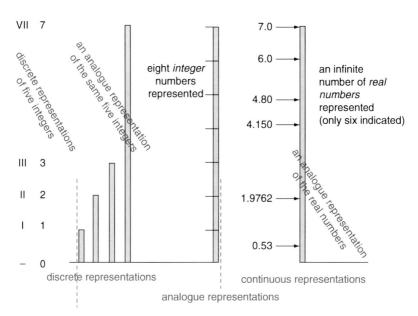

Fig. 1.1 Discrete versus continuous representations

If the *integers* are represented by vertical bars whose length is proportional to the integer value being represented, then this is an analogue representation. So the bar representing the integer "two" is twice is long as the one representing the integer "one". To the left of these vertical bars are two discrete representations of these five *integers*: the most common one, the decimal-system digits 0, 1, 2, 3 and 7 (which is, of course, also the digital representation, most symbols are not digits). This is not an analogue representation because "2" gives no indication that it represents a value that is twice, or even any bigger than, the value represented by the "1" – there is no correspondence between the representations and the values they represent. On the far left is the Roman-numeral representation, which doesn't use digits but is discrete. Notice, however, that in this representation we do tend to get longer strings of characters as the numbers being represented get bigger – e.g. II is twice as long as I, and VII is shorter than VIII – but not consistently – e.g. X and IX are both shorter than VIII. Perhaps this representation is 'semi-analogue'?[10]

The vertical bar to the far right is an analogue representation of some *real numbers*, and although the range is also zero to seven, it does (in principle) represent an infinite number of real numbers.

Notice also that the set of vertical-bars on the left is an analogue representation of the *integers* and it is also discrete – there are five distinct bars (if we include the 'nothing' bar representing the integer zero). In the combined *integer* representation immediately to the right, the full bar can be used to represent just eight integers – there are eight discrete representational points on the bar (illustrated with horizontal lines).

To repeat: the distinction we will use is between discrete (sometimes digital[11]) and continuous (always analogue). The point of the foregoing is to make clear that my choice is simplistic but not misleadingly so.

For Norman: "We are analog beings trapped in a digital [he means 'discrete'] world" of our own making (p. 135). His substantial elaboration of how human strengths do not match the characteristics of discrete systems – hence, computers are awkward – echoes many of my concerns.

To return to our central concern: Is the computer computing correctly? This is an important issue, because IT systems are controlling ever more aspects of our lives, from the bank's IT system dictating personal solvency to the IT system that monitors the local nuclear power station. Yet it is a question that we do not know how to answer with certainty. Worse than this, in many applications simple repeat calculations are not possible because, for example, they are far too long and involved which is precisely the reason why a computer system was used in the first place. Even straightforward tests of the computer system (such as seeing if the bank's computer and your hand calculation generate the same balance for some specimen deposits and withdrawals) may not be practical.

For example, you just can't fly a few aircraft into Heathrow one afternoon when it's not too busy in order to test whether a brand new air-traffic control (ATC) IT system is working correctly. To do a halfway decent job of testing the new ATC system, the pilots would have to be persuaded to run through the gamut of dangerous manoeuvres (if not actually crash a few airliners) in order to ensure that the new system responded correctly. It was even less likely that the President of the USA, one Ronald Reagan at the time, could have given permission to hold even a small nuclear war in order to test the proposed '*Star Wars*' missile-defence system.[12]

It is true that in both cases, some simulation of the required situations is possible. Simulation however, by its very nature, is not the same as the real thing, often not at all the same thing. Testing by simulation introduces another level of uncertainty into the interpretation of test outcomes: does the simulation omit something crucial? It is, of course, exactly the unrecognized situations that, by being unacknowledged, will not be built into simulation tests. Someone decides what to simulate, and how. It is not just possible but virtually <u>guaranteed</u> that unanticipated aspects of the real-world problem will not be represented in the simulated tests – because no one had realized either their presence or their significance. Examples abound in military and safety-critical applications of computer technology because important aspects of such systems can only be tested by simulation.

A case in point is the tragedy that occurred on July 3, 1988: the cruiser USS *Vincennes* shot down a commercial airliner, Iran Air Flight 655. Why this appalling accident occurred has no simple answer. But indisputably, the *Vincennes*' highly sophisticated IT system, called *Aegis* together with its human operators, misidentified the airliner as a hostile military jet fighter about to attack.

No small part of the reason for this tragic blunder was that the *Aegis* system was designed and tested by means of simulations. You can bet that none of the simulations used in the testing involved a commercial aircraft flying quite low (it had just taken off for a short hop across the Straight of Hormuz) and straight towards the vessel under attack. After all, there is really no possibility that a commercial airliner will be cruising low through a battlefield while the battle is in progress (or so the test designers presumably reasoned).

According to Lee's detailed report,[13] *Aegis* was designed for open ocean operation not the relatively close combat it found itself in on this occasion. The *Aegis* system designers very reasonably assumed that any non-friendly aircraft flying low and straight towards the ship under attack must be assumed to be hostile and eliminated as quickly as possible, and in the narrow Straits there was far less decision time than the open-ocean test simulations had probably allowed.

From bank balances to battle-field management and *Star Wars* may seem like a big jump, and it is. But the problems posed by modern computer technology run right through all applications and may, in fact, be worse in the seemingly 'harmless' applications, primarily because we do not pay such close attention to the possibility of error. Some people view with admiration the undoubted marvels made possible by this new technology, others are appalled by them. The extreme responses are right here, but this is not a black-or-white issue.

Computers do have a tendency to polarize humanity. When people first come into contact with computer systems the response is typically love or hate, to put it crudely. For the lovers,[14] a smallish but rapidly growing group who are seduced by the possibilities for control and thus power, the response is primarily fascination – computers exert an irresistible allure for these people. They find computers seductive.

The majority of mankind, however, shies away from the technical detail of programming, either overawed by this mysterious and powerful technology, or repulsed by simple distaste for the cold, rational precision necessary to master these invasive machines. Whatever the reasons behind this bimodal response pattern, it is a worrying situation. With computers insinuated into all aspects of our lives, people should not respond by burying their heads in the sand in the hope that they can ignore this new technology and get on with their lives in blissful ignorance of it. Nor should the response be uncritical, the unquestioning commitment of blind infatuation. Currently, this strategy of 'pretend it's not happening' does work to some extent, but as IT systems continue to infiltrate and eventually saturate the fabric of society so the head-in-sand response will become less effective. In the long term it will lead to personal crisis and societal disruption.

Many people have issued lengthy warnings about the threat to society of the rise of a computer elite. The pronouncements of these modern Cassandras vary from misconceived and alarmist[15] to reasonably measured and appropriate. Unfortunately, it is specimens from the former category that tend to capture the popular imagination and make a big impact. Apocalyptic visions tend to get snapped up by the media. We would all much rather learn about, say, computers becoming more powerful than human brains and thus consigning humanity to a subservient role, than about the continuing frustrations and lack of major progress in artificial intelligence research.[16]

Perhaps most surprising of all – if surprising is the word, alarming might be better – is the fact that the computer technologists who actually wrote the program don't understand it very well either. "Gee, I've never seen it act this way before," is the telling confession of a system designer.[17] One of my goals in this book is to make it quite clear why this odd (to put it mildly) situation occurs, and why it should not be surprising (even if still alarming).

I must warn you at the outset that there are no clear-cut solutions to the problems. However, if I can succeed in explaining the scope of the problem, and the reasons why the obvious solutions do not work, I will have contributed significantly to the search for an appropriate computer technology, or more appropriate uses of the current technology.

Summarizing this introduction:

- IT systems are everywhere, and will continue to infiltrate the lives of all of us.
- We cannot easily check that an IT system is computing correctly.
- IT systems all fail: sometimes immediately and spectacularly, sometimes unobtrusively just once in a while, and sometimes in any combination of these two extremes.
- IT-system failures vary from production of blatantly incorrect results to failure to produce a desired result.
- The interplay of a variety of causes means that all large IT systems are unmanageably complex.
- IT-system complexity is discrete complexity rather than complexity based on continua.
- If, by chance (combined with exemplary practice and much effort), an IT system is constructed with no possibility of failure behaviour, we can never know this.

The root of the problem is the programming technology, and an important non-technical element is the irresistible allure that it has for certain people. The computer technologist is all too often an addict. Like shooting heroin, computer programming is an activity that it is hard to maintain in nothing more than a casual take-it-or-leave-it relationship.[18] The computer is a seductive device; it lures the unwary programmer into domains of excessive complexity and surprising behaviours that just keep emerging. Nothing is easier, and more difficult to resist, than to construct a program that is totally beyond the programmer's conceptual grasp. This program will cause the computer to do totally unexpected things; it will also cause the computer to fail to exhibit confidently expected behaviour. But the worst part is that, however much scrutiny we subsequently subject the program to, once in the computer it will always produce surprises of this sort.

In order to understand why, you will need a (somewhat) detailed appreciation of the basics of the technology. The necessary understanding, however, does not demand a slog through the minutiae of binary arithmetic, nor computer hardware details, which is, of course, all to the good. You won't even have to learn a programming language, I'll just conjure up bits and pieces of a mythical one as and when we need them.

Endnotes

1. This quote comes from *The Day The Phones Stopped* by Leonard Lee (Primus, NY, 1992). This book documents and presents in a non-technical account of many of the horror stories of computer systems going wrong.
2. A true story adapted from Lee's book introduced in the previous note.
3. Computer Scientists, Antony Finkelstein and John Dowell provide a readable short outline in "A Comedy of Errors: the London Ambulance Service case study," and recommend the full analysis of P. Mellor, "CAD: computer-aided disaster" in *High Integrity Systems*, vol. 1, no. 2, pp. 101–156, 1994.
4. A short summary of the TAURUS debacle can be found at http://www.scit.wlv.ac.uk (accessed 03/02/09).
5. One of the results in a Standish Group survey reported by Ted Lewis in the July 1998 issue of *Computer* magazine (p. 107).
6. From "The Economic Impacts of Inadequate Infrastructure for Software Testing", US Department Commerce Planning Report 02–03, May 2002.
7. Quoted by Leonard Lee (see note 1, above) p. 203: it was General B. Randolph, former commander of the US Air Force Systems Command who said this in 1990.
8. Even our simple example is, in fact, a reality of IT-system failure in 2009. The multi-million pound IT system to manage the payrolls of all three armed forces in the UK has been "a familiar tale of growing costs and cock-ups. Barely anybody in the service seems to have received the right pay; and £29m in over payments have had to be recovered." Reported in Private Eye, no. 1234, 17 April to 30 April, p. 28.
9. Donald Norman's *The Invisible Computer* was published by the MIT Press in 1998.
10. The Arabic numerals, the digits themselves, also exhibit this 'semi-analogue' property: in the number system we use e.g. all number representations above "9" are bigger than all those below "9", and all those greater than "99" are bigger than those below "99", and so on. Our 'place system' for representing numeric values, the digital system par excellence, embodies a fundamental analogue characteristic under Norman's view.

11. For most people, 'discrete' is a much less comfortable adjective than 'digital'. It is, however, the correct general term. 'Digital' is just a special case of 'discrete' representation, and most components of computer programs are not digits, but other discrete objects such as characters, keywords and names. Curiously, modern computers are typically called digital computers because the electronic basis is discrete states, usually two distinct states that are most commonly represented with the digits 0 and 1. These distinct states could just as easily be represented by any pair of non-digit symbols, A and B, say, which would only be a little awkward when binary arithmetic is involved. The more accurate term 'discrete computer' jars, so we will stick with 'digital' when accurate and when it conforms to customary usage, but otherwise we will use 'discrete.'

12. The Strategic Defence Initiative (SDI) launched by President Reagan in March 1983, quickly dubbed *Star Wars*, required IT systems in roles that they could never, in practice fulfil. An illuminating critique of the SDI programme was given by David Parnas (an eminent Professor of Computer Science) to accompany his resignation from his consulting role in the project: D.L. Parnas, *Software aspects of strategic defense systems*, Comm. ACM Dec., vol. 28, no. 12, pp. 1326–1335, 1985.

13. These details are the subject of Chapter 9, pp. 214–240, of Lee's book (see note 1).

14. The amazing functionality offered by the Internet and World Wide Web has generated a whole new breed of computer lovers, but these are very different from the lovers of computer programming; it is this latter, much smaller, group that I am focusing on, their thrills come from constructing programs not from ranging across the world whilst sitting comfortably at home. Interestingly, the growth of the Internet can be taken as an example of how large IT systems ought to be developed, see Aaron Sloman's case for this in his article *The iSoft Affair* at www.cs.bham.ac.uk.

15. "Computer One," a novel by Warwick Collins (Marion Boyars Publishers Ltd; new edition, 1997) is fiction, but the author's premise, i.e., that the ongoing expansion of networked computers and systems over the next 40–50 years will result in final net-control of world energy sources and production, was persuasive to many. Using the platform of *The Spectator* (8 Oct. 1994) Collins presented his musings as a real and scary likelihood. My tongue-in-cheek deflation was also published in *The Spectator* (15 Oct. 1994, p. 27), and now we must wait just a couple more decades to see who was right.

16. The UK's BBC television broadcast a *Horizon* programme on the 24 October 2006 that claimed (disingenuously, in my view) to explore the 'what if' scenario when computers will be as powerful as the human brain. It quoted an entrepreneur, Ray Kurzweil, who claimed that this equivalence, "the singularity", will happen by about 2012 without questioning either his basis for this prediction or what 'more powerful' means in this context. After all computers are already much more powerful than human brains in terms of speed and accuracy of both calculation, and information storage and retrieval. My prediction, which I wrote to the producer, is that 2012 will arrive and "the singularity" will be as distant as ever just like the all previous predictions concerning Artificial Intelligence – not for nothing is this known as the science of *hopeware*. (but see R. Kurzweil, "*The Singularity is Near*", Viking Press, 2005). In this case, we only need wait a couple of years.

17. Norman (see note 9) gives this quote as the surprising, but not-uncommon, response of the person who designed the system.

18. *Cyberpunk: Outlaws and Hackers on the Computer Frontie* by Katie Hafner and John Markoff (Simon and Schuster, 1991) tells the story of seemingly hereditary computer addiction in the USA – both father and son are smitten. The father happens to earn a living (working for the National Security Agency) fulfilling his personal preoccupation with computer systems, but the son (somewhat accidentally, it seems) messed up thousands of computers on November 2, 1989, with a small code-hacking experiment of his own. In another of their stories, the authors relate the tale of a computer fanatic who has been ordered by a California court to undergo treatment for his addiction to computer hacking.

Part I
The Joy of Programming

The hacker's creed

We believe that all instructions are created equally crucial to the correctness of a program, and that all programmers, of whatever programming language, operating system preference, or methodological predisposition, have an inalienable right to work without distractions, unlimited access to the keyboard, the liberty to try whatever might work, and the pursuit of every detail in their quest for a good enough program.

Chapter 2
The Happy Hacker, Love at First Byte

King Kong was only 18 inches tall – in movie making every-thing is possible.

(Peter O'Toole in *The Director*)

The Hollywood school of unreality can create whatever is required. It devises stunts such that whatever is required seems to be made manifest. It's the great illusion fantasy, and we love it. Similarly, computer technology (which, incidentally, has majestically pushed back the limits of fantasy made real in the film industry) is virtually unconstrained. It is almost free of the millstones of reality, and this is no small part of the allure. In programming everything is possible.[1] This is as true for the programmer as it is for the Hollywood director, which is to say that it's almost true. Where it is not true turns out to be crucial, as we shall see when it comes to issuing guarantees that the programmer's creations are correct.

In this chapter I shall explain how and why it is that certain specimens of humanity, who otherwise seem fairly normal and come from good homes, get hooked on computer programming. The problem certainly seems to occur more (much more) in the male than the female of the species, and it also strikes the young more frequently than the, let us say, mature individuals. Males in the years surrounding puberty seem to be definitely the most susceptible which is not at all surprising where issues of infatuation are concerned.

As I said, even the most level-headed can be struck down by the happy-hacker syndrome (henceforth HHS).[2] Indeed, I myself am proof of this. Yes, I have to admit it, I was a victim. It struck me in the early twenties, but only missed me earlier because in those dim and distant days home computers in the UK were no more than a gleam in Sir Clive Sinclair's spectacles. It was at University that I first gained access to computer technology. Even then my exposure was very limited, and quite peripheral to my main reason for being there which was to obtain a degree in chemistry.

My chemistry degree course was three long years, and by the end of the first I had grave doubts about chemistry being the life for me. But after another year my doubts had vanished, in their stead was a firm conviction that I was not cut out to be chemist. It's hard to put a finger on what exactly it was that I did not like about chemistry. Certainly, the endless washing up held no attraction for me (an inherently distasteful

D. Partridge, *The Seductive Computer: Why IT Systems Always Fail*,
DOI 10.1007/978-1-84996-498-2_2, © Springer-Verlag London Limited 2011

task at the best of times). This coupled with the olfactory issue, at times a supreme miasmic event which had to be experienced to be believed, was a definite negative. Day in, day out sloshing about with dangerous substances was probably the clincher. It was not the known explosives and poisons that were worrying so much as the ones whose life-threatening capabilities were still being uncovered.

Benzene is a case in point: for a year or more we used it as a substitute for Fairy Liquid – it easily dissolves away incrustations that treat soap and water with utter disdain, it evaporates quickly (which eliminates the drying-up chore), and it is relatively cheap. Then one day, while up to my elbows in the stuff and at the centre of a pall of benzene vapour, a freshly printed directive from the Prof arrived. The gist of it was that benzene was poisonous, carcinogenic, etc. and all benzene-related activities were thus to be abandoned forthwith.

You can perhaps imagine that to a young, red-blooded person, in their prime, and looking confidently forward to a lot of prime-time activity in the next few years, such happenings were a very real disincentive. However, with only one more year to go, I decided to stick it out to the end, but to avoid chemicals as much as possible.

It turned out that in the third and final year the student was allowed to specialize, to choose a particular branch of chemistry as the area for a substantial project. For me there was no choice, theoretical chemistry just had to be my area of specialization. Theoretical chemistry is effectively a branch of mathematics whereas the other areas of specialization all involved that which I had forsworn – i.e., use of chemicals. In theoretical chemistry all that is required is a pencil, paper and an armchair, although a liking for calculation (not to mention an ability to do it) is also a help.

The theoretical chemist finds fulfilment calculating energies of molecules and of chemical reactions. This sort of mathematics typically requires the use of quantum mechanics (which we will not be delving into, rest assured). Quantum-mechanical calculations involve a lot of the usual messing about with numbers – i.e., additions, multiplications, etc. They also involve integration which is a particularly tricky species of mathematical manipulation invented by Sir Isaac Newton during his Easter holidays.

One of the awkward features of integration is that we don't know how to do it exactly on many elaborate mathematical structures, but there are exhausting ways to get it approximately correct, as approximately correct as you wish (time and energy permitting).[3] The upshot of all this is that, although a pencil and paper is all that is required in principle, human life is too short to take the in-principle route, and the few months available to me was hardly time to get started. So in practice, computers must be used which, as we all know, are just fast and accurate adding machines. The sort of number crunching exercise that my quantum-mechanical calculations involved was just the right stuff for computerization.

Consequently, I had to forego my Easter hols (much like Sir Isaac, although I don't know who was twisting his arm and forcing him to invent the differential calculus) and attend a programming course. Needless to say, I was not delighted by this intrusion of the educational world on my Easter break. But given that it would, in effect, permit me to avoid chemicals for the remainder of my degree course, I was prepared to make the sacrifice.

The computer programming language on offer was called FORTRAN, FORTRAN II. Much to my surprise I liked FORTRAN. In fact, within a week I loved it. Now, as a professional computer scientist, this is an embarrassing admission.

"Why such a speedy emotional entrapment?" you might well ask, puzzled by this almost instantaneous infatuation that I have confessed to. I now ask myself the same question, I didn't at the time, of course. Whilst being tumbled along in the midst of a growing romantic attachment one never does, does one? But now, with some few decades and many thousands of lines of FORTRAN between me and that first close encounter of the computational kind, I think I can explain everything.

Fundamentally, it is a question of power, power and the satisfaction of the 'look ma, no hands' phenomenon. A final significant factor is the personal, and at the same time non-personal, nature of human-computer interaction. It's just you and the machine trying to work things out, the rest of humanity is effectively excluded, prevented from intruding.

This last point raises a complex issue, one more in the realm of the sociologist than the computer scientist. So I'll say no more about it for the moment, except to note that it may be at the root of why males are readily afflicted with HHS while females appear almost immune. When you have gained a better appreciation of the technical details that underlie this *liaison dangereux*, we can usefully begin to explore the more nebulous psychological aspects of the problem. There is, I will argue, a significant macho element to software engineering disasters.

Having constructed a good program, we are left with the feelings of power and satisfaction that a successful computer program engenders in the programmer. The notion of power comes from having an exceedingly complex and intricate machine do your bidding. For the reader who views computers as normal home appliances like electric kettles, I might point out that back in the dark ages when I got hooked my university possessed <u>one computer</u>[*] for the use of everyone. So getting control of this beast – a large room full of electronics – may well have been more satisfying to the closet megalomaniac than successfully instructing a modern laptop, but the same principle still holds: the successful programmer has gained control of an intricate and powerful machine. (But note: today most mobile phones[4] are more powerful computers than my room full of whirring machinery – card reader, card punch, tape readers both paper and magnetic, crude printer, massive disc storage device, air conditioning and, oh yes, the central processing unit.)

One can quite easily make a computer number crunch or data shuffle for long periods churning out vast quantities of results with very little programming effort. In fact, it is all too easy to make a computer repeat the same series of computations endlessly (endlessly until someone pulls the plug that is). This is actually one of the problems with this technology, and we will revisit it in due course.

---

[*] Definitional use of special terms, which is also usually the first mention, are italicized and under-lined; they are also Glossary entries. Subsequent use is also italicized if there is a need to empha-size the special meaning used in this book for a word or term that has a different everyday meaning. Because I use bold for programming language keywords, I am left with underline for ordinary emphasis, and occasional foreign words are also italicized.

The great satisfaction that programming can provide stems from the stringent demands of most programming languages in conjunction with the absence of limitations on what might be achieved – in programming it seems as though everything is possible if you, the programmer, are smart enough. What testosterone filled young man is going to throw in the keyboard and admit that they're not smart enough – especially when he can quickly and quietly try whatever comes into his head?

The obsessive concern for detailed correctness exhibited by most computers means that significant programs never work first time. After hours, maybe days of pondering the programmer submits his best effort to the computer which returns the program virtually instantaneously together with a whole catalogue of errors it has found; the programmer (if he wants to remain a programmer) has no option but to think again. This to-and-fro process can continue for very long periods until eventually the programmer gives up, or the computer accepts the program as *grammatically correct* and performs the computations that it specifies.

Suddenly, after repeated rejections, the behaviour that your program has specified emerges from the computer (although often not exactly the behaviour that was expected). However, the computer is finally doing your bidding, and the resultant feeling of satisfaction and power is not surprising. Actually, the computer is, of course, doing your program's bidding, but that's a start. The challenge then is to make yours and your program's biddings identical.

By sheer persistence and intelligent reasoning (the relative mix of these two quantities can vary considerably) the programmer succeeds in compelling the hitherto superior machine to obey his instructions. You, the programmer, start out as the servant spending long periods laboriously sorting out all the errors so quickly and surely spotted by the computer, but once the last error has been corrected, the tables are turned – the computer has no choice but to compute for as long and as tediously as your program specifies. An acceptable program (acceptable to the computer that is) is a powerful object, a talisman of the technological age, and the programmer is (of course) the witchdoctor.

In short, programming is a game. It is a private game. You are free to blunder at the keyboard, no one will laugh at you, and when you succeed they will be mightily impressed. Programming is fun, very private fun. There's no one to ridicule your more feeble efforts. All mistakes and blunders can be kept strictly between you and the machine which doesn't, of course, exhibit any judgemental behaviour. So that's how I, and many thousands of others, got hooked, although I wasn't affected by the introspective allure of the exercise, of course. But then, in the memorable phraseology of Mandy Rice-Davies: I would say that wouldn't I?

'Game' is actually too broad a word for the particular phenomenon that we are considering. It is misleading because it suggests the presence of attendant qualities like luck and chance which don't really come into the programming game. One can, it is true, get something right in a program quite by chance, and good luck never comes amiss in life, but serendipity in any of its manifestations has no real part to play in the game of programming.

This state of affairs is unusual in the gaming world. Most games, it seems, include a good portion of luck, and people presumably want it so. It provides an element of unpredictability to game outcomes. However good the player, there is no guarantee that they will win. Chess is perhaps the popular game that comes closest to being devoid of fortuitousness. It is also a complex game that computers have come close to mastering – anybody but a real chess expert will lose to the best chess-playing computers.[5] I'm not at all sure that there is any causal relationship between the chanceless nature of chess and the high quality of chess-playing computers, but there just might be. The allure of chess and that of programming have a number of features in common.

Those of you who have either dabbled with a home computer or have children or partners that do so will have noted the hours that can be consumed locked with this machine in a struggle for supremacy. It might be Dungeons and Dragons, a war game, surfing the Internet or whatever, but computer games often rival the popularity of television as a face-to-screen activity in the modern world. Television is easier, you just sit back and take what comes more or less, the brain can be put on idle for the duration. But when facing a computer screen considerable high-geared brain-work is absolutely essential.

Computer games can constitute a considerable mental challenge, and they offer you the opportunity to influence events. Success demands concentration and commitment but many are prepared to give it, and for extraordinarily long periods of time. Programming can be viewed as the next step along, a further enrichment of person-machine interaction.

Computer games, however elaborate, contain inherent limitations.[6] The avid computer gamer soon hits up against some of these limitations, and needs to move on. The onward move is often to a new game, but the significant step forward, the one that opens up a whole new and virtually limitless challenge, is the move to become a programmer. Computer games are programs. The scope and limitations built into any particular game are, in a general sense, imposed by speed and memory limitations of particular computers but how these general constraints become manifest in the game depends upon the programmer. To a significant degree, the limitations and opportunities within any computer game are determined by the time, skill and imagination of the person(s) who wrote the program. So, when the excitement of computer gaming begins to pale, the solution is to become a programmer and invent your own computer games. The future then is determined by you, and its limitations are yours too.

The lack of limitations is much the same as the lack of limitations in writing a murder mystery: there are certain fixed points, like someone has to be murdered (or appear to be), but there are infinitely many ways to actually write the story. The real limitations are determined only by the limits of the writer's imagination.

A peculiarity of the programming game is that the rules are open and loose at a general level, but they are tight, fixed (and often quite pedantic) at the detailed level – i.e., the rules about what constructions the computer system will actually accept and act upon.

The general framework of the programming game is:

[a.] spend considerable time writing a program
[b.] give it to the computer

[c.] the computer immediately rejects it indicating numerous errors

[d.] spend time sorting out the errors, and modify the program

[e.] go back to step [b.]

This series of five steps may not strike you as an obviously fun thing to do, but you should be able appreciate that it is a challenge. Fun, after all, exists only in the brain of the player. It is not an inherent property of certain activities. In this game the human intellect is being pitted against a sophisticated electronic machine, an incredibly fast and accurate machine. There is, however, no laughing at the inevitable human errors and blunders. There is no peer pressure. All your weaknesses and inadequacies are just between you and this machine which is lightning fast, unerringly correct and totally committed to the contest, but in an entirely unemotional way. The rest of humanity is excluded from the duel; the rest of the world might well not exist.

What may strike you about my list of five steps (if you're really paying the proper attention) is that it describes an endless procedure. I have in fact omitted some crucial details. Step [c.] should really describe alternative outcomes: the rejection given above, and an acceptance of your program as a *grammatically correct* one. When your program gets the green light rather than the usual red one, as it were, you suddenly become the driver of the machine. The computer has no alternative; it must now do exactly what your program tells it to do (which is usually not quite the same as what you thought you had told it to do). At this point you've won (but just a battle, not the war). The human intellect comes out on top just as it should. Man triumphs over machine yet again. With this victory securely in your pocket, you are free to move on and fix up the program to get precisely the behaviour you intended, or maybe elaborate on the current program to try to make the machine do something just a bit more demanding, or something totally different. And the game goes on.

In fact, the game has only just begun. Once the computer has accepted your program and starts to do what your program dictates, that's when the real fight begins. The next battle is to get the emergent behaviour to be exactly what you want it to be – no more and no less. It is mostly this activity that eats up years of system-development time on large IT projects.[7]

How come? The program must be correct before the computer will accept it? This is true, but there are two very different levels of correctness to master. The first, is *grammatical correctness* – have you got the detailed structures of the program instructions correct? If yes, then the next level of correctness (the really tricky one) is: *behavioural correctness*, does this correctly structured program instruct the computer to do what you want it to do? Is the program behaving correctly?[8]

Computers operate like your worst nightmare of an English teacher. Suppose you text[9] or email a friend with: "Is their room in your car for me. I need to know immediately?" and your friend replies: "Sorry, your question was grammatically incorrect, please correct it and try again." You might well be miffed, but that's how computers behave: they will make no attempt to interpret the meaning of your program until the program is grammatically correct – every comma and semicolon is precisely where it should be (and similar-sounding words must be spelt correctly).

I realize that my explanation of the lure of computers may be unconvincing to the non-susceptible and to those who have never risked being smitten. Like train spotting, bird watching and other forms of minor lunacy that various of us indulge in, if that's your thing then the irresistibility is obvious, but if you're immune to a specific affliction it is next to impossible to appreciate the nature of that particular compulsion.

A compulsion to practise and experiment with playing various pieces of music on, say, the piano might be a somewhat better analogy with the activities of those afflicted with the HHS. This musical madness is not primarily acquisitive like train spotting and the similar collecting obsessions that so many of us are prone to exhibit. Exploring the possibilities of a musical score is a much richer activity, and one whose reward is a good deal less tangible rather like programming, although there clearly are a number of significant differences between what the musician and the programmer aim to produce.

I don't expect the hardened anti-computerists amongst you to be convinced by the foregoing, but I hope that if you tackle the subsequent chapter on what it means to program a computer you will begin, at least, to appreciate why some individuals do fall in love at first byte.

So what progress towards the necessary understanding have we made with this confessional chapter?

- To some, programming is an alluring man-machine tussle that ultimately promises to put great power in the hands of the man.
- The first challenge (the easy one) is that a program must be _grammatically correct_ before a computer will accept it.
- But the (much) bigger challenge is getting an accepted program to cause the computer to behave in precisely the way you want it to behave; it is _behavioural correctness_ that is the really big problem.

By looking quite closely into the nature of programs we will begin to develop an appreciation of the enormity of this latter challenge in the next chapter.

Endnotes

1. There are many things that we know that computers cannot do, and will never be able to do – see _COMPUTERS LTD What they really can't do_ by D. Harel (Oxford University Press, 2000) for a very readable explanation of the many fundamental limitations of modern computer technology. But these are the technical limitations on the _size_ of various computational problems.

   "The great thing about software [i.e., a computer program] is that it allows a computer to do almost anything. Actually, this isn't quite true. In reality, software allows a computer to do anything – almost." So said David Lubar on page 20 of in his 1995 book _"It's Not a Bug, It's a Feature: computer wit and wisdom"_ published by Addison-Wesley.

   In chess playing, for example, no computer will ever be able to compute all of the alternative moves and countermoves through to all win, lose or draw endpoints – there are just too many of them. So no computer (nor human, of course) will ever play perfect chess which is precisely what makes it an interesting game. Nevertheless, computers now play very high quality chess, and it is unclear how good they will eventually become, but we know they'll never be perfect. In this book we are concerned with the lack of similar clear limitations on the quality of solution that computers can be programmed to produce rather than the well-defined limitations on the size of certain problems.

The surprisingness of this size constraint is exemplified in the story of the Chinese Emperor who wanted to reward a local sage. "Give me some rice," said the sage.

"Some rice!" The Emperor spluttered, "Not gold, or silver, or precious stones?"

"No. Just give me the rice that results from one grain on the first square of your chessboard, two on the second, four on the third, and continue doubling up through all 64 squares."

"Well, the rice is yours," declared the Emperor who did not know that he had just promised more rice than existed in the world.

2. I use the word "hacker" in its older, and (I think) more appropriate meaning, i.e., someone who is addicted to computer technology. In more recent times the word has been hijacked and forced to carry the meaning of someone who gains illegal access to computer systems which is, in my view, merely one of the diversions that the hacker indulges in to satisfy his craving. Steven Levy's book *Hackers: heroes of the computer revolution* (Penguin, 1984), introduces many of these characters.

3. Mathematics is full of useful numbers that can only be calculated approximately. The square root of 4 is 2, because $2 \times 2 = 4$; hence we write $\sqrt{4} = 2$. So what's the square root of 2, written $\sqrt{2}$, the number that when multiplied by itself gives 2, i.e. $\sqrt{2} \times \sqrt{2} = 2$? Like its more famous relative *Pi* (the ratio of the circumference of a circle to its diameter), $\sqrt{2}$ can only be calculated approximately. In the case of $\sqrt{2}$ we have:

$$\sqrt{2} = \frac{1}{2} + \frac{3}{8} + \frac{15}{64} + \frac{35}{256} + \frac{315}{4096} + \frac{693}{16384} + \dots \text{ the add-ons are getting smaller and smaller,}$$

but each one added on gives us a more accurate approximation to the square root of 2. However, there is no end to these add-ons; it is an infinite series. Infinite series are not so mysterious. Just divide 10 by 3 and you'll see what I mean.

4. Following the 'phone connection: something of a modern manifestation of the old game, but with the possibility of serious money attached, is the current enthusiasm for the entrepreneurial whiz-kid to write an 'application' for the iPhone – iPhone Apps and the like. It is true that with Gigabytes of memory to play with the pressure to compress cannot be as intense, but nevertheless App creation does appear to echo some aspects of the early days of programming.

5. As Gary Kasparov demonstrated in his famous 1997 encounter with IBM's Deep Blue chess-playing computer, the best can sometimes be beaten. Contrary to many gee-whiz descriptions of the marvels of artificial intelligence, this one-off event showed nothing more than that Kasparov is human, and has his off days. It may not have escaped your notice that more than a decade on from that supposed breakthrough computers are still not contenders at World Chess Championships. Some claim this is because the human chess experts are excluding the chess programs to preserve human supremacy; others point out that Kasparov played a computer program and a team of human experts who 'adjusted' the Deep Blue system after every game, and no stand-alone program is good enough to compete. But did Kasparov stand alone? And so on … A substantial reflective article by Kasparov can be found on pages 2 and 3 of *The New York Review of Books*, 23 Jan. 2010.

6. Steven Johnson in his book *Emergence* (Penguin, 2001) holds up modern computer games as examples at the forefront of self-adaptive (i.e., 'emergent' in his use of the word) software, but admits that their adaptivity is far from open-ended learning. As is usual with these descriptions of *hopeware*, he consults the ever-optimistic (despite decades of failed predictions) crystal ball: "A few decades from now [2001], the forces unleashed by the bottom-up revolution may well dictate that we redefine intelligence itself, as computers begin to convincingly simulate the human capacity for open-ended learning." p. 208. And it may well not. Indeed, it will certainly not, unless some huge leaps forward in the field of Machine Learning (ML) occur and surprise us all. Geoff Hinton, who knows as much about ML as anyone, once described ML as: a complex and difficult problem composed of very many, very complex and very difficult

subproblems (if I remember him correctly – I'm sure the gist is right). We only have a decade to wait on this prediction.

7. The long-running saga of National Air Traffic Services' £699m IT system for their new Swanwick centre is well-documented. When already multi-millions over budget and years late, the developers claimed to be working on 1,260 known bugs, i.e. known errors, in the system which were (optimistically) reckoned to be "fixed" at a rate of 70 per week, although each such week's work introduced about 10 new bugs according to Professor Les Hatton in a letter in *Computer Weekly*, 7 Jan. 1999, page 11. Nearly 2 years later *Computer Weekly* (5 Oct 2000) had the following front page story: **More bugs hatch in new air traffic control IT systems** – a rise from 200 to 217 was reported.

8. My neat distinction between grammatically correct and behaviourally correct is really not so clear cut. But for the purposes of my argument it is not misleadingly simplistic. Even with formal languages, such as a programming language, syntax and semantics (grammar and behaviour, respectively) are not well-defined, disjoint concepts, but they form the basis of a useful distinction for many purposes.

9. Curiously, the accepted norms of mobile-phone texting explicitly eschew the syntactic precision that a computer demands. But then a text message is for human comprehension; it is not instructions for a machine.

Chapter 3
The Reluctant Programmer

If it weren't for bugs [i.e. errors], the average computer program could be written in about two hours and thirty minutes. Add a few bugs and the process expands to eight or nine months.[1]

So how do we induce these wondrous machines to do our bidding? Ultimately, we have to program them. Much is made of this mysterious skill that some small portion of humanity is blessed with, while the rest are condemned to stand back and watch in awe – regrettably, a response legitimized by unwavering repetition from the dawn of modern computing until today. Those that are so blessed might want to skip this chapter and the next, perhaps just touching down on the summary bullet points (in order to absorb my take on this skill).

The following text bite is a record of the moment when the very first programmer (curiously, a young lady, the daughter of Lord Byron and soon to be the Countess of Lovelace) first met the very first computer, Charles Babbage's Calculating Machine.[2]

While the rest of the party gazed at this beautiful instrument with the same sort of expression and feeling that some savages are said to have shown on first seeing a looking glass or hearing a gun, Miss Byron, young as she was, understood its working and saw the great beauty of the invention.

Miss Byron was exceptional in this party, but this is not the way it has to be. Anyone with a modicum of intelligence and the free time to concentrate for half an hour won't necessarily become a hotshot programmer but he or she will be able to appreciate the rudiments of the craft. That is all I am aiming for with this chapter. Armed with this appreciation in place of the blank space in your brain, where ignorance of programming used to be, you will be thoroughly equipped for an expedition into the depths of the problems and possibilities that computer technology engenders. You will be able to 'see' why large IT projects can never totally succeed.

The air of mystique that typically surrounds the programming of computers is due partly to our ignorance – we the computer technologists and educationalists. We don't know how to teach this skill effectively (in fact, we don't really know what this skill ought best to be). It is still a relatively new skill, and one that is still changing in nature, and may well change fundamentally (as you'll find out if you persist sufficiently in your reading of this book).[3] We are now much better at teaching

D. Partridge, *The Seductive Computer: Why IT Systems Always Fail*,
DOI 10.1007/978-1-84996-498-2_3, © Springer-Verlag London Limited 2011

programming than we used to be, but there is still a long way to go, of that I am sure. My bold claim to be able to impart to you the basics of this skill in half an hour is not quite as boastful as it may seem at first sight. For all that I hope to get across is the rudiments of programming – nothing sophisticated, nothing conceptually too complex, but the essential details nevertheless.

Blaise Pascal, the French philosopher, is credited with the insightful remark that "things are best at the beginning." This pithy observation is often right on when applied to large computer programs (as we shall see), but with respect to teaching programming it is, I'm pleased to report, wide of the mark. So, although the passage of time does many of us no favours, one beneficial outcome for our present purposes is that I am now able to provide you with an appreciation of computer technology without first leading you through a host of irritating trivia. In the old days (the bad old days, to be more precise) it was considered *de rigueur* to subject the newly enquiring mind to a long drawn-out set of initiation rights – basic electronics, flip-flops, binary arithmetic, logic gates, bits, bytes, nanoseconds, etc. In this more enlightened time, I am able, you will be relieved to learn, to dispense with all this mental foreplay and get immediately to the central (and much less tedious) issues.

We start by viewing the computer as a two-part device: a *processor* that can check, store and then follow a list of instructions and do what they tell it to do, and a *memory:* a collection of *storage boxes* that can each hold a single number and be given a label.

The processor can only obey certain instructions. It can't do just whatever we wish to tell it, in whatever way we might wish to tell it. There is nothing too special about this restriction. Most complex machines exhibit similar limitations. For example, an organ can only play the selection of notes that it was designed to play. There may be infinitely many combinations of these notes (some of which will be music) that can be played on a given instrument, but there will also be some notes that cannot be played.

The set of possible instructions that the programmer must choose from is defined by a *programming language*, and a specific list of such instructions is a *computer program,* or just a *program*. So programming is the task of devising a list of allowable instructions that will cause the computer to do exactly what you want it to do. The vast majority of possible instruction lists the computer cannot do anything with at all. It just grinds to a halt, or continues following instructions in a circular fashion until someone notices, and pulls the plug.

So there are good programs that cause the computer to do something sensible, and there are bad programs that it cannot obey in any sensible way. The latter set is much bigger than the former (or so it seems), and the novice programmer usually finds a lot of them very quickly before he or she generates one of the good programs.

What are the sorts of things that these mysterious instructions get the computer to do? And where do these *storage boxes* come into the story? Not quite by chance these two questions answer each other. The sorts of things that computers typically do is to calculate numbers and store them away, in labelled boxes. There is a need for somewhere to store these numbers so that they may be used again later in the program, hence the *storage boxes*. This is beginning to make a computer sound a bit like a mechanical squirrel, merrily salting away numbers rather than hazel nuts. This is not a particularly well-balanced view, but it will do no harm for now.

Let's have an example:

ADD 1 TO 3 PUT RESULT IN X

This might be a typical instruction. It is instructing the computer to add the number 1 to the number 3 and to put the resultant sum in the box labelled "X". How do we know that there is a *storage box* labelled "X" in this particular computer? Well we don't, and this will be a sensible instruction only if the computer has a spare *storage box* to label "X". But, assuming a spare box is available, it will automatically be labelled "X" as soon as the computer determines from such an instruction that a box labelled "X" is needed (see Fig. 3.1).

When the *processor* has performed the action stated in this instruction, what has changed? Nothing earth shattering it's true, but a *storage box* has been labelled "X", and this box should have gained a number, the number 4. So when the computer has followed this instruction, <u>*executed*</u> it (to use the jargon), its *storage boxes* will look like this:

X	–	–
4	–	–

Note: just 3 of the many *storage boxes* are illustrated and only one is currently used.

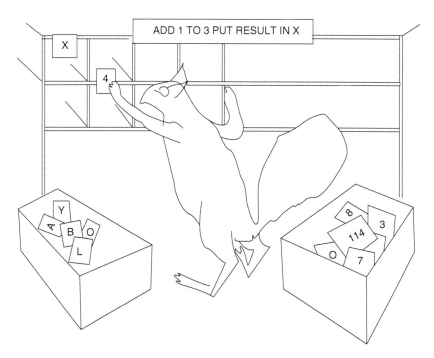

Fig. 3.1 The 'squirrel computer' at work

Can we check this result? Yes, we can instruct the computer to print out the number in the box labelled "X" – i.e., print the value of "X". We might add a PRINT instruction to obtain the following program:

```
ADD 1 TO 3 PUT RESULT IN X
PRINT X
```

If the computer *executes* this small program correctly (and it invariably does), we will see the number 4 printed out. This happens because to the computer PRINT X means print out the number in the *storage box* labelled "X". It does not mean: print out the character "X".

A point to note is that after the computer has obeyed the PRINT instruction the number 4 will still be stored in the box labelled "X". The processor doesn't remove it from the box when it prints out the value; it just takes a look and leaves it alone. This number in box X will remain as 4 until we either turn off the computer, or we instruct the computer to put a different number in box X in which case it will first discard the box's current number – i.e., the 4. A single box can only hold one number at a time but any amount of different numbers can be placed in a given box one after another during the course of a computation. Each new number placed in a box causes the previous number to be discarded.

The computer works through its instruction list, i.e., it *executes* the program, from top to bottom (unless otherwise explicitly instructed as we'll see in the next chapter). So it is crucial that the PRINT instruction follows the ADD instruction because it is unreasonable to ask the machine to print out the number in box X until after you've instructed it to put a number in box X. That is just simple good sense, is it not?

So now you've not exactly written but at least been a party to the writing of a program. This short list of two instructions is a computer program. Admittedly, it is neither a very exciting nor a very ambitious program, but it is a respectable computer program nonetheless. In order to clearly demonstrate both the allure of programming and the dangers that lurk therein, we do need to delve just a little more deeply into the intricacies of this mysterious practice.

One point that the alert reader should be puzzling over is, why bother with the labelled boxes? Why not reduce the two-instruction program to a single instruction? The single instruction that I'm suggesting is:

```
ADD 1 TO 3 AND PRINT RESULT
```

This is in fact an eminently sensible program. If all you want is to find out the sum of 1 and 3, then this single-instruction program is the way that you would elicit a computer's help to solve your problem. But usually we wish to do something more ambitious, and then the labelled boxes prove to be essential. The *storage boxes* provide us with somewhere to stash away newly computed results for future use in subsequent computations later in the same program. Rather like the squirrel stashing away nuts until they are needed later in the year (just to squeeze this analogy quite dry).

As an example, we can now instruct the computer to use the number in box X to calculate some further number. Let's add to our embryonic program:

ADD 1 TO 3 PUT RESULT IN X
PRINT X
MULTIPLY X BY X PUT RESULT IN Y

In the last instruction we've introduced something new. Instead of instructing the computer to do something with specific numbers (such as 1 and 3 in our first instruction), we have asked it to do something with labelled boxes – in fact, with the box labelled "X". If you're thinking that this doesn't make much sense (i.e., multiplying a box label by a box label), you're right – it just proves that you do think logically after all. But this is a sensible instruction (provided the processor has a spare box to label "Y" handy) because the computer knows that this final instruction means 'multiply the number in the box labelled "X" by the number in the box labelled "X"'. After the execution of this program we can review the state of the computer's *memory*, its *storage boxes*, and the situation will be this:

X	Y	–
4	16	–

The next unused *storage box* has been commandeered and labelled "Y", and the correct value, which is the value in box X multiplied by the value in box X, has been placed in it. This is, of course, just a long winded way of saying 'square the number in box X', but then long-windedness is often part of the price that we have to pay in order to get computers working for us. However, as we shall soon see, powerful shortcuts are also possible.

So what exactly is a *computer program*? It is simply a sequence of instructions that tell the computer to do one thing, then the next thing, then the next, etc. The computer obeys the instructions one after another, from the first (at the top of the list) to the last (at the bottom). The order in which the computer works through the program, which is not always as simple as top-to-bottom, imposes a <u>*flow path*</u> on the program. Figure 3.2 shows the bare program, and the program with its *flow path* superimposed. In this and all subsequent *flow-path* illustrations, the *flow path* starts at the open circle and ends at the filled-in one.

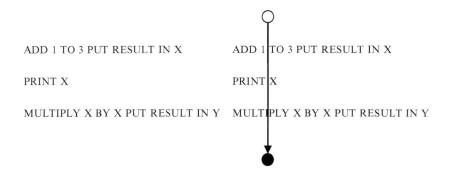

ADD 1 TO 3 PUT RESULT IN X

PRINT X

MULTIPLY X BY X PUT RESULT IN Y

Fig. 3.2 The three-line program and its flow path

Before we move on, notice that the instruction:

MULTIPLY X BY X PUT RESULT IN Y

does contribute to a good program in the short list of instructions given above because the box labelled "X" does contain a number (it is put there by the first instruction) at the point in time that the computer *executes* the multiplication. If we interchange the first and third instructions in our program (or the first and second) then we would obtain our first bad program. As a result of exchanging the first and third instructions, we would be instructing the computer to first MULTIPLY X BY X PUT RESULT IN Y, and one of two things will happen.

First, the computer will check and accept the program as *grammatically correct* (because each instruction on its own is correctly structured), then it will begin *executing* this program. Either the computer will grind to a halt, and send us an error message indicating that box X does not contain a number (and hence it cannot do the specified multiplication), or worse it will compute away happily with whatever number happens quite fortuitously to be in box X (perhaps a random number, perhaps a leftover from the previous program). The worst outcome of all would be that the number that just happens to be sitting in box X at the start of the program is 4. This will, of course, give exactly the answer we anticipated (as a result of the second instruction PRINT X), but for exactly the wrong reasons. So, on seeing the program's correct output, the observer would be tempted to wrongly infer that the program was correct.

"Not a big problem" you might be tempted to think to yourself. After all, the answer was correct, and if had been incorrect we would immediately have noticed that something was wrong. Anyway the chance that we would get such a right answer in such a serendipitous way is very small. It is similar perhaps to the likelihood of being struck by lightning on a clear sunny day, and we typically don't let this exceedingly low-probability event affect the pursuance of our daily lives.

This is all true and reasonable, but only in the context of an utterly trivial program like the one we have developed. Programs tend to be much more complex, and their real purpose is to compute results that we don't already know. This means that the above situation does not hinge on the correct answer emerging quite by chance. Any reasonable-looking answer will present us with exactly the same problem. Only if we check slowly and tediously through the whole program can we begin to develop some confidence that an answer that looks correct is in fact correct (or incorrect). But do remember the bank-balance example: a hand-checking exercise will not deliver any certainty of the general correctness of the program being checked.

So where are we on the path to understanding this technology?

- We know the basics of programming technology: *a computer program* is a list of instructions, each selected from a *programming language*, that tell the *processor* how to manipulate symbols (in our case, to add and multiply numbers) and what *storage boxes* of the *memory* to put the results in.
- Once your program is accepted as *grammatically correct*, the computer will *execute* it, and the behaviour it specifies will emerge; a behaviour that depends

on the precise order of the instructions. Programming thus demands a high proficiency in all-round trivia management (from instruction order to *storage-box* naming).

- The instruction sequence dictates a *flow path* through the program, i.e., the order in which the computer will *execute* each instruction.
- The resultant emergent behaviour may be correct, i.e., what you intended, or incorrect, not what you intended.
- But even when the snippets of observed behaviour look to be correct, the full details of the causal links between correct behaviour and your intentions are hard to verify. So, general correctness of IT-system behaviour will remain a faith-based property.

But anyway: congratulations. You've just written your first program. It was a piece of cake really, composing three instructions and putting them together sensibly to produce a good program. Moreover, it is a program that you fully understand – I hope (any reader who is hesitant about affirming this can still read on, all is not lost, but you'll have to take an awful lot on trust).

Endnotes

1. Quoted by David Lubar on p. 53 of his collection of computer wit and wisdom entitled *It's Not a Bug: It's a Feature* published by Addison-Wesley in 1995.
2. The quotation is from the reminiscences of Mrs. De Morgan (wife of the famous mathematician), its date is early 1830s, and it is to be found in B. V. Bowden's useful early compendium, *Faster than Thought* (published by Pitman, London, 1953), p. 20.

   Miss Byron, later Lady Lovelace, is often given the title of "the first programmer" for the work she did with Charles Babbage on his very early computers.

   Of related interest is the way one of the great seducers, Lord Byron the poet, lurks behind the scenes in this saga. In sum, he supplied the first programmer, the only lasting product of his short married life, and also produced a daughter with the stepsister of Mary Shelley (the author of *Frankenstein*, whose creation of emergent chaos will also have a part to play in this book).
3. In the dark days of my own infatuation, computer memories were very small and so a significant part of the challenge was to find slick ways to compress programs, and even slicker ways to reuse or double use memory locations of the machine. Today, the challenge is squarely on maximizing ease of program understanding with program size no longer an issue, and memory location usage banished from programmer control.

Chapter 4
Cooking Up Programs

Trivia Pursuit

In 1991, on June 26th and again on the 27th, the AT&T tele-phone systems in Washington, DC, Los Angeles, Pittsburgh and San Francisco collapsed and were inoperable for 5 to 10 hours. Millions of people were isolated, and businesses lost millions of dollars as a direct result. After patching up the system and getting it working again, DSC Communications, the company responsible for the computer systems involved, eventually tracked down and corrected the error: it took 5 months (and many man-years), and deep within two million program instructions, it was discovered that a programmer had acciden-tally typed a wrong character – a "6" instead of a "d".[1]

As the above story illustrates: there are no trivial details in computer programs, every character is potentially crucial. The goal of this chapter is to introduce all of the programming detail that you will need, and the nature of the complexity that then emerges. Complexity and detail: the combination of these two properties is more than a match for the best brains that *Homo sapiens* can muster.

Many of the more painless introductions to computer programming try to encourage the novice by likening programs to recipes: the list of instructions that specify a computation for the computer is just like a list of instructions in a cook-book that specify a culinary exercise for the cook. This analogy is both helpful and somewhat misleading; like all analogies it can be pushed too far.[2]

At the moment we are still on solid analogical ground, and I hope that you can, without too much trouble, view our simple program as a recipe for computing and printing out the sum of 1 and 3, and subsequently squaring the value of X to put the result in box Y.

Few readers, I would hazard a guess, are finding the computation with Xs and Ys really gripping. It probably serves best to confirm the suspicion that, despite all my preliminary protestations to the contrary, programming is not at all fun for anyone with interests that extend beyond numbers, letters of the alphabet and how the two may be jumbled together in diverse ways. More than this, it is so boring that you'll leave it to the freaks who like it, and take your chances with the future impacts of the technology in blissful ignorance, comforted by the knowledge that at least you

D. Partridge, *The Seductive Computer: Why IT Systems Always Fail,*
DOI 10.1007/978-1-84996-498-2_4, © Springer-Verlag London Limited 2011

tried. The joy of programming may be very real for some (odd) people, but then so are the pleasures of masochism.

The good news is, however, that, although knowledge of *storage-box* labels and numbers is crucial to a proper understanding of computer technology, you now have the necessary knowledge. This leaves me free to move on, and move up, to a more user-friendly example.

To many people it is the total simulations of humans, often with superhuman (if somewhat alien) powers, that epitomize the extremes of modern computer technology. I mean the walking, talking and thinking robots of fiction: R2D2 and C3PO of the blockbuster films (that other *Star Wars*), or the *Daleks* of the long-running UK television series *Dr. Who*. These highly complex machines (which we will assume they are) are, of course, limited to the world of fiction for now (and the foreseeable future), but they will not always be, and it is the computer programs running on their fancy electronic circuits that determines their capabilities to a large extent.

A tame *Dalek*, after elocution lessons (to soften the harsh strangulated delivery) and some judicious re-programming (or a wire-snipping frontal lobotomy to be on the safe side), might prove to be a valuable adjunct to the home of the twenty-first century. However, once the cachet of being the first *Dalek* owner in the golf club has evaporated, and everyone has one, their real worth will be called into question. Beyond functioning as a particularly ugly pot stand, a mobile dustbin or a garden gnome it is hard to imagine the really useful functions which they might perform. But if they're programmable (and I'm also assuming that they are) then, of course, the functions of a *Dalek* are (apart from the physical constraints of the hardware and the world we inhabit) constrained only by the limitations of the programmer.

Let's suppose we want to extend the functions of the *Daleks*. The intergalactic marketing company needs a new selling point in order to shift its stockpile of millions. Notice that the highly mobile, compact and aggressive machines are ideally suited for shopping, especially when the force is with them. So, we'll develop a shopping program for installation within the mental menials. We'll start small, and (rest assured) we'll stay that way, although program complexity will grow and grow.

Cutting right through all the necessary preamble to the average shopping expedition–i.e., putting the cat out, locking the house door, parking the car, etc. – we'll focus on the details of the task once inside the local superstore that contains everything that the rational shopper could possibly want. What is this "everything"? It is, of course, up to the proud owner of the *Dalek* supermarket-cruiser model to decide. In accord with the time-honoured tradition our mechanical shopper is in possession of a shopping list – a list of the desired commodities. So what must this *Dalek* be instructed to do in order to shop with its shopping list? Here's a first stab at the basis of a suitable program:

1. read first item on list
2. locate this item in the store
3. place item in trolley
4. read next item on list
5. locate this item in the store

6. place item in trolley
7. read next item on list
8. ...

This is, of course, not a proper program: it is not couched in terms of a programming language – there are, for example, no box labels in these instructions. But this is a design for a program, a *plan*. We just need to expand each of these *plan instructions* into readily computable details – i.e. the instructions of our programming language, such as **PUT-INTO**s, etc.

The above list of high-level instructions is a plan of our desired program. Well, it's the beginnings of a plan. In programming, as with many of life's complexities, it is wise to plan at a general or high level before diving into the full necessary details. If, for example, you're organizing a wedding, then you plan the general sequence of events before worrying about the detailed composition of the bride's bouquet.

Each *plan instruction* is refined into more detailed *plan instructions* and eventually to programming language instructions. When all the original plan instructions have been so refined, we have our program. This process of systematically developing a program from a plan is known as *stepwise refinement* (and is further explained in the next chapter).

Take the first *plan instruction*: read first item on list. In order to avoid the (currently) insoluble problem of a robot clutching, and attempting to visually decipher, a list of items hastily scribbled on crumpled notepaper by the busy owner, we'll assume that the owner has a means of entering the shopping list into the *storage boxes* of the *Dalek*'s on-board computer – by means of WiFi and a keyboard or iPhone, for example. So the list is resident inside the robot in *storage boxes* labelled "A", "B", "C", etc. – we will not worry about the owners who require more than 26 items (they will just have to send the robot shopping more frequently, or do some shopping themselves).

So, on crossing the threshold of the chosen shop, the robot's storage boxes might look like this:

A	B	C	D	E	F	G	H
eggs	bread	milk	meat	soap	bran	honey	apple

The first high-level instruction might then be refined directly into programming-language instructions (it is sufficiently simple that we do not need any intermediate plan refinements); it becomes the first piece of a program that we shall call **SHOP**:

SHOP

COMMENT read first item on list
    PUT A INTO CURRENT-TASK
    PUT 0 **INTO** A

I have included the original *plan instruction* as a **COMMENT** – i.e. just information for the human reader; such **COMMENT**s are ignored by the computer. The two programming language instructions (the two **PUT**s) that constitute our programming of the **COMMENT**ed action are indented to show that we mean them, and only them, to be interpreted as the programming-language refinement of the **COMMENT**. These *program style* guidelines are no more than a visual layout device to help you and me 'see' how the program 'works'; to the computer they mean nothing.

The program instructs the robot's computer to copy the item in box A into a box labelled "CURRENT-TASK" – this is the commodity that it is going to find and put in its trolley. It is also instructed to delete this commodity from its shopping list so that it knows that the box-A item has been taken care of. After executing this small piece of program its *memory*, i.e., its *storage boxes*, will look like this:

A	B	C	D	E	F	G	H	CURRENT-TASK
0	bread	milk	meat	soap	bran	honey	apple	eggs

Notice that box labels are not, in fact, restricted to single letters of the alphabet; boxes can be labelled with any combination of characters that the programmer cares to choose.

The robot now needs to locate this first item (the value in box CURRENT-TASK) within the superstore. Let's refine the second original *plan instruction* and expand it into a more detailed plan. This refinement step might give us:

COMMENT locate this item in the store
    categorize item in CURRENT-TASK
    consult supermarket layout plan
    find desired category of items
    plan route to where desired category located
    go to this location
    survey items until item in CURRENT-TASK found

Even this sixfold expansion will require further refinement steps before it can really constitute a proper program – e.g., in precisely what way is the robot to 'survey' all the items in a given category? What happens if the item is not found? But (you'll be pleased to learn) it will do for our purposes.

The next development of our shopping program then is to substitute our refined instruction sets for the *plan instructions* from which they were developed. This gives:

SHOP

COMMENT read first item on list
    PUT A **INTO** CURRENT-TASK
    PUT 0 **INTO** A

COMMENT locate this item in the store
    categorize item in CURRENT-TASK
    consult supermarket layout plan
    find desired category of items
    plan route to where desired category located
    go to this location
    survey items until item in CURRENT-TASK found

3. place item in trolley

COMMENT read next item on list
    PUT B **INTO** CURRENT-TASK
    PUT 0 **INTO** B

COMMENT locate this item in the store
    categorize item in CURRENT-TASK
    consult supermarket layout plan
    find desired category of items
    plan route to where desired category located
    go to this location
    survey items until item in CURRENT-TASK found

6. place item in trolley

COMMENT read next item on list
    PUT C **INTO** CURRENT-TASK
    PUT 0 **INTO** C

COMMENT locate this item in the store
    categorize item in CURRENT-TASK
    consult supermarket layout plan
    find desired category of items
    plan route to where desired category located
    go to this location
    survey items until item in CURRENT-TASK found

9. …

Notice that our embryonic program is now a mixture of undeveloped *plan instructions* (each prefaced by its original number), more detailed *plan instructions* and programming-language instructions; each block of instructions is indented below the original *plan instruction* (**COMMENT**ed) that it was refined from and so has replaced.

This program is quite complicated, but it is still just a list of instructions that the computer will obey in sequence from top to bottom. The flow path of this more complicated program is the same straight arrow as we saw in the simple three-instruction program in the previous chapter. Figure 4.1 illustrates these two views of the program. They are not very different, but this is all about to change.

Clearly, if we're going to persist with this program it will be a very repetitive list of instructions. After the first block of instructions (up to and including the one prefaced by 3) every subsequent group of three instruction blocks (two **COMMENT**ed blocks and a numbered, unexpanded one) is directing the computer to do almost exactly the same thing over and over again. Now this is exactly what computers are good at, and people are not. It's one of the important strong points about computers. But the construction of such a program is very tedious for the programmer.

The computer technologists soon spotted this unattractive possibility and took steps to eliminate it. But Mrs. Beeton, in her classic "Household Management" (with perhaps a counterclaim to be the first programmer), took the same steps

SHOP	SHOP

COMMENT read first item on list
    PUT A **INTO** CURRENT-TASK
    PUT 0 **INTO** A
	COMMENT read first item on list
	    PUT A **INTO** CURRENT-TASK
	    PUT 0 **INTO** A

COMMENT locate this item in the store
    categorize item in CURRENT-
    TASK
    consult supermarket layout plan
    find desired category of items
    plan route to where desired
    category located
    go to this location
    survey items until item in
    CURRENT-TASK found
	COMMENT locate this item in the store
	    categorize item in CURRENT-
	    TASK
	    consult supermarket layout plan
	    find desired category of items
	    plan route to where desired
	    category located
	    go to this location
	    survey items until item in
	    CURRENT-TASK found

3. place item in trolley	3. place item in trolley

COMMENT read next item on list
    PUT B **INTO** CURRENT-TASK
    PUT 0 **INTO** B
	COMMENT read next item on list
	    PUT B **INTO** CURRENT-TASK
	    PUT 0 **INTO** B

COMMENT locate this item in the store
    categorize item in CURRENT-
    TASK
    consult supermarket layout plan
    find desired category of items
    plan route to where desired
    category located
    go to this location
    survey items until item in
    CURRENT-TASK found
	COMMENT locate this item in the store
	    categorize item in CURRENT-
	    TASK
	    consult supermarket layout plan
	    find desired category of items
	    plan route to where desired
	    category located
	    go to this location
	    survey items until item in
	    CURRENT-TASK found

6. place item in trolley	6. place item in trolley

COMMENT read next item on list
    PUT C **INTO** CURRENT-TASK
    PUT 0 **INTO** C
	COMMENT read next item on list
	    PUT C **INTO** CURRENT-TASK
	    PUT 0 **INTO** C

COMMENT locate this item in the store
    categorize item in CURRENT-
    TASK
    consult supermarket layout plan
    find desired category of items
    plan route to where desired
    category located
    go to this location
    survey items until item in
    CURRENT-TASK found
9. ...
	COMMENT locate this item in the store
	    categorize item in CURRENT-
	    TASK
	    consult supermarket layout plan
	    find desired category of items
	    plan route to where desired
	    category located
	    go to this location
	    survey items until item in
	    CURRENT-TASK found
	9. ...

Fig. 4.1 Two views of the program

decades earlier when she realized that her recipes were becoming repetitive. Here's an example of her insight.

WOODCOCK, ROASTED

Ingredients. Woodcocks, toast, bacon, butter for basting, good Brown gravy (p. 195), watercress.

Method. The skin of these birds is particularly tender, therefore they must be plucked very carefully. They are prepared and cooked in the same manner as Snipe (*see* **Snipe, Roasted**, p. 622).[3]

In order to reduce the size of her cookbook, Mrs. B. does not repeat details unnecessarily. Instead of explaining how to make "good Brown gravy" yet again in this recipe she refers the cook to the page where he or she will find the detailed recipe; it functions as a 'subrecipe' to be referred to and used within the more extensive recipes. In addition, the details of how to conduct the actual roasting of a Woodcock are the same as the details of how to roast a Snipe. Actually, the two roasting subrecipes are not precisely the same, and this is an important point. If you turn to page 622 for the **Snipe, Roasted** recipe you will find no mention of Woodcocks, of course. What the cook is supposed to do is to follow the **Snipe, Roasted** details but with "Woodcock" substituted for "Snipe" throughout. An obvious piece of commonsense – a general commodity which you and I possess in abundance, but computers do not.

So when we introduce subrecipes, called *subprograms*, to shorten our total program, they may be exact repeats (like "good Brown gravy") or they may be similar repeats (like roasting woodcocks and roasting snipes). In the case of similar repetitions, you will see how the necessary substitutions must be spelled out precisely for a computer.

Computer programs are then shortened in exactly the same way: that is to say, a repeated segment of a program can be written out just once and references to it (like Mrs. Beeton's page numbers) are placed wherever in the original program (now called the *main* program) this *subprogram* is needed. As a consequence, programs become much shorter (as do recipe books), but there is a cost as there is also a cost to the Beeton-following cook.

The cost is composed of increases in both time and complexity: it takes the cook (and the computer) longer to follow through the instructions if they are spread around the book instead of being all together in the form of a simple list on one or more consecutive pages. It is also trickier for the cook to actually locate and follow a precise set of instructions when these instructions occur here and there in the book. It is this latter increase, the increase in complexity, that is by far the most important one with respect to computer programs; it is also badly misrepresented in the cookbook analogy.

For the cook is, of course, the computer executing a recipe, and the basic operations of a computer when following program instructions are effectively error free; so, an increase in program complexity should have no measurable effect on the accuracy with which the program is processed.

So where exactly does this important increase in complexity become manifest in the world of computer technology? It is an increase in complexity for the programmer, not for the computer, i.e., for Mrs. Beeton rather than for the cook – for those who just hate to see a good analogy abandoned before its usefulness has been totally exhausted. The program must be precisely correct in every detail because the computer will follow it unerringly but blindly, and it will exercise no commonsense whatsoever.

Let's go back to specifics in order to give some detailed substance to these points. Assume you are the cook: consider what sequence of actions you must perform in order to roast a Woodcock.

While collecting the ingredients, after fetching the butter you must leave this recipe and turn to page 195 in order to find details of the Brown gravy required. Having made the necessary gravy, you must then return to the Woodcock recipe, at the point immediately following the reference to "good Brown gravy", and then make sure that you have the watercress to hand. Having done so, you progress to the **Method** part. After carefully plucking the bird you must stop reading the Woodcock recipe, turn to page 622, and start following the **Snipe, Roasted** recipe but with "Woodcock" mentally substituted for every mention of "Snipe". Once you've completed the **Snipe, Roasted** recipe you return back to where you left off the **Woodcock, Roasted** recipe and continue on from there.

Notice that recipe following has become a discontinuous process. The simple *flow path* has become more complex; it no longer merely echos the instruction sequence. In order to follow a recipe that contains references to subrecipes you must jump around in the cook book as determined by the page numbers that are provided. Mrs Beeton's esteemed cookbook is a simple list of sentences that can be read in sequence from beginning to end. But the cook executing the **Woodcock, Roasted** recipe follows a more complex, discontinuous path through (part of) the book. Figure 4.2 illustrates the *flow path* of the cook who is following Mrs B's Woodcock recipe.

So the cost of avoiding repetition by referencing subrecipes is both the time and the trouble needed to jump around in the cookbook. Exactly the same costs are associated with programs written by programmers who seek to avoid repetition of program segments by writing them out only once and then referencing them whenever required in the main program. Except that, as mentioned above, the cost is to the programmer for it is he who must construct this discontinuous program. The computer will accurately follow whatever non-sequential *flow path* the program dictates; it is the burden of the programmer to ensure that the discontinuities he specifies are really the ones that he wants – i.e., precisely the ones that cause the desired behaviour of the program to emerge.

Let's make this notion of discontinuous programs concrete by rearranging our earlier, simple sequential, but repetitive program.

The repeated segment is:

```
COMMENT read next item on list
    PUT ? INTO CURRENT-TASK
    PUT 0 INTO ?
```

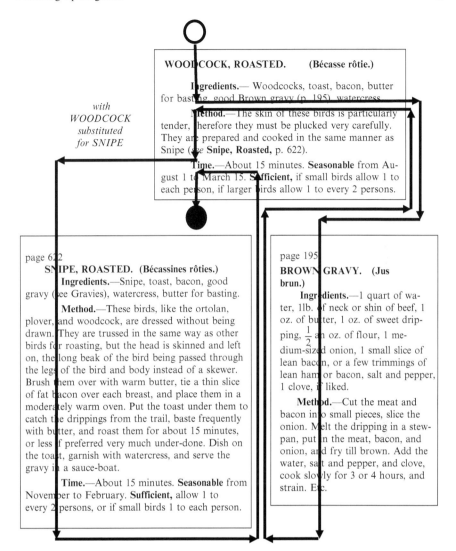

Fig. 4.2 The *flow path* of the Woodcock-roasting cook

COMMENT locate this item in the store
      categorize item in CURRENT-TASK
      consult supermarket layout plan
      find desired category of items
      plan route to where desired category located
      go to this location
      survey items until item in CURRENT-TASK found

If you're also wondering about the question marks in this proposed *subprogram*, they are not mistakes; they are not correct either. We must replace them with something that is acceptable to the computer. The question marks occur in precisely the positions where the repeated segments of the original program do not in fact repeat. In the first case there is an "A" in both positions, and in the second case there is a "B". This segment of a program is the analogue of Mrs. Beeton's **Snipe, Roasted** recipe, and you will recall that we had to substitute "Woodcock" for "Snipe" when we used it from within the **Woodcock, Roasted** recipe. In programming terms we might call Mrs. Beeton's subrecipe the **Game-Bird, Roasted** recipe. When it's used for Snipe we substitute "Snipe" for "Game-Bird"; when it's used for Woodcock we substitute "Woodcock" for "Game-Bird"; and so on. The term Game-Bird is just a general term within the subrecipe, and we substitute the name of a specific game bird for all occurrences of "Game-Bird" each time the general subrecipe is used as part of a specific bird-roasting exercise.

Now to the question marks: they should be replaced by a box label. I shall choose the label "NEXT-ITEM" in order to remind us of what it is that we are dealing with in this part of the program. Let me also give this whole *subprogram* a name, **READ&FIND**, so that we may refer to it from the *main* program, **SHOP** (computers prefer to associate names with such *subprograms* rather than Mrs. Beeton's page numbers). This is what we now have:

SHOP

COMMENT read first item on list & locate this item in the store
    DO READ&FIND **WITH** A **AS** NEXT-ITEM

3. place item in trolley

COMMENT read next item on list & locate this item in the store
    DO READ&FIND **WITH** B **AS** NEXT-ITEM

6. place item in trolley

COMMENT read next item on list & locate this item in the store
    DO READ&FIND **WITH** C **AS** NEXT-ITEM

9. place item in trolley

SUBPROGRAM READ&FIND

COMMENT read next item on list
    PUT NEXT-ITEM **INTO** CURRENT-TASK
    PUT 0 **INTO** NEXT-ITEM

COMMENT locate this item in the store
    categorize item in CURRENT-TASK
    consult supermarket layout plan
    find desired category of items
    plan route to where desired category located
    go to this location
    survey items until item in CURRENT-TASK found

This two-part program – that is, *main* program (named **SHOP**) and the *subprogram* (named **READ&FIND**) – should cause the computer to do exactly the same computation as our earlier repetitive monolithic program. The computer will work through the list of instructions in the *main* program, when it encounters the first **DO** instruction (the third line, or first instruction, in the *main* program, **SHOP**), it stops there and zips off to the named *subprogram* (just as the cook leaves the Woodcock-roasted recipe to find out how to make "good Brown gravy" on another page).

On arrival at **SUBPROGRAM READ&FIND**, the **WITH** A **AS** NEXT-ITEM part of the **DO** instruction tells the robot's computer explicitly to substitute "A" for "NEXT-ITEM" when it follows the instructions within the subprogram; this is analogous to the cook who must follow the instructions for the **Snipe, Roasted** subrecipe, but substituting "Woodcock" for "Snipe" throughout. So now when the computer follows the instructions in the *subprogram*, each mention of the box label "NEXT-ITEM" is treated as if it were a reference to the box label "A".

One box has two labels – "NEXT-ITEM" is an <u>alias</u> for "A". The computer's *memory* will thus look like this when it starts to execute **SUBPROGRAM READ&FIND** for the first time:

NEXT-ITEM								
A	B	C	D	E	F	G	H	CURRENT-TASK
eggs	bread	milk	meat	soap	bran	honey	apple	

So, the first instruction in the *subprogram*,

PUT NEXT-ITEM **INTO** CURRENT-TASK,

causes the value "eggs" to be copied to become the value in the box CURRENT-TASK – i.e. the computer behaves <u>as if</u> the instruction is

PUT A **INTO** CURRENT-TASK.

The second instruction in the *subprogram*,

PUT 0 **INTO** NEXT-ITEM,

will result in the value in box NEXT-ITEM (which is an alias for "A" remember) to be replaced by 0. After this the computer's *memory*, its set of *storage boxes* will look like this:

NEXT-ITEM								
A	B	C	D	E	F	G	H	CURRENT-TASK
0	bread	milk	meat	soap	bran	honey	apple	eggs

When it has finished following the instructions in this *subprogram* it will automatically jump back to where it came from, that is the instruction following the **DO** instruction that sent it off in the first place. (Just as the cook will return to page of the **Woodcock, Roasted** recipe when finished making the "good Brown gravy" on page 195, and set about sourcing watercress.) In our case, the robot will return to perform the fourth instruction in the main program, viz. "place item in trolley".

The next instruction:

DO <u>READ&FIND</u> **WITH** B **AS** NEXT-ITEM[4]

results in all references to box NEXT-ITEM being transformed into references to box B. The aliasing arrangement has been changed by the **WITH** part of the instruction.

The computer's *memory* will look like this as it starts to work through the *subprogram* for the second time:

	NEXT-ITEM							
A	B	C	D	E	F	G	H	CURRENT-TASK
0	bread	milk	meat	soap	bran	honey	apple	eggs

The first instruction in this *subprogram* copies the value "bread" to the box CURRENT-TASK, and the next instruction resets the value in NEXT-ITEM (in effect box B) to zero. At this point the *memory* looks as follows:

	NEXT-ITEM							
A	B	C	D	E	F	G	H	CURRENT-TASK
0	0	milk	meat	soap	bran	honey	apple	bread

The rest of the instructions in the *subprogram* will cause the robot to locate and retrieve a loaf of bread. After this, all the instructions in the *subprogram* have been completed, and the computer returns to process the sixth instruction in the main program, and so on.

The *flow path* of the complete program is no longer an explicit reflection of the simple instruction sequence. It is much more like the discontinuous series of recipe-following actions that the cook must undertake in order to roast a woodcock in the Mrs Beeton way. The main difference is that in our program the same *subprogram* is executed on three separate occasions (whereas, "good Brown gravy" and **Snipe, Roasted** happen to be needed only once each when roasting a Woodcock). On each repetition our program uses a different memory box as NEXT-ITEM, which is what makes the repetitions useful.

It is as if the cook has a pile of three different game birds to roast, and so he follows the **SNIPE, ROASTED** recipe three separate times: once with "Woodcock" substituted for "Snipe", then with "Partridge" substituted for "Snipe", and perhaps finally with "Quail" substituted for "Snipe".

Figure 4.3 illustrates the now *subprogram*med program and its *flow path*. Notice particularly that the program is still a simple list of instructions, and, from this viewpoint, not very different from the earlier version. However, the *flow path* illustrated is totally different from the earlier straight arrows.

The program, as written, may well be finished but it only causes the robot to shop for exactly three items. The original shopping list contained eight items, but we can easily cause our shopping robot to complete its task. We just add the following instructions to the bottom of our main program:

<u>**SHOP**</u>

COMMENT read first item on list & locate this item in the store

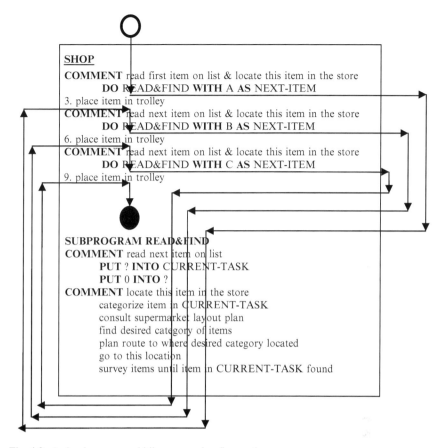

Fig. 4.3 A simple sequence hiding a complex *flow path*

DO <u>READ&FIND</u> **WITH** A **AS** NEXT-ITEM
3. place item in trolley

COMMENT read next item on list & locate this item in the store
    DO <u>READ&FIND</u> **WITH** B **AS** NEXT-ITEM

6. place item in trolley

COMMENT read next item on list & locate this item in the store
    DO <u>READ&FIND</u> **WITH** C **AS** NEXT-ITEM

9. place item in trolley

COMMENT read next item on list & locate this item in the store
    DO <u>READ&FIND</u> **WITH** D **AS** NEXT-ITEM

12. place item in trolley

COMMENT read next item on list & locate this item in the store
    DO <u>READ&FIND</u> **WITH** E **AS** NEXT-ITEM

15. place item in trolley

COMMENT read next item on list & locate this item in the store
    DO <u>READ&FIND</u> **WITH** F **AS** NEXT-ITEM

18. place item in trolley

COMMENT read next item on list & locate this item in the store
    DO <u>READ&FIND</u> **WITH** G **AS** NEXT-ITEM

21. place item in trolley

COMMENT read next item on list & locate this item in the store
    DO <u>READ&FIND</u> **WITH** H **AS** NEXT-ITEM

24. place item in trolley

SUBPROGRAM <u>READ&FIND</u>
COMMENT read next item on list
    PUT NEXT-ITEM **INTO** CURRENT-TASK
    PUT 0 **INTO** NEXT-ITEM

COMMENT locate this item in the store
    categorize item in CURRENT-TASK
    consult supermarket layout plan
    find desired category of items
    plan route to where desired category located
    go to this location
    survey items until item in CURRENT-TASK found

Notice that the **DO** instruction replaces two instructions from the original plan. So, the remaining plan instructions (all repetitions of "place item …") retain their original numbering 3, 6, 9, and so on.

This new version of our program is condensed by eliminating the repetition of the details of reading and locating, but it's still a bit tedious because it remains very repetitive (it is also configured only for shopping lists of exactly eight items).

We need to take just one more step into the finely detailed world of programming in order to see how we can avoid this repetition and shop with ease for just as many items as we wish. Well almost. There are physical limitations on the size of numbers than any computer can handle, but they are typically way beyond the numbers than humans can usefully handle, and certainly larger than any real shopping list.

So far, we have allowed the computer to simply work sequentially down through the list of instructions in the *main* program, and then it is finished (although **DO** instructions cause it to have to break off this main list and work sequentially through **SUBPROGRAM READ&FIND**). Because we have allowed the computer to operate in this simple beginning to end fashion it has meant that whenever we want it to compute some more, we must add some more instructions to the end of our *main* program. This seems reasonable, and it is, but there are also further shortcuts that the programmer can take.

Instead of simply allowing the computer to start at the top of our *main* program, work down through the list of instructions, and finish when it reaches the bottom, we can force it to return back up and re-*execute* of some of the earlier instructions. This is, for obvious reasons, called *looping*. We can force the computer to repeatedly *execute* a chosen list of instructions as many times as we wish. As you can perhaps appreciate there is real power resident in this possibility, for with just a few instructions repeatedly obeyed by the computer we can keep the machine busy for very long periods of time computing what amounts to lengthy sequences of results.

One snag with this simple idea, which you may be puzzling over, is that there seems very little point in getting the computer to repeatedly obey exactly the same sequence of instructions. Once more your logical reasoning is spot on – such exact repetition is likely to be pointless. So what we in fact do is we change the instruction sequence slightly, but significantly, each time the computer re-*executes* the *loop* sequence. Thus the computer computes something different on each repetition of the *loop* sequence. This should come as no real surprise for we did just this with our *subprogram* **READ&FIND**. In this *subprogram* we changed the actual box that NEXT-ITEM referred to each time we reused the *subprogram*. It was only this substitution for NEXT-ITEM that caused the robot to find a different item each time the *subprogram* was used.

Close inspection of the *main* program, **SHOP**, above will reveal that the only difference in the repeated blocks of instructions is the **DO** instruction. And the only difference between successive **DO** instructions is the label of the box to be substituted for NEXT-ITEM in the processing of the *subprogram* named (i.e., **READ&FIND**). So if we can arrange for the correct sequence of labels to appear in a single **DO** instruction each time we get the computer to repeat this instruction, we will have solved our problem. For the moment I'll again use a question mark to indicate that a detail remains to be sorted out, and first show you how we might obtain the *looping* behaviour itself.

In most programming languages there is a variety of instructions that cause the computer to return to some earlier (higher up) point in the instruction list and continue back down repeating what it has already done. Here's one popular *loop* structure:

REPEAT

    COMMENT read next item on list & locate this item in the store
        DO READ&FIND **WITH** ? **AS** NEXT-ITEM

    3. place item in trolley
UNTIL ??

Typically this **REPEAT-UNTIL** structure causes the computer to repeatedly *execute* all of the individual instructions listed between the **REPEAT** and the **UNTIL**. In this case just the **DO** and "place" instructions (recall that the computer ignores **COMMENT**s). As it stands this is fine for getting a lot of work out of the computer with only a little programming effort, but of course the computer will never stop this repetition. After re-*executing* the *loop* instructions some number of times, stopping the repetition is usually desirable, if not essential. The use of a *loop* structure thus introduces a two-way split in the program's *flow path*, a *branch point*: at the end of the *loop* the computer may either re-*execute* the *loop* instructions, or continue on down and *execute* whatever instructions follow the *loop*. The use of a <u>*branch condition*</u> determines which of the alternative *flow paths* is taken when a *branch point* is reached.

What is the *branch condition* we need (I've marked its place with a double question mark)? In this particular case the robot should be programmed to shop for a list of items, and naturally it should cease shopping when it reaches the end of its shopping list.

So, we'll complete the **UNTIL** instruction with a *branch condition* that tells the robot to stop shopping when it reaches the end of its shopping list. Something like

UNTIL list is empty

should do the trick (remember we've been deleting each item, by replacing the box value with 0, before we sent the robot off to find it).

Now we have a short list of instructions that embody a potentially very long *flow path* (around and around the *looping flow path*). This is because the computer may go around the loop hundreds, thousands or millions of times before the shopping "list is empty" (not in our program, which is limited to 26 items, but in general). In Fig. 4.4 we see the by now familiar illustrations: a simple list of instructions and a not-so-simple <u>*flow structure*</u> which is <u>all</u> the potential *flow paths* in the program.

In this particular case, if the shopping list is e*mpty* it will go straight down and so reach the end of the program. But if the shopping list is *not empty*, it will take the branch left (from the reader's viewpoint) and up to re-*execute* the *loop* instructions.

Large programs usually contain hundreds or thousands of such *branch points* in their *flow structure*. So the particular path that a computer weaves through the alternative potential *flow paths* is determined by the specific values in certain *storage boxes* (the ones specified in each *branch condition*) at the instant when the computer reaches each *branch point*. In Fig. 4.4 the two paths out of the *branch point* have been labelled with the specific *conditions* that determine which route it will take. In all future *flow-structure* illustrations the *branch points* will not be labelled, but you should realise that they could be and that they are, in effect, for the computer. But for us who seek merely to grasp the rudiments of program complexity, such labelling would be unnecessary clutter. However, for the programmer grappling with unsatisfactory emergent behaviour, these *branch conditions* are, of course, vital details needed to inform his understanding. He must deal with all the clutter.

Finally, notice that in this figure the program still appears to be (and indeed still is) a simple list of instructions, but that superficial simplicity hides a complex *flow structure*. It is this hidden structure that directly determines what behaviours will emerge from a program.

We are almost finished with program development, so stay with me just a little longer. All that remains is to replace the single question mark with the proper object. What is the purpose of the **WITH**? **AS** NEXT-ITEM part of the instruction?

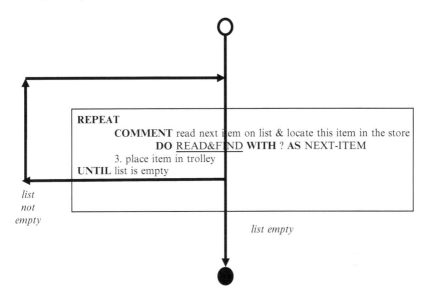

Fig. 4.4 A short list of instructions hiding a very long *flow path*, a *loop*

Cast your mind (or even your eyes) back to when I first mooted this loop idea. We planned to use a *loop* structure in order to enable the robot to shop for as many items as a given list specifies without having to keep explicitly repeating the **DO** and "place in trolley" instructions. And the sequence of **DO** instructions differed only in the label used in each of them. The actual values to **PUT-INTO** NEXT-ITEM were "A", "B", "C", "D", etc. So, on each fresh loop back through the **DO** instruction we need the question mark replaced by the next letter in the alphabet after starting at letter A.

If you'll allow me to slip in two new programming instructions at this eleventh hour, we've finished. The two instructions, **SET** and **SET-NEXT**, are used to cause the computer to start at the beginning of the alphabet and to step through it, one letter after another. The result is that our **PUT-INTO** instruction actually works through the shopping list, starting at box A, then box B, etc. just as it should.

SET alpha-letter **AS** A

REPEAT

> **COMMENT** read next item on list & locate this item in the store
> > **DO** READ&FIND **WITH** alpha-letter **AS** NEXT-ITEM
> 3. place item in trolley

> **SET-NEXT** alpha-letter

UNTIL list is empty

This gives us our finished program, which is:

<u>SHOP</u>

SET alpha-letter **AS** A

REPEAT

    COMMENT read next item on list & locate this item in the store

        DO <u>READ&FIND</u> **WITH** alpha-letter **AS** NEXT-ITEM

    3. place item in trolley

    SET-NEXT alpha-letter

UNTIL list is empty

SUBPROGRAM <u>READ&FIND</u>

    COMMENT read next item on list

        PUT NEXT-ITEM **INTO** CURRENT-TASK

        PUT 0 **INTO** NEXT-ITEM

    COMMENT locate this item in the store

        categorize item in CURRENT-TASK

        consult supermarket layout plan

        find desired category of items

        plan route to where desired category located

        go to this location

        survey items until item in CURRENT-TASK found

Actually, this is not a finished program because it still contains plan instructions that would eventually need to be refined into programming-language instructions, but it's finished enough for our purposes. Notice that the program is still no more than a simple list of instructions, but its *flow structure* is far from a similarly straight and simple arrow, as Fig. 4.5 illustrates.

Flow through **SUBPROGRAM <u>READ&FIND</u>** will occur many times on the average shopping expedition (as many times as there are items on the shopping list). However, each repeated flow through will be different: the robot will be shopping for a new shopping-list item each time.

So, if the programmer is desirous of checking some aspect of the *subprogram* computation, he will need to be aware of the full range of box values that could differ on each repetition. In our simple case, the difference amounts to no more than the value of box NEXT-ITEM. Hence, the value of this box is a crucial detail of the computation when the computer is executing **SUBPROGRAM <u>READ&FIND</u>**.

Just as flow *branch points* each require explicit *branch conditions* as part of the understanding that a programmer must be aware of, so *loops* especially (and all *flow paths*, in general) require explicit knowledge of the individual *storage-box* contents to support the necessary understanding. As with *branch conditions*, we shall not be augmenting *flow paths* with the critical *storage-box* values either. Again we do this to cut down on clutter; the programmer will only do this at his peril. The details of the *storage-box* value changes during the *execution* of a program are a further aspect

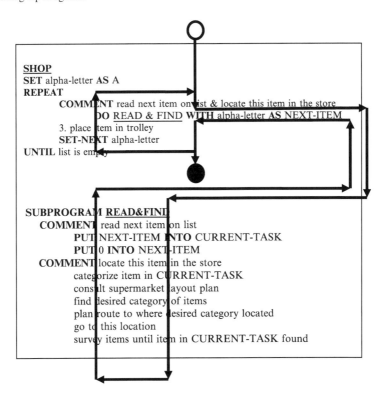

SHOP
SET alpha-letter **AS** A
REPEAT
        COMMENT read next item on list & locate this item in the store
                DO READ & FIND WITH alpha-letter AS NEXT-ITEM
        3. place item in trolley
        SET-NEXT alpha-letter
UNTIL list is empty

SUBPROGRAM READ&FIND
    COMMENT read next item on list
            PUT NEXT-ITEM INTO CURRENT-TASK
            PUT 0 INTO NEXT-ITEM
    COMMENT locate this item in the store
            categorize item in CURRENT-TASK
            consult supermarket layout plan
            find desired category of items
            plan route to where desired category located
            go to this location
            survey items until item in CURRENT-TASK found

Fig. 4.5 Superficial simplicity hiding considerable complexity

of detailed complexity that we shall henceforth ignore. The take-away message is: far from exaggerating program complexity, I'm slashing it down to basics.

For all those readers who are not closet hackers and refuse to be charmed by such tinkering with programs, the end is nigh; in fact, we've reached it already. So for you who are thoroughly fed up and bored by the foregoing pages of tediousness the good news is that it is finished. If you can understand a significant amount of the programming trivia that I've just been pushing in front of you then you are in a position to develop a proper appreciation of my subsequent arguments about the scope, limitations and dangers of modern computer technology.

If, on the other hand, you have followed the foregoing with ease and enjoyment, and even feel tempted to develop this program further, beware! You are obviously susceptible to the HHS. Resist the growing feeling that ploughing on through the rest of this book will simply be a waste of potential programming time. Say 'No' to programming before you get hooked.

So, you're not a programmer (unless you were before you started this book), but you should now have some useful insights into the technology. Let me list them:

• All programs are simply a list of instructions that the computer will follow mindlessly.

- The instruction list may be reduced in length by making repeated segments into a single instance of a _subprogram_ which is _executed_ repeatedly from the _main_ program.
- Other repeated instruction segments may be included in a _loop_ structure that directs the computer to repeatedly _execute_ the instructions included within it.
- Use of a _loop_ structure introduces a _branch point_ where the _execution_ sequence may either go around the loop or not.
- This list of instructions, the program, then determines a complex _flow structure_ (as the collection of all potential _flow paths_), but makes no effort to expose it.
- It is the _flow structure_ (in conjunction with _branch conditions_ and specific _storage-box_ values) that directly determines the program behaviour that emerges.
- _Stepwise refinement_ from _program plan_ to programming language instructions is introduced and contrasted with _ad hoc_ concoction of programs.
- Some _program style_ guidelines (just **COMMENT**s and indentation as a layout feature) were introduced as an aid to human comprehension.
- _subprograms_ and _loops_ reduce program size but increase _flow structure_ complexity.
- Consequently, the programmer attempting to eliminate an error, or otherwise modify the emergent behaviour, can only work by rearranging the list of instructions but must think in terms of the _flow structure_ repercussions.

The wrenching dislocation between manipulating the list of instructions in order to modify the _flow structure_ it determines is a demanding mental exercise in itself; it's made (much) worse because it's dependent upon a myriad of other details, any one of which can wreck the outcome – as we shall see in the next chapter.

Endnotes

1. This true story is told at much greater length and with full details by Leonard Lee in _The Day the Phones Stopped_ (Primus: New York, 1992).
2. One important difference between programs and recipes is that programs are constructed to be followed precisely, whereas recipes will always (and are usually expected to) admit some latitude for interpretation. You never get precisely the same cake twice, but you should always get precisely the same computation from an unchanged program – however many times you require the computer to _execute_ the program (to exercise the jargon).
3. _Mrs Beeton's Household Management: a complete cookery book_, by Isabella Beeton, Ward Lock: London. This famous nineteenth century tome of 1,680 pages, which ranges from cookery through to "servants' duties", has been through many editions and was a UK standard for decades.
4. I employ the convention of underlining for all _main_ program and _subprogram_ names, and bold for the name itself where the subprogram is specified, but not bolded for references to the name. In this way we can visually distinguish between a _subprogram_ name designating a segment of instructions as a _subprogram_, and a _subprogram_ name that is an instruction for the computer to go to the named _subprogram_ and _execute_ the instructions it contains.

Chapter 5
Recipes for What?

The $18 million Hyphen

On July 22nd, 1962, the Mariner I *space probe to Venus lifted off the launch pad at Cape Canaveral. A few seconds later it was destroyed by mission control when it began to behave erratically, thereby threatening a crash landing back on Earth. A minor equipment malfunction had, apparently, activated a small and very rarely used piece of the total program in the probe's computer system. This small program was missing a hyphen – the most expensive hyphen in history.*[1]

Another version of this story has a minus sign instead of a hyphen as the micro glitch with the macro cost – a confusion of two symbols that are visually very similar but interpreted differently in a computer program. Computers, remember, don't visualize their programs, they simply obey the codes they are given.

You have been exposed to the basic difficulty of programming, i.e., the programmer must work with a list of instructions but he must think in terms of a complex *flow structure*. The goal of this chapter is to show that the detailed intricacies, which complicate the programmer's task, extend beyond, way beyond, the constraints of logic or rationality.

The intricate web of constraints to be managed also escalates rapidly as program size grows – the manageably small all too soon becomes the unmanageably large.

In dealing with this complexity growth, rational or logical reasoning has a role, but so does style. *Program style* manifest as good program layout, informative **COMMENT**s and judicious name choices can help a great deal, but it can all too easily become a hindrance. Stylistic awareness and competence are bound up with visual aesthetics: they are crucial aids to the struggle in the programmer's brain to 'see' how the program is doing what it is observed to be doing. Hence the severe negative impact when stylistic devices are misleading.

At this point I hope that you can appreciate some of the intricacies of programming, but this is just a beginning. We'll probe a little deeper to make it quite clear what is demanded of the programmer. I trust that the programming exercise was not a total blur in your brain. But even if the experience was for you more of a mystery

D. Partridge, *The Seductive Computer: Why IT Systems Always Fail*,
DOI 10.1007/978-1-84996-498-2_5, © Springer-Verlag London Limited 2011

tour than a journey of enlightenment, all is not lost. In either case, you are now in a position to appreciate that programming is a demanding task, and what the nature of these demands is.

The programmer must possess the ability to mentally manage large quantities of fine-grained detail. The order of the instructions is important: sometimes precise order is crucial and sometimes it makes no significant difference. Sometimes the constraints on order are looser – for example, a certain statement must precede (or be inside) a loop structure. Sometimes the ordering constraints are interrelated such that the specific way that one restriction is satisfied changes the details of other constraints which may or may not already have been dealt with by the programmer.

There are examples of all of these elements of program complexity in our small program. A simple order constraint would be that our shopping robot must know what the next item on the shopping list is before it attempts to locate it in the superstore. In our program, the instructions to 'read next item on list' must precede 'locate this item in the store.' That's pretty obvious (I hope). But what about the instruction **SET-NEXT** alpha-letter? Can it precede the instruction currently above it, i.e., 3. place item in trolley? The answer is, Yes. Logically, or rationally (if that's preferred), these two instructions can exchange places and the program's emergent behaviour is not affected. However as we shall soon see, hard on the heels of such firm logical constraints are softer (in terms of behavioural correctness), but vital, stylistic ones.

What about moving the **SET-NEXT** instruction above the **DO** instruction that precedes the 'place'one? This time the answer is, No. Such an interchange would wreck a crucial ordering in the program. Why? **SET-NEXT** moves the shopping process on to the next shopping list item by moving the value of "alpha-letter" on to the next letter of the alphabet, and you shouldn't do this until the robot has identified, located and retrieved its current shopping list item. This logical constraint makes obvious sense, does it not?

What would be the effect of this error? Perhaps not much, actually. The robot would always fail to shop for the first item on the shopping list.[2] That may be all that would happen, and so the error could go unnoticed for some time. Or the robot owner might notice that he or she never gets the first item on the shopping list, and elects to live with this glitch by putting something unwanted as first item or repeating the first item later in the list.

This strategy of learning to live with the recognized glitches of IT systems is commonplace. Every organization does it. This is because working around the known problems with an IT system is often cheaper, quicker, easier and far less risky than trying to get the problems fixed. The known errors are often no more than a nuisance; it is the unknown ones that can quietly wreak major damage before their existence is recognized.

Another constraint in our program is that our mechanical shopper must always put a copy of the next item (say "milk" from box C) into box CURRENT-TASK before it puts a zero into the shopping-list box (box C in this case). To get these parts of the program the wrong way around will result in a robot that shops only for "0"s, whatever that might mean. The robot happily fills its trolley with nothing and proceeds to the checkout? The robot returns empty handed to report that none of your items were available? The robot continues shopping fruitlessly until it's reported to the store manager who flips its cutout switch and telephones the owner? The robot stalls on the first "0", and awaits human intervention? You and I may hazard guesses, but the outcome will be precisely determined, one way or another, only by programmed detail.

The human shopper similarly misinstructed would know immediately that something is amiss, but the human can (and will) apply commonsense and intelligence. The robot possesses neither, and hence the program must be precisely correct in every detail in a way that instructions for humans need not be.

So you can see, I hope, what I mean about fine-grained complexity of programming. What sort of mind does it take to manage the mass of detailed complexity necessary to construct programs successfully? Folklore has it that a logical mind is what is needed. I'm not so sure; I'm also not sure what the sign of a logical mind actually is – traditionally educationalists equate it with an ability to do mathematics. Certainly, reasoning about program instruction order constraints does appear to depend on a ability to think clearly and rationally about process details. This is not formal logic but 'logical' is a word that begs to be used in this context.[3]

So now we've constructed a computer program, nothing approaching the 25 million lines that control NASA's Space Shuttle, but we've constructed a real program, nevertheless. We've also seen something of the variety and scope of constraints that a programmer must manage.

We've constructed a program and I choose the neutral word "constructed" advisedly. It carries no meaning as to how the program was put together. The methodologically correct computer scientist might well want to say they we have concocted a computer program, cobbled one together – paying little more than lip service to systematic program development.

I'd probably have to agree, but the point of the foregoing was not to exemplify good programming practice. It was to begin to convey the intricate complexities of the task. This was a legitimate demonstration despite the fact that use of a good program-design technique will drastically reduce the complexities of the task. For, although use of such a technique could have eliminated much of the complexity that we found in the development of our small program, it was a very small program.

The vast increase in the number of instructions that a professional programmer is called upon to manage soon overwhelms the complexity reduction that systematic development of a program brings with it. However, any help is still better than no help at all.

The program that we came up with was not designed and developed step-by-step in a systematic manner, although we did progress, in one or more refinement steps, from a *program plan* to detailed programming-language instructions for (parts of) this plan. This is the proper way to develop programs, and the only way (that holds any chance of success) when developing large IT systems. The overall plan of the task is systematically refined to yield a final program composed of many interacting parts, each of which causes the computer to execute a well-defined subtask. *Stepwise refinement*, a process of systematic program development, was illustrated in the previous chapter.

Divide and conquer is a well-known strategy for dealing with large problems that threaten intractability, or worse, be they opposing armies or IT system applications.

Consider both the time involved and the chances of eventual success if you try to reconstruct a jigsaw puzzle with all the pieces in one heap, face down. It is not impossible, but with little more to go on than whether each two or three individual pieces seem to fit together, you will make very many mistakes (including many that you never realize are mistakes) and you'll probably never complete the correct picture anyway. This is what we might call the 'concocting' method of jigsaw-puzzle construction. In reality, it is no method at all.

The systematic, step-by-step alternative exploits to the full the picture to be reconstructed. You first turn all the pieces face up, then you partition the initial jumble of pieces into various subgroups such as edge pieces, sky pieces, reddish-brown pieces, etc. You then work with each of these small and selected subsets of pieces in an attempt to reconstruct just one small part of the final picture, and so on. In this way you will make fewer mistakes and probably achieve the final goal in a reasonable time.

Constructing programs is much trickier, but a similar sort of divide-and-conquer, systematic approach seems to be the most effective way of tackling the overall task. With our program we were juggling relatively few instructions, and this feat was more or less manageable (more for some people and less for others). Conceptual juggling with 10,000 instructions is not possible for anyone. At this level of complexity we must have a program design and management scheme to assist us.

In much the same spirit as this is not a 'how to program' book, it is also not the intention of this book to subject the reader to a full course on the principles of program development and the consequent *programming style*. With respect to program layout styles, my intent is: to give you a taste of *style* as derived from *stepwise refinement*; to make it clear that such stylistic effort is an important collection of machinery for lessening the gap between *flow structure* and the list of program instructions; and finally to demonstrate the inherent weakness of this idea.

The fundamental *stylistic* intuitions behind lessening the complexity gulf between a simple list of instructions and the convoluted *flow structure* that yields the program's behaviour are:

- *modularity*: complexity is reduced by a structure within which blocks of instructions (i.e. modules) each compute a well-defined subtask of the overall behaviour desired.
- *encapsulation*: every effort is made to keep a maximum of the implementation details of a module (e.g., specific box labels) isolated within the module, and to reduce to a minimum the information that must flow from one module to another.
- *flow-structure visualization*: layout of the program instruction list is designed to infer the *flow structure*.

The good news is that we have already been exercising these desiderata in our programming effort. Yes indeed.

A *structured* or *well-structured program* is one that embodies these *stylistic* principles, and reveals its *flow structure* to the human eye, insofar as that is possible. Such structure can be naturally achieved by using a systematic development procedure, such as *stepwise refinement*, and we have done some of this en route to our small program.

Look at Fig. 5.1, it makes explicit the relationship between our high-level plan for the robot shopper and the program module that we developed from it.

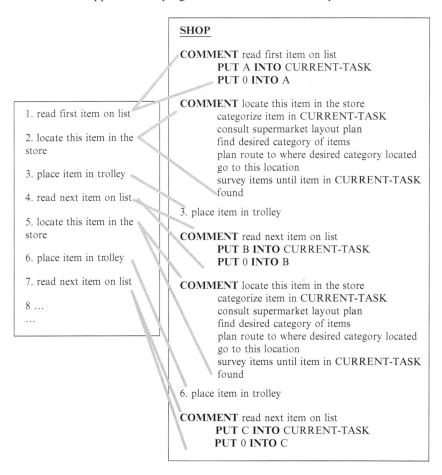

Fig. 5.1 Our high-level plan refines to program modules

Each element of the initial plan (the list of operations on the left of Fig. 5.1) is a subtask of shopping, and each becomes a module of our developing program. Visually, I emphasize this modularity by adopting the following *stylistic* layout rules:

1. separate modules with empty lines
2. preface each expanded module with a **COMMENT**, a header outlining the operations that the module should cause the computer to perform (and these

COMMENTed statements derive from, or are exact copies of, the original plan statements)

3. the refinement of each module (into either program instructions, further high-level instructions, or a mixture of both) is indented under its header **COMMENT** as a visually obvious block

Within Fig. 5.1, we can clearly see that the "read" and "locate" elements of the original plan have been refined separately into **COMMENT**ed blocks of program instructions, while the unrefined "place" elements remain unchanged.

The layout of the (partially) programmed version helps us visualize this modularization: each program module is headed with a **COMMENT** instruction that states what the module should cause the robot to do. Furthermore, each block of program module instructions is indented under its introductory **COMMENT** so that by scanning down the left-hand side of the program, the programmer can quickly pick out the modules and sub-modules. The program, which (as far as the computer is concerned) could just as easily be a monolithic single list of instructions, has been divided into modules.

The concept of 'understanding' programs merits a book all to itself; this is not that book. By *program understanding*, which we take as crucial to IT system development and useful survival, we mean an appreciation of the *flow structure* and various program-instruction decisions (such as stepping through the alphabet by choosing to use two instructions both placed in the main **SHOP** module). The nature of the necessary appreciation is such as to facilitate both debugging and further system development. Figure 5.1 is an attempt to make explicit the basis for the necessary understanding of the (partial) program in the right-hand panel.

Let's look at the next step from linear *flow-structure* program to our final loop structure with a subprogram; Fig. 5.2 illustrates these relationships.

By eliminating repetition and adding a *loop* (in this case **REPEAT-UNTIL**) to permit flexible and (almost) unlimited shopping lists we have lost the simple transformations of Fig. 5.1. In Fig. 5.2 we see the repetitive segments of the left-hand panel collapsed into the *subprogram* reference (**DO** READ&FIND) plus plan-statement number 3, and then further arrows (within the right-hand panel) illustrate how the *subprogram* reference has been transformed into the *subprogram* body (i.e., the two **COMMENT**ed modules).

Maybe you don't see these transformations all that clearly? This is exactly the point. Even with our very small program, layout conventions can only go some way towards helping the programmer visualize the all important *flow structure* of his program. It is crucial that the smaller, neater and more powerful final version, gained at the cost of *flow-structure* complexity, is indeed equivalent in program behaviour sketched out in the initial plan. *Stylistic* principles manifest as layout conventions, systematically developed in refinement steps, help us to assure ourselves of this equivalence, but they fall far short of a complete guarantee.

Indeed, they can become something of a problem themselves. Whilst I was constructing Figs. 5.1 and 5.2 I found two significant layout mistakes that I had made

```
SHOP                                      SHOP
                                          SET alpha-letter AS A
COMMENT read first item on list           REPEAT
        PUT A INTO CURRENT-TASK                    COMMENT read next item on list
        PUT 0 INTO A                               & locate this item in the store
                                                       DO READ&FIND WITH
COMMENT  locate this item in the store                 alpha-letter AS NEXT-
         categorize item in CURRENT-                   ITEM
         TASK
         consult supermarket layout plan          3. place item in trolley
         find desired category of items              SET-NEXT alpha-letter
         plan route to where desired           UNTIL list is empty
         category located
         go to this location
         survey items until item in          SUBPROGRAM READ&FIND
         CURRENT-TASK found                      COMMENT   read next item on list
                                                        PUT NEXT-ITEM INTO
                                                        CURRENT-TASK
3. place item in trolley                                PUT 0 INTO NEXT-ITEM

COMMENT   read next item on list            COMMENT locate this item in the store
          PUT B INTO CURRENT-TASK                    categorize item in CURRENT-
          PUT 0 INTO B                               TASK
                                                     consult supermarket layout plan
COMMENT locate this item in the store                find desired category of items
        categorize item in CURRENT-                  plan route to where desired
        TASK                                         category located
        consult supermarket layout plan             go to this location
        find desired category of items              survey items until item in
        plan route to where desired                 CURRENT-TASK found
        category located
        go to this location
        survey items until item in
        CURRENT-TASK found


6. place item in trolley
```

Fig. 5.2 Repetitive simple program modules are further refined

with the program versions in Chapter 4. As you can imagine, I had checked and double-checked my programs. I am not a professional IT system programmer, but I can mount some considerable claim to expertise in this area.

So how did I make these layout mistakes? Easy, anyone can do it, and all programmers do it from time to time. If complex detail becomes a challenge with a 20-line program just imagine how this issue escalates when grappling with hundreds of thousands or millions of lines of code.

As a hardened, but rehabilitated, programmer I saw these errors and immediately fixed them quite easily, and that capability is no small part of the overall delusion. Many an energetic and mentally agile young man[4] could quite quickly and easily construct our final program with no preliminary plan, no step-by-step derivation of modules, no **COMMENT**s and no visual layout of the modules. Such boring foreplay he will dismiss as a waste of time with the evidence of his working program to back up his claim.

The big mistake is to think that their positive experience with small programs can be extended to large programs with just a bit more effort. An interested and committed brain of the right sort can construct satisfactory small programs out of nothing (with a degree of retrospective error fixing permitted). Creative ad hoc-ery is the basis of this process, which is challenging, exciting and immensely satisfying once the 'puzzle' has been solved and your program works as it is supposed to do. However, no brain, or even cooperating collection of excellent brains, stands any chance of constructing large IT systems without meticulous planning and systematic program development. Even then success is by no means a foregone conclusion irrespective of both budget and schedule considerations.

From such a realization, the answer to the question of why large IT systems cost so much, take so long to build, and then work so poorly, is obvious. The difficult question would seem to be: how are they ever completed at all? Well, sometimes they're not, at least, not as useful products.[5]

It is reasonable to think that the counsel of perfection (which I've been seriously considering) is to refine the entire *program plan* to program instructions, and then *execute* the resultant program on a computer. This will identify any small grammatical mistakes as well as confirm (I hope) that the shopping behaviour emerges just as it should. As we know from the bank-balance example back in Chapter 1, the emergence of specific behaviour as expected does not prove that the program is in a general sense correct, but it would serve to assure me that I might well have avoided the most obvious blunders. But would it even do this?

Notice that to produce an executable program considerably more work needs to be done to replace the plan and high-level instructions that still remain in our final version, work that itself will inject further opportunities to make mistakes. But, much more importantly, if I had done all this further development correctly and yet included my two significant layout errors, what would I have learned? In a word: nothing.

This is because the layout of a program is purely an aid to help the human brain appreciate the *flow structure* of a program; the computer ignores it. We know that **COMMENT**s are ignored but so are empty lines and indentations. The computer simply moves from one executable instruction to the next (either sequentially next, or as directed explicitly by **DO** or **REPEAT-UNTIL** instructions), and it does what the instructions specify. Figure 5.3 illustrates our program with its helpful structured layout, and the same program as processed by the computer.[6]

What this means is that the structured layout, helpfully reflecting the supposed *flow structure*, has no necessary connection with the actual *flow structure,* nor with the logical breakdown of the task. What the human brain perceives of the program's *flow structure* may be total fiction. It is the programmer's task to make sure that this is not the case, and, of course, it never is – never total, that is.

However, even ignoring layout mistakes, it is usually the case that some aspects of the layout structure are fictional simply because changes have been made to the programmed instructions but not to the layout. Why? Well because there is no pressing need to change the layout structure (the computer ignores it) and the

```
SHOP                                    SHOP
SET alpha-letter AS A                   SET alpha-letter AS A
REPEAT                                  REPEAT
      COMMENT read next item on         DO READ&FIND WITH alpha-letter AS
      list & locate this item in the    NEXT-ITEM
      store                             3. place item in trolley
            DO READ&FIND WITH           SET-NEXT alpha-letter
            alpha-letter AS NEXT-       UNTIL list is empty
            ITEM                        SUBPROGRAM READ&FIND
      3. place item in trolley          PUT NEXT-ITEM INTO CURRENT-TASK
      SET-NEXT alpha-letter             PUT 0 INTO NEXT-ITEM
UNTIL list is empty                     categorize item in CURRENT-TASK
                                        consult supermarket layout plan
SUBPROGRAM READ&FIND                    find desired category of items
  COMMENT  read next item on list       plan route to where desired category
      PUT NEXT-ITEM INTO                located
      CURRENT-TASK                      go to this location
      PUT 0 INTO NEXT-ITEM              survey items until item in CURRENT-TASK
  COMMENT locate this item in the store found
      categorize item in CURRENT-
      TASK
      consult supermarket layout plan
      find desired category of items
      plan route to where desired
      category located
      go to this location
      survey items until item in
      CURRENT-TASK found
```

Fig. 5.3 Two views of our program – ours and the computer's

programmer is just trying out some program change with the intention to go back and make the layout changes once he's happy with the program-instruction changes. For reasons of forgetfulness, laziness, continued uncertainty about the program changes and pressure to move on to resolve other (the 'real') difficulties with the IT system, the layout changes do not get made. After all, they will have absolutely no effect on how the IT system actually works (or doesn't, as the case may be).

Changing the program instructions in order to get the computer to do what you want is fun and self-absorbing – try this neat idea, see what happens, and then try that, and so on. But writing **COMMENT**s and adjusting layout to reflect the changes involves not one iota of amusement or challenge. It is pure drudgery. So no wonder such mundane and boring housekeeping activities are left till later, and later, like tomorrow, is always in the future.

Succinct and accurate **COMMENT**s are something of an art in themselves. They require careful phraseology, short yet precise, founded on a decent mastery of English (in our case). Neither of these qualities is typically found in abundance in computer whiz-kids. Ambiguous, or downright misleading, **COMMENT**s can be worse than no **COMMENT**s.

Other 'structure' that I have slipped in to help human perception is the names that I have chosen. They help you and me appreciate what's going on because of the meanings that these English words carry. For the computer they carry no meanings whatsoever other than arbitrary *storage-box* labels, or *subprogram* labels. So, just like helpful layout, helpful labels can be a genuine aid to program insights. However, they can also be a major source of misdirection for exactly the same reasons.

Figure 5.4 illustrates how injudicious naming and **COMMENT**ing can be a severe impediment to *program understanding*. Any consistent name substitution will have no computational effect, and absolutely anything at all can be written in the **COMMENT** instructions. For example, our **SHOP** program illustrated in Fig. 5.3 is exactly the same to the computer as the one in Fig. 5.4.

```
WAGER
SET nothing AS A
REPEAT
        COMMENT make a low bet
                DO BID WITH nothing AS NEXT-BET
        3. place item in trolley
        SET-NEXT nothing
UNTIL list is empty

SUBPROGRAM BID
  COMMENT  reduce bet
        PUT NEXT-BET INTO GAME
        PUT 0 INTO NEXT-BET
  COMMENT find new game to play
        categorize item in GAME
        consult supermarket layout plan
        find desired category of items
        plan route to where desired category located
        go to this location
        survey items until item in GAME found
```

Fig. 5.4 A disguised program for the robot shopper

The final principle that remains unillustrated is *encapsulation*, which is closely tied to the principle of *modularity*. The *encapsulation* principle stipulates that details, such as box labels and elements of a composite operation, are kept within a module as much as possible.

Thus "CURRENT-TASK" labels a box that contains the name of the item being 'shopped for' at any moment in time. The finding and retrieving of this item all occurs in the subprogram **READ&FIND**, so we can limit the *scope* of this particular box label to the module that is **SUBPROGRAM READ&FIND**, which is itself composed of two sub-modules – one to determine the item to be found, and the other to do the finding. The *scope* of a box label is all the modules of the program in which that box's value can be used or changed.

Why is it a good thing to limit *scope*? It localizes the potential effects of this box label. This means that if we want to alter it, or alter how it is used, or suspect it of being party to erroneous program behaviour, we have only a small part of our program to inspect when attempting to assure ourselves of its role in the overall IT system.

An example of operation encapsulation is provided by our need to step through the alphabet when processing the shopping list. The 'stepping through' operation is composed of two elements: setting up the operation to start at the letter "A", and then progressing from one letter to the next. These two components (manifest as instructions **SET** and **SET-NEXT,** respectively) are both located within the main **SHOP** module. Logically, they do not have to be.

The robot needs to move on to the next box on its shopping list (so the next letter of the alphabet) when it has read and found the current item. It can do this at the end of **SUBPROGRAM READ&FIND**. So we could move the instruction **SET-NEXT** from the **SHOP** module to the bottom of the **READ&FIND** *subprogram*; everything will work fine, but the 'stepping through' operation will be split between two modules which themselves could be separated by hundreds of other modules. Such a dispersion of what is conceptually a single, composite operation is not going to help *program understanding*, and such an understanding is the key to effective and accurate program modification.

However, look again at our program (the left panel of Fig. 5.3). You might notice that NEXT-ITEM is not restricted to just one module of our program. It occurs in both. Why? A stylistic blunder? No, of course not. This box label is the single piece of information that needs to be communicated between our program modules. The *subprogram* needs to know exactly in which box it will find the item to be shopped for, and the main program arranges for this box to contain the correct succession of items on the shopping list. These decisions are all a matter of judgement biased by other judgements; they are not the outcome of cold logic. *Encapsulation* cannot be total because non-communicating modules are in effect separate programs. But what is communicated, between which modules and by what means are all judge-mental issues more or less constrained by logical necessities.

So logical, or rational, thinking is not the whole story behind programming success – once again in the small, it might be, but in the large it definitely is not. A good IT system will be stylistically sound, and sometimes the simplest logical approach runs contrary to the best stylistic solution. The competent IT-system developer has a logical mind tempered by stylistic appreciation in order to be fully cognizant of his options and the long-term costs of his system-design choices. Such complexity management skills are not required for the small-program hacker because he'll crack the emergent problems and any new requirements with sheer ingenuity and perseverance.

Far too many recruitment agencies and project managers have absolutely no appreciation of the mix of skills really required for IT system development. Anyone with an interest in, or aptitude for, programming can land such a job. Employing hackers to develop large IT systems is the short route to emergent chaos, but it happens all the time.[7]

Notice also that fine-detailed choices can impact directly (and worse, indirectly) on overall IT-system behaviour. The project manager who maintains an ignorance of crucial design choices, through inability or inattention, coupled with hackers at the code face largely winging it, flying by the seat of their pants, means that emergent chaos is to be expected sooner rather than later. If the IT company does have program development and *documentation* standards, they are easily satisfied after the 'real' programming has been done. For example, a stipulated ratio of **COMMENT**s to programming-language instructions is quickly and easily satisfied with a sprinkling of bland, if not downright misleading, **COMMENT**s after the program has been written.

A good number of the above-listed problems are clearly the programmer's fault – he chose misleading box labels; he failed to update a **COMMENT** when he changed the instructions; he dispersed composite operations unnecessarily across modules; and so on. So he's only got himself to blame for his problems, and the IT-system contractor must shoulder the blame for employing such a poor programmer.

Yes, but this all presumes that the person grappling with program *bugs* or trying to extend an IT system's behaviour is the person who also constructed the program in the first place – called greenfield programming. This is not usually the case. Firstly, no one person constructs a large IT system: it is a team task. Secondly, such expensive IT systems are constructed over years, and debugged or extended over decades whilst programmers come and go from month to month. Even if the original programmers happen to be around when called upon a few years (or just months) later, their grasp of the program's fine detail (which was always tenuous) will have faded or simply vanished.

So the general (and much worse) problem is that someone other than the original programmer will be faced with the task of completing or extending, or tracking down an error in a very large program that he is seeing for the first time. There should be extensive *documentation* of the original IT system development to help the new man get to grips with the program. But *documentation* such as manuals and design documents are just like program **COMMENT**s. They have no effect on system behaviour and so suffer from exactly the same faults. A well-written, accurate design document, like a well-written and accurate **COMMENT**, can be a great aid to understanding crucial program details. But inaccurate ones, whether well-written or not, can be very misleading. This problem is compounded by the fact that the new man has no easy way to distinguish the accurate from the inaccurate guidance he gets.

Software system maintenance is long-term process of sustaining system usefulness and usability. It involves tracking down and removing errors (old persistent ones and newly emergent ones) – known euphemistically as *debugging* – as well as enhancing system behaviour to accommodate new requirements both those of the business itself, and those due to hardware developments. Ease of *program understanding* is the key to efficient and effective IT-system maintenance, and *well-structured* and well-*documented* programming is the route to the requisite understanding.

The hacker, as I'm sure you are now aware, has for very good reasons of his own a horizon that makes the average politician, with an election looming, appear very far-sighted by comparison. Getting the program to 'work' is his major goal, and as soon as that happens, it's job done. Long-term maintenance will be done by someone else, so it's someone else's problem. But when development itself starts to stretch across years, *maintenance* becomes an element, perhaps the dominant one, of even the development process. Rewriting **COMMENT**s, readjusting layout and changing box labels will have absolutely no effect on how the program works, and it's very boring to boot. So, what's the chance that it gets full attention?

In sum, computer technology is certainly not all bad, nor all good. I suppose I should say that the technology itself is neutral and that it is the use that we humans make of it that turns it into a force for good or for evil (or at least something less than good). I would say this, except I don't believe it is true.

Computer technology is not neutral; its seductive and invasive nature makes it a technology that we must keep a very careful eye on, but even then we will only succeed in slowing its escape from our control.

So what has the current chapter added to our knowledge vis-à-vis programming technology and IT systems?

- Programming demands mastery, on a massive scale, of fine grained complexity springing from a network of constraints: some logical, some stylistic and some an ill-defined combination.
- Principles of *program style* and *structured programming* – such as, *modularity*, *encapsulation*, and localization of *scope* – minimize complexity and so facilitate *program understanding* through *flow-structure visualization*.
- Principles of *program style*, naturally developed through *stepwise refinement*, are made manifest through layout conventions, and can significantly facilitate understanding of the all-important *flow structure*.
- Poor, incomplete and outdated stylistic aids, a natural consequence of the HHS, can seriously misdirect *program understanding*.
- IT-system *documentation*, such as design diagrams and notes, can similarly assist *program understanding*, or misdirect it.
- Programming in the small is totally different from large IT system development – size really does matter.
- Whiz-kid hackers are the worst IT-system developers.
- IT-system *maintenance* is first introduced as a further aggravation in our quest for high-quality IT systems.
- A lot of IT-system *maintenance* is *debugging*, i.e., finding and fixing errors.

In this chapter I've provided you with examples of the detailed intricacies with which the programmer must grapple. I've introduced style and structure as weapons to combat the resultant complexity of programs (but weapons with a double edge). This led us on to the crucial role of *program understanding* as the basis for IT-system *maintenance* which is, all too often, an element of system development as well as of long-term system usability.

Adding, or making changes to, program instructions, either maintenance or initial development, has the goal of causing the correct behaviour to emerge, but I've fudged this issue of program correctness. It is obviously important and in the next chapter we'll get to grips with it. The introductory bank-balance example showed that correctness is not the simple issue it might seem, even with a simple problem.

Put IT-system correctness in the context of a very complicated task, such as managing all our medical records on a national scale, and it is hardly surprising that in addition to the problem of getting the computer to do what you want it to do there is the issue of <u>what</u> we should want it to do. What is correct behaviour?

Many computer scientists would dismiss much of my commentary out of hand. A computer program is a well-defined, formal object and so should be developed by formal methods thereby getting it correct first time with a sound basis for knowing it's correct. All the difficulties of poor program *structure* and misleading *style* would then vanish.

In the next chapter we'll see what they mean, and why it is not an answer.

Endnotes

1. Another snippet from Leonard Lee's collection *The Day the Phones Stopped* (Primus: New York, 1992).
2. For those who like to check their grasp of the relevant details, I'll explain why these changes will cause the robot to always overlook the first item on the shopping list. Below is our program with the proposed exchange of instruction positions.

   When the execution of the program begins, "alpha-letter" is set as "A" (i.e. to point to the first item on the shopping list), but on first entry to the loop, the SET-NEXT instruction moves "alpha-letter" along to point to "B". This means that the first jump to SUBPROGRAM READ&FIND will be with NEXT-ITEM aliased to box B, and not box A as it should. So the first item shopped for will be the item in box B, the second item on the shopping list. On next re-entry at the top of the loop SET-NEXT will move "alpha-letter" along to box C, and so all will proceed as intended with just the first item missed.

   A further error is to be expected with a shopping list containing only one item, because that will be skipped and the robot will be required to read and locate a second item that does not exist. This is a special case of another probable general error ('probable' only because we have not clarified what the "list is empty" stopping condition will be, nor what the shopping-list boxes contain beyond the designated items). With all shopping lists, the robot will be trying to shop for a final, non-existent item (as the result of a jump to SUBPROGRAM READ&FIND after SET-NEXT has moved "alpha-letter" on from the final list item) before it reaches the test "list is empty" at the end of the loop (part of the UNTIL instruction).
3. Formal logics are precisely defined reasoning systems, but they are not formalizations of our everyday logical or commonsense reasoning. To take a very basic example: logical inference from known facts to new ones. We might have the logical reasoning rule that 'if A is true then B is also true', perhaps written within the logical formalism as: **if** A **then** B. Let's turn this into a concrete example by choosing A and B as things that can be true or false (indeed must be only either true or false): A could be 'you are hungry', and B could be 'there is food in the refrigerator', both of which may independently be true or false. So, our specific reasoning rule now becomes: **if** *you are hungry* **then** *there is food in the refrigerator*. Now how does formal logic stipulate that we reason with this rule? If it is true that *you are hungry* then the rule permits you to infer that *there is food in the refrigerator*. This line of reasoning fits perfectly with commonsense reasoning. All well and good, but what about when you are not hungry? In formal logic terms: *you are hungry* is false. Is there still food in the refrigerator? In the world that you and I inhabit: of course there is, but formal logic insists that we cannot conclude this.

There might be food in the refrigerator, and there might not be. We just do not know. If A is false in the logical rule then, in formal logic, we are not entitled to conclude anything about the truth of B.

4. Or young woman if only she could work up enough enthusiasm for the activity.

5. Some of the following IT disasters were mentioned in the introductory chapter, but I'll recap here because this list is barely credible. The list of abandoned IT systems is long, some abandoned (or redirected) during development and others similarly treated after delivery. Many large IT systems are in use, only after rescaling and retargeting, changes that are not usually publicized (for obvious reasons). In March 2009, the UK's Ministry of Justice abandoned its IT project to track criminals from sentence to release after 5 years of development costing hundreds of millions of pounds (BBC News, 13/03/2009). Also in the news (and likely to run and run for some years yet) is the UK government's IT system for the National Health Service in which additional to all the usual program-correctness issues there is the massive extra complexity of constraints introduced by privacy issues surrounding personal medical records. Aaron Sloman (www.cs.bham.ac.uk) uses this system as an example of why such large IT system projects "are almost all doomed to fail."

   This is not a new phenomenon: in the1990s, the London Ambulance Service system (In 1994, P. Mellor wrote an article called "CAD: computer-aided disaster" and published it in a journal called *High Integrity Systems* vol. 1, no. 2, pp. 101–156), and the International Stock Exchange: Taurus project were both abandoned after repeated simplifying 'redesigns', repeated failure to meet development deadlines and costs escalating by tens of millions of pounds (www. scit.wlv.ac.uk accessed 03/02/2009); the Prison Service scrapped a £350 million project "in favour of two smaller ones"; a welfare benefits IT system was abandoned after £25 million spent on it; and so on.

6. Actually, it's worse than this because inside the computer the nice line-by-line separation of instructions that we still see in the right panel of Fig. 5.3 is also removed. It is replaced by a 'newline' character, say "%". In which case the computer is actually *executing*:

   SHOP%**SET** alpha-letter **AS** A%**REPEAT**%**DO** READ&FIND **WITH** alpha-letter **AS** NEXT-ITEM% 3. place item in trolley%**SET-NEXT** alpha-letter%**UNTIL** list is empty%**SUBPROGRAM** READ&FIND%**PUT** NEXT-ITEM **INTO** CURRENT-TASK%**PUT** 0 **INTO** NEXT-ITEM%categorize item in CURRENT-TASK%consult supermarket layout plan%find desired category of items%plan route to where desired category located%go to this location%survey items until item in CURRENT-TASK found.

7. During the recent decades in which Computer Science has become a recognized degree course in most Universities the intake has grown and grown. But sometime around the turn of the millennium applications to read Computer Science at Universities suddenly slumped. This triggered considerable consternation and consequent searching for the reasons. One of the popular explanations that emerged was that a general misconception that whiz-kid programmers were just what was needed for IT system development resulted in the view that three years spent at a University getting a degree in Computer Science was a waste of time for the self-taught competent programmer. As a committed Computer Science teacher, I like to believe that this explanation is a significant contributor to the dire state of IT-system development, and it just might be.

Chapter 6
Programs: The Good, the Bad, and the Verified

> *The construction of a computer program from a set of basic instructions is very similar to the construction of a mathematical proof from a set of axioms.*

> (D. Knuth, *The Art of Computer Programming*[1])

In the previous chapters we've seen how test cases are used to probe the correctness of computer programs – from wondering about the bank's IT system that generates our personal statements, through robot shopping issues, to the tragedy of shooting down airliners. We'll now revisit the inadequacies of testing and continue our quest for what a 'correct' IT system might be, and how (some believe) we might just achieve this ultimate goal. Testing is a doomed strategy, and a significant contributor to our IT-system woes. Formal verification, proving that a program is, in general, correct is the (much) better alternative. We need to flesh out these claims.

This is a demanding chapter, but necessarily so in its entirety because I want to expose the real complexity of proving a program correct. In recognition of the unreasonable demands this issue makes on the 'amateur reader', several explicit opportunities to cut and run are included.

Computer science is (or should be) a mathematical science. If only we would realize this, and insist on its practice, programming would cease to be the conglomerate of dubious activities outlined in the previous chapters. A program would become a verifiably correct construct just like a mathematical theorem. We could prove that our IT system is correct in general (i.e. for all possible inputs), instead of fiddling with the correctness of individual test cases and having to trust that general correctness also holds true.

The big mistake in all of the earlier chapters is to focus on the correctness of details instead of the correctness of the general principles. Once these general principles are verified as correct, i.e. mathematically proven to be correct, then the stepwise development of module details can also be guaranteed correct. And so on, to deliver a certifiably correct program, a verified IT system.

This might sound tricky, but remember that computer science (again like mathematics) is a world invented by the computer scientist. Unlike the classical scientist (e.g., the physicist or biologist who doesn't deal the cards, but just gets to play the

D. Partridge, *The Seductive Computer: Why IT Systems Always Fail*,
DOI 10.1007/978-1-84996-498-2_6, © Springer-Verlag London Limited 2011

odds), the computer scientist actually deals his own cards from a deck that he has stacked; so he has no one to blame but himself if his hand is less than perfect.

As this opening provocation implies, computer science is a different sort of science. In this chapter this idea will be fleshed out to present the positive case behind the belief that the computer technologist really ought to be able to guarantee the behaviour of his program, in general. In subsequent chapters, we'll progress to why such guarantees are just not possible by any known means, but first the good news.

Early on, the notion of good and bad programs was introduced – the former are the desirable ones, they instruct the computer to compute something useful for us, the latter category is where we dump all the failures. There is a rich variety of failures; they fill a complete spectrum from those that fail to gain acceptance by the computer – i.e., fail to start – to those that contain endless loops and will fail to finish of their own accord. The middle region of this spectrum of failure is where we find programs that do start but then crash to a halt before proper completion of the program, and, more worrying, ones that compute smoothly through to the end but fail to compute what was wanted. Most worrying of all are programs that compute smoothly but deliver plausible erroneous outputs. Bad programs may instruct the computer to compute something, but that something is typically nonsense or, more worryingly, just not what we think it is – so we misuse it. Computers will readily compute non-sensical results of course if that is what our program instructs them to do.

Suppose that our Dalek, supermarket cruiser model, when released in the local superstore promptly begins filling up its trolley with box upon box of eggs until it exhausts the supply on the shelves and ends up brandishing its (deactivated) ray gun in frustration at the unforgivable scarcity of eggs. Then, if we presume that its owner is not in fact planning the egg-feast of the century, we must conclude that something is going wrong, but what?

Perhaps the on-board computer is malfunctioning? Perhaps it's not following the **SHOP** program properly? Perhaps the **SHOP** program is wrong – it needs *debugging*? This latter possibility is by far the most likely one.

Suppose that we closely inspect the **SHOP** program, we couple this inspection with a little thought, and we pay close attention to program detail. Suddenly, we notice a tiny spelling error, for example, in **SUBPROGRAM READ&FIND** the first two instructions (ignoring the **COMMENT**) might be:

PUT NEXT-ITEM **INTO** CURRENT-TASK
PUT 0 **INTO** NEXT-ITEN

and back in the main part of the program we also find:

SET-NEXT alpha_letter

These three instructions are each grammatically correct, and so could easily contribute to a sensible computation. Yet, the outcome is the shopping robot with an insatiable demand for eggs; it is easy to see why, isn't it? (Hint: check every character and refer to end of chapter note 2 if a full explanation is both required and desired.)

This was most probably not what the houseperson wanted, nor what the programmer intended. This version of the **SHOP** program is composed of correct programming-language statements, and there is no problem with the logic of the sequencing. We might then, with some justification, call this a correct program and in that sense a good program, but it is a bad program with respect to the programmer's intentions and the robot owner's expectations. These two aspirations should coincide as the program *specification* which is a statement of desired program behaviour, precisely what it should do.

The point here is that 'good' and 'bad' as labels for two bins into one of which every program can be quickly and correctly deposited were used as a convenient fiction. At your newly acquired level of programming acumen, this fiction must be abandoned for something closer to the truth. We must concentrate on a misty borderline where many of the important questions lurk, but the boundary where correctness actually ends and the bad programs begin is disconcertingly blurred.

The more technically minded reader, the hotshot programmer skimming this book just to kill time during a power failure, or the mathematician toying with the idea of moving on from pencil and paper, will probably have been struck by my disinclination to talk about correct and incorrect programs. They will most likely have been irritated by my childish notion of good and bad programs.

"That," they will claim "is the root cause of the unsatisfactory situation that we now find ourselves in, i.e., not being able to clearly distinguish between desirable and undesirable programs. Correct programs are what we strive for; all others are completely unsatisfactory, 'bad' if you like. A well-defined notion of correctness is the keystone to a robust and reliable computer technology." So, a program is *correct* if its behaviour is as specified. Then if the *specification* is couched in a formal language (a formal logic, for example), it should be possible to prove whether or not a given program correctly implements its *specification*. We will then be able to guarantee that the program is in general correct, rather than test for correctness on specific examples which can at best only reveal that we can find no errors,[3] so it might be correct in general. But it might not.

This (or words to much the same effect) is roughly the manifesto of what I might term the computationally correct computer technologists, the formal computer scientists. This is a major branch of the anti-hacker party, one of the groups that are appalled by the prevalence of concocted computer programs on the loose in society. Their plan to do something about it centres on putting computer technology on a firm mathematical basis – one based on logic, as opposed to, say, statistics, i.e. an up-front proof of correctness rather than an after-the-fact attempt to build a probability of correctness by repeated testing of the program.

This all sounds well and good, does it not? It must be right to insist that a program is correct before we allow it to be used – for banking, for routing telephone calls, and certainly for controlling the identification and destruction of hostile missiles. The occasional wrong number or failure to connect within the telephone system can be accepted without undue societal disruption – a lack of absolute perfection is both accepted and perhaps even expected. But the downing of a transpolar jumbo jet from time to time as a result of a misidentification by a computer system is altogether another story, and one to which we must return.

To a reasonable approximation, the quality of a product is dependent upon the effort put in to improve it, and that in turn equates roughly with the cost of production. In a telephone system the engineers are likely to stop short of striving for total correctness at some point where cost and quality dictate – i.e., when the system works well enough and further improvements would cost too much. But this simple economic argument does not hold for a *Star Wars* system. Total correctness is required and the cost of achieving is not an issue. The computer programs controlling the radar-based identification of incoming objects and controlling the aiming of the laser guns are required to work correctly, always.

The goal of perfection with software artefacts (unlike bridges and buildings) does appear to be within the bounds of possibility, because a piece of software, a program, is a mathematical abstraction – a formula like $2 + 2 = 4$, or $(1 + 3) \times (1 + 3) = Y$ from our initial program.[4] But the formula embodied in a real IT system will be a lot more complicated. However, it should be possible to get such formulae perfectly correct, and to verify that you have done so by proving their correctness. The special nature of programs leads to the temptation to believe that both of these desirable goals are attainable.

So programs being abstract formulae can (like mathematical formulae) be subjected to a treatment that yields further abstractions such as mathematical theorems – i.e. it is possible to construct a *formal proof*, and so verify, that programs are *correct*, absolutely correct like a proven theorem in mathematics. Here's a theorem:

An odd number multiplied by itself always gives an odd number.

This version of the theorem is not a mathematical formula, but it could be – I'm just being user friendly for as long as possible. What is this theorem telling us? Just that for any odd number you care to choose, multiply it by itself (i.e. square it, in more technical language), and the result will always be another odd number.

Is it true? Let's see: $3 \times 3 = 9$, $5 \times 5 = 25$, $1 \times 1 = 1$ and $273 \times 273 = 74529$. It does seem to be true for these four test cases, but we can't possibly check all possibilities (because there is no end to the possibilities). Just like program testing, we've tested four cases and found no errors in the claim, so it might be a true theorem. However, there might be an odd number (amongst the infinity of odd numbers) that when multiplied by itself gives an even result, and it only takes one such number to invalidate our supposed theorem, our conjecture.

How can we know that it is true for all possible numbers? Clearly, we can't test them all, but we can prove it for the general case of any whole number. Let's use the label N for any whole number. So what we need to prove is that $N \times N$ is always an odd number if N is an odd number. Here's a proof:

The odd theorem

Proof that if N is an odd number, then $N \times N$ is also an odd number
Assume that N is an odd number, any odd number:
in which case N can be rewritten as
$(2 \times M + 1)$ where M is a whole number, odd or even.

(continued)

The odd theorem (continued)

Square this representation of N:

$(2{\times}M{+}1) \times (2{\times}M{+}1) = 4{\times}M^2 + 4{\times}M + 1$

The expression on the right-hand side of the equals sign must always be odd,
because the first two terms must be even for every value of M,
(because 4 times any whole number <u>must</u> give an even number)
and if you add 1 to an even number the final result is odd.
Therefore <u>every</u> odd number multiplied by itself results in an odd number.

Now we can be absolutely certain that any odd number squared will yield an odd result. Furthermore we can be certain of this without checking even one single test case – we have proved the general case. **The odd theorem** is true.[5]

If that was too easy, and the theorem too obvious anyway (although obviousness is not always a good guide to truth), here's another theorem. It's tougher to prove, and immaterial to the flow of the book, but it's somewhat surprising and it uses **the odd theorem** – but feel free to skip it, no penalty will be incurred.

The square root of 2 is not a fraction.

What is it asserting? It is saying that the square root of 2 (i.e., the number which multiplied by itself gives 2: usually written as $\sqrt{2}$) cannot be written as one whole number over another, a fraction like $\frac{3}{2}$ or $\frac{7}{4}$ or $\frac{213}{333}$, etc. This is odd (at least it is odd to even wonder about such things), but it is also surprising. Think about it. There are an infinite number of such fractions and the square root of 2 ought to be a respectable number, yet we cannot find a fractional number that when multiplied by itself yields 2 as the result. Not being able to find such a fraction may just mean that we haven't looked hard enough. After all, there are an infinite number of such fractions, so they can't all have been examined. Perhaps the fraction that is the square root of 2 is hiding from the searching mathematicians, and it just happens to be not one of the ones tested so far?

In truth, not many are devoting time to the quest for this elusive fraction, quite probably none at all. Why not? Because the mathematicians have proved that this fraction does not exist. The proof goes like this:

The root-two theorem

<u>the square root of 2 is not a fraction</u>

Assume that the square root of 2 is the fraction $\frac{n}{m}$ in its simplest form
(e.g., $\frac{3}{6}$ can be simplified to $\frac{1}{2}$ by dividing top and bottom by the common factor 3, hence I am stipulating that there is no common factor in top and bottom numbers), where n and m can otherwise be any whole numbers.

(continued)

The root-two theorem (continued)

So, we are going to assume that the square root of 2 is a fraction, $\sqrt{2} = \frac{n}{m}$

Square both sides of this equation, we get: $2 = \frac{n^2}{m^2}$

Rearrange this equation to give: $2 \times m^2 = n^2$

This equation tells us that n^2 is an <u>even</u> number (because it is equal to 2 times another whole number, namely m^2).

Therefore n must be an even number (because odd squared always gives an odd number – **the odd theorem**).

Thus we can say that $n = 2 \times r$, where r is (of course) half of n.

Substitute $2 \times r$ for n in the above equation, we get:

$2 \times m^2 = (2 \times r)^2$

Multiply out the right side gives:

$2 \times m^2 = 4 \times r^2$

Divide both sides by 2, we get: $m^2 = 2 \times r^2$

Hence m must also be an even number (same argument as used for n above).

Now we have reached the point where n and m must <u>both</u> be even numbers (i.e., both divisible by 2).

This contradicts our starting assumption

– i.e., that the fraction $\frac{n}{m}$ was in its simplest form.

If a sequence of valid reasoning steps leads us to a contradiction,

then our initial assumption must be invalid,

i.e., the square root of 2 <u>cannot</u> be represented by $\frac{n}{m}$

where n and m are whole numbers with no common factor.

Hence the square root of 2 cannot be represented as fraction.

This gives you the flavour, I hope, of the activity known as mathematical proof. This particular example happens to be a proof by refutation: we assume the opposite of what we believe to be true and show that it cannot be true.[6]

Notice that we reason through a series of steps from some starting assumptions through to a conclusion. This is analogous to a computer working through a list of instructions from a starting number through to some computed resultant numbers. Or equally, although perhaps less obviously, it is also like a robot's computer working through its **SHOP** program starting with a shopping list to finish with a trolley full of all and only the listed items.

In the case of our **SHOP** program we would like to prove that starting from the assumption that the robot is given a valid shopping list, its program will *execute* it and stop with a trolley containing exactly those items on the original list. Now we need to see how on earth a computer program could be proven to be correct in a manner similar to that used by mathematicians to push the boundaries of mathematical knowledge forward with absolute certainty.

This sort of mathematical or logical juggling as in **the root-two theorem**, although home ground to the mathematician, is a bit alien to normal people. So let me give you another theorem, one that non-numerically minded readers should find more comfortable, and one that also has particular importance with respect to my general claims about the seductive nature of computer technology.

There is a theorem about colouring maps. It states that with at most four colours the countries on any conceivable map can each be coloured such that no two countries of the same colour have a common border. This is **the four-colour theorem** (although a mathematician would be likely to couch it in more abstract terms), if it's called a theorem it should be true, provably true. It is, I think, quite surprising that the cartographer knows for sure that four different coloured pens are guaranteed to be quite sufficient for all his needs.

Just try to generate a counterexample. You draw the countries absolutely any shape you like. You can wrap countries around each other to your heart's content; don't be constrained by a supposed need for readily defendable boundaries and the like. Just draw whatever weird shapes you wish. It will still be possible to colour the resultant map with no more than four different colours, and each country will stand out as a different-coloured shape from all of its neighbours.

In the interests of efficiency, and to further induce you to complete the exercises as you read this book, Fig. 6.1 provides four such maps which should be coloured in as attempted refutations of the four-colour theorem.

By colouring these four maps, you are, of course, testing the theorem. If all four colouring-in attempts succeed without the need for more than four colours, then all you can conclude is that the theorem might be true. You've tested it and found no problems. But what if one of your maps did require a fifth colour? What would that show?

Because this is a proven theorem, it would almost certainly show that you've not been inventive enough, and you need to try again. In general, however, it is worth noting the asymmetry between successful and failed tests. Nothing short of all possible tests succeeding (which is impossible for infinite domains like the numbers) can prove correctness, but a single failed test can prove incorrectness. Exactly the same line of general reasoning tells us that successful tests can never confirm that our program is correct, but a single failed test confirms that our program is incorrect.

The original statement about the need for at most four colours – i.e., the four-colour theorem – is a theorem (rather than a conjecture) because it has been formally proved. I cannot present this proof you might be relieved to learn. A good reason is that this book is too small to hold the full proof; an equally good, if not actually better, reason is that I don't understand the actual proof. However, my lack of understanding is based on the seductive quality of computers as much as on my lack of mathematical competence.[7] In essence, this proof is based upon a mathematical argument that there are a fixed number of alternative different kinds of maps and a fixed number of ways to try to colour them. The catalogue of all alternatives in this case runs into hundreds of thousands (compare the two alternatives for whole numbers – odd or even), so the only way to work through them systematically

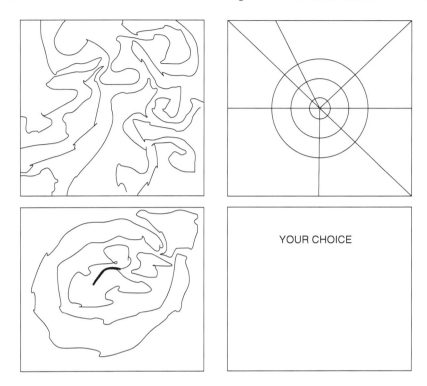

Fig. 6.1 Possible bases for a refutation of the four-colour theorem

in reasonable time is to use a computer. "The use of ad hoc programs to analyse large numbers of cases in very large proofs has proved highly controversial. Doubts about correctness are the ostensible objection, but the difficulty of understanding the resulting proofs may be a more fundamental objection."[8] Once more, computer power has opened up the scope of accepted practice (in this case, formal proofs that are based on proving all possible alternatives), and somewhere a line has been crossed into contentiousness due (in no small part) to concerns about understanding a large computer program.

A proof then is a series of formally justified steps from some accepted true assumptions (the axioms and premises, if you want to get technical) to the conjecture in question. A proof demonstrates that an initially conjectural statement can be derived, by means of a sequence of sound transformations (such as squaring both sides of an equation to obtain a different but equivalently valid equation), from some others statements that are true, hence it is also true. Once the conjecture is proved true, it becomes a theorem.

A program, just like a proof, is typically presented as a sequence of symbols written on paper (or on a computer screen, the actual medium is immaterial). However, their persuasive similarities run much deeper: if you follow a series of proof steps you prove the theorem true; if you obey the list of instruction steps in a program you prove what output the program will generate from its input. The key point here is that the program input, all the intermediate transformations and the output must be reasoned about in general, otherwise we are just hand executing a test case. The odd theorem is reasoned with any odd number, N, not with a specific whole number such as 3 or 5. It is this abstraction from specific inputs that makes theorems so powerful.

Here is another opportunity to skip about seven pages, or even more to touch down on the bullet-point chapter summary, and then move on.

In our **SHOP** program we would have to start our reasoning with any (valid) shopping list, say, S. The proof then works through the program instructions deducing their effect on S which in our case is a sequence of n boxes labelled from the alphabet, starting at "A", where n is a whole number between 1 and 26. This is not easy, even for the experts, but let's have a taste of the reasoning required.

Here is our program:

SHOP
SET alpha-letter **AS** A
REPEAT
    COMMENT read next item on list & locate this item in the store
        DO READ&FIND **WITH** alpha-letter **AS** NEXT-ITEM
    3. place item in trolley
    SET-NEXT alpha-letter
UNTIL list is empty

SUBPROGRAM READ&FIND
COMMENT read next item on list
    PUT NEXT-ITEM **INTO** CURRENT-TASK
    PUT 0 **INTO** NEXT-ITEM
COMMENT locate this item in the store
    categorize item in CURRENT-TASK
    consult supermarket layout plan
    find desired category of items
    plan route to where desired category located
    go to this location
    survey items until item in CURRENT-TASK found

A major part of proving that this program is correct would be to prove that the **REPEAT-UNTIL** loop instructions will correctly process any shopping list S containing any number of items from 1 to 26. In general, we can say that we have n items to shop for, and we'll represent our general list as $S(n)$, where (because of our chosen alphabetic labelling) n must be a whole number from 1 to 26. So $S(n)$ is a sequence of boxes $s(1)$, $s(2)$, etc. up to $s(n)$. $S(n)$ is the shopping list of n boxes, and $s(n)$ is the final box on the list. Any box in the list might be referred to in general as $s(i)$ where i must be a whole number between 1 and n,[9] and any sublist (a list of i consecutive boxes) is $S(i)$. Now we have enough formal machinery to deal with our shopping list in the necessary generalities.

What does "correctly process" mean? Well, because **SHOP** is using the **READ&FIND** subprogram to identify and collect each item in S, it must *execute* the **DO** instruction n times (there are n items in $S(n)$). Furthermore, it must do so in the sequence $s(1)$ then $s(2)$ then $s(3)$ etc. up to $s(n)$. Of course, if our robot only has one item to shop for then there will be no $s(2)$ and $s(3)$, $s(1)$ will also be $s(n)$, so we are still being too specific. We can use i, as introduced above, to generalize enough.

So, we can say: the **DO** instruction must be executed n times in the order where i starts at 1, increases by 1 each time, and is used for the last time when $i=n$.

Let's look at the **SHOP** module and prove that it is correct (in this one aspect at least). To do this we must begin with our general input statement about the structure of our shopping list, S. We must then progress through our program generating statements about the structure of S as it is transformed by the program instructions we encounter. Each such statement must be a general statement that will be true of all valid shopping lists.

We start by stating the properties of our general shopping list, $S(n)$, and of our pointer i which will be used to specify how our program progresses through $S(n)$ when controlled by the **REPEAT-UNTIL** instruction. The symbol i is used as a convenient substitute for the alphabet that is our box labels, i.e. $i=1$ refers to A, when $i=2$ it refers to B, and so on.

The input assumption can then be stated as:

shopping list is S(n) where n has a value between 1 and 26 (incl.), and all n boxes contain items to be shopped for.

This statement allows us to characterize the structure of our initial shopping list as:

$i = 0, i < n$
shopping list S(n) is S(i) zeroes followed by S(n) items.

We are stating that initially there are no zeroes in the shopping list; all n boxes contain an item to be shopped for, and we are keeping track of both the value of i and its relationship to the value of n.

So why do we bother to include a statement about $S(i)$ when $i=0$? This seems to refer to nothing. Why not simplify and say the shopping list at this point is just $S(n)$ items? The answer is that we generate a more elaborate statement about the shopping list because this captures its general structure throughout the whole computation. Part of our program successively replaces each shopped-for item with a zero in the shopping list, S. So the computation progresses by gradually replacing shopping-list box values, the $s(i)$s, from beginning to end with zeroes.

Figure 6.2 gives the bare bones of how we might prove that our program loop correctly processes the shopping list. The top and bottom boxes in Fig. 6.2 give the general shopping list before our program works on it, and what should have happened to the same list after our program has finished, respectively. The proof process must show that given this initial general structure of a shopping list (illustrated in top box), the program statements will transform it in such a way that we do indeed get the structure that we intended (as shown in the bottom box). And to help see where we are going, I have conjured up the crucial intermediate structure that anchors the transformation (illustrated in the middle box).

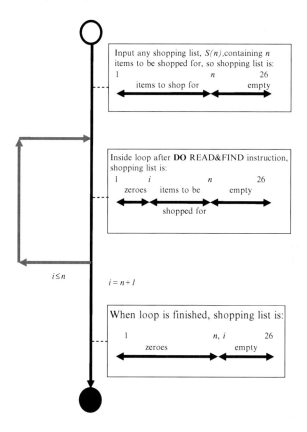

Fig. 6.2 The bare bones of a small proof

Thus, in general during this computation, our shopping list will be an initial sublist of zeroed boxes (the items already shopped for) followed by a sublist of items still to be shopped for as illustrated in the middle box of Fig. 6.2.

At the outset all items are still to be shopped for so the sublist of zeroed boxes is non-existent, length zero in our formal notation, i.e. it is $S(i)$ when $i = 0$. As the computation proceeds the sublist of zeroed boxes grows and the sublist of items to be shopped-for shrinks, hence our general characterization of the shopping list in terms of these two sublists.

At this point, the reader whose had more than enough of program proofs, or is unsettled by formalisms like $S(n-i+1)$, should: jump forward to Fig. 6.3; glance over it to see what they've side-stepped; and move on about three more pages to the following text.

In order to prove that the REPEAT-UNTIL loop in our <u>SHOP</u> program does indeed correctly process any valid shopping list, we must start with the general shopping list (as diagrammed in the top box of Fig. 6.2).

Then we must work through the program generating and inserting statements about the structure of $S(n)$, the value of i and its relationship to n as determined by

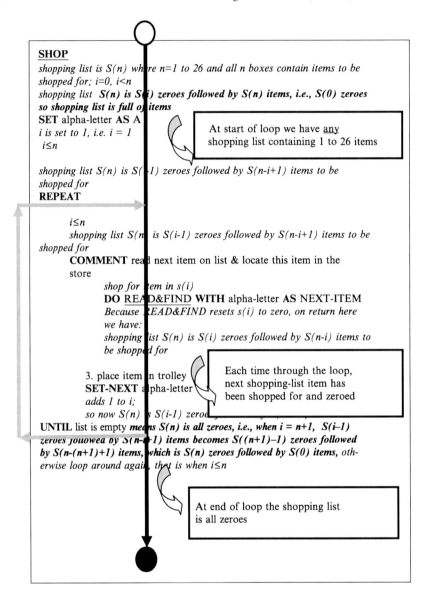

SHOP
shopping list is S(n) where n=1 to 26 and all n boxes contain items to be shopped for; i=0, i<n
shopping list S(n) is S(i) zeroes followed by S(n) items, i.e., S(0) zeroes
so shopping list is full of items
SET alpha-letter AS A
i is set to 1, i.e. i = 1
i≤n

> At start of loop we have <u>any</u> shopping list containing 1 to 26 items

shopping list S(n) is S(i-1) zeroes followed by S(n-i+1) items to be shopped for
REPEAT

    i≤n
    shopping list S(n) is S(i-1) zeroes followed by S(n-i+1) items to be shopped for
    COMMENT read next item on list & locate this item in the store
      shop for item in s(i)
      DO <u>READ&FIND</u> **WITH** alpha-letter **AS** NEXT-ITEM
      Because READ&FIND resets s(i) to zero, on return here we have:
      shopping list S(n) is S(i) zeroes followed by S(n-i) items to be shopped for

      3. place item in trolley
      SET-NEXT alpha-letter
      adds 1 to i;
      so now S(n) is S(i-1) zeroe...

> Each time through the loop, next shopping-list item has been shopped for and zeroed

UNTIL list is empty *means S(n) is all zeroes, i.e., when i = n+1, S(i-1) zeroes followed by S(n-i+1) items becomes S((n+1)-1) zeroes followed by S(n-(n+1)+1) items, which is S(n) zeroes followed by S(0) items, otherwise loop around again, that is when i≤n*

> At end of loop the shopping list is all zeroes

Fig. 6.3 The proof structure re-linearizes the program

the changes that our program instructions introduce. Some of these statements are obvious (I hope), but many of these new statements are neither obvious nor easy, especially in a program loop.

If our program loop is indeed correct, then we will end up with our original shopping list transformed into the structure diagrammed in the bottom box of Fig. 6.2.

Loops are particularly tricky because within a loop we must find general statements that are true for every repetition of the loop. I have inserted these statements below in italics.

SHOP
shopping list is S(n) where n=1 to 26 and all n boxes contain items to be shopped for; i = 0, i < n
shopping list S(n) is S(i) zeroes followed by S(n) items, i.e., S(0) zeroes so shopping list is full of items
SET alpha-letter **AS** A
i is set to 1, i.e. i = 1
i ≤ n
shopping list S(n) is S(i − 1) zeroes followed by S(n − i + 1) items to be shopped for
REPEAT
    i ≤ n
    shopping list S(n) is S(i − 1) zeroes followed by S(n − i + 1) items to be shopped for
    COMMENT read next item on list & locate this item in the store
        shop for item in s(i)
        DO READ&FIND **WITH** alpha-letter **AS** NEXT-ITEM
        Because READ&FIND resets s(i) to zero, on return here we have:
        shopping list S(n) is S(i) zeroes followed by S(n-i) items to be shopped for
    3. place item in trolley
    SET-NEXT alpha-letter
    adds 1 to i;
    so now S(n) is S(i − 1) zeroes followed by S(n − i + 1) items
UNTIL list is empty *means S(n) is all zeroes, i.e., when i = n + 1, otherwise loop around again, that is when i ≤ n*

SUBPROGRAM READ&FIND
Shop for item in s(i)
COMMENT read next item on list
    PUT NEXT-ITEM **INTO** CURRENT-TASK
    PUT 0 **INTO** NEXT-ITEM
    sets s(i) = 0
COMMENT locate this item in the store
    categorize item in CURRENT-TASK
    consult supermarket layout plan
    find desired category of items
    plan route to where desired category located
    go to this location
    survey items until item in CURRENT-TASK found

These italicized insertions, some flesh on the bones of a proof, which have mysteriously appeared, must each be justified as the result of program-instruction transformations. We start from statements that characterize the program's input (our shopping list) and work through to statements that characterize the program's final behaviour (a shopping trolley full of shopping). Only then can we prove that if we start with any valid shopping list, the **SHOP** program will always end up with a trolley containing exactly the listed items – i.e., the program is proven correct in a general sense.

It what sense is the annotated program above part of a proof of the correctness of our program? Each of the italicized statements is a transformation of the previous ones as defined by the intervening program instruction just like the statements of a mathematical proof are transformations justified by the laws of arithmetic.

Let's see how we do a couple of these transformations. We'll start with an easy one.

SET alpha-letter **AS** A is the program instruction to start the robot shopping at the first list item. In terms of our proof notation, this is the action of setting $i = 1$, so this is precisely the proof statement immediately following. However, we can also state something else that must be true, namely $i \leq n$. How can we justify this? Well, the initial proof statement says that n is a number from 1 to 26, and no changes to n have been made. Given that $i = 1$, then it must also now be true that $i \leq n$.

Our proof elements are not all as obvious and easy as this. For example, immediately on return from the subprogram, that is immediately following the **DO** instruction, we have the following statement about our shopping list's structure:

S(n) is S(i) zeroes followed by S(n − i) items

Next we find the (plan) instruction:
3. place item in trolley.

This has no effect on the shopping list structure, but the very next instruction,
SET-NEXT alpha-letter,

certainly does; it moves the computation along to the next shopping-list box. In terms of our substitute for these alphabetic labels, i, it adds 1 to whatever value i has. So this instruction has caused i to become $i + 1$. As i is used in our statement about the structure of $S(n)$, which has not changed, we must substitute $i − 1$ for all occurrences of i in order to maintain our statement about the shopping list structure as true (the old i is the new $i − 1$, e.g., if i was previously 3, it has now become 4, so all expressions using i must replace all occurrences of i, which are now 4s, with $i − 1$, which will be 3).

Let's do this substitution:

S(n) is S(i) zeroes followed by S(n − i) items
becomes
S(n) is S(i − 1) zeroes followed by S(n − (i − 1)) items
which simplifies by the rules of arithmetic to:
S(n) is S(i − 1) zeroes followed by S(n − i + 1) items
and this is how the crucial end of loop statement is derived.

What do these italicized statements prove? To begin with, we can see that the loop will finish when all shopping list items have been reset to zero, and, because this resetting is only done in **READ&FIND** just before it locates an item, we can conclude that all shopping-list items are located.

Notice also that we have exactly the same statement about the structure of our shopping list, namely:

S(n) is S(i − 1) zeroes followed by S(n − i + 1) items,

in three different places in the program:

1. before the loop is first entered;
2. at the beginning but inside the loop, so at the position of the start of every execution of the loop; and
3. at the end but inside the loop, so at the position just before every repetition (and the final exit).

If the loop is to be correct then (1) and (2) must be the same because first entry comes from above and nothing is done to change the shopping list by the **REPEAT** part of the loop instruction. Similarly, (2) and (3) must be the same because after the first entry all subsequent re-entries come directly from the **UNTIL** part (caused by the stopping condition not being true, i.e. list is not empty), and checking the stopping condition also does nothing to change the shopping list. It merely determines whether the loop is to be repeated, or the program is finished.

The fact that these statements are all true and all identical goes a good way towards proving that our loop structure is correct. However, this statement about the structure of our shopping list, its zeroed elements and its items to be shopped for, is far from obvious – to put it mildly. Considerable creativity is required for a program proof just as for a mathematical proof. Notice also that the proof statements in italics are arguably more complicated than the program instructions that we are attempting to prove (and so they are, at least, equally subject to mistakes).

But on the positive side: notice also that a proof reduces the tortuous flow structure, which testing must grapple with directly, to a straight line (an echo back to our original simple programs and all programs as lists of instructions). This view of the power of proofs is illustrated in Fig. 6.3. However, few readers will have trouble appreciating that this powerful reduction in complexity only comes at a price. The price involves both the creative effort of composing just the right characterizations of the computation (e.g. the sublist of zeroes that is initially empty) and of correctly managing considerable new complexity (all the italicized interjections).

The input statement that the shopping list is all items and no zeroes has become transformed on the exit from the loop (i.e., when list is empty stopping condition is true) to a statement that the shopping list is all zeroes (both bolded in Fig. 6.3). Furthermore, this has been achieved without recourse to the necessity to consider the looping behaviour explicitly. In effect, the careful construction of the statement *S(n) is S(i − 1) zeroes followed by S(n − i + 1) items* (explained above in its three occurrences) has factored out any need to consider the looping behaviour explicitly. It has captured the general effect of the loop and so we can ignore the specifics of any particular iteration.

Just as a formal proof stands as a testimony to the absolute truth of a theorem, so a program proof guarantees the correctness of what the program does for every possible usage – i.e., for all possible (valid) shopping lists presented to the **SHOP** program. This is just the sort of guarantee we would like to be able to get with the IT systems that run our lives.

A formal proof of program correctness is thus a very strong statement to make. If the local bank could make this claim for its accounting program then you would have a cast iron guarantee that your monthly bank statement was always correct. Or would you?

Computer scientists made all these connections (between mathematical theorems and programs) many years ago with the result that proving programs to be correct – i.e., proving that the desired output will always be generated when the program is given an appropriate input – is widely thought to be the key to ensuring that programs don't make mistakes, or do anything unexpected. Sophisticated analogues of mathematical proof have been developed in order to make the mathematical proof idea readily applicable to computer programs.

What does "correct" mean exactly, now that we have this mechanism of formal *proof*? In the context of generating proof-based guarantees, *a correct program* is: one that computes exactly what was stipulated in the *specification*, and the formal *proof* supplies the guarantee that this will always be so for every usage of the program.

The *specification* for the **SHOP** program might have been something like:

Write a program that would cause the robot to collect together all of the shopping-list items.

This first attempt at a problem *specification*, however, clearly leaves much unsaid. How many items maximum and minimum? What sort of items? We must surely rule out some things, things like double-decker buses, a new partner and happiness. They are not valid items to put on a robot's shopping list.

What are the assumptions about when and how this program is to be used? Implicit assumptions in a *specification* are the fertile ground for system failures, and so to be avoided at all costs.

The *specification* given above implies at least one item in the shopping list, but logically a shopping list might contain zero items, might it not? The program as written accepted shopping lists with no items (i.e. empty lists), but, because it goes through the **READ&FIND** subprogram before checking for an empty shopping list, a robot shopper given an empty shopping list would end up in a tangle. The implicit minimum shopping list length, imposed by the details of our program (i.e. first read and find before empty-list test), is one item. Similarly, further program details (the decision to label shopping-list boxes with single letters of the alphabet) limited acceptable shopping lists to no more than 26 items. Notice that both of these restrictions were made explicit in the proof statements, and so our proof that the program is correct imposes unspecified limits to shopping lists.

But if the owner of the shopping Dalek gives it a list of 56 items to shop for, it will not collect these 56 items in its trolley. It is hard to say (in the absence of further detail) exactly what will happen, except that we can be sure that as far as the owner is concerned the robot will behave incorrectly. Yet the program was proved correct, wasn't it?

This point about shopping-list length is actually illustrating a general and important point about computer programs and their correctness. There can be, and with large programs there always will be, a clash between the programmer's specification (his yardstick for assessing correctness) and the system user's expectations (his or her yardstick for correctness). Correctness for the programmer is not necessarily so for the user.

The root of this problem appears to be that the *specification* is incomplete: thus the **SHOP** program *specification* really should specify minimum and maximum shopping-list lengths. This is easily done, and leads us onto three important criteria of program *specifications*, the first is:

- they must be <u>complete</u>.

A sensible and reasonable requirement is it not? Actually, it isn't. Consider the questions of what items the owner can include on the robot's shopping list. Any potentially complete specification is going to have to say what sort of items are valid shopping-list items. This is impossible to pin down precisely. A possible approach to this item-validity requirement would be to specify that the valid items are only the sort of things that can be purchased in a neighbourhood superstore. But this is little more than a general guideline for the busy houseperson to know what can be put on the robot's shopping list and what cannot. It is a similarly loose constraint for the programmer to work to when devising the **SHOP** program. There's a lot of latitude for interpretation by both parties, and when their interpretations don't coincide, something is bound to go wrong.

The second major criterion of program *specifications* is:

- they must be <u>precise</u>.

As the Iranian commercial airliner cruised towards the US battleship being harassed by small gunboats around it, the battleship captain assumed that if his sophisticated, computerized identification system reported that the unknown plane was a fighter swooping in for attack, then that's what it was. The designers of the plane-identification module within the total system presumably felt free to assume that any non-friendly plane on a direct course for the ship during a battle was a hostile fighter. A mismatch of interpretations or a lack of precision in the original specification (a requirement to distinguish carefully in all situations between commercial and military aircraft) had tragic consequences.

However, when the robo-shopper (UK model) continues to whiz endlessly around and around Tescos on a fruitless quest for a squeezy bottle of fat-free butter for its American owner, a similar mismatch of interpretations may be blamed. But apart from the owner perhaps being forced to spread animal fat on his toast, the consequences could hardly said to be severe.

Send the shopping Dalek for "paste" and it might end up with a jar of fish paste in its trolley, or it might be wallpaper paste. It all depends upon how the programmer has programmed the robot to deal with locating its items in the store. If the program was constructed to search for the first occurrence of each desired item in, say, an alphabetically ordered list, then the robot will retrieve fish paste not wallpaper paste.

The point of this is not to insist that the houseperson must tell the robot before it is sent on a shopping spree whether the shopping is for a weekend of DIY rather than a picnic in the country, it is to draw out a last essential criterion of program *specifications*:

- they must be <u>unambiguous</u>.

This requirement is to ensure that the correct IT-system behaviour for every legal input is determined by the system *specification* rather than by how the program happened to be written.

To the hardened hacker all these finicky problems may seem unimportant because the problem *specification* and, if necessary, the program could quickly be changed to deal with any of them – e.g., one fruitless circuit of the store and the robot abandons its attempt to shop for that item. This suggested solution, as usual, misses the point.

Sure, any programmer worth his salary could correctly fix up these small, but missing, links between the problem *specification* and the program constructed. The problems are obvious within a twelve-line program, but within a hundred-thousand-line program the existence of a problem may be far from obvious until too late. Even when the existence of a problem is known finding its exact location can be a challenging task, to say the least. Finally, having found the source of the problem (or believing that you have), it must be fixed without disrupting any other system behaviour.

In fact, it is exactly these trivial flaws which are the hardest to locate in large programs, major blunders are usually relatively obvious, where "trivial" and "major" here refer to amount of wrong instruction rather than importance of the resultant wrong behaviour of the computer system.

The ever-circling robot may be exhibiting a behaviourally obvious flaw, but this may be caused by trivial element of the program (remember, every program symbol is potentially crucial). There is no systematic relationship between size of behavioural problem and amount of program structure that must be changed to eliminate it. Big problems may derive from single-symbol errors, as the Mariner probe demonstrated, and minor behavioural problems may necessitate a major program redesign and rewrite in order to correct them.

Having discovered these dents in the correctness of our program, we can hammer them out by adding riders to our original problem *specification*. The resultant *specification* might go something like:

> *Write a program that accepts a list of at least one, but no more than 26, valid items (where a valid item is something that might reasonably be purchased in a superstore) and collects together the listed items, with the proviso that if any particular item cannot be found after one complete circuit of the store, shopping for that particular item will be abandoned.*

We may now have something much closer to a correct program, given that this overblown statement is the problem *specification*. But notice that it is not complete, nor free of imprecision, nor totally unambiguous:

- <u>incompleteness</u>: What should happen if the item is either too big to fit in a trolley, or the trolley is full before the shopping list is finished?
- <u>imprecision</u>: The *specification* provides only a vague description of the notion of a "valid item", the phrase "something that might reasonably be purchased in a superstore" is hardly a precise characterization of what items the robot must be able to shop for.
- <u>ambiguity</u>: What's "a complete circuit of the store"? Is it a circuit around the outer aisles of the store? Is it an inspection of the commodities summary for each aisle? Is it a double traversal of each aisle, once on one side and once on the other? There are many alternative, and equally valid, detailed mechanisms to program that will satisfy this part of the *specification*.

The really bad news is that a problem specification can <u>never</u> be free of these three sources of error (with the possible exception of abstract mathematical problems).[10] If you think that this small problem statement has become rather puffed up by our attempts to be complete, precise and unambiguous, consider what a similar expansion of the *Star Wars specification* might look like; it will be a bloated leviathan, impossible to comprehend in its totality, and necessarily still lacking at least a few of the riders whose importance has not yet been recognised.

The reader without a penchant for mathematical proof procedures – i.e., a normal person – will probably be puzzling at this point over why we should contemplate going into all the gruesomeness of mathematical proof for our small program when we can see by inspection that it is correct, and does what we want. If this sentiment strikes a chord with you then you failed to fully appreciate the simple bank-balance problem in the introductory chapter.

Can you really determine the correctness of this program by staring at it and perhaps jotting down some labelled boxes with numbers in them? The truth is that you can't.

Hence the reason why computer scientists are so very keen on this notion of proving that programs are correct: testing is fundamentally flawed (it can only show the presence of errors, never their absence[11]) whereas proof holds the promise of an absolute correctness for the program, in general. The analogy with the mathematical notion of proving theorems correct is almost irresistible: don't test for the presence of individual errors, prove their complete absence. I don't propose to go further into how these proof-of-program-correctness advocates go about their work – this is not that sort of book, as I said at the beginning. But I have given you a flavour of the general idea.

So what has this proof chapter shown us?

- An IT-system *specification* is a complete, precise and unambiguous statement of what the desired IT system should do.
- A *correct* IT system is one whose behaviour is exactly as *specified*.

- Testing can never deliver a guarantee of IT-system *correctness*.
- Programs are, however, well-defined symbol structures just like mathematical formulae, and thus hold the promise of being *proven correct*.
- Mathematical proof, the time-honoured mechanism for demonstrating the correctness of well-defined symbol structures, has its strengths and weaknesses especially in relation to IT systems.
- IT systems, by virtue of sheer complexity, have significantly muddied even this neat mathematical idea.
- Both proofs and *specifications* of IT systems will be large and complicated 'objects' just like the programs.
- There are some fundamental problems with IT system *specification*, and a major source of difficulty is explained in the next chapter.

In sum, (to rework a valuable soundbite) anytime a computer scientist puts his arm around you and tells you not to worry because the computer in control of your well-being is directed by a proven program and so can't possibly go wrong, that's the time to be really worried.[12] In the next chapter we'll see yet another reason why. For, in fact, even the proof idea can never deliver the guarantees that we would like, and that it seems to promise.

Endnotes

1. A strong statement from an eminent Computer Scientist and given in his set of books (sometimes known as the Bible of Computer Science): D. Knuth, *The Art of Computer Programming*, vol. I, preface, page ix, 1968.
2. Notice that at the end of the second instruction the box label is NEXT-ITEN, not NEXT-ITEM. The result will be that the 'eggs' value in box NEXT-ITEM will not be replaced by a zero. Add to this the observation that the SET-NEXT instruction is not moving shopping along, because it refers to alpha_letter and not to alpha-letter as it should. Hence, the robot will keep finding 'eggs' in box A as its next item to shop for.

    If you needed to read this note to find the *bugs* in so few lines of program, then just imagine the problem of searching in two thousand, or two million instructions.
3. C.A.R. Hoare, in his defence of IT-system quality despite our inability to construct program proofs, makes the point that testing gains value if it is used to test not the IT system itself but the methods that were used to produce it. But the use of system errors to track down inadequacies in the production process assumes two crucial points: first, that the programmer will resist directly fixing his IT system, and dig back in time in order to find the root causes of the observed error; and secondly, that the documentation exists to support this investigation. This paper entitled How Did Software Get So Reliable Without Proof? was published in 1996 in Springer's LNCS FME'96, pages 1–17.
4. Our original program (with a final PRINT instruction added) is:

    ADD 1 **TO** 3 **PUT RESULT IN** X
    PRINT X
    MULTIPLY X **BY** X **PUT RESULT IN** Y
    PRINT Y

    It is a program that computes a numerical value in box "Y" and prints out this value. Our computer *executes* this program and prints out the result: 16. Is this program's output correct, and, if so, is it correct for the right reasons? Despite the fact that this travesty of a useful program can only compute one result, we can, nevertheless, prove that this result is correct.

> **ADD 1 TO 3 PUT RESULT IN** X
> $X = 1 + 3$
> **PRINT** X
> *The value (1 + 3) is printed out, and X = 1 + 3*
> **MULTIPLY** X **BY** X **PUT RESULT IN** Y
> $Y = X \times X$ *and* $X = 1 + 3$, *so* $Y = (1 + 3) \times (1 + 3)$
> **PRINT** Y
> *The value (1 + 3) × (1 + 3), which the rules of arithmetic tell us is 16, should be printed out.*

Hence, the value 16 is the correct output and it is generated as anticipated, i.e., it is not the result of some fortuitous but rogue calculation.

5. The boxed text will be more of an obvious proof for some people than others. Every proof assumes a certain level of accepted knowledge: this one could not, for example, include all the relevant axioms of basic arithmetic. Why is 4 times any whole number an even number?

   A proof also relies upon an acceptance of the truth of every step and transformation given. For example, are you sure that $(2 \times M + 1)$ squared is $4 \times M^2 + 4 \times M + 1$? I could have got it wrong in many ways, e.g. $4 \times M^2 + 2 \times M + 1$, and the proof still works fine even though it would now have a bad error in one step.

6. An acceptance of this chunk of text as a proof that the square root of 2 cannot be a fraction is to some extent an act of faith. The less mathematics you know, the more that faith is required to believe that what the proof tells you is true is indeed true. But all proofs are faith objects, because the reader must accept that all the transformations presented are valid. Are they?

   In the middle of the proof, for example, we are asked to accept that because n^2 is an even number n must be an even number, and the basis for acceptance is given as **the odd theorem**. But **the odd theorem** only tells us that an odd number squared always gives an odd number. It says nothing about even numbers, does it?

   Implicitly it does, of course, because all whole numbers must be either even or odd. There are only two possibilities. There are also examples of even squared numbers, e.g., 4 is even and the square of 2. So n^2 in the proof can be an even square, because we know they exist. It can't come from squaring an odd number (that only delivers odd squares), so n must be even. There are no other options.

   This attempt to justify faith in this element of the proof (without recourse to **the even theorem**, which we haven't proved) rests on the realization that the full scope of parity possibilities with respect to whole numbers is two: every whole number must be either even or odd (with the possible exception of zero adding another more general twist). This feature of defining all alternative possibilities (just two, odd or even, in this case) gets expanded to the point of absurdity (some would say) in some modern computer-based proofs (see next note).

7. The four-colour theorem attained theoremhood with the aid of a computer. Not too surprising, at least not more so than the fact that such things can be proved at all. However, this book was produced with the aid of a computer, but these two uses of the word "aid" are crucially different. I could have written this book without the assistance of a computer. It would have been slower and more painful; it might have been better or worse, but it could have been done. People still do it all the time (I think). But the proof of the four-colour theorem was made possible by a computer. The proof wasn't just aided by a computer. It was based on massive, precise computation, and couldn't have been done without a computer.

   The potential truth of the four-colour conjecture was first mooted in 1852. In 1879 a proof was published. This proof was accepted for eleven years when a nosey mathematician discovered a fatal flaw in the proof; so, in 1890 it was no longer a proof and the four-colour proposal was once more reduced to a conjecture. At the time of writing, there is a computer-based proof (K. Appel, W. Haken and J. Koch "Every planar map is four colourable," *Illinois Journal of Mathematics,* vol. 21, pages 429–490, 1977), and the four-colour theorem has set a new longevity record – at least in some circles. There is an informed body of opinion that is dubious about the whole nature of the computer-based proof; they ask the question, is it a mathematical proof in the time-honoured sense of the term? If not, is there now a new sense to be considered? As is the way with computer programs, the program that proved the four-colour theorem is much too complicated for most mathematicians to fully grasp, to grasp even the essence of the proof to a degree that they can satisfy themselves that it is a valid proof. They just have to accept it on trust, or not, as the case may be.

The computer has introduced a new ingredient, what is it? Computers are just fast adding machines, and adding machines are themselves just a means of doing fast and accurate mental calculation. But in our current state of sophistication with regard to computer technology, this sort of garden-path argument will not be meekly accepted. We know that computer technology can introduce new, emergent properties by taking us into domains of hitherto unimagined complexity. The computer-based proof of the four-colour theorem is an example of just this.

The computer was employed in the proof for something like 50 days of computation. It explored some 2,000 alternative maps and tried some 200,000 colouring schemes on them.

There may be mathematical arguments about whether the catalogue of different maps and the alternative ways of colouring them is provably the full set of alternatives (just one overlooked could wreck the proof) – like odd and even being the full set of alternatives for whole numbers. But there is also, of course, the question of whether the program used was correct. Did it properly explore all 2,000 alternative maps and all 200,000 colouring schemes? Or did it miss one, or not do one properly?

8. The problems caused by "computer proofs" is the topic of Alan Bundy's *Boole Lecture* entitled "A very mathematical dilemma" (published in 2006 in *The Computer Journal*, vol. 49, no. 4, pages 480–486), and the Four Colour Theorem is one of his three examples.

9. This is not true: because we chose to move along to the next item before the branch condition for the end of the loop is checked (i.e. **SET-NEXT** alpha-letter precedes **UNTIL** list is empty), the loop will repeat when $i \leq n$ (i.e. there is another item to shop for); when the loop exits, we will have $i = n + 1$ – the shopping list is empty but we move to a possible next item before checking. So the true statement is that i must be any whole number between 1 and $(n + 1)$, not n. This could cause an error, e.g., when shopping list is 26 items, alpha-letter is Z after locating last item, so what will happen when **SET-NEXT** tries to move in on to the 'next' letter? This glitch is easily fixed, but first it has to be recognized and maybe one of the strengths of program proofs is that they force the programmer into a thorough examination of the relationships between all elements of the program.

10. Elsewhere (D. Partridge and A.P. Galton, "The specification of 'specification,'" *Minds and Machines*, vol. 5, no. 2, pages 243–255, 1995), we have thoroughly exposed the problems of specifying programs.

11. This pithy put-down of what is probably the major activity in IT-system development was voiced by the late Edsger Dijkstra, one of the pre-eminent computer scientists and a fierce advocate that general proof of correctness is the only sensible route for the programmer to pursue.

12. A quip that regularly does the rounds of meetings where 'testers' and 'provers' face each other across the table is: Suppose that you are given the choice of flying on one of two airliners. The flight control software of one has been exhaustively tested, and of the other it is totally untested but has been proven correct. Which plane would you board?

Chapter 7
Going to Ground with Symbols

As far as the propositions of mathematics refer to reality, they are not certain; and as far as they are certain, they do not refer to reality.

(A. Einstein, 1921[1])

Our excursion into formal proof and theorems was undertaken in order to get a feel for how we might prove that a program is in general correct. This was explored because we have established that the testing of programs, quite apart from being a long, drawn-out process, can never deliver the sort of assurance that we would like to have. Proven IT systems do not exist, and consequently, the behaviour of the various IT systems, upon which modern society increasingly relies, will always contain surprises.

But is the promise of program verification, i.e., an abstract proof for an IT system, really the lifeline to a safe and secure technology? In the previous chapter, *specification* of the task was introduced as an essential prerequisite to program correctness with respect to formal proof. But even at this early stage, we began to see that there are inevitable weaknesses in every IT-system *specification* – the three villains identified were incompleteness, imprecision and ambiguity.

Let's be charitable: assume that we are discussing complete, precise and unambiguous *specifications*, the resultant programs, and proofs that they are correct. What have we got? We have a guarantee that the abstract program (the complex formula) is a correct mechanism for always achieving the behaviour stipulated in the *specification*.

However, we can achieve nothing with this abstract program. In order to actually get something done – e.g. a new Dalek actually bringing home the streaky bacon – the program must be loaded into a physical machine, a computer. At this point the program becomes *grounded*, and at precisely this point our troubles really begin. What is this *grounding* that I claim is so problematic?

Consider a simpler formula than the **SHOP** program, let's say the equation 2 + 2 = 4. It is possible to prove that this equation is correct given the necessary basic definitions of the numbers, 1, 2, 3, 4, etc. and of the two symbols "+" and "=". If this is done, what have we proved? In programming terms we have proved that the symbol structure, the formula, "2 + 2" will always equate to the symbol "4". How can we use this new-found and guaranteed knowledge?

D. Partridge, *The Seductive Computer: Why IT Systems Always Fail*,
DOI 10.1007/978-1-84996-498-2_7, © Springer-Verlag London Limited 2011

Easy. If a rich relative dies and leaves you £2, and in the same week a lottery pays out £2 in your favour, you can be sure that your personal wealth has increased by a total of £4. Why can you be absolutely sure of this? Because you know for certain that 2 + 2 = 4.

What you have unconsciously done in applying the abstract certainty of the equation to a real-world situation is you have _grounded_ all the symbols in reality. How did you do this? You 'equated' the first symbol "2" with your £2 inheritance, and the second symbol "2" with your £2 winnings. You have also 'equated' the "+" symbol with the process of putting your two lots of money together. The proven equation then guarantees that you have "4", but "4" what? The answer is £4, of course. Figure 7.1 illustrates this successful exercise in symbol-structure grounding.

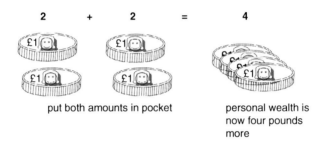

Fig. 7.1   A simple grounding of a simple equation

This example of symbol grounding is hardly suggestive of a knotty problem. Perhaps Einstein was having an off day in 1921 when the chapter-opening quotation was secured? We seem to have quite easily and painlessly transformed the certainty of mathematics into a certainty in reality. After banking your two financial windfalls, you can be certain that you are £4 richer without counting the total, because "2 + 2" is guaranteed to equal "4". The abstract truth of the equation was _grounded_ in financial transfers to give a truth in reality, a truth about concrete objects.

What's wrong here? In order to see how you are being led astray, and why Einstein was right all along, consider another example.

Your deceased relative did not in fact hold you in high esteem, so your inheritance is a derisory 2 pence. Your lottery win, however, remains solid: £2 is your prize. Now, if you simply equate 2 pence with the first "2", and £2 with the second "2", you must be certain that your personal estate is worth "4" more. But 4 what more? Is it £4 more, or 4 pence more?

We, who are sophisticated numeric-symbol grounders, know that these are both wrong answers. We made a hash of the original _grounding_. You cannot add 2 pence to £2 and get 4 of anything. Well, to be honest, you can get 4 lots of 50.5 pence, but how would you know to _ground_ the "4" with this odd sum? After all, we use the _grounding_ to tell us what we have "4" of. It is blatant cheating to determine your new total wealth (by some other means), and then go back to the equation to make the grounding consistent. Figure 7.2 illustrates this unsuccessful attempt to ground our simple equation in reality.

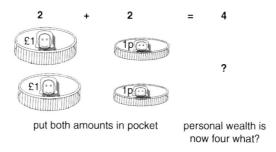

Fig. 7.2 A simple grounding that does not work

So what was the big mistake? Perhaps you can't ground the first "2" symbol with one sort of object (i.e. pennies) and the second "2" symbol with a different sort of object (i.e. pounds). Alternatively or additionally, the "+" symbol may not be equivalent to putting these two pairs together.

The former reservation suggests that all the numeric symbols must be grounded with the same sort of object. But we can surely add 2 apples to 2 pears and end up with 4 fruit?

However, if we add 2 drops of water to 2 drops of water, we are likely to end up with just 1 (bigger) drop, not 4. If we try to add 2 drops of nitro-glycerine to 2 drops of nitro-glycerine, we are unlikely to be around to count the number of pieces that result! Figure 7.3 illustrates these two unsuccessful attempted groundings.[2]

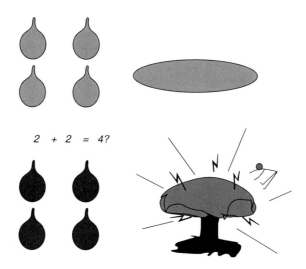

Fig. 7.3 Two attempted groundings: one bad and the other lethal

But view this water experiment in terms of volume (or weight) of water, then the *grounding* work just fine: 2 cc of water added to another 2 cc of water delivers 4 cc of water. Reality is multi-dimensional, thus the necessary *grounding* is always the result of a choice, a choice that biases our interpretation of subsequent, related aspects of reality.

The real-world action of putting drops of water (or nitro-glycerine) together cannot be equated with the abstract operation denoted by the "+" symbol in mathematics – this grounding is invalid. In reality (almost) anything can (almost) always happen. In abstract symbol systems, however, the options for the result of an operation are always limited and well-defined. It is always the case that "2 + 2" equals "4", there are no other possibilities. But where in the world this sure knowledge can be cashed in is an open question.

The shopping robot, attempting to add 2 more oranges to the 2 already in the trolley, might end up with 4, but might not: one orange might slip from the mechanical hand; one might bounce out of the trolley when dropped in; one might fall right through the trolley, etc.

We might say that 'adding' oranges in this manner is in reality a much more complicated operation than the one the symbol "+" represents. The simple *grounding* is only approximately correct. Or we might say that it's simply wrong (as with the pounds and pence example). In either case the result is the same: the necessary *grounding* results in a loss of the certainty that the abstract scheme seemed to promise.

Clearly, even with the simplest of mathematics, it is impossible to provide a *grounding* rule that will always work. This is just another way of saying that it is impossible to know for sure where, when and how the certainty of a mathematical result can be applied to reality. So Einstein, as you might have suspected, was right all along.

How does this *grounding* problem surface in modern computer technology? The Dalek shopper, as we've seen, can easily slip up with the oranges. This particular programming task is, in fact, a minefield of *grounding* problems. But there's nothing particularly special about the robo-shopper and the problem of *grounding* its symbols. The only thing that can be guaranteed once a program is *executing* in the physical world is that there are no guarantees.

The robot shopper must be *grounding* symbols in many different ways all the time. Its programs must generate symbol structures that become transformed into electronic signals for the motors that drive it around, and move its arms and hands to secure the various shopping-list items.

In the previous chapter we embarked on a proof that the **SHOP** program terminates with a trolley full of the shopping-list items. Actually, for each shopping-list item the program terminates by sending signals to the motor activators so that the robot will physically pick up and place the located item in its trolley. There was then no chance of *proving* that the **SHOP** program correctly filled a trolley with the shopping-list items. The best that we might really hope to prove about the **SHOP** program was that it issued seemingly appropriate motor signals at the right times – i.e., after locating each desired item. Our proof exercise stopped far short of even this: we attempted to prove only that every valid shopping-list was always processed appropriately.

We've already considered a number of reasons why our reasoning that the robot has 4 oranges in its trolley might not be secure. There are many more ways that reality can (and will) step in to undermine any abstract certainties.

Suppose that one orange fell on some eggs and broke 2 of them. Or suppose the robot's wheels slip on a squashed rotten orange. It might end up either constantly trying to approach the counter but getting nowhere because of the slippage, or simply groping with its arms unable to reason why the oranges are not within reach having issued the necessary commands to the wheel motors. The possibilities for a failed shopping expedition, despite a perfect **SHOP** program are, of course, endless (which is one major reason why such mechanical menials are not available, and will not be for the foreseeable future).[3]

The formal proof idea can deliver a certainty of equivalence between a problem statement about a desired computation and an abstract program. But in order to get real computations performed we must transform our abstract program (i.e., merely a symbol structure) into a concrete program (i.e., a physical representation within an actual computer). Even when we neglect the further groundings in the world outside the computer, the question arises of how can we be sure that our actual program *executing* on a real computer is an absolutely correct realisation of our proven abstract program? The truth is, we cannot. In addition, we can never be sure that the *grounding* of the program in reality does not introduce new problems (such as a limit on the number of items that can be packed in a trolley). Elsewhere,[4] the phrase "wrenching metamorphosis" has been used to contrast the reality of the move from abstract symbol structures to *grounded* IT systems. Contrast the tacit implication of the verificationists that this transformation need introduce no more than minor perturbations.

You might be tempted to think that I have chosen an example that is particularly awkward to *ground*. Our robot shopper is required to interact with the world, constantly and in quite complicated ways (although the average human shopper is more likely to consider the necessary actions of shopping mind-numbingly boring rather than challengingly complicated). "Surely," you might feel impelled to suggest, "when computers, which are adding machines after all, are limited to mathematical manipulations" – number crunching as its affectionately known – "then the symbol-grounding problem largely vanishes. Does it not?"

The short answer is: "No, it does not." It my have escaped general notice but all my examples have dealt with only whole numbers, _the_ _integers_. Numbers with decimal points, numbers like 2.5, 35.091, etc. – known as _the_ _real_ _numbers_ – cannot be *grounded* accurately in a digital computer. This is because the abstract notion of real numbers is a continuum (i.e. any two such numbers have an infinite number of real numbers between them) and their representation inside a digital computer is necessarily discrete.

Figure 7.4 illustrates this point: the *integers* 59 and 60 (to pick two at random) are discrete values with no intervening *integers*, and can be represented exactly in a digital computer. But consider the *real numbers* 59.0 and 60.0. These two values may, or may not, be exactly representable.[5] Firstly, this depends upon whether 59.0, for example, is precisely the number we want, or whether this is an approximation to, say, 59.000001. And, if it is the latter, then the issue is whether the hardware of a particular computer is capable of representing the desired accuracy. In addition, there are an infinite number of real values between 59.0 and 60.0. Figure 7.4 illustrates some of these. No computer can accurately represent an infinite number of different discrete values. All digital computers can only offer a patchy (some

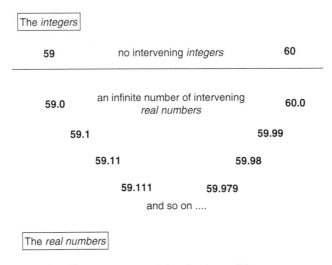

Fig. 7.4 Two sorts of numbers – one easy and the other impossible

values can be more accurately represented than others) and approximate representation of the *real numbers*. And worse, each computer may offer a different approximation with a different patchiness, dependent upon the hardware and software used to implement the *real numbers*.

Digital hardware must limit the accuracy of *real-number* representations, and so only certain discrete samples from the abstract continuum are available for the computations.

On a clear day in June of 1996, Europe's pride and joy, the massive Ariane 5 rocket, lifted from its launch-pad in French Guiana to deliver two 3-ton satellites into orbit. It was a mission that would establish European supremacy in the commercial space business after 10 years of development and a $7 billion investment. But after only 39 seconds into the flight, it was exploded two-and-a-half miles up because the on-board IT system had calculated a number that was too big for its designated *storage box*. This (seemingly) minor fault, which had never occurred in the 23 previously successful launches of the Ariane series, caused a cascade of IT-system faults that in turn led to a dangerously out-of-control rocket.[6]

On the 25th of February 1991, a Patriot missile was launched from its base in Dhahran, Saudi Arabia, to intercept an incoming Scud missile. In the Patriot's on-board computer, time-reckoning software had necessarily approximated the representation of a crucial time lapse; this approximate *grounding* accumulated an error (between the number in the computer and real time) of about 1 second during 300 hours of continuous use (of the missile battery). At the time of firing the on-board representation of time was about one third of a second out: the Patriot missed the Scud by about 500 metres and 28 American soldiers were killed when the Scud hit its target.[7]

Computers, you may be surprised to learn, "never do [real-number] arithmetic exactly, except by accident."[8] The rest of the time we get approximately correct answers. But before you rush to recheck your bank account, you should realize that a monetary approximation to more than a couple of decimal places of pence is, for most intents and purposes, totally accurate. Do you care if your balance is £120.7628 or £120.7629? No, you are content that it is £120 and 76 pence.[9]

Formal proof of program correctness is a potentially powerful tool to help us tackle the important problem of program correctness, but it is only one tool that has something to contribute to the problem of ill-behaved and surprising computer systems; it is by no means a complete solution, even when all the current dreams of proof automation and practical viability of large-scale proofs have been realised.

In summary:

* *Grounding* is an interpretation of a symbol structure in terms of some real-world phenomena – e.g. the decimal number that appears next to "Final Balance" on my bank statement is taken to be the amount in pounds that I had in the bank on the date given (another symbol structure to be *grounded*[10]).
* If an IT system is to be used to impact on the real world, the symbol structures of the program, just like those in mathematical formulae, must be interpreted in terms of real-world phenomena – parts of the program must be *grounded*.
* Grounding is not rule-governed; it is a matter of choice and so shatters certainty of abstract behaviour.
* Formal verification of programs (or parts of programs) is a potentially useful tool for grappling with IT-system correctness, but it can never be a complete answer.

Having led, perhaps dragged, you through the ins and outs of program correctness, and exposed you to the somewhat esoteric notion of formal proofs of program correctness, we might usefully expose one of the great mistakes that non-scientists make about scientists.

This misapprehension is that scientists prove things to be true, and so can operate with certainties. Following this hooptedoodle chapter we get back right on track in order to see why programs may usefully be considered as rather special machines – soft machines. But first a word from the great and good.

Endnotes

1. Einstein's observation occurs in an article entitled "Geometry and Experience," which can be found between pages 232–246 in *Ideas and Opinions*, edited by C. Selig and published by Crown Publishers: New York in 1954.
2. You are strongly advised not to try this experiment at home, or anywhere else.
3. Curiously, it is the more intellectual aspects of human intelligence (activities like chess playing and formal problem solving) that are most easily reproduced with computer programs. Artificial intelligence researchers know that progress towards a world-champion chess playing computer is far more advanced (because it's far easier to specify) than progress towards a house-cleaning robot.
4. In an exhaustive critique of abstract proof as a route to program verification, Nelson uses the evocative phrase "wrenching metamorphosis" to describe the *grounding* problem. D. A. Nelson, "Deductive program proofs: a practitioner's commentary", *Minds and Machines*, vol. 2, no. 3, pp. 283–307, 1992.

5. Even exactly 59.0 is potentially problematic because the real numbers are not typically stored as we would view them. So 1,000,000.0, for example, which is 10^6, can be more compactly stored as 10 and 6, meaning that the number represented is the first value (in this case 10) multiplied by itself the number of times given by the second number (in this case 6). In this case there is no problem, but in general we can find that the value regenerated is not quite the same as we think it should be because the computer is working with one representation and we are working with another.

6. The IT system in the Ariane 5 had been previously used with repeated success, and had not been changed. All that had been changed was the power of the rocket motors – Ariane 5 was more powerful than its predecessors. As a result it flew further than previous rockets in its first 39 seconds. So 'distance flown' (a number computed by the inertial guidance system) was a bigger number than it had ever been previously, and most importantly, it was a bigger number than the IT-system designers had allowed for. Consequently, it overflowed the designated *storage box*; the guidance system shut down and issued an error message; this message (which will be just a digital code within the computer) "looked like flight data – bizarre and impossible flight data"; another IT sub-system used this spurious 'flight data' to execute a drastic flight-control 'correction'; the rocket swerved dangerously off course; and a built-in self-destruct mechanism did what it was designed to do. James Gleick tells this story in "A bug and a crash" (www.around.com/ariane.html – accessed 13/10/2008).

   Yet another example of discrete-system fragility; this example also exposes a 'hole' in the IT system, a promiscuous opening that allowed an 'external' change (more powerful rocket motors) to crash (or literally, explode, in this case) the complete system.

7. Steve Homer writing in *The New Scientist* (14 Nov. 1992, pp. 32–35) tells this story together with a number of others; his main point is not the problems caused by approximation of the real numbers, but the problems stemming from the continual use of old computers. The Patriot missile, originally designed in the mid 1960s with the aim of shooting down aircraft, had been extensively modified 25 years later to intercept much faster missiles. The basic approximate representation (i.e. grounding) of timing data was not improved; it was good enough for hitting aircraft but could fail tragically when the much-faster missiles were its targets.

8. This somewhat surprising, but true, statement appeared in The Guardian Online (Thurs. 1 Dec. 1994) after it came to light that an Intel Pentium chip for real-number arithmetic contained errors, and sometimes computed wrong results. Thomas Nicely (a professor at Lynchburg College in the USA) is credited with finding, or at least publicizing (as Intel already knew, apparently, but weren't declaring it) the problem towards the end of 1994.

9. It is exactly these mismatches between reality and the abstract computation that provide the basis for so-called 'skimming' frauds: an illicit module in the bank's IT system 'collects' the £0.0028 (or 0.28 pence) that your transaction generated, but you won't miss. It does this, say, 1 million times a day, and each day it has accumulated something like £2,800, and no customer feels cheated.

10. In the USA and in the UK symbol strings are grounded differently for dates. For example, the symbols "9–11", if not so tragically memorable, would be the 9th of November in the UK, but it is, of course, a US symbol string and so grounds out as the 11th of September.

Chapter 8
Hooptedoodle 1 – The Proof of the Science is in the Pudding

scientific thinking means that all things must be proved before it is believed that they are

(John Patten, Secretary of State for Education and Science, 1992–1994[1])

Richard Lindzen of MIT has produced conclusive empirical proof that manmade global warming is a farce.[2]

In this optional chapter, an attempt is made to dispel the myth that scientists as a breed operate in a totally dispassionate, rational way objectively proving the truth of facts about the world. By this means, the scientists have vastly increased the sum total of human knowledge, an ever-growing pile of proven truths about the way the world works.

It is true that the beavering of boffins has added enormously to the sum of human knowledge, but that is about the only thing that is true in the preceding paragraph. Scientific knowledge is not proven, it is never a certainty, and what is actually accepted or rejected by the scientific community can be as much a result of efficient in-fighting, effective publicity, canvassing of the right people, friends in high places, etc. as it is of some inherent scientific merit of the work.

As we have already acquired a healthy suspicion of (not to mention practical competence with) the mechanism of logical proof, we might as well start there. Logical deduction, you may recall, is the only mechanism that can deliver certain results. "Deduction" as well as "logic" (or "logical") are words with multiple meanings.

If by "proven" we mean certain knowledge, then the process by means of which the proof was obtained can only have been logical deduction.

> "Subject to your correction, I should judge that the watch belonged to your elder brother, who inherited it from your father. He was a man of untidy habits. He was left with good prospects, but he threw away his chances, lived for some time in poverty with occasional short intervals of prosperity, and, finally, taking to drink, he died. That is all I can gather."
> "Amazing Holmes."
> "Elementary my dear Watson. Simply the power of deduction coupled with precise observation and a store of knowledge."

Such dialogue might Conan Doyle have given to his indefatigable crimebusters at some point in their collaborative adventures. But Sherlock Holmes' reasoning powers, impressive as they may be, are not based on logical deduction at all. The super

D. Partridge, *The Seductive Computer: Why IT Systems Always Fail*, DOI 10.1007/978-1-84996-498-2_8, © Springer-Verlag London Limited 2011

sleuth's technique is swashbuckling deduction at best, and that bears as much similarity to logical deduction (the stuff that proofs are made of) as chalk does to cheese – and this is probably being overgenerous.

Logic and proof are tightly coupled notions that are easy to grasp, but even easier to misconstrue. Set off by John Patten's pronouncement, on his elevation to the ministerage, that scientific thinking means that all things must be proved before they are; constantly surprised by the attempts of apologists to 'explain' why this might be considered more or less correct; and spurred on by the low-volume but relentless flow of pseudo-science articles in the press: I offer this short clarification of what scientists don't do, and why not.

No scientist has ever proved any general claim about our world, and no sane one has ever expected to do so. The hallmark of a scientific theory (if we have to choose just one) is that it can be <u>disproved</u> – i.e., the theory is open to possible refutation without any possibility of confirmation as a true theory. For, although proof and disproof may seem to be complementary notions, opposite sides of the same coin, there is in fact no plane of symmetry between them. Scientific theories must always be potentially disprovable; they are never provable. In a nutshell: this is because scientists must work from observations of particulars to general rules or principles, or theories (call them what you will). This flow of reasoning from the particular to the general is induction, the opposite of deduction. An inductive generalization is at best a possible truth, and just one counterexample can switch its status to that of a known falsehood.

As an example consider the disoriented child in the old UK television advertisement who asked his mother if it was possible for a man to be Prime Minister (PM) of Britain. We were meant to infer that the child had observed, throughout his ten long years of life in the 1980s, that the British PM was always a woman. From his (possibly) very large set of specific observations, he framed the general theory that the post of Prime Minister was, in Britain, reserved for the female of the species. It is true that his question must have been prompted by some misgivings about the correctness of his theory, but that's beside the point which is that, no matter how many more times he witnesses the leader of the opposition get a handbagging from his opposite number, the female-only-PM theory would never be proved correct.

Repeated observation corroborating a theory cannot prove that the theory is correct, but a single observation of a counterexample brings the theory crashing down. Thus proof is impossible, but disproof can be simple and easy; it all depends on the theory. For a theory to qualify as 'scientific' disproof must be possible. Hence "God works in mysterious ways" is not a scientific theory. For what possible event could show it to be false? Joseph Heller's words given to Yossarian in *Catch-22* "He's not working at all. He's playing. Or else He's forgotten all about us." must always remain pure speculation. For how and whether God works or not is a non-scientific theory; this does not mean it is worthless or meaningless, it just means that its value is to be found outside science. This is not because we cannot prove it to be true; it is because we cannot possibly disprove it.

The female-only-PM theory could easily be proved incorrect. One single observation of a grey man installed in number 10, and the theory is disproved, or refuted.

It was Sir Karl Popper who earlier last century laid out the full argument for scientific progress being one of theory refutation rather than confirmation or proof.[3] Later philosophers of science have refined this idea to account for the fact that clear refutations have sometimes been ignored, and seemingly good theories have failed to be adopted by the scientific community. Cold, hard logic is not the whole story; it never will be in a community of humans jockeying for position individually and in pressure groups.

In 1962 an American philosopher, Thomas Kuhn, published a slim but seminal volume *The Structure of Scientific Revolutions* which surveyed the history of science and attempted to put the logical infrastructure in its proper context of a human community. Scientific in-groups provide mutual support for commonly held beliefs, and they vigorously put down the outsiders who hold competing theories. It has been noted more than once by disgruntled young scientists that a radical new theory is only accepted when the resistance finally dies – literally.[4]

Even this notion of disproof is seldom applied within a framework of cold logic that the layman tends to perceive in the barren, rational world of the scientist. The reality is that the logic is attenuated, flexed, coloured and alloyed by personal ambition as well as by social pressures.

The "cold fusion" saga as well as the much more recent (but less celebrated) "bubble fusion" controversy highlighted many of the more colourful aspects of science.[5] Cold fusion is a potentially safe, very cheap, and effectively limitless source of nuclear energy. It is based on a notion of cramming hydrogen molecules together so closely that they fuse and release a lot of energy – nuclear fusion at room temperature. Supposedly this can be done quite simply by using an electric current to drive the hydrogen into the natural interstices of a metal bar (the metal used was platinum).

The big question is can it be done? The surprising answer is – most probably not. The shattering announcement (from the University of Utah in the USA) that successful cold fusion experiments had been achieved was made in 1989. Ever since, there have been many attempts to reproduce the phenomenon. A very few claimed success, but most reported failure. Respected and competent scientists can still be found to argue (with a wealth of supporting 'facts') both the positive and the negative answers. How can this be?

There are lots of reasons, not the least of which are: the fantastic worth of such a discovery (hence claims of secrecy, and gagging by patent attorneys); the embarrassment it would cause to the scientific establishment which has been persuading governments to plough billions of pounds into 'hot' fusion research with very little to show as a result. But one particularly interesting spin-off from the controversy reveals the poverty of the simple notion that theories can be refuted by a single counterexample.[6]

Failure by competing scientists to observe the cold fusion phenomenon when they repeated the published cold-fusion experiments was dismissed by the believers in cold fusion with the assertion that the experiments had not been repeated correctly: for example, the platinum bars were impure, or too pure, or too new, or too old, etc. The set of possible reasons for refusing to accept a scientific finding is limitless. The notion of cold, hard scientific facts is just another myth.

Consider also the reliability of what we observe: human perception is unreliable, as any decent magic show will confirm. Another path to contamination of the pristine logic is the one bordered by human intuition and commonsense. The scientist cannot afford to trust such notions. It is, for example, absurd to believe that the Earth is round and that Australians are thus walking upside down, or that jumbo jets can fly. But these and many similar, thoroughly implausible notions do appear to be true.

A thoroughly implausible theory that most people these days would bet on is that the Earth revolves around the Sun, and not vice versa. It was not always so, and certainly doesn't appear so from the standpoint of the earth-bound observer. From his solid and unmoving vantage point, he has repeatedly seen the Sun rise in the East, go over the top, and disappear down on the other side.

Copernicus is often credited with dreaming up this idea which was recognized as quite absurd and sensibly rejected by his peers. But early in the seventeenth century Galileo decided to champion this theory against the might of the Church which took the very enlightened attitude that if the Bible was to be reinterpreted, then the cause of the reinterpretation must be rigorously demonstrated. Galileo, however, a pillar of the scientific establishment thought that his personal belief in the controversial idea should be sufficient for general acceptance. The Church, however, was not about to budge, even for a Galileo.

Under considerable pressure either to provide evidence in support of the theory or to withdraw it as a supposedly established theory, Galileo presented a simple analysis of the relative effects on the Earth's seas of the Earth revolving about the Sun: the conclusion of his analysis was that should be one high tide every day and that it will occur about noon – see Fig. 8.1.

The sceptical ecclesiastics took away this supposed demonstration of the theory. They soon, however, got back to Galileo with the awkward point that actually, high tides are generally observed to occur *twice* in every 24 hours, and they move steadily around the clock from day to day.

But Galileo was not the sort of scientist who would permit inconvenient small facts to hinder the development of good theory. Quite unfazed by these apparent refutations of the Copernican theory, he dismissed them as merely due to 'secondary effects' and thus not significant contradictions.

The Church failed to appreciate these points and so finally hauled him over the coals for heresy. At which point he quickly saw sense.[7] It may well be true that over the course of the subsequent 250 years scientific controversy has lost some of its colour, and that may be to the good.

Scientific thinking is not commonsense thinking; it is not even commonsense thinking with the rough edges knocked off and polished up a bit. It is an entirely different kind of thinking. Wolpert's small book, *The Unnatural Nature of Science*,[8] makes this all quite clear. Who, for example, would believe that a bullet fired horizontally from a gun held 3 ft above the ground will drop to the ground at the same time as a bullet simply dropped (at the same instant as the other is fired) from a height of 3 ft. Science tells us that this will indeed happen; commonsense tells us that the fired bullet will travel for a much longer time before eventually falling to the ground.

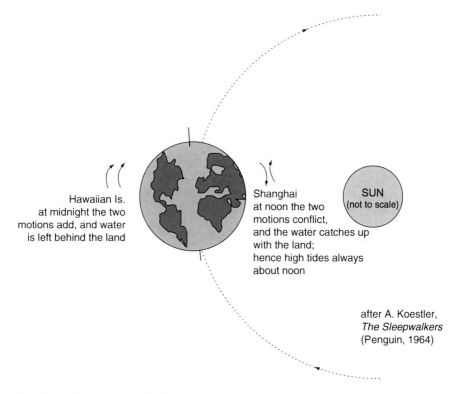

Hawaiian Is.
at midnight the two
motions add, and water
is left behind the land

Shanghai
at noon the two
motions conflict,
and the water catches up
with the land;
hence high tides always
about noon

SUN
(not to scale)

after A. Koestler,
The Sleepwalkers
(Penguin, 1964)

Fig. 8.1 Galileo's 'proof' of the heliocentric theory

Closer to home for most readers who may well be missing out on the gun culture but not the car one: can an object be travelling in one direction and at the same time be accelerating in the opposite direction? Of course not, is the commonsense answer. Actually, it happens every time you apply the brakes in your car.

So where does this notion of proof come in? Surely it can't have been invented as merely an abstract notion with no application? Of course, it could have. Mathematicians and logicians do that sort of thing all the time. It's the cognitive equivalent of the mountaineer's far-flung pinnacle of windswept, icy rock. They go for it because it's there. But many of the champions of proof and logic are also very practical people, or can at least provide a practical justification for their efforts as is required if they want to survive in this time of utilitarian science. A formal proof does provide a guarantee that what you end up with is absolutely correct, subject to certain provisos. The question then is: why can the scientist not use this powerful notion? To appreciate the answer to this we need to unpick the mechanism of proof just a little.

What is a proof? It's a chain of reasoning that starts from a set of basic assumptions, and progresses through a series of steps in which new pieces of information are logically deduced – and can thus be added to the fund of basic knowledge from which the further deductive steps will be taken. Deductive logic delivers guaranteed implications (provided the basic assumptions are correct, complete and non-contradictory); inductive logic can do no such thing.

What is this powerful reasoning mechanism that can deliver the ultimate goods? The essential mechanism is trivial: from true general rules and true facts we can logically deduce further facts which are also guaranteed to be true. Here is one such general rule derived from our Chapter 6 proof of **the odd theorem** (where the use of bolded upper case and italics indicate that this is the language of logic, and not everyday English):

IF *we have any integer* **AND** *it is multiplied by 2* **THEN** *the result is an even integer*
and here is a related fact:

4 times any integer is the same as that integer multiplied by 2 and the result multiplied by 2 once more.
The logical deduction from these two assumptions is:
4 times any integer is an even integer.

This small deductive exercise expands the bald statement of the truth of our deduction in the original proof. This deduction was implicit[9] in the proof given (and also illustrates the arbitrariness of the rule-fact distinction). It is long chains of such deductive reasoning, drawing on many rules and facts that can lead to interesting, surprising and provably-correct new information.

Strict logical reasoning, however, does not always accord well with human common-sense, rational reasoning. One of the basic mistakes of non-formalists is to fail to distinguish between the language of formal logic and the everyday language of English. They can look similar, identical even, but mean very different things. Very carefully phrased English can be closely equivalent in meaning to statements in logic, but casual English can be wildly wrong despite a superficial resemblance.

Whilst walking along the beach, at Dawlish in Devon, with a friend who happened to be scientist. We encountered a notice that proclaimed:

> IF THE YELLOW FLAG IS FLYING
>
> IT IS SAFE TO SWIM

"I wonder," mused my companion, "whether it's safe to swim when the yellow flag is not flying."

"Of course not!" is the commonsense response, but formal logical reasoning can come to no firm conclusion either way; it has nothing to tell us when the conditional part of a rule is not true. As a statement in logic (which it was not, of course) we can have no idea of whether it is safe to swim or not when the yellow flag is not flying. This is quite counterintuitive; it is, however, logically correct reasoning.

So can proven information be guaranteed even if the reasoning that leads to the proof is a bit adrift of rational commonsense reasoning? The reality is that mathematicians are (despite all appearances to the contrary) only human and they make mistakes. In addition, the deductive logic running through a proof is typically based upon other accepted truths, such as the laws of arithmetic. Our earlier small proof of **the odd theorem** did this; it also relied on the fact that all integer number must be either odd or even. Impeccable application of deductive logic can be wrecked by an (often implicit) erroneous assumption anywhere in the chain of reasoning. The chapter endnote to this theorem explains the non-obvious validity of one such implicit assumption in this proof.

It is estimated that mathematicians publish some 200,000 theorems (i.e. interesting, proven, new knowledge) every year. A number of these are subsequently shown to be erroneous – i.e. not proven at all. The history of mathematics is littered with proofs that were accepted for years and then subsequently shown to be wrong.

The famous map-colouring conjecture (reminder: no more than four different colours will ever be needed to colour the countries on a map in order to ensure that no two countries of the same colour have a common border), for example, was thought to be proved true in 1879. This supposed proof stood for 11 years before another mathematician spotted a fatal flaw in it. It remained unproved, relegated once more to a mere conjecture, for more than half a century. An elaborate computer-based proof was published in the 1970s; it is currently subject to much debate as to its significance and validity (see end notes to Chapter 6)

Finally, even when the formalists do get it right there is a real gulf between the formal frameworks within which certain presumptions can be proved true, and the empirical world within which scientists can champion their presumptions only as not-yet-disproved.

Formal theories, as Bertrand Russell once observed, preserve the notion of provable correctness, but at the cost of not saying what they are talking about in the real world. This *symbol-grounding* problem was the subject of an earlier chapter, and so will not be repeated here. Although mathematicians and logicians can use logical deduction to prove that certain relationships between symbols are true, there are quite a few reasons why scientists cannot directly transfer this certainty to their activity of furthering our understanding of the world.

I have of necessity skated quickly over a number of patches of thin argument in this chapter. How scientists actually go about their business as scientists, and the reasons why certain theories gather support, or not, both with and without problematic observations, are all tricky issues. The problem of the rise and fall of scientific theories, and the steady increase in the sum of human knowledge bear some considerable similarity to that of the ebb and flow of interest rates, and the availability of credit – dramatically illustrated on a world-wide scale in 2008. In both cases, those in the know are sure that there are important relationships, but they are equally sure that no one really understands exactly what the relationships are. The scientific endeavour is both rich and interesting but not the concern of this chapter which is merely to demonstrate why disproof not proof is the overriding characteristic of the scientific. To paraphrase John Patten and provide something a good deal closer to the truth: scientific thinking means that all things must be potentially disprovable before it is believed that they might be. This is far more awkward and ugly than the original, but sadly the truth sometimes is.

An example of contrary evidence not leading to (what we now take to be) correct refutation of a theory is found in observations of the planet Mercury.[10] For many years it was observed by astronomers that this planet did not quite traverse the sky on the trajectory that Newton's Laws predicted. But as Newton's Laws were well-tested and corroborated by many other observations and experiments in the physical world, and the discrepancy in Mercury's path was small, this minor flaw was not thought to be significant. It was perhaps an inaccuracy introduced by the measuring devices, an experimental error, and certainly not a basis for challenging the validity of Newton's wide-ranging and spectacularly successful theories.

Nevertheless, Einstein's General Relativity Theory predicts exactly the observed discrepancy, and it is now taken as an important refutation of Newtonian mechanics rather than an inconvenient glitch. We now believe that the Sun's gravitational field bends the light from Mercury, and we see it the planet displaced slightly from where we would predict it to be – rather like the sight of an object under water when viewed through the water surface, we see it displaced from its true position.

Endnotes

1. This quotation is from the then Minister for Education and Science who wrote an article for *The Spectator* arguing for the merits of religious teaching. This fundamental misinterpretation of the nature of science was not much more than a (misguided) passing reference, but it was from our political leader in this field, and it did get widely publicized.
2. See the Global Warming 'sceptics' website for a wealth of 'proof' claims – http://scienceandpublicpolicy.org

   For example: December 8, 2009.

   "Richard Lindzen of MIT has produced conclusive empirical proof that manmade global warming is a farce. See here, for example:

   Yes, the earth was getting warmer. It's always warming or cooling. Surely these idiots realize this. And you would think that they had the common sense that God gave a boiled turnip and realize the earth's climate is driven largely by the sun, and to a lesser extent by such factors as volcanism."

   "To disprove the AGW [i.e., manmade global warming] science

   You need to look no further than the missing greenhouse hotspot. Many studies have tried to locate it, but it is nowhere to be found. Every single computer climate model predicts its existence.

   It's interesting that every single global climate model uses the CRU data as it initial values, which is now known to be faked. Therefore the models produce fake results.

   It is not up to the detractors to prove a negative, it is up to the proposers to prove their hypothesis is correct using the scientific method. Which includes releasing all data, methods and results so other scientists can duplicate the hypothesis. Otherwise it's just some rigged, fudged, faked up computer program."

   All this would be more amusing if it were not potentially so serious.
3. It was Sir Karl Popper's seminal book *The Logic of Scientific Discovery* (published in German, 1930s, translated into English, 1960s) which laid out the objective foundations of scientific progress. It was left to later writers, such as T. Kuhn (*The Structure of Scientific Revolutions*, 1962 – see note below for details), to then explain why this logical process of conjecture, test and refutation was so often flouted by the scientists.
4. Kuhn quotes both Charles Darwin and Max Planck on the point that new theories are not accepted on merit, the latter writing in his autobiography: "a new scientific truth does not triumph by convincing its opponents and making them see the light, but rather because its

opponents eventually die" (p. 151, 2nd edn). Thomas S. Kuhn's book, *The Structure of Scientific Revolutions*, was published by the University of Chicago Press in 1962 with an enlarged 2nd edition in 1970.

5. A number of books exploring this most bizarre episode in modern science (which is still continuing) are available:

Too Hot to Handle by Frank Close (Penguin, 1990)

A British professor of physics tells the tale of what *Time Magazine* hailed as "the greatest discovery since fire."

Cold fusion: The scientific fiasco of the century by John R. Huizenga (OUP, 1992).

An American chemistry and physics professor was co-Chairman of the U.S. Department of Energy Cold Fusion Panel which investigated the phenomenon.

Both academics tell much the same story and are at pains to explain the details of the supposed phenomenon – probably tough going for the chemically unenlightened. The stories are, however, quite readable and fascinating even if the much of the technical details are ignored. Neither author is in any doubt that the phenomenon called 'cold fusion' (i.e., nuclear fusion at room temperature rather than at millions of degrees Centigrade) has not been demonstrated and almost certainly never happened.

In the current millennium, claims for a new version of cold fusion have been made and similarly challenged by other scientists who failed to replicate the phenomenon reported. The new claims are that nuclear fusion has been observed in the collapse of bubbles in liquids; hence the name "bubble fusion."

On March 8, 2006, *Nature* magazine published an online article under the title, *Bubble bursts for table-top fusion; Data analysis calls bubble fusion into question*, by UCLA researchers, namely Brian Naranjo, under the supervision of Seth Putterman (doi:10.1038/news060306-3). This article was attacked as "misinformed, unpublished, web- posted, non-peer reviewed ... relied on sources with undisclosed conflicts of interest with competitors, [and it] set into motion a federally mandated two-year investigation. ... The *Nature* March 8, 2006 article alleged actions that constitute fraud, bubble fusion data fabrication, and quoted UCLA's B. Naranjo as stating: "The probability of getting such a poor match for neutrons produced by fusion is one in more than 100 million –virtually impossible." This webpost verdict from a UCLA graduate student was portrayed by the *Nature* reporter as true without accurately investigating the facts." (from http://pesn.com/2008/08/27/9501491_BubbleFusion_vindicated/ accessed 25/03/09) ... and so this new debate rumbles on.

The thoroughly up to date example is the disagreements over Global Warming – is it happening? If so, are mankind's actions a significant causal factor? Sceptics claim that the case for manmade global warming "has not been proved" – of course it hasn't, because this sort of hypothesis can never be proved. It has to be a question of weight of evidence for and against these hypotheses. However, with the complexity of the 'Earth's-climate' system far exceeding that of the unmanageable IT systems, the truth of these hypotheses will always be a matter of argument – even though it's primarily a 'predictable' analogue system.

The hypothesis that our climate is warming and that human activity is a significant contributive factor is an important scientific hypothesis, but one for which either clear proof or even indisputable refutation seem equally unlikely.

6. This sort of disagreement also highlights the difficulties surrounding another touchstone of science: repeatability. But if an experiment is not repeatable (i.e., the attempted repetition fails to deliver the original outcomes), what does this mean? The attempted repetition was carried out incompetently? The original descriptions were incomplete, or wrong, with respect to the experimental procedure and/or the measurements recorded? There are endless ways that either of these questions can be answered in the positive, and no easy way to conclude that either is not the reason behind failure to repeat.

7. Arthur Koestler in *The Sleepwalkers* (Penguin, 1964) recounts this tale in great detail. This book documents the way science has stumbled along in the dark for centuries not knowing where it was going or even recognizing when it got there. Despite Koestler's arguably anti-scientific stance, his book is revealing reading for those with a stubbornly persistent belief in

the clarity and rationality of the scientific enterprise. The author concentrates on Copernicus, Tycho Brahe, Kepler and Galileo.

8. Lewis Wolpert's book, *The Unnatural Nature of Science* (Faber and Faber, 1992), is an eminently readable, non-technical explanation of how and why scientific thinking is not just formalised commonsense thinking, but an entirely different (and somewhat alien) mode of thinking.

9. Still implicit is the fact:

   2 multiplied by 2 is the same as 4 as well as many others, such as the definition of an even number being that it divides exactly by two, and the necessary relationship between multiplication and division. Which facts and rules are explicitly included in a proof and which are left implicit is largely a matter of taste and judgement with respect to minimizing proof size and including all 'non-obvious' assumptions. But 'obviousness', of course, is highly person specific, so the notion of a complete proof is no more clear-cut than that of a complete *specification* for an IT system (see Chapter 6).

10. Kuhn on page 155 in his 2nd edition (see book details above) states: "Einstein, for example, seems not to have anticipated that general relativity would account with precision for the well-known anomaly in the motion of Mercury's perihelion, and he experienced a corresponding triumph when it did so."

   Kuhn gives further references to the book and letters that support this claim.

Chapter 9
The Soft Machine

When Claude Shannon, a pioneer information technologist,
was asked if he thought machines could think, he replied:
You bet. I'm a machine and you're a machine, and we both
think, don't we?[1]

As the opening quotation indicates, the notion of what is (and what is not) a machine is not as simple and straightforward as casual expectation might suggest. But at this point in our story the question of whether organisms, such as you or I, might sensibly be thought of as machines – sometimes called meat machines – need not be broached. The less emotive question is: are programs some sort of machine? And following on from this: why does it matter?

Programs are artefacts, but what sort of man-made things are they? Are they like bridges and buildings? Or are they like cars and cranes? Are they like poems, or other works of art? Or are they something unique, a new type of artefact? So far, there has been no shortage of special pleading, so why stop short of making the case for an entirely new sort of product of human ingenuity. However, we shall see that there is no compelling reason to invent a new category of artefact.

I am assuming here that programs are not primarily works of art, although some might want to argue that the best ones are this as well. Programs are _engineered_ artefacts. The persons who design and build them professionally are often called _software engineers_ – not that titles prove anything, but they are indicative of the way the wind is blowing.

In a previous chapter we examined and rejected the academic computer science proposal for proving that programs are correct. This requirement of correct programs is indeed the counsel of perfection, and therein lies the fatal flaw as we saw in the grounding chapter. Reality does not admit mechanisms of perfection: there are no perfect motor cars, no perfect buildings, and no perfect computer systems. In fact, it is altogether rather odd to talk of perfect cars, say – and even more odd to contemplate the notion of a correct car. Why is this? Cars and buildings are engineered artefacts and so are computer systems.

The obvious answer is that cars and computer systems are very different sorts of machines, and anyway, the claim is not that the computer hardware itself is perfect, but that the program which controls it is, or can be – this program is known as the _software_ of the system. If we can ensure that the controlling software is correct,

D. Partridge, *The Seductive Computer: Why IT Systems Always Fail,*
DOI 10.1007/978-1-84996-498-2_9, © Springer-Verlag London Limited 2011

then we will have reduced the overall problem of, say, target identification and laser gun aiming to one of mechanical and electronic reliability. We will have ruled out one major subsystem as a potential source of overall system imperfection. This does not solve the general problem but it does reduce its scope.

The basis for the formal-proof idea was the observation that programs are well-defined symbol structures just like formulae in mathematics. As well as being like mathematical formulae, programs are also like conventional machines. Programs contain no moving parts that can wear out; computers do but programs don't. However, a program is, in some quite meaningful sense, a machine.

Consider our standard formula: $2 + 2 = 4$. A computer program that contained this information could well be part of a general program for computing the sums of arbitrary numbers – i.e. for doing addition.

We type two numbers into the program; it computes with them; and it prints out the total. The program is then an adding machine. It exhibits exactly the same set of behaviours as the old-fashioned adding machines which required that a handle be turned a certain number of times, etc. in order to compute the resultant total. An abacus with a similarly proficient operator could also reproduce the behaviours of the 'adding' program.

In fact, if you were totally isolated from the particular adding machine (computer program, mechanical adder or abacus) such that you gave the input numbers to an operator, who then went off, did the calculation on one of these three devices, and returned to give you the answer; the three alternatives would be indistinguishable from their behaviours. There might be quite noticeable speed differences, and even accuracy differences, but in terms of basic capabilities we simply have three different ways of doing the same set of things.

The mechanical adding machine is, everyone would agree, a 'machine' in the normal sense of the word. So the computer program, once installed in a computer, behaves as if it were part of a machine. The combination accepts the raw materials (some numbers), works on them, and generates a final product, the sum total.

In the typical modern manifestation, precisely what this program-computer machine does is determined by the program. Although there are exceptions,[2] it is overwhelmingly the case that an understanding of the program is also an understanding of program-computer machine. This viewpoint provides us with a basis for treating computer programs as machines, machines constructed of software – *soft machines*.

An adding-machine may have any amount of software components, from almost total to none. In principle, the mix is a matter of choice. Nowadays the mix usually chosen is task-specific software components (i.e., bits of programming) and general-purpose hardware components (often electronics wizardry).

Our earlier **SHOP** program was part of a conventional type of machine, the supermarket-cruiser robot. The programmed part allowed the owner to specify his or her list of items to be shopped for, and it determined how the list of items was to be processed – e.g. started at left end, replaced item by zero to signify that it has been 'shopped for', etc. The rest of the machine was (or would be, if it existed) electronics, motors, wheels, etc. – i.e. quite conventional machine stuff.

The programmed part could also be constructed entirely out of cogs and gears, as indeed the very first computers were. It's a cumbersome way to construct programs, and the resultant machine is slow, prone to breakdown and very expensive, but it's possible. There is essentially a choice for any desired computation, a choice between constructing an entirely physical mechanism, or a combination of a general-purpose physical mechanism and task-specific programmed instructions.

Consider the possibility of a shopping robot that is (mis)designed as an entirely physical machine. In the worst case both the shopping list and the way it is processed are fixed and predetermined. So the robot will always shop for exactly the same items in exactly the same way, with no opportunity for the owner who has tired of eggs, bread, milk, meat, etc. to vary the family diet. No opportunity that is, short of taking a soldering iron, hacksaw and wire snippers to rearrange the insides of the unimaginative menial.

A better design (better because it would permit the flexibility of varying the items in the shopping list) would make the shopping list contents programmable but the shopping-list processing mechanism fixed by the physical innards of the robot. This choice of hardware-software partitioning is entirely reasonable, it does however fix (assuming the average owner is not going to delve inside it wielding the requisite tools) the details of how the shopping list is to be processed. Our original design, opting to program both the shopping list and its processing details, gave the user (who is able to program, it must be said) full flexibility to change these details of how the overall machine will function. More realistically, it gave the software technicians back at corporate workshops a freedom to deal with emergent problems by reprogramming.

These days the physical mechanism is largely electronic in nature, and thus a bit less physical than cogs and gears, but it is the combination option that we go for – a basic physical machine and a sophisticated set of programming instructions. So modern programs are simply that part of the computational mechanism which we choose to construct out of software (all programs are called software in contrast to the hardware of the physical machine); it is simply more efficient and economical to opt for this division of the overall computational task.

Building soft machines is the preferred option, this choice is however the result of "an offer that can't be refused"; it is dictated by convenience, cost and power. The inevitable result is that modern computer technology is dominated by programming. But by choosing this option for constructing sophisticated computers we impose the subsequent problem of having to ground our abstract science in reality before a practically useful machine is obtained.

The computer technologists' great achievements rest in no small way on the decision to construct primarily soft machines. By taking this route they are able to work with highly flexible, potentially guaranteeable symbol structures abstracted away from much of the concrete detail that would further cloud the issues.

The unavoidable consequence is, however, that the soft machine must be grounded, and the act of grounding must (by its very nature) eliminate provability and hence certainty from the range of possible characteristics that the resultant machine can exhibit. The great mistake of some computer scientists is to pretend that this loss may not occur (e.g. if the hardware is properly constructed[3]), or to refuse to accept that when it occurs it will inevitably introduce more than a minor perturbation to their well-understood, perhaps proven, abstract construction. The smallest symbol in error can wreck the largest program, remember, and the fact that this is so is due to the way the computational world has been created.

Having the largest system hostage to the smallest error was the creators' choice. It is not a necessary feature of all computational worlds as we shall see. It is, however, a necessary consequence of the desire to have a computational world within which the possibility of guaranteed results was best preserved.

More succinctly, the soft machine must confront reality at two interfaces, and when it does it will be twisted and distorted in ways that can never be fully formalized. This must be recognized, but perhaps it need not be tolerated. In order to avoid it we must be prepared to forswear any hope of guaranteed correctness in complex computer systems.

To recap:

- There is no valid reason to limit the notion of a machine to hard components.
- A computer program is a machine, a _soft_ _machine_.
- An IT system is composed of a hard machine (usually electronic components) and a _soft machine_, a computer program.
- In principle, the relative mix of hard and soft components in an IT system is entirely arbitrary.
- In practice, IT systems are primarily _soft machines_.
- The _soft machine_ becomes _grounded_ within the hard components of an IT system (the computer hardware), and the IT system as a whole is then _grounded_ by the context in which it is used, and its inputs and outputs are interpreted.
- Even this initial _grounding_, which cannot be avoided for a _soft machine_, wrecks the scope for formal proofs of IT system correctness.

Having completed the explanation of why the computer technologists, who build programs for our modern computer systems, cannot import mathematical certainty into their constructions, it is time to move on. So we can't prove that the bank's computer always computes the balance of our accounts correctly, but if it doesn't it must be simply because some programmer gave it a wrong instruction. Computers only do what they are told, so why don't we just make sure that we tell them what to do correctly? Why indeed?

Endnotes

1. This quotation comes from an article by J. Horgan in *IEEE Spectrum*, April 1992.
2. In the context of the *grounding* problem (a subject initiated in Chapter 7), the hardware computer tends to intrude on a 'full' understanding of the program-computer machine in just those cases where *grounding* is equivocal – e.g., when timing is important or when the necessary real-number concerns stray into the holes and inaccuracies of the hardware approximations.
3. C. A. R. Hoare, a professor of Computing at Oxford University has written of "correct implementations" by which he means that the soft machine can be transformed into a 'hard' (i.e. real-world) machine with no changes in its behaviour. But even when we agree to exclude the unavoidable difference between the fallibility of all real-world mechanisms and the potential for infallibility of abstract mechanisms, there is still a variety of detailed reasons why this

'perfect transformation' can never be realised. Nelson, for example, describes the inevitable differences between the soft machines that dominate modern computer technology and the 'hard' machines of modern electronics technology. The article is, " Deductive Program Verification (a Practitioner's Commentary)" in *Minds and Machines*, vol. 2, pp. 283–307, 1992.

As the earlier chapter on grounding symbol structures made quite clear, although the computer scientist creates his own world, the fact that it must operate in reality means that there are no correct implementations of the abstract symbol-manipulation schemes – where 'correct' here means that perfect grounding is obtained, i.e., the programs grounded in real computers behave in precisely the same way as the abstract program whose behaviour has been proven to be correct.

To illustrate this issue with a familiar example: the mathematics of collisions of perfect, inelastic spheres – i.e., the activity for which practical proficiency is one of the signs of a misspent youth – is well developed and would allow us to prove that a given configuration of snooker balls may be cleared in one break with a series of precisely specified cue strokes. The fact is, of course, this series of strokes, even if precisely carried out by a Dalek (hustler model) will not, in reality, guarantee that the table will be cleared.

The problem resides in the lamentable fact that the equipment designers and manufacturers haven't produced a correct implementation of the abstract mathematical scheme. Table cushions do not give precisely the same bounce everywhere. The balls are not perfect spheres, they are not inelastic, and sometimes they're dusty, etc.

The inventor of the perfect snooker-playing robot may wish to complain that the reason why his provably perfect player does not win any tournaments is that the table and ball designers have not yet done a good enough job. There is some truth in this charge, but it would be the height of foolishness to continue refining the perfection of cue-shot calculation and execution by his robot while awaiting the emergence of a correct implementation of the mathematics – a perfect snooker table. There are computer scientists who are, in effect, doing just this.

Chapter 10
Computers Only Do as They're Told

<u>one Hal of a problem</u>

"Are you sure it's necessary to revive any of them, Dave? We can manage very well by ourselves. My on-board memory is quite capable of handling all the mission requirements."

...

What had gone before could have been a series of accidents; but this was the first hint of mutiny. Bowman felt that he was walking on eggs as he answered:

"Since an emergency has developed, I want as much help as possible. So please let me have manual hibernation control."

"If you're still determined to revive the whole crew, I can handle it myself. There's no need for you to bother."

...

"I want to do this myself, Hal," he said. "Please give me control."

"Look, Dave, you've got a lot of things to do. I suggest you leave this to me."

"Hal – switch to manual hibernation control."

"I can tell from your voice harmonics, Dave, that you're badly upset. Why don't you take a stress pill and get some rest?"

(Arthur C. Clarke, 2001 *a space odyssey*, p. 146)

This small exchange, between the (up-market) IT system, Hal, and the human user, Dave Bowman, may be taken as an example of one of the classic problems in computer programming: a fundamental mismatch between what the programmer has told the computer to do, and what the user wants the computer to do. As you can see, it is the programmer's telling rather than the user's that tends to hold sway with the computer. So the 'telling' that we are considering here is that of the programmer, and he does it by means of a program.

If there's one thing that you can say about computers it is that, unlike children (and many grownups for that matter), computers do what they are told – and only what they are told. This sort of observation is often trotted out by some wise old owl when the misbehaviour of an IT system is being discussed on a casual basis. It is meant to imply that a computer can never be blamed for its undesirable actions

D. Partridge, *The Seductive Computer: Why IT Systems Always Fail*,
DOI 10.1007/978-1-84996-498-2_10, © Springer-Verlag London Limited 2011

because misbehaviour implies a spontaneity and novelty of action that is at odds with the constraint that computers can only do what they are told.

If the IT system behaves incorrectly then it's simply because someone foolishly told it to. But the question of the correctness, or appropriateness, of computer behaviour is not (as we now know) this straightforward. In this chapter I'll explain why this viewpoint is dangerously simplistic.

The casual assertion of computer obedience is, of course, true. Slavish obedience of computers is more part of the problem than a solution. Crucially the statement is not: 'computers only do what you intended to tell them to do.'

Fans of Lewis Carroll's Alice might recall the occasion when the White Queen tried to program her.

> "Can you do addition?" the White Queen asked. "What's one and one and one and one and one and one and one and one and one and one?"
> "I don't know," said Alice. "I lost count."

Of course, Lewis Carroll predated the computer age and so he wasn't making a point about computer technology, but we can use this snippet to good effect nevertheless. The list of instructions that the White Queen uttered constituted a perfectly good program. Alice, however, couldn't *execute* it correctly which is not surprising because humans are not computers. You and I would have exactly the same trouble as Alice did.

Just suppose that Alice had listened carefully, waited for the White Queen to cease, and then paused for a moment before saying confidently, "eleven" or some similarly plausible result. The chances are high that the Queen would not know if Alice was right or wrong. The Queen, who uttered the list of instructions (the program), would not know exactly what she had in fact just told Alice to do. She would know that she had instructed Alice to add a large number of ones together, but she would not know precisely how many. Therefore the Queen would not know if Alice had done as instructed or not.

With the White Queen as the programmer and a more confident Alice as the computer this exchange captures the sort of problem that daily confronts the IT-system builder. It's not quite the same problem because computers will follow instructions much more reliably than Alice (or you or I for that matter, I'm not getting at Alice here). Also, the list of instructions will be recorded somewhere in such a way that the programmer can refer back to check exactly what he told the computer to do. These two riders on the similarity claim suggest that the programmer should be able to boost his confidence that the computer did what it was told to a far higher degree than the White Queen could hope to achieve. After all, in an age before tape recorders, the royal program was gone, dissipated into the ether, chasing echoes of the Big Bang. The White Queen's verbal program was just not available for subsequent, close re-inspection. In addition, Alice's computational reliability was certainly at the low end of the computational-reliability spectrum populated by modern electronic computers.

The modern reality, it turns out, is that the programmer can be no more certain than the White Queen would have been if confronted with a confident "eleven" from Alice. This is not because of uncertainty as to whether the computer was doing as it was told, but because of uncertainty about what exactly it was told to do. This claim should be surprising. The programmer can view his program on a screen for hours, or print it out on paper and take it home for virtually endless close scrutiny. Why can he not determine exactly what the computer has been told to do? Am I hiding something from you? Well I am, as you well know; what I have glossed over is the complexity inherent in the programs that constitute modern IT systems. As we saw when we played computer with our small program in an attempt to determine its correctness, the human mind does not take happily to focusing down and working meticulously through a series of precise instructions for long periods of time. Some minds will stick at it for longer periods than others, but all minds will, sooner or later, insist on breaking away from the tediousness of the task and revert to the altogether more comfortable mode of flitting to and fro, dabbling with, and sampling, possibilities on a higher conceptual plane – i.e., however hard you rein in your brain it will not play computer well for very long. Remember, we experienced this refusal of the brain to knuckle down and play computer on a very small program. Now imagine the enormity of the task when faced with 100,000 instructions instead of a dozen or so!

Alice was also tested with a simple program, and her failure was partly due to the human limitations on short term memory. The list of additions was too long and too repetitive to memorize as well as presented too fast for her to deal with on the fly as it were. IT systems are altogether more complex, much more complex.

Consider our first programs: the first a non-complex and rather tedious object, and the second, the **SHOP** program, which was considerably more complex. The payoff for enduring the program-development chapters (or the cost of skipping over them) is that the rest of the book has been, and will continue to be, based on the principles exemplified in these simple examples. These programs will continue to provide us with concrete examples of all the computational phenomena that need to be considered.

The **SHOP** program, although definitely non-trivial, is still not a very complex object, and certainly not a complex program. Nevertheless, it is difficult to be sure exactly what it has (and hence we have) told the computer to do. Look at this:

```
SET alpha-letter AS A
REPEAT
    DO READ&FIND WITH alpha-letter AS NEXT-ITEM
    3. place item in trolley
    SET-NEXT alpha-letter
UNTIL list is empty
```

It is the main part of the **SHOP** program (with the **COMMENT** omitted). What does it all mean? However much you felt comfortable with each of these instructions when the program was originally developed, it is a fair wager that by now (especially if you have not ploughed through to here in one read) your mental grasp will have slipped to some degree – if not almost totally.

Such recall failure is not to be taken as yet another indication of your unsuitability for the programming life. It just means that you are more or less human with respect to your ability to memorize masses of intricate detail. Assuming that you are not one of the pathological cases of total non-recall, it is likely that the average hotshot programmer will not do much better.

What the competent programmer will do is quickly refresh his grasp of the details of why each instruction is as it is in any small group of instructions. That, however, is not the point; the important point is that the human brain is incapable of keeping in mind a precise recollection of more than a very few fine details at any one time. Our earlier brief encounter with 'playing computer' and with proofs of program correctness should leave you in no doubt about the validity of this assertion.

The capable programmer can thus mentally roam over a large program and reason about (and so understand) the details of successive small groups of instructions. But the mental grasp of each new group will necessarily displace or degrade the understandings of the previous groupings.

Whatever it is exactly that we've told the computer to do, we can be reasonably sure that the computer will do it accurately, and that's all to the good but it doesn't solve our problem. So the apparent force behind the true claim that computers only do what you tell them to do is illusory, because the root of the problem lies buried elsewhere.

So, how does the programmer hope to get to grips with precisely what his program has told the computer to do?

When dealing with a technology that involves literally thousands (and often millions) of fine details, every one of which is potentially crucial, we can never be sure what exactly it is that we've told the computer to do. A large program is merely a long sequence of instructions. Figure 10.1 illustrates such a program in which the long sequence (actually not very long, only about 100 instructions) has been broken into four columns in order to achieve a compact representation.

Even the most casual reader will realize that the program instructions in Fig. 10.1 are illegible, and the more astute reader will also realize that the four columns of instructions are identical. Why is this?

This is because we now need to defocus. As with IT-system development, so with *program understanding*, it is a mistake to start with the details; you should home in on the details once their context is understood. So now we will concentrate on general program structure as a route down to instruction detail. From this viewpoint, the fine structure of the individual instructions is irrelevant, so I have eliminated this source of potential distraction in the large-program illustrations.

I have reduced the individual instructions to the point of illegibility which also happens to have the added bonus of allowing large-program illustrations to be reasonably sized. This ploy also makes the further salient points:

1. A really large program presents itself as simply a very long list of instructions, individually non-meaningful – it is a blurred mass of code, in effect, at first sight.
2. Good, bad and terrible programs are indistinguishable when viewed simply as a long list of instructions. (This point is more forcibly made by using the instruction list of Fig. 10.1 for Fig. 10.5 and again for Fig. 13.1.)

a large program -- a long sequence of instructions

Fig. 10.1 Quite a lot of program instructions (in four columns) – the casual view

By looking closely at a (real) program, we can always be sure of the individual instructions, both exactly how they are ordered, and what, in general, the computer will do with each one. But the totality of what the program instructs the computer to do in detail and in every conceivable starting situation is unknown, perhaps unknowable.

If the task is to determine what the program tells the computer to do, then fine instruction-level detail is not the place to start. The *flow structure* provides a better route towards a hope of understanding a large program.[1] It gives us a high-level indication of what we have told the computer to do, and from this global perspective we can begin to focus down on details. Figure 10.2 shows the *flow structure* for our large program – the simple straight arrow is no more than a vague memory.

Programs are classic examples of the adage that the whole is greater than the sum of the parts. Remodelling this old saw for the current context: the range of possible behaviours of a program is greater than the collection of individual instructions. In the context of a program, John Donne's observations concerning man in his world apply perfectly to programming language instructions:

> No instruction is an island, entire of itself;
> every instruction is a piece of a program, a part
> of a subprogram;

if a character be washed away by the sea, the
SHOP program is the less,
as well as if the **SUBPROGRAM READ&FIND**
were,
as well as if a subprogram of thy friends or thine
own were;
any lost character diminishes an instruction, because it is involved in the program;
And therefore never send to know why the program failed;
It failed because a single instruction, or just a
single character, was in the wrong place in relation to the rest.

There is nothing mysterious in this situation. It is merely a result of the generation of unmanageable complexity. As we have seen, quite small programs soon begin to push beyond the limits of manageable conceptual complexity. Each instruction on its own is simple and straightforward, but within a program no instruction is on its own – "an island entire of itself." It is enmeshed in a *flow structure*.

Within a program each instruction is embedded in a precise context – i.e., the actual numbers sitting in each labelled *storage box* at the time the computer comes to *execute* the instruction. It is impossible for us to keep in mind precisely the correct set of numbers and their associated labels as we think through a program. The problem is actually

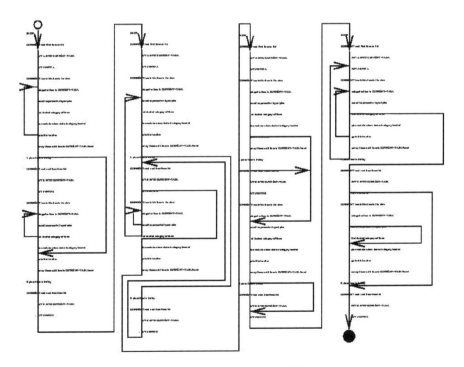

Fig. 10.2 A large program with the flow structure made explicit

worse: we have to bear in mind all the possible sets of numbers, i.e., the whole range of possible contexts for each instruction as determined by different starting numbers and successive iterations of instructions in a loop. Even when we elect to focus on only one possible set of numbers and play computer with the help of a pencil and paper, it is very difficult to keep our concentration focused down at the tediously low level of these box-number changes for a substantial period of time. On occasion, we can do so successfully, but what we can never do is be sure that we have succeeded.

You might be tempted to think that conceptual manageability can be gained by only considering small portions of the program at a time if we divide the whole into an organized collection of more-or-less independent bits, and this is to some extent true. The previous flow structure (Fig. 10.2) is indicative of a well-organized program. Figure 10.3 illustrates all the more or less independent bits.

As mentioned earlier, a major strategy in computer program design and development is divide and conquer. We are urged to *modularise* our large programs – i.e., break them up into a collection of more or less independent modules. Our use of the program **SUBPROGRAM READ&FIND** illustrates this strategy. The *main* program, **SHOP**, took care of the problem of selecting the NEXT-ITEM to be shopped for, and finally (after following the **READ&FIND** subprogram) it directed the robot to place the retrieved item in the trolley. This particular *modularisation* of the program should limit any concerns about the way the robot finds the NEXT-ITEM to the details of the instructions within the subprogram.

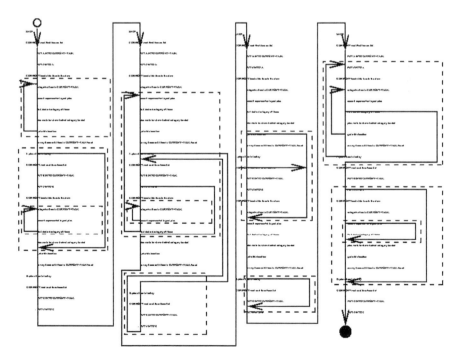

Fig. 10.3 More or less independent bits in the context of some complexity

Such *modularisation* reduced the effective complexity of the program. If we want to reassure ourselves about the details of the way the robot has been told to find items, then we need only examine the instructions within **SUBPROGRAM READ&FIND.** Quite independently, we can then inspect the *main* program in order to build our confidence that the retrieved items are appropriately dealt with (at least we could if we had refined the high-level instruction 3 down to the level of programming language detail, which of course we would have to do before we had a complete working program).

I don't say that this approach has suddenly, at one bound, solved our problem of determining what it is exactly that we have told the computer to do. What I do claim is that it has reduced the complexity of the *program-understanding* problem. This claim may be less than self evident with respect to our small program composed of only two modules, but it becomes indisputable when we are faced with a well-designed, multi-module extravaganza as opposed to a multi-thousand-instruction monolithic alternative – the former version is by far the more easily manageable, or, more accurately, the less unmanageable.

Each *module* has only one *flow path* in and one *flow path* out, this means we can reason about each of these modules <u>almost</u> independent of the rest of the program. We just have to take into account the single route in and the single route out – *modules* are almost "islands". The *modular* program is a string of "islands" (and some "islands" within "islands"). Such a <u>*well-structured program*</u> has a linear flow structure from *module* to *module*; Fig. 10.4 makes clear the module-to-module flow structure of Fig. 10.3.

Such *well-structured* programs are not always possible, but, by striving to achieve this degree of clean line, simplicity of flow and elegance, conceptual manageability of the program will be maximised. Thus the scope for surprising errors is minimised. Large programs exhibiting this quality of structural elegance deserve to be ranked with the best of humanity's well-designed complex artefacts – such as the fine cathedral at Rheims.[2]

So *modularisation* is a great boon to the computer programmer wrestling with a large program, but the story is not one of all gain untainted by any bad news. Earlier (Chapter 4), we transformed a repeated sequence of instructions into a single *subprogram module*. The gain could be seen as a shorter program at the cost of a more complex *flow structure*. There are also time costs to subprogram *modularisation*. The computer uses extra time to locate each named subprogram and to transfer its attention from where it is (presumably at a **DO** instruction) to the subprogram specified (which will be one of many possibilities). Then control must be transferred back again when execution of the subprogram is complete.

Computers are lightning swift (almost), but this extra work caused by the presence of subprograms may be done many millions of times in a large program, and this all adds up. So take it from me that significant slowdowns are deceptively easy to generate in highly subprogram-modularised, large programs.

Modular design is always a good thing, and generally so is *subprogram modularisation*. But ultimately, this latter aspect of *modularisation* exemplifies design choice, and not one that has a great deal to do with cold hard logic.[3]

The good news is, however, that slowing down the computer is typically not a major problem, although the *Star Wars* enthusiasts might disagree (as incoming

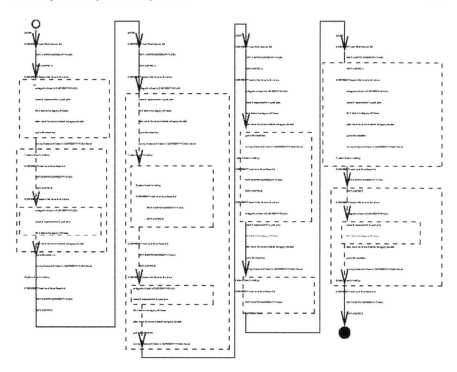

Fig. 10.4 *Modularisation*: a technique for straightening arrows

missiles are raining down all around while the computer is still trying to decide whether it has detected a hostile missile or not). The bigger problem caused by subprogram *modularisation* is lack of continuity in the flow of the computation, and the consequent negative impact on *program understanding*. We can see an example of this in our small program.

Suppose we wish to reassure ourselves of the reliability of our **SUBPROGRAM READ&FIND**. This program module was constructed to compute NEXT-ITEM to be shopped for, and to locate this item in the store. By just focusing on the subprogram itself we can determine that it seems to do this okay, provided that whenever the computer comes to *execute* the instructions in the *subprogram* there is a suitable value in the box aliased with the label NEXT-ITEM.

Now the actual aliasing operation does not occur within this subprogram; it is done by a <u>non-local</u> instruction, i.e., an instruction outside of the *module* under scrutiny. So, in order to check out the instructions in our subprogram we must switch our attention to elsewhere in the program to determine: first, the location of <u>all</u> the **DO** instructions that can cause the computer to jump to **SUBPROGRAM READ&FIND**, and second, how, within <u>each of</u> these **DO** instructions the **WITH** part is set up to do the aliasing.

Now, in our little example program this is not a big problem. We can quickly see that there is only one **DO** <u>READ&FIND</u> instruction in the *main*, **SHOP**, program and that the **WITH**-part uses the value of alpha-letter to achieve the necessary aliasing. We then have to switch attention to the instructions that set up the values of alpha-letter; there are two of them: one that sets an initial value "A" and one that changes the value to the next letter of the alphabet – **SET** and **SET-NEXT**, respectively. This all seems okay.

But just imagine even this small task embedded in many thousands of instructions. We would have to scan through all the rest just to be sure that there was not another **DO** READ&FIND instruction anywhere. And then, if this is not bad enough, consider the case where different **WITH** parts use entirely different mechanisms for aliasing, some using perhaps further non-local values.

The task is then expanded to tracing back through all possible preceding instruction sequences (which may involve other *subprograms* and *loop* structures) in order to locate the instruction that last set the value that each **WITH** part uses.

When a program needs fixing or extending, the programmer needs to fully understand the *flow structure* of (in conjunction with the labelled boxes involved in) the instructions that he is about to alter. This understanding can only come from a detailed study of the *flow paths* of the actual program. Tracing back along all possible *flow paths* from somewhere in the centre of a large, *well-structured* program (see Fig. 10.2) is demanding enough, but consider this task in relation to another large program, the one illustrated in Fig. 10.5.

a large program —— a long sequence of instructions

Fig. 10.5 Another long sequence of instructions – just like Fig. 10.2?

It doesn't look to be a cinch, but it doesn't look like too much of a challenge for the hot-shot programmer. However, look deeper. Figure 10.6 illustrates its flow structure. It's a mess. Such (lack of) structure is known ruefully as *spaghetti-code*.

There are virtually no *modules*, and consequently there are no simpler views. This is it! No arrow straightening is possible. Brave programmers have nightmares about such programs. Imagine trying to make changes, or find errors, within such computational turmoil (and never forget every character is potentially crucial – perhaps that should be, lethal). Almost any instruction within *spaghetti code* can be reached via countless different *flow paths*. Finally, before we leave this stomach-churning atrocity, remember the public face of this unholy mess, Fig. 10.5. It looks quite harmless doesn't it? In fact, it looks surprisingly like the well-structured large program of Fig. 10.2.

If the pinnacle of *well-structured* programs is composed of elegant complex objects that rank alongside the cathedral at Rheims, the other end of the scale of structural complexity – the end we might call chaotic complexity, and hence ultra-complexity – fits more aptly next to a Heath Robinson contraption. It may work okay, but that knowledge comes as a bit of a surprise when first looking at the internal structure.

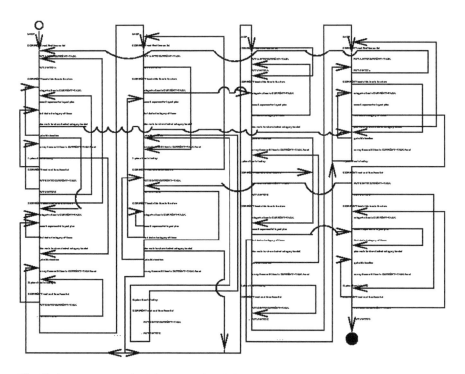

Fig. 10.6 A programmer's nightmare – Fig. 10.5 nothing like Fig. 10.2

As you can well appreciate, I hope, the use of *subprogram* modules necessarily causes discontinuities in the flow of a computation through a program. This means that we must be prepared to follow these discontinuities in our efforts to reassure ourselves that the program is doing what we wanted it to do, or to rationalize why it is doing whatever it is that we observe it to be doing – i.e., to gain an understanding of the results that the program generates when it's instructing an actual computer.

A classic example of the danger associated with the view that computers only do what you tell them to do somehow precludes surprising and unexplainable behaviour in computer programs can be found in the stone age of computer technology.

In the late 1940s Arthur Samuel was at the University of Illinois. He and his colleagues were desirous of obtaining one of the latest electronic marvels – a computing machine. At that time the vacuum-tube filled monsters that passed for computers were very few and far between, and even if you had the money (which Samuel didn't) there weren't any for sale. It was a case of if you want one, build one, but this also takes considerable money. As it happened, there was to be a world checker (i.e. draughts) championship in the neighbourhood the following year, so Samuel and his colleagues hit upon the crazy idea of building a primitive checker-playing machine whose success would provide a platform for the necessary large-scale fund raising.

Once the general strategy had been formulated, detailed plans were laid. With commendable modesty the group decided that they had set themselves a non-trivial programming task as well as a challenging electronics problem of actually building a computing machine. It was thus decided that they had better start writing the checker-playing program immediately, i.e., at the same time as they started to design the small computer itself. This programming part of the project fell to Samuel, who thus found himself in the unenviable position of writing a program in an unspecified programming language for a machine which had not been built!

Needless to say, this program was never completed and neither was the computer, but Arthur Samuel did go on to write a very successful checker-playing program for the first large-scale, general-purpose computers marketed by IBM. Samuel was by this time an IBM employee and hardware reliability was, in these early days, somewhat precarious, as one might expect. IBM found it necessary to extensively test each new machine before shipping it out to the customer. So at a time when large computers were an extremely scarce and thus an expensive commodity (the late 1950s and the 1960s) Samuel was surrounded by hitherto undreamt-of computational resources in need of exercise.

The happy outcome from this fortuitous co-occurrence of needs and wants resulted in a factory basement full of large computers all playing checkers with themselves – i.e., each computer contained two checker-playing programs locked in checker combat with each other. While many copies of the same checker-playing program divided into pairs and pitted one against another might well serve to exercise the computers for long periods, it is not clear what Samuel would have gained from such an exercise. But many different checker-playing programs similarly organized constituted a real tournament from which an overall winner could be expected to emerge. This is, of course, what he did. He experimented with random variants of his basic program, and by selecting the winning versions for further experimentation he eventually developed a very powerful checker-playing program. (A very early venture, and still one of the most successful ones, into IT-system development through simulated evolution.)

The remarkable feature of the final program was that it could consistently beat Samuel himself. It is true that Samuel did not claim to be an expert checker player, but it is equally true that he did not tell his final program how to beat him. He merely told it how to play legal checkers and how to automatically experiment with minor variations in its strategy of play. However, given this basic information and a lot of playing time, the result was a program that illuminates a further angle on the poverty of bald statements like:

Computers only do what you tell them to do.

Another example also comes from the dark ages of programming, and it serves to exemplify the way the task of programming has radically changed during its few decades of existence – I refer to the phenomenon of *one-liners*. *One-liners* is an early programmers' game in which the objective is to pack a maximum of instruction into as small a program as possible such that it causes the computer to perform a number of actions for totally non-obvious reasons. The best *one-liner* concocters were often the best programmers because programming expertise was a rather different sort of quality then. In those early days, when computer memories were small and computers were slow, the name of the (programming) game was to save storage space and to shave microseconds off program running time. Computers were a scarce resource and had to be used with maximum efficiency. The good programmer could hand-craft the most exquisitely compact programs, and he did this by finely timed reuse and double-use of the few available *storage boxes* – sometimes, for example, exploiting the numeric code by means of which the computer happened to store part of an instruction as a number in the computation performed by that instruction! What this led to was dense programs whose ultimate expression was the program in one line – the one-liner.[4]

Information density is seldom found to correlate with transparency, and programs are not an exceptional medium in this respect. The early programs, while being wonders of micro-engineering, tended to be conceptually opaque – i.e., it was very difficult to determine how the program was doing what it was observed to do. This was, of course, the major source of enjoyment derived from the *one-liner* game – challenging one's colleagues to determine what it was that your exquisitely crafted micro-program tells the computer to do.

But now times have changed: information density is no longer a requirement; conceptual transparency to support *program understanding* is the overriding need. The fact that computers only do what they are told to do is neither here nor there.

So what has this chapter added to the sum of our knowledge?

- Computers most assuredly do only what we tell them to do.
- What we've told a computer to do must be distinguished from what we believe we've told it to do.

- Knowing what you've told a computer to do is impossible to establish with certainty.
- A program *module* has only one flow-path in and one flow-path out.
- *Well-structured* (i.e. modular) IT systems can be contrasted with *spaghetti-code* systems, and the former considerably assist the task of knowing what you've told the computer to do.
- Modern IT-system design and development still suffers from the puzzle solving-and-setting practices that were important in the early days of programming, such as the *one liner*. This remains a detrimental element of the allure of programming.

At this point we have reached the end of the crash course in the nature of programming. Having ploughed through assiduously to this endpoint, most probably you could not program yourself out of a paper bag. However, it was never meant to be that sort of crash course. What you can now do, I hope, is appreciate the enormous complexities and inevitable uncertainties of the task, and hence the unavoidable problems with the products – i.e., large IT systems.

The next chapter, the final one in this section, is entirely optional. It explains what I take to be a further intriguing twist in the complexity-simplicity feature of computer programs and human reasoning processes. Beyond this readily-skippable hooptedoodle chapter, with a sound knowledge of the basics of modern software technology now resident in some portion of your brain, we begin to explore the implications of this technology, first on certain individuals, and subsequently on society as a whole.

Endnotes

1. IT-system *flow structure* is just one, perhaps the most important one, of a variety of representations of the dynamics of a computation – 'data-flow diagrams', for example, are another popular aid to IT-system understanding. Do not assume that *flow structure* is the key that will fling the door open to full *program understanding*; it just provides one useful view of what's going on in general. F. P. Brooks in his book *The Mythical Man-Month* (Addison-Wesley, 1975; reissued with additions 1995) stresses the point that such representations of computations (and he lists a number of alternative and competing ones) can help, but they fall far short of solving the problem of *program understanding*.
2. Brooks again (see note above) first used Rheims cathedral as a motif for elegant complexity with respect to programs.
3. In the first figure below, five rectangles enclose five occurrences of the same four program instructions which occur in the linear *modularisation* illustrated in Fig. 10.4. So the IT-system designer's choice would be to accept the linear *modularisation* or to create a *subprogram* module of these four instructions and then replace each boxed set of the four instructions by a single **DO** instruction. The program would be shorter but the *flow structure* would be more complicated. Which is preferable? It depends upon many factors, and even when they are all assessed the choice will still be a matter of creative judgement. The resultant decisions should be designed to maximize understanding of the current and future versions of the IT system. For example, are the five occurrences of the identical instruction groups likely to be subject to change, and are they all likely to be subject to the same change pressures, or is one or more likely to diverge from the others?

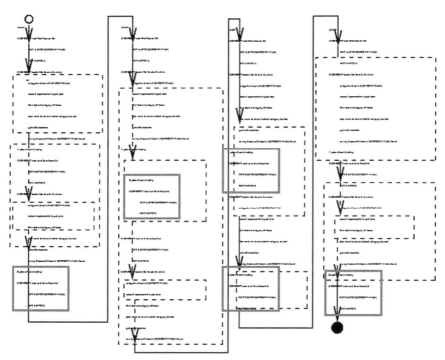

the straight–line flow structure of a modularised program

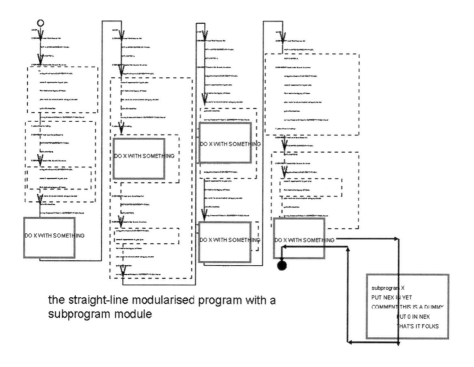

the straight-line modularised program with a
subprogram module

But assuming we are happy to treat all five equally: we can create a *subprogram* (named **X**) and replace the five identical blocks of four instructions with a reference to the *subprogram*, i.e., **DO X** ... . By so doing we have reduced the size of our program (ten instructions fewer) and localized this repeated operation in the one subprogram, but we have, of necessity, introduced a more complex flow structure. This figure below illustrates this strategy but with the explicit flow structure to, and back from, the *subprogram* only shown once (it exists for all five **DO** instructions).

4. The macho allure of the one-liner is captured in the 1983 quotation to be found on page 111 of D. Lubar's *It's Not a Bug; It's a Feature* (Addison-Wesley, 1995):

> It's a big boost to the ego to write code that works and that nobody else can read. It's bad practice, but often almost irresistible.

attributed to Jim Butterfield

Chapter 11
Hooptedoodle 2: Recursing Through Tescos

> *"What's a wally?"*
>
> *"A wally is someone who doesn't know what a wally is."*
>
> the recursive definition of 'wally'

For those either unconvinced of the sheer complexity of programs or simply thirsting for more, another important source of computational power, and one with particularly intriguing complexity properties, is the notion of *recursion*.

It is an intriguing notion because tremendous computational power can be packed into very few instructions – it's computational nuclear power. As with all powerful phenomena, which nuclear fission epitomizes, the user must be wary of the attendant dangers. In the case of recursion, it is can be used for the worst of *one-liner* activities, but, if used wisely, it exhibits a powerful transparency. Programming with recursive structures is in some real sense utterly simple, and in yet another, equally real, sense it causes a giant step up in conceptual complexity. We shall home in on this notion slowly.

Closely related to the tension between simplicity and complexity, recursion appears to be an example of a computational process that is unsupported by brain architecture, and thus it is difficult for humans to execute recursive processes. The management of the computational details is difficult, without training and practice, and yet 'what the computer has been told to do' is quite transparent in general.

Let's continue with our shopping robot example, but start afresh. Here is the, by now, familiar plan of a solution, assuming a shopping list is available.

1. read first item on list
2. locate this item in the store
3. place item in trolley
4. read next item on list
5. locate this item in the store
6. place item in trolley
7. read next item on list
8. etc.

D. Partridge, *The Seductive Computer: Why IT Systems Always Fail*,
DOI 10.1007/978-1-84996-498-2_11, © Springer-Verlag London Limited 2011

I trust that you can see that this is becoming repetitive. Although we might program the computer that controls our shopping-robot with this very tedious program, we, who have now progressed well beyond the category of utter-novice programmer, would immediately know that a *loop* structure will do the trick much more succinctly, say:

REPEAT
    read next item on list
    locate this item in the store
    place item in trolley
UNTIL no more items left on list

I hope that you feel thoroughly at home with this little pseudo-program, if not, then skip back to the early part of this book where we developed a very similar one. The **REPEAT-UNTIL** structure causes the computer (and hence our robot in this little piece of science fiction) to repeatedly read next item, locate it, and put it in its trolley. It will continue repeating these three instructions until its shopping list is empty which is, of course, just the right time to stop shopping and pay for all that has been amassed (another problem, but one that I shall neglect).

This *loop* structure has allowed us to condense a large number of instructions into just five lines of program – five lines that can deal with a shopping list of any length. Clearly, the use of a *loop* structure is a good idea, but we've been over this ground earlier. So what's new?

Suppose that shopping lists were restricted to only one item, what would the necessary shopping program look like? All you would need for the **SHOP** program is:

SHOP
    read first item on list
    locate this item in the store
    place item in trolley

A piece of cake (as they say) as a programming challenge, but a program of limited use. We really must deal with shopping lists that contain more than one item.

Consider this possibility:

SHOP
    read first item on list
    locate this item in the store
    place item in trolley
    SHOP for rest of list

What have I done here? The **SHOP** program now uses the SHOP program to achieve its goal (I'll continue with the earlier stylistic convention of bold-underline for *main* program and *subprogram* names, and underline without bold for references to these names). I've programmed myself into an ever-decreasing circle (and we all know the unfortunate outcome of this type of activity).

Before I extricate myself with one bound, notice that this programmed example of ever-decreasing circles does have a certain logic about it: shopping for a list of items can quite sensibly be viewed as determining, locating and retrieving the first item on the list followed by shopping for all the rest of the items on the list. This is a recursive description of shopping which means that I've described shopping in terms of shopping. Clearly a circular notion, but one that has great simplicity and power when properly handled; not all circularity needs to be vicious (but note, not all recursion is benign).

So how do we extricate the computer from the endless circularity of this program that I've called **SHOP**? The answer is simple, possibly obvious even. If shopping is viewed as taking care of the first item on the list followed by shopping for the remaining items, the obvious point to stop shopping is when there are no remaining items – i.e., the rest of the list is empty. So let's preface the circular reference to continue shopping with a condition that instructs the robot to continue shopping only if there are further items on the remaining shopping list (i.e. the remaining list is not empty) – eminently sensible I would have thought.

Here's the improved, and no longer viciously circular, program:

SHOP

read first item on list
locate this item in the store
place item in trolley
IF rest of list is not empty **THEN** SHOP for rest of list

This is a *recursive program*: we have instructed our robot how to SHOP in terms of SHOP, but in a way that is both logically correct and quite simply conceptualized.

We obtain a simple program for shopping by thinking of shopping as determining, locating, and retrieving the first item on the list, and then shopping for the rest of the items on the list until there are no more. I would hope that you can agree that this characterization of shopping has an obvious simplicity about it. (For those readers who feel that shopping could hardly be otherwise, please suspend judgement on the power of recursive strategies until we get to more ambitious examples.)

An obvious question here is can the computer cope with this style of convoluted program? Rest assured, it can. Let's give our computer-controlled robot a shopping list, and set it loose in a selected superstore. Here's the shopping list:

tin of baked beans
half a dozen eggs
a tomato

Given the *recursive program* **SHOP**, let's work through the sequence of operations that will ensue – i.e. we'll hand *execute* it. When the robot's computer brain first begins to follow the **SHOP** program, it is instructed to read the first item on the list: it reads: tin of baked beans. The second instruction causes it to set off to find this popular delicacy, and when found, the third instruction tells it to pop the tin of beans in its trolley. That's the first three instructions followed, and the first item on the original shopping list has been dealt with.

The rest of the shopping list now looks like this:

half a dozen eggs
a tomato

The shopping task has now been reduced to shopping for these two items.

The computer is faced with the final instruction in the **SHOP** program. At this point the rest of the list is clearly not empty and so it *executes* the **SHOP** program, as instructed, using the rest of its shopping list. So now it is back at the beginning of **SHOP** with this two-item shopping list.

It reads the first item on the rest of the shopping list; it is: half a dozen eggs. It finds the egg counter and puts half a dozen eggs in its trolley. That's the top item dealt with according to the first three instructions, and now it's reached the fourth instruction for the second time. At this point 'the rest of the shopping list' is:

a tomato

Although not a big request the list is certainly not empty, so it must once more *execute* the **SHOP** program with this one-item shopping list.

Now (and this is where it gets really exciting!), the robot reads that a tomato is required, it finds tomatoes, and puts one juicy red specimen in its trolley. At this point in the shopping computation, the last item in the shopping list has been successfully dealt with so the rest of the list contains no items (i.e. it's empty). The fourth instruction is next, but this tells the computer to continue shopping only if the rest of the shopping list is not empty.

So what does the computer do? Nothing, it has finished executing the **SHOP** program, because there are no more instructions following this fourth one. With its trolley containing a tin of baked beans, half a dozen eggs together with a tomato, the success of the shopping activity must be admitted. Therefore the program looks like it works okay. (There is in fact a bit more computational tidy-up involved in the *execution* of recursive programs, but I'm glossing over it for the moment.)

Actually, the programmer who is on the ball will not be altogether satisfied with our recursive program for robot shopping. He or she is likely to point out that things will go wrong if we present our metal menial with an empty shopping list. The everyday response to this criticism might be that if you are stupid enough to send your robot shopping with an empty shopping list you just get what you deserve. As a logical point, however, it's unassailable: loose the robot in the store, with our program **SHOP** and an empty shopping list, and trouble is guaranteed.

Why? Well, it will be parked in the entrance to the shop, trolley at the ready, trying to read the top item from an empty list – this cannot be done! So the program will stall (or 'hang up'), and consequently so will the robot because it is controlled by the program.

So, although it is not good practice to send robots shopping with empty shopping lists, it is even worse practice to write programs that are vulnerable to human stupidity and thoughtlessness, or to artful bloody-mindedness. Luckily, we can fix this logical weakness in our program quite easily: we just need to move the stopping condition so that it does not attempt to deal with the top list item unless the shopping list is non-empty. Here's the better version:

SHOP
    IF the list is empty **THEN** cease shopping
    read first item on list

    locate this item in the store
    put item in trolley
    <u>SHOP</u> for rest of list items

Now I've added an explicit instruction to stop the shopping activity. In the context of a more realistic shopping program this would have to be an instruction for the robot to set off in search of the check-out, but in this vastly oversimplified example, I've just told it to stop.

It is time to move on to a more ambitious example in order to provide better support for my contention that recursive programming offers great simplicity and overwhelming complexity all in one neat package. But before I do, consider briefly an English description of our **SHOP** program:

SHOP
If the shopping list is empty, then there is no shopping to do.
Otherwise determine, locate, and retrieve the top item on the list, and then shop for the rest of the list.

The first sentence (paraphrasing the first program instruction) is simply and obviously true, is it not? The next four instructions, which are only *executed* by the computer if the list is not empty, are paraphrased by the second sentence. This is also plausibly true. I won't say "obviously true" because the notion of shopping is generally ill-defined, and we have developed a rather special meaning for it. So let's really move on to an equally simple but more well-defined problem.

Assume that we want the robot to be able to compute how many items are on any given shopping list – i.e. determine the length of a shopping list. This is not a problem that should tax the computational capacity of the average household robot, but we will have to supply a program to actually do the calculation.

Writing a program to compute the length of a list is not a major challenge for the competent programmer, but there are two rather different ways to go about it. The non-recursive thinker will start developing a loop structure that steps along the shopping list one item at a time, and adds one to a storage box value at each step. When it reaches the end of the list, then the final value accumulated in this box will be the number of items in the list (provided that the initial box value was set to zero). This is a tricky little program for the neophyte programmer; here it is:

PUT 0 **IN** LENGTH
IF list is empty **THEN PRINT** LENGTH and stop
REPEAT
    ADD 1 **TO** LENGTH **PUT RESULT IN** LENGTH
    discard current list item
UNTIL remaining list is empty
PRINT LENGTH

I'm using a box labelled "LENGTH" to accumulate the final list length. The second instruction is just to take care of the possibility that some smart alec might ask our robot, how many items are in an empty list? The **REPEAT-UNTIL** loop then steps through the list, adding one to the value in box LENGTH for each item it finds, until it reaches the end of the list. Finally, the value in box LENGTH, i.e. the number of items in the list and hence its length, is printed out.

Now consider the recursive approach to this problem:

The length of an empty shopping list is zero.

Acceptable as true without more ado, I hope.

The length of a non-empty shopping list is: 1 plus the length of the list without its first item.

Slightly odd, but similarly, obviously true, if you think about it. So let's do that. It will probably help if we call a list with its first item removed, the *tail* of a list. So the *tail* of our earlier beans-eggs-tomato shopping list is:

half a dozen eggs
a tomato

and the *tail* of this list is:

a tomato

and the *tail* of this list is an empty shopping list (which is hard to illustrate clearly, but in future I'll do this with " empty list"). An empty list, of course, has no *tail* because it has no first item that can be removed. And remember, the length of an empty list is zero. Let's rephrase the second half of our recursive definition:

The length of a non-empty shopping list is 1 plus the length of the tail of the list.

If this is not obviously true for you, then take an example, say, our beans-eggs-tomato list. This is a non-empty list, so the second half of our recursive definition should apply. This tells us that the length of this list is:

1+ (length of eggs-tomato list)

and the eggs-tomato list is length 2, so the total length becomes:

1 + 2

which is 3, and is the correct length of the original list.

But we know the dangers of justifying the correctness of programs using specific tests, so I won't push this too hard. It is really the logic of the definition that I want you to accept as obviously true: the length of a non-empty list just has to be 1 plus the length of its tail, doesn't it? From an acceptance of this definition we can provide a complete re-definition of the list-length problem, it is:

The length of an empty list is zero, and
the length of a non-empty list is 1 plus the length of its tail.

Notice that this is a recursive definition: the length of a non-empty list is defined in terms of length. But it is defined in terms of the length of a shorter list (a tail must always be shorter than the list it came from, no?). The length of the shortest list, the empty list, is given simply as zero. It is the interaction of these two aspects of our recursive definition that save it from endless circularity.

So, we have a simple restatement of our original problem; it is composed of two ludicrously obvious statements. It is also directly re-writeable as a computer program:

LIST-LENGTH
IF list is empty **THEN PUT** 0 **IN** LENGTH
IF list is not empty **THEN PUT** 1+(LIST-LENGTH of tail) **IN** LENGTH

This is a much simpler program than the earlier looping one (it is also more complex but we'll get to that aspect shortly).[1]

This program is composed of two instructions. The computer will execute one or the other (dependent upon whether the list it has is empty or not), and the program is then finished. Figure 11.1 illustrates this *flow structure*.

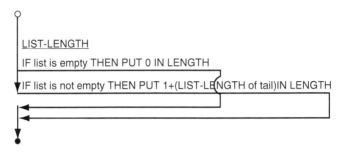

Fig. 11.1 Flow through one instruction or the other

The two instructions are both constructed to put a value in a *storage box* labelled "LENGTH". The first instruction simply puts a zero in this box, but the second instruction has to first compute the value to be put into the *storage box*. The computation that is required is to add one to the length of the tail of the list. But before it can add the one, it must first compute the length of the tail of the list. To do this it is sent off to do this computation and come back with the answer. The flow structure for this program is then more accurately illustrated in Fig. 11.2.

The two instructions of this program, which constitute a complete program to compute the length of a shopping list, are both straightforward recastings of the recursive definition given in English. Thus, to the extent that the English definition is obviously correct, so is the recursive program. This is my point about the simplicity of the recursive approach to programming, and it gets more forceful as the problems that we tackle become trickier. The jump in complexity, which I also promised, is to be found in the way that the computer must process such a program. In order to make this complexity crystal clear for those readers who are really getting into this programming business and think that such a two-instruction program must be a cinch to hand execute, let us begin to play computer with this small, but recursive, program.

First, we'll need a specific shopping list to try it out on. How about our old favourite, the Sunday-breakfast list?

tin of baked beans
half a dozen eggs
a tomato

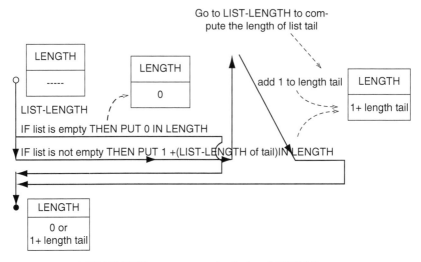

LIST-LENGTH computes a value for box "LENGTH"

Fig. 11.2 Discontinuities in the *flow structure* of a recursive re-entry

Using our recursive **LIST-LENGTH** program: the first instruction tells the computer to do something if the list is empty, but it is not. So we drop down to the second instruction which tells the computer to do something if the list is not empty. This is the case with our three-item shopping list, so what does the computer have to do? It is instructed to put a value in the box labelled "LENGTH". What value? The value obtained by adding 1 to (LIST-LENGTH of tail) – i.e. it must add 1 to the result of computing the **LIST-LENGTH** of the eggs-tomato list.

So at this point towards the end of the second instruction, when the computer wants to do a simple addition and put the result in box LENGTH, something more than a simple addition is required. Before it can do the addition it must compute the length of the tail of the original list.

Computers can do this suspension of current computation, restarting another, and later returning to finish the previously suspended one with no trouble at all. They can pile up these suspended computations and subsequently return to them all in the correct order and complete them all with unerring reliability. They can, moreover, do this even if the new computation is a re-reference to the current, suspended, computation. In our case, the new computation is to compute the LIST-LENGTH of tail – i.e. LIST-LENGTH of eggs-tomato list – while within the program **LIST-LENGTH** and suspending the addition of 1 to the result it now needs.

Such behaviour, it turns out, is mechanistically quite simple and straightforward, and hence it is quite easy to instruct a computer to do it. But such behaviour is quite alien to the average human brain. We mix up the suspended computations and cannot return to complete them accurately. This is my point about the leap in complexity that recursive programming causes. The increase in complexity is with respect to human understanding of the mechanistic details of the computation specified in the recursive program.

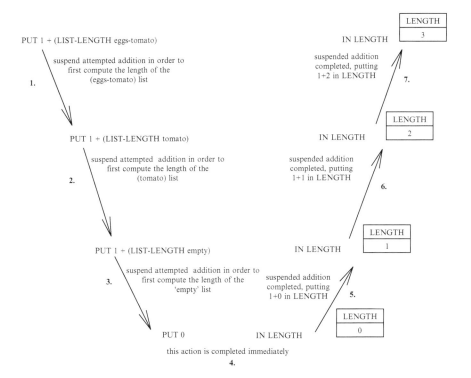

In an attempt to clarify this we can illustrate the recursive computation as shown above. In order to compute the length of the beans-eggs-tomato list, the computer will have to manage the illustrated sequence of events.

This diagram is read from top left down to bottom centre and then finally up to top right. The sequence of actions within the overall computation is given by the numbers **1.** to **7.** (in bold).

Each time the addition computation is suspended in order to first compute the length of the tail of the list, I have illustrated this as a step down in the diagram. As you can see there are three steps down. This because the original list was three-items long. The computer is quite happy to do thousands of such step-downs, if the program demands it. They are caused by the recursive structure at the end of the second instruction in our program: each time it tries to compute the length of a non-empty list it is instructed to first find the length of the tail of that list.

What saves this program from endless stepping down is that the successive list tails will always be shorter than their predecessors, and ultimately an empty list tail will be reached.

At this point our program can use the non-recursive, first instruction which computes the length of an empty list as zero – this is the first completed computation and is illustrated as the bottoming out of our step-down procedure. At this point the computer steps up to resume the suspended addition of 1 + (<u>LIST-LENGTH</u> empty list), this becomes 1 + 0 which completes this computation. It has now computed that the length of the list, a tomato, is 1. Having completed one execution of the program, it steps up to next suspended addition with just the information needed to complete it, i.e. 1 + (<u>LIST-LENGTH</u> a tomato) which it now can complete as 1 + 1. Finally, it steps back up to complete the first suspended addition, and again it has just the information needed to complete it. So, 1 + (<u>LIST-LENGTH</u> eggs-tomato) becomes 1 + 2, and the final answer of 3 is computed, which is of course correct.

How does a computer manage the complexity of suspended computations that must be completed in the proper order? 'Very easily,' is the answer. All it requires is one (in this case) of those sprung plate stackers that can be found in cafeterias: a stack of clean plates is put in, and it sinks down to present the top plate (the last one put in) to the next customer. When this plate is removed, the stack pops up a bit and presents the next plate (the second from last plate put in) ready for the next customer. If no more reloading happens, then eventually a customer removes the last plate (which was the first one put in) and the stack is empty.

This mechanism is a *pop-up stack*, or a 'last in, first out' (hence LIFO) mechanism. In the computer, of course, we do not bother with stainless steel cabinets and springs, we just implement the essential function of this device – items can be pushed onto a *stack*, and can be removed, and the order of removal is the reverse of the order in which they were put in.

This stack mechanism is exactly what's needed to make a recursive program work. In the case of our above example, a copy of the program **LIST-LENGTH** is made whenever it is needed – that is whenever the program needs to compute the <u>LIST-LENGTH</u> of a list. Whenever a computation needs to be suspended in order to compute something else first, the current copy is pushed onto a stack, and the new computation is started. Conversely, whenever a computation terminates, the value computed is fed into the suspended computation on the top of the stack which is popped off and restarted. When the stack is empty, the complete computation is finished.

Humans, we are forced to conclude, do not have stack mechanisms in their brains. Hence getting one's head around the correct sequence of suspended and restarted computations is not at all easy.

Figure 11.3 illustrates the *flow path* of the actual computation required to compute the length of a three-item list, "(b,e,t)", using the **LIST-LENGTH** program. As can be seen the circularity inherent in using the same two-instruction program four times, each new usage nested inside the previous one, is managed by making <u>four copies</u> of both the program instructions and the necessary *storage boxes*, and by keeping track of which copy of the program goes with which copy of the *storage-box* values. A computer, however, can and does do this all automatically.

Such recursive computation may strike you as unnecessarily complex, and it is for you the human programmer, but for the computer it is quite simple and straightforward (although time-consuming as well as storage consuming, I admit). Never forget, though, that the big problem with IT systems is not so much computation time and storage requirements; it is for the human to understand what he has told the computer to do (and recursive programming's contribution to this requirement is contentious given its logical-simplicity and mental-complexity characteristics).

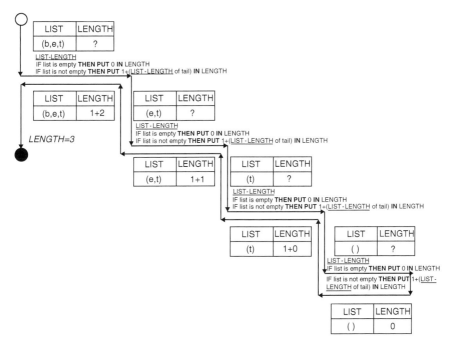

Fig. 11.3 A *flow path* generated when computing the length of list "(b,e,t)"

In addition, this particular recursive program is an unnecessarily complex and inefficient way to compute the length of our shopping lists, but consider one last enhancement of this problem in order to fully appreciate the power of recursive programs.

It might be a good idea if the shopping list was organized into categories. Then our robot might acquire all of the listed veggies before it sets off for, say, dairy products – recursing without the cursing perhaps. Let's devise such a list, and group different commodities together in, say, parentheses with hyphens connecting the words of individual items. A typical shopping list might then be:

(tin-of-beans tin-of-tomatoes)
(eggs cream milk)
(coffee)
(tomato lettuce apples)

This is, of course, not the only way to divide up such a shopping. Another houseperson might structure the same items rather differently:

(tin-of-beans tin-of-tomatoes)
(eggs)
(cream milk coffee)
(tomato lettuce)
(apples)

These two shopping lists are both lists of sublists, one sublist of individual items for each category chosen. Now, what is the length of these shopping lists? The answer depends upon what exactly is meant by this question. There are at least two reasonable interpretations. The first version of our categorized shopping list contains four sublists and is therefore of length four, but it contains nine individual items and so could be of length nine. If we choose this last interpretation of the question, then what is a recursive characterization of the problem? As usual, we start simple.

If the list is empty then its length is zero.

But what if the list is not empty? The first element of such a list is no longer a single item, but a sublist of items.

If the list is not empty then its length is the length of the first sublist plus the length of the tail of the list.

Clearly (I hope), the total length (i.e. number individual items) in such a list is the number in the first sublist plus the number in all the rest of the sublists. It couldn't be otherwise, could it? Again the recursive reformulation, which can be programmed directly, has a surprising simplicity and obvious truth, once it has been stated.

I shall resist the temptation to press on with this example, but notice that the recursion itself is no longer as simple as it was – i.e. the length of a non-empty list is defined in terms of two recursive references (rather than the usual, one) to lengths of lists.

What is most surprising is, I think, that such a restatement of the problem is not merely a restatement, but it is also very close to a computational procedure for computing the solution – i.e. the restatement is almost a program. This then is my contention concerning the simplicity of recursive techniques for programming. The complexity aspect is grounded in the fact that the necessary computational mechanism appears to be difficult for the human brain to reproduce – i.e., there are no plate-stacking mechanisms in our brains. There is some interesting support for this contention in the sorts of English sentences that we do and do not readily understand.

Some years ago George Miller[2], an American psychologist, probably most famous for his "magic number 7 ± 2", provided a graphic illustration of the severe limitations on the recursive computational power of the human brain. His examples did not involve mathematics (the usual playground of recursivists), but sentences in English.

Let's begin with a refresher course in English grammar (a more off-putting start to a paragraph is hard to imagine!). How many adjectives can precede a noun in English? It's a trick question. The answer is zero, one, two, ... many, in fact, as many as you like. Classical English grammar does not put a limit on the number of adjectives that may correctly precede a noun. We can say "the green, cold, fresh, wet, wavy, spine-tingling, awesome, punctilious, tendentious, spiteful, glowing, bemedalled, tired, selfish, tasselled, Uralian, vicinal, wall-eyed, dictionary-plundering author." If tempted to do so, take a big breath first, and don't be too disappointed if your listener is gone by the time you finish. But however antisocial such use of English may be, it is quite grammatically correct. Here are the grammar rules that cover it:

Noun-phrase **is** Article **followed by** Adjective-list **followed by** Noun
Article **is** THE **or** A
Adjective-list **is** *nothing* **or** Adjective **followed by** Adjective-list
Adjective **is** GREEN **or** COLD **or** FRESH **...**
Noun **is** AUTHOR

The main point about this sparse grammar is that the rule defining grammatical adjective lists is recursive – the term "Adjective-list" is used to define "Adjective-list". But we now know that such circularity is not necessarily a recipe for either endlessly chasing one's own tail, or for an impossible feat of self-contortion. Recursive definitions, when well constructed (as this one is), can be succinct yet powerful.

If I transcribe the third grammar rule into English, it will read as follows:

An adjective list is either nothing, or it is an adjective followed by an adjective list.

In other words we can have zero adjectives or as many as we like in an adjective list. While it is true that we can pack as many adjectives as we like in front of our nouns and still claim to be speaking or writing English, we never use more than 27 (or thereabouts), and usually only two or three at most. Whatever the reason for our conservative attitude towards adjective lists, it is not because our brains cannot cope with the recursion that may be involved in generating and comprehending long lists of adjectives. It seems more likely that our tendency to use only short adjective lists is related to the limitations on short-term memory (roughly a limitation on the number of things we can keep in mind simultaneously – Miller's magic number).

The reader may recall Alice's problem with the addition of a long succession of ones that the White Queen demanded. This is a somewhat similar problem: a long sequence of similar objects with no framework of interrelationships that would assist memorization.

It seems unlikely that our lack of linguistic verbosity with respect to adjective lists has anything to do with the fact that linguists find it most convenient to define this grammatical structure in terms of a recursive rule. But elsewhere within the linguistic repertoire of a native English speaker it appears that recursive processing is required, but is only supported in a minimal way. Consider the following sentence.

The road the dog crossed was busy.

Not much problem with that, I trust. Let's beef it up a bit:

The road the dog the cat chased crossed was busy.

Awful! But it's English with just the same underlying grammatical structure as its predecessor. The difference is that the first sentence has just one embedded phrase, "the dog crossed" while the second had two, and, most importantly, one of these two is embedded inside the other. So the overall sentence exhibits a three-level embedding. What does understanding (or generating) such a sentence involve? It involves suspending processing of the noun phrase while processing the embedded structure and then subsequent return to the noun phrase when its associated verb is encountered after processing the embedded structure. This is just like the recursive processing that the computer finds so easy.

A word of warning: just because it seems like the processing of these sentences is like recursive computation – i.e. suspend, process subtask, and resume – we've really no idea whether it is or not. But it is difficult to devise a more plausible alternative, and, if we assume this mechanism, it explains why we find such sentences difficult to understand, even though we readily understand simpler sentences with the same underlying structure.

Here's some grammar rules for this structure in English sentences.

Sentence **is** Noun-phrase **followed by** Verb **or** Noun-phrase **followed by** Sentence **followed by** Verb **or** *nothing*
Verb **is** WAS BUSY **or** CROSSED **or** CHASED ...

The rule for a noun phrase we've had before so I'll not repeat it. As you can see the first rule is recursive, and the recursive reference (the occurrence of "Sentence" in the right side of the first rule) is embedded between two other grammatical structures.

This sort of recursion is different from that which occurred in our rule for defining adjective lists. In that rule the recursion simply followed another grammatical structure. It is the occurrence of this embedded recursion that seems to force us into the classical recursion processing mechanism, i.e., suspend, stack, start something new – finish it, unstack, restart. When trying to comprehend a sentence of this structure we must suspend processing of the initial noun phrase in order to process the embedded sentence, which may itself contain any number of further embedded sentences. Finally, we must return to complete the suspended processing by associating the correct verb with its previously encountered noun phrase.

Even though these subsequent 'completions' (i.e. noun phrase and verb) are all in order – actually reverse order, the last-suspended noun phrase goes with the first-encountered verb – the human brain cannot manage more than about two of them. Whereas an appropriately programmed computer (or suitably automated cafeteria) would not have the slightest trouble parsing and rephrasing such sentences, however many embedded sentences they contained.

So what? Some may take comfort from this non-trivial excursion into the world of recursion from the conclusion that brains and computers seem to work in fundamentally different ways with respect to recursive processing at least. Hence brains are not computers. Some people do take comfort from this sort of observation, but it is not the main purpose of this chapter.

The conclusion that I wish to point to is that of Miller: that the human brain does not seem to be a recursion-processing mechanism. From this conclusion I offer one further observation: we must then expect that the human brain will have great difficulty when its task is to follow closely a long sequence of recursive processing. This makes it difficult for humans to maintain a detailed understanding of recursive programs. Ordinary, non-recursive programs present enormous challenges to the human intellect. Recursive ones can present even greater difficulties at the level of detailed mechanism. Yet curiously, at a higher (logical?) level, recursive programs can represent beautifully simple reformulations of what would otherwise be very complex problems.

Endnotes

1. On viewing this very small recursive program:
   LIST-LENGTH
   IF list is empty **THEN PUT** 0 **IN** LENGTH
   IF list is not empty **THEN PUT** 1+(LIST-LENGTH of tail) **IN** LENGTH

   the thoroughly logical thinker would point out that even in it, there is unnecessary clutter. For all lists are either empty or not empty, there are no other possibilities as the earlier *flow-structure* illustrated (Fig. 11.1). This illustration was, however, designed to avoid this issue; it was in fact not accurate.

   The presence of an **IF-THEN** instruction is indicative of a *branch point* in a *flow structure*: the computer will take one *flow path* of the branch if the *branch condition* specified (such as 'list empty') is true, and it will take the other branch if it's not true. Notice, however, that the second **IF-THEN** instruction was not illustrated as a *branch point* in the *flow structure*. This was because the, although there is a potential *flow path* straight down from the second **IF-THEN** instruction to the end of the program, it can never be used. The logic that lists can only be empty or non-empty tells us this.

   This is because it would only be used if it is <u>not</u> <u>true</u> that the list is not empty – i.e., only when the list is empty. But this is precisely the *branch condition* that will cause the computer to obey the first **IF-THEN** instruction, so when the list is empty the second instruction will never be reached. Thus, one potential branch of the second *branch point* can never be followed in any computation. Figure 11.4 illustrates this unusable part of the flow structure and calls it "the impossible gap". So, although an **IF-THEN** instruction incorporates a *branch point* and so always offers two *flow paths*; logical analysis of these particular *branch conditions* that tells us that, in this particular case, one of these *flow paths* is not 'real' – it cannot ever be used; it is 'dead'. (A large-scale example of the closely associated *dead-code* problem is discussed in Chapter 13.)

   So, whenever the computer is executing our small program it will always follow either the first **IF-THEN** instruction, or the second – always one, and never both. These two instructions are thus more accurately written as one **IF-THEN-ELSE** instruction, as follows:

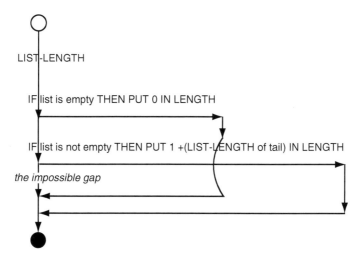

Fig. 11.4 The real flow structure

LIST-LENGTH
IF list is empty **THEN PUT** 0 **IN** LENGTH
ELSE PUT 1+(LIST-LENGTH of tail) **IN** LENGTH

Now the computer will only follow the **ELSE** part of the instruction if it doesn't follow the **THEN** part which it will do if the particular list it is computing with happens to be empty. So it will only compute with the **ELSE** part when it has a non-empty list. This is just what we want, and just the same as the earlier version of this program. We have two logically equivalent alternative programs. Figure 11.5 illustrates the flow structure of the logically better version.

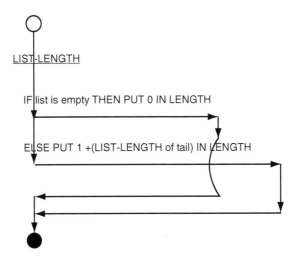

Fig. 11.5 The neater version

From a logical point of view the second version is preferable. It's more concise, and it doesn't make the computer go through the unnecessary check for a non-empty list once the empty-list test has failed (if a list is not empty then it must be non-empty, so why bother checking?). But is it simpler for the programmer? Does it make *program understanding* easier? When faced with this version the programmer (who may be required to alter or extend this program) must now make the logical deduction about the **ELSE** part only being used when the list being processed is non-empty – this is no longer explicitly written in the program. It is an arguable choice, and once again not one that is purely logic based.

This is a simple example, but, like most other arguments is this book, it becomes many times more forceful when scaled up into a realistic context of a 10,000 instruction program. The necessary logical deductions become many and much more complex, and then there is a very real decision about how far to push your program towards its logical bare-bones, and how much logically redundant structure to leave in for the sake of easing of human comprehension.

2. The psychologist George Miller investigated the size of short-term memory (roughly: how many items can we keep in mind at the same time). He concluded that the number was seven plus-or-minus two, i.e. typically five to nine. In some lesser-known experiments he probed the human ability to comprehend English sentences with embedded phrases, sentences such as:

> The movie that the script that the novel that the producer whom
> she thanked discovered became made was applauded by the critics.

It's grammatical but contains too many embedded clauses for the human brain to process properly, yet it is quite systematic. You can appreciate this if the sentence is laid out two-dimensionally in its proper groupings.

```
The movie                                      was applauded by the critics.
        that the script                                    made
            that the novel                               became
                that the producer                discovered
                    whom she thanked
```

Or, more simply, with better phrasing, it becomes:

She thanked the producer who discovered the novel that became the
script that made the movie that was applauded by the critics.

It is a rephrasing that changes the emphasis of the sentence from the applauding of the movie to her thanking the producer. Does it change its meaning? Does the indigestible nested version have a coherent meaning? Not to me, but for a computer – no problem. (Well, no more of a problem than 'meaning' in general for a computer.) Would the ability to process such nested sentences constitute an advance from natural-language processing to super-natural language processing?

Miller's experiments led him to conclude that everyone could handle one embedded clause, some could handle two, but everyone had trouble with three or more. The source of this information is: G.A. Miller, "Thinking Machines: Myths and Actualities", *The Public Interest*, vol. 2, pp. 92–97, 99–108, 1966.

Part II
The Way of the Seducer

The aim of the first section of this book was to instruct the novice in the rudiments of the craft of programming. The goal was <u>not</u> to transform every reader into a programmer, but to make clear the basics of the task:

- The nature of its detailed complexity.
- The unsolved problems concerning good, bad, correct and erroneous programs.
- The major ways that these problems are being addressed.
- And the controversy about how they should be addressed.

You now know why there is no easy answer to the question: "Is this program correct?" You now have sound reasons to be thoroughly suspicious of anyone who is prepared to answer "yes", or even thinks that this question has a clear-cut meaning.

We have surveyed the technical issues that challenge and attract active young minds to the programming game. The basis for this allure is puzzle solving just as it is for crosswords and Sudoku, but puzzle solving that is fundamentally creative and virtually limitless. For some, the programming game holds a fascination that resembles an unhealthy fixation far beyond a compulsive need to do the crossword regularly. These extreme cases exemplify, and so help explain, the general allure that is a negative force in operation (to some degree) within all IT-system development and maintenance projects.

In this section I wish to explore the consequences of this technology in IT systems – i.e., large programs out and about in our world. We will explore the repercussions of the interaction between the brittle basis of programming technology and its compulsive character. In particular, we'll be concerned with the consequences of the seductive nature of the technology that lures even the most scrupulous programmer into situations of unmanageable conceptual complexity. Couple this with our inability to guarantee the behaviour that will emerge from all but the most utterly trivial programs that we write, and it is not at all difficult to see why the makings of chaos are at every programmer's fingertips.

First, let's take a complete break from the minutiae of programming, and consider the nature of the relationship between man and machine that gives rise to the Happy Hacker Syndrome (HHS). It may be possible to shed some light on this gender-specific compulsion if we briefly explore the nature of human-human intimate relationships in the context of computer technology. After that, we return to the more technical problems to which this intimacy contributes.

Chapter 12
Intimate Relationships
of the Computational Kind*

Is it better to have a wife or a mistress?

accountant: *a wife, because being married brings with it defi-nite tax advantages.*

lawyer: *a mistress, because if it comes to separation the cost of a divorce is avoided.*

computer programmer: *both, because then you can tell your wife you're with your mistress, and you can tell your mistress you're with your wife, and so spend all of your time on the computer!*

Such a politically incorrect joke may rightfully be scorned in this age of equal-opportunity enlightenment, but underneath its superficial sexist theme, there is another that is precisely the right, sad commentary.

A central thesis of this book is that some people (typically young males) become immoderately enamoured of computer systems, and as a result are lured into program-ming for all the wrong reasons. When in the grip of this close relationship with computers they use their machine with great facility but little responsibility. The programs that they produce tend to be both amazing and poorly designed.

Luckily, perhaps, the computer besotted show little propensity to apply themselves to the production of large IT systems, preferring to 'interact' with their new best friend – they experiment with changes to existing programs that control the machine's behaviour, they explore the possibilities for breaking into supposedly protected systems, etc. The happy hacker is a pathological case. He is the extreme development of a poorly-understood, yet dangerous feature of modern computer technology.

As is the nature of extremes the happy hacker is not thoroughly representative of the general problem, but in him we can see most clearly certain traits that are present in the majority of computer users although less obviously so simply because they are less

---

* The first draft of this chapter was written for me by a good friend and erstwhile colleague, Ken Paap, a professor of cognitive science affiliated with the Department of Psychology at San Francisco State University. His draft remains the substantial core of the current version, although I should explicitly exonerate him with respect to the supposed joke. He bears none of the respon-sibility for it. It is part of the padding I added.

D. Partridge, *The Seductive Computer: Why IT Systems Always Fail*,
DOI 10.1007/978-1-84996-498-2_12, © Springer-Verlag London Limited 2011

developed. However, the root cause of the unhelpful allure is to be found within these strange, close encounters of the computational kind. It might be useful to try to develop our own understanding of this intimate relationship in order to better appreciate the dangers of its less extreme but almost ubiquitous analogue. No one (to my knowledge) has yet probed at all deeply into the nature of person-machine seduction, so we only have the thoroughly human analogue to go on. Consequently, that is where we must start.

Why do people fall in love? What are the ingredients for a close personal relationship? Answers to these questions may help us to understand the seduction of the hacker, or even enable the rest of us who find ourselves regularly in the close proximity of computers to develop better relationships with these complex artefacts. And for those who have forsworn all contact with computer technology, it might provide them with a rationale for their abstemious choice.

Psychologists who study these matters (the person-person ones) believe they have uncovered three essential ingredients for a close relationship: interdependence, emotion, and intimacy. As in any good stew, the ingredients must complement each other; we shall eventually examine their interrelationships, but let's start with each individually – interdependence is the first on the list.

When two lives become intertwined, a close personal relationship is likely to develop. If Michael's actions frequently affect Jane's, and Jane's actions and reactions influence Michael's situation, then they are not likely to remain socially indifferent. But will the scales tip towards love or towards hate? Equity theory says that it all depends on the balance between give and take. If Jane perceives that she incurs most of the costs (i.e., does most of the giving) and that Michael enjoys most of the benefits (i.e., does most of the taking), the relationship is not equitable.

There is a fair amount of evidence which suggests that inequitable relationships are doomed to failure. Partners who perceive that their relationship is equitable are more confident of staying together, more content, and less likely to have affairs with others. They evaluate the fruits of their relationship more positively and, consequently, have more positive (and less negative) feelings towards the relationship.

The importance of interdependence in building a close relationship suggests that it is more than coincidence that the happy hacker quickly throws himself into frequent and diverse interactions with his computer. Nothing interesting is going to happen when contact is infrequent or if frequent contact is limited by the habitual repetition of the same old activity. The attraction of any given computer game will eventually evaporate and the longevity of the fascination probably correlates well with the scope for continued novelty within the limitations of each game. Now that you have an understanding of the programming game, you can readily appreciate how the happy hacker might find it a richer and more varied activity than hanging out with his here-to-fore best friend (although the root of the problem may be that he never had this social option in the first place[1]).

Of course, the quality of the first interactions is as important as quantity. Studies have shown that the perceived equity in a budding romance is as good a predictor of long-term satisfaction and the desire to continue the relationship as judgements solicited several months into the affair. The happy hacker must have experienced at least some early rewards, whilst the hater's first encounter probably seemed unjust and inequitable.

Equity theory holds that each partner should accumulate about the same amount of benefit and incur about the same amount of cost. Reality doesn't always seem to follow equity theory. There are, for example, some significant gender differences. Men become distressed with their relationship when they perceive themselves under-benefited, whereas women suffer more distress when they perceive themselves over-benefited. Perhaps computers are too self-sufficient to need mothering. It may take the masculine perspective to feel close to a partner that does most of the giving.

Another chink in the armour of equity theory is research that shows that the success of long-term relationships is best predicted by the sum of benefit and cost, not the difference! This can be explained if one assumes that partners feel responsible for each others needs. That is, the more each person feels responsible for the other, the more benefits each receives as the other meets his or her needs and the more costs each incurs in meeting the other's needs. Equity may be important in the early stages of a relationship, but meeting each other's needs is what matters in the long run.

In Peggy Clark's terminology[2] the rules governing giving and receiving in a mature intimate relationship are 'communal' rather than 'exchange'. That is, benefits are given, non-contingently, in response to a partner's needs rather than as a tit-for-tat accounting. People in intimate relationships, overwhelmingly, follow communal norms and they and their partners feel best when they do so. For the happy-hacker-computer relationship the strengths and weaknesses of each are extremely complementary and tending to one another's distinctive needs is simply more natural than giving benefits on an exchange basis where one partner may be more predisposed to monitoring the degree of equity.

This analysis seems to apply readily to the seduction of the happy hacker. The computer is far superior to the human in its ability to calculate, follow instructions, and do so without error, but its power lays dormant awaiting interaction with the programmer. Although limited in attention and error-prone in performance, the programmer offers the promise of creative genius. Each _needs_ the other. Their interdependence is of critical proportion. Apart they are your average Joe and a not-so-heavy tin box; together they may travel where neither man nor machine has gone before.

If interdependence in the form of fulfilling mutual needs is the meat of the matter, then emotion is the spice that adds that special zest and flavour to the relationship. The two ingredients are complementary. Interdependence means that one partner's actions will often interrupt the goal-directed behaviour of the other. In the two-process theory of emotion this interruption produces arousal, but the arousal is consistent with a variety of specific emotions and must, consequently, be interpreted within the framework of the current situation. If Jane's interruption blocks Michael's goal and he perceives that the misdeed was voluntary, intentional, and preventable, then Michael reacts with anger. But if the action was benign, the resultant high arousal may simply strengthen his positive regard for Jane. The computer has the happy hacker at great advantage for the smitten human knows that the computer has no voluntary control over its rejection of the programmer's silly mistakes. Its fastidiousness is endearing, not nagging, to the happy hacker. Furthermore, when the last of the _grammatical_ errors is discovered and removed, the computer's actions enable goal attainment. The seemingly endless cycle of program submission and correction is broken, arousal rises, and the successful programmer naturally feels warm and fuzzy towards this marvellous partner.

An additional allure of the computer may actually derive from its literal warmth and its flawless competence in carrying out instructions. Warmth and competence are the two most powerful personality traits underlying judgments ranging from first impressions to group stereotypes. Warmth includes perceived friendliness, helpfulness, and trustworthiness and is metaphorically based on concrete physical experiences. The classic studies by Harry Harlow of infant macaque monkeys showed that the monkeys sought comfort and safety from a surrogate mother who was soft and warm (from a 100-W bulb) rather than a wire-mother who provided the sole source of nourishment. Consistent with the idea that physical and psychological warmth are linked from early life experiences recent research on the neurobiology of attachment reveals that the insular cortex becomes activated in response to both physical and psychological warmth. This framework motivated Williams and Bargh[3] to demonstrate that holding a hot cup of coffee rather than an iced coffee leads to "warmer" judgments (e.g., more generous, caring) of an individual who is described immediately after the warming or chilling physical experience. Thus, it is entirely possible that a torrent of positive emotions directed toward the computer is augmented simply because hardware engineers have still not completely solved the heating and cooling problem[4].

People are motivated to maintain a positive self image. One potential danger in a close relationship is that it can endanger the maintenance of the self image. When partners are engaged in a task that is relevant to the self-evaluation process, comparisons are triggered. What tasks are relevant? Certainly those that are our responsibility. If Michael and Jane are both taking a programming course, and Jane must consistently play the role of the teacher, then Michael's self image will be degraded in comparison to Jane; this unleashes negative emotions such as jealousy. The happy hacker is not subject to jealousy – not because he is a better person, but because his partner, the computer, does not compete in tasks relevant to evaluating his own self image. Michael does the programmer's job, and the computer does its job. Together, man and machine can bask in one another's reflected glory.

If the meat of seduction is interdependence, and emotion provides the spice, then what are the vitamin-rich vegetables necessary for long-term growth and commitment? The psychology of interpersonal attraction informs us that the final ingredient is intimacy; a process by which one partner expresses important self-relevant feelings and information to the other, and as a result comes to feel understood, validated, and cared for. Now even the happiest of the hackers are rarely caught confessing their sins or sharing their hopes for the future with their computer; it is even less likely that the computer will reciprocate with relevant self-disclosures of its own, but some of the aspects of intimacy do seem possible.

One such aspect is the privacy of the man-computer interaction discussed at length earlier. Our enamoured dyad is insulated from the rest of the world. Long drawn-out exchanges, many resulting in failure on the programmer's part, are confidently trusted to the machine's knowing silence – not a word will leak out; no chance of even the slightest whisper in an 'outside' ear.

One way to validate a partner's beliefs and personal worth is to be accepting of faults in a non-judgemental manner. Without rebuke the computer patiently corrects the programmer's error-prone instructions. The intimate relationship between the happy hacker and his computer is built on many of the qualities that most people quickly detect when they interact with the (in)famous ELIZA program.[5]

The response to a valid set of instructions is output that encourages the programmer to continue. The error messages caused by invalid instructions redirect his attention. The computer is so responsive to the programmer's every input, that it is difficult to resist the temptation to view the computer as a knowing partner.

The frustrated neophyte sees the computer as stupid and uncooperative. The happy hacker is engaged in a goal-directed partnership – the computer is thus seen as an invaluable accomplice at the very least, and more probably as 'someone' with whom the personal relationship goes way beyond the demands of mere business.

When a specific segment of the program first runs correctly, the hacker exclaims: "We've licked that part." When the computer displays the desired output, the programmer's idea has been validated, and many such sessions substantiate his personal worth.

In sum, a state of intimacy that at first blush seems far-fetched is part of the close relationship between the happy hacker and the computer. Through the computer's co-operative and guiding responses, the hacker has found someone who understands him, values his talent, cares for him, and needs to be cared for – intimacy of the highest order!

But why is it that Michael may sometimes opt for a computer rather than Jane as his partner in close and constant companionship, and yet Jane is not likely to want to substitute inanimate electronics for a real live Michael? The evidence, both anecdotal and more scientifically based, all indicates that computer dependency or computer addiction is overwhelmingly a male failing.

Jane and the rest of her sex are very seldom drawn into prolonged close encounters with computers. One might attempt to pass off this quite dramatic gender difference as just another example of the well-known fact that women are simply more sensible, more stable, etc. than men. But I feel that there must be more to it (However, as a male, I would, wouldn't I? – to borrow, once more, the timeless observation of Mandy Rice-Davies). Can there be something of the prehistoric hunter, a call on our evolutionary heritage, in the nature of the programming game? This seems unlikely. Or approaching from the opposite direction: is the maternal instinct so firmly grounded in live warm bodies that cold electronics always gets a similarly cool shoulder from individuals of the other sex? For there does seem to be an 'object-centredness' about the computer-dependent's relationship with his computer, and this seems to follow an inability to develop the usual relationships with other people.

A further twist to this comfortable notion that the happy hacker and his computer have an intimate relationship that parallels the typical man-woman one is given by the evidence that the computational partner is usually seen as male, not female.[6]

Boats, aircraft, cars, etc. are typically female on those occasions when we attribute a gender to them, but computers are invariably male. What does this quite surprising observation signify? That the human relationship from which insights on compulsive programming might be drawn is male homosexual, not heterosexual?; that the idea of a sexual bond is misleading, it's the male camaraderie of fun and games, or in its more earnest manifestations, exploration, mountaineering, etc.? The happy hacker and his machine are Burton and Speke, or Hilary and Tensing, not Antony and Cleopatra, nor Darby and Joan. Perhaps it's similar to the male-male bond that has sustained many of the amazing feats of human endurance that pepper the historical record. Do we now see it sustaining the computer addict through long cold nights hunched over a keyboard peering at his display screen on a quest for who knows what program, or other computational accomplishment? With freezing fingers barely able to feel the keyboard, an icy wind whistling under the attic door, only a single Mars Bar left, and the end of the adventure nowhere in sight: is this the new breed of selfless, questing man?

An ever-ready answer to the question of why hackers are male is: it's cultural. Boys play with trucks and trains, and girls play with dolls. The reason for this is that it is largely a realization of the parents' expectations – they reinforce the cultural norms of play in their children, and block or obstruct deviant play at an early stage. There's nothing innate in these behaviour differences that divide according to gender. It's simply the inevitable expression of the pressures of cultural norms. On the other hand: the mother who buys a sailor doll for her little boy is just storing up trouble for the future – the non-culturalists might assert. The nature-or-nurture debate has raged for centuries and ranged over most aspects of human behaviour. I mention it here not because it solves our problem, but for completeness. The computer hacker is a relatively modern phenomenon to which this ancient debate will apply. Our problem may be viewed as nothing new, just another manifestation of the man-machine syndrome – a bias imposed by cultural context.

Whatever the reason, we do see this gender difference with respect to computers, and it's causing considerable concern in the educational world. Applications to study computer science in higher education are only about 10% from females, and this figure seems to be falling rather than rising. More anecdotally, but with some empirical basis, I can say that females tend to make very good computer software developers, not hot-shot programmers (which are generally trouble in the commercial world of software development) but disciplined, responsible and highly competent programmers who can also communicate effectively in this domain of high complexity.[7] How much of this is because only the really dedicated women will fight against the current in this male-dominated area, and how much might be attributable to the fact that the girls are more naturally resistant to computer seduction? I don't know. I'd very much like to be able to argue for the importance of the latter reason. But, in truth, this is a totally open question.

What might we extract from this dip into human psychology that could shed light on why programming is compulsive, but almost exclusively for males?

- Male-female close relationships are not symmetrical.
- The tireless, non-judgemental and (apparently) endless novel responses of a computer supply the interdependence required for a stable close relationship.

- An entity capable of endless and inexhaustible giving may be more attractive to males than females.
- For a sustained relationship, the creative genius needs interaction with the ever-ready and lightning-fast machine – but why primarily males?
- Males (more than females) tend to perceive, and resent, under-benefit in a relationship; this never happens when the partner is a computer.
- The intimacy, based on total guaranteed privacy, can be expected to encourage a close relationship – all faults are accepted without rebuke.
- The non-competitive computer never challenges self-image – another primarily male weakness when developing a close relationship.
- The happy hacker has found a partner that:

  (a) Understands him
  (b) Values his talent
  (c) Cares for him
  (d) Needs to be cared for (perhaps led rather than mothered)

  What more could a man want? Or a woman? But perhaps she too readily sees through this perception whereas a socially isolated male does not?

- Perhaps it's a male-male bond not a male-female one; the drive is to scale new heights with his amazing partner, not to isolate themselves in a bond of mutual admiration?

This chapter only begins to try to answer the question of 'Why males?', no more than a few hints and suggestions are offered. It may, however, be a useful start for others to work from.

One final point before we return to more technical matters: a radical solution to the societal problems engendered by the susceptibility of males to computer seduction is to employ only females as IT-system developers!

Endnotes

1. In *Computer Addiction?* (Taylor & Francis: London, 1989), the book based on her PhD research, Magaret Shotton presents a wealth of empirical data to support the idea that the apparent sex difference is quite real, although perhaps not a simple fact (e.g. far less females are interested in computers, but within this very small group computer-dependency was no less likely than with males). She concludes that computer dependency tends to be a result of an introverted personality, and not its cause – i.e. it's people who can't cope with the complexity and unpredictability of other people that may turn to the computer (and not that an attachment to computers leads to a rejection of people). She further contends that for these computer-dependent people the computer can offer a source of inspiration, excitement and intellectual stimulation, and can create an environment which is positively therapeutic. But notice that the proposed benefit is only for the hacker himself (and perhaps for his immediate circle of acquaintances who might find some relief from the need to try to interact with this awkward person, although spouses, for example, can experience a traumatic loss of personal contact). This claim in no way goes against my case for the detrimental effects of this phenomenon on

the technology, and ultimately on society which relies on it. Our happy hacker may well feel great when faced with a recalcitrant program, but others may well suffer when the products of his epic and uplifting struggles are finally used to control some aspect of their lives.

2. In 2002, M.S. Clark, S. Graham and N. Grote, published "Bases for giving benefits in marriage: What is ideal? What is realistic? What really happens?" (pp. 150–176) in *Understanding marriage: Developments in the study of couple interaction* edited by P. Noller and J. Feeney and published by Cambridge University Press.

3. In 2008, L. E. Williams and J. A. Bargh, argued that physical warmth induces psychological warmth in an article in the journal *Science* (no. 322, pp. 606–607) entitled "Experiencing Physical Warmth Promotes Interpersonal Warmth."

4. It is somewhat ironic that attachment theorists have stressed the importance of warm physical contact with caregivers during infancy for developing healthy normal relationships in adulthood whereas the thesis offered here is that the a strong attachment between programmer and computer can be maladaptive for both the programmer and the programs he produces.

5. The ELIZA program, designed long ago by Joseph Weizenbaum in the USA to simulate the responses of a non-directive therapist, can, occasionally and for short periods, engage a human in a seemingly meaningful and intimate dialogue. Thus a number of apocryphal tales exist which tell of persons who quickly latched on to this program as an intimate friend, one that seemed to understand their problems (but see note 1, next chapter).

6. Shotton again (see note 1 above) states that:

   "It was extremely interesting to note that those who personalized and anthropomorphized their computers always referred to them as male, no doubt because they felt the qualities of the computer reflected those considered to be masculine traits" (p. 194)

   And Neil Frude in *The Intimate Machine* (Century: London, 1983) reports on a study by two American psychologists, Scheibe and Erwin, who

   "found that pronoun references [by the subjects to their personal computers] were very common. The machine was referred to as "it", "he" and "they" but, perhaps significantly, never as "she"" (p. 62).

   David Lubar in his compilation entitled *It's Not a Bug, It's a Feature* (Addison-Wesley, 1995) repeats the observation that

   "These computers are so human in their reactions that chess players sitting down to play with one, after half a dozen moves, have begun referring to it no longer as 'it' but 'he'." (p. 153)

7. Equally lacking in sound empirical justification, it is widely believed that women also produce the best software user manuals.

Chapter 13
Programming with Flair

Until now even the most profound thinkers have usually attempted to explain things in terms of a relative handful of causal forces. For even the best human mind finds it difficult to entertain, let alone manipulate, more than a few variables at a time.

(Alvin Toffler, *The Third Wave*)

Returning to the formal specifics of modern computer technology: we now need to see why such fascination coupled with the detailed intricacies of the programming task cannot be given a free rein within society. What is so insidious about the emotionally committed programmer? Surely, there are not really very many of these totally besotted programmers? Computer addiction is a relatively rare dependency. The few addicts are perhaps largely confined to their own personal computers isolated in attic bedrooms or in academic ivory towers. What harm can they really do in the world at large?

The good old iceberg seems to be a particularly apt analogy here. The happy hacker and the few like-minded specimens constitute the small but quite visible tip of the iceberg. It is, however, not this tip that does the damage. Its significance is as a flag to warn of the vast, invisible bulk hanging beneath it. It is, of course, this invisible 90% that redirects unwary ships. So it is also with computer programmers. It is easy to appreciate the problem in its extravagant manifestation in the happy hacker, this, however, is but a signal that should draw our attention to the much larger problem hidden within the programming community – the invisible bulk that does the real damage.

In truth, the pathological cases of HHS have not reached epidemic proportions, and many of the stricken adolescents shake off the worst of the problem on emergence from these troublesome, tail-end years of growth. But the HHS, unlike pregnancy, is not an all-or-nothing condition; it is endemic in its low-grade form in the majority of programmers – or software engineers, or whatever their more grandiose job title may be. At bottom, I'm claiming that the HHS is to varying degrees quite unbelievably widespread within the subculture of persons who design, develop or maintain computer programs. Because of its ubiquity, much of the work

D. Partridge, *The Seductive Computer: Why IT Systems Always Fail*,
DOI 10.1007/978-1-84996-498-2_13, © Springer-Verlag London Limited 2011

of program construction and maintenance is, in actuality, program concoction and patching instead of systematic design and development.

As long ago as 1976, Joseph Weizenbaum warned of the happy hacker, and called him "the compulsive programmer". He noted, however, that what the afflicted does with his time is interact with the machine rather than construct large software systems to serve some practical purpose.[1] Since the time of Weizenbaum's remarkably prescient writing, global Internet computer gaming has opened a whole new sphere of addiction for his "compulsive programmer."

The compulsive programmer may spend a lot of his time working on big projects, but he never finishes the job. This is partly because the chosen problems are open-ended and overambitious in the first place, and partly because he lacks the self-discipline that is necessary to bring a large software project to a satisfactory conclusion. In addition to getting the program to exhibit the desired behaviours, true completion means structuring and **COMMENT**ing the code as well as completing the technical documentation – all boring and unnecessary from the compulsive programmer's viewpoint.

So the computer addict is not the major source of the problem. He is merely the extreme case that has served to exemplify the insidious nature of computer technology. It is all his non-addicted, but not unaffected colleagues, the vast majority of the world's programmers that I am considering. Let me call them "programmers" for brevity, but bear in mind that my simple, and nowadays not very prestigious, label is meant to take in all of the more high-falutin' job titles if the title holder is actually responsible for program structure at a technical level – titles such as systems analyst and software engineer.

Now, if the actions of all these programmers really are suspect, several further questions should spring to mind. Why do otherwise responsible citizens indulge in this socially irresponsible behaviour? And why do we let them get away with it?

Commercial markets often have built-in self-regulation – i.e. good products survive and their producers flourish while the bad competing products are killed off by insufficient sales. But such market forces are manifest more in some markets than others. Why is the IT-systems market one in which such market pressures are largely inoperative? Not only might we expect poorly engineered IT systems to be stifled by the dynamics of the commercial world, but even earlier in the process we might expect software companies, in the guise of their quality control mechanisms, to filter out these dodgy programs long before they ever become bad products.

This last possibility is undermined by the fact that software production can be, and often is, a cottage industry. All you need in order to set up business is an Internet connection, a computer, a brain of the requisite type, and some space in which to park all three. Although minimal setup requirements may be a contributing factor, they are not the root of the problem, as you should know by now. Let's first deal with why this aberrant behaviour is all too common when the otherwise model citizen gets his hands on a computer keyboard.

There are number of component elements to the answer to this question, but the basic one is that the programmer just gets sucked under, slowly but surely, down into the depths of unmanageable complexity – quite unknowingly, and even directly against his will when he is quite aware of the proximity of this dangerous undertow.

The current from low complexity to the conceptually unmanageable is very strong, almost invisible and (most importantly) sweeps the programmer along commonly imbuing within him a warm and cosy feeling of progress and personal achievement. Like so many of the sinister 'forces' in fiction, every step along the path to the point of no return is accompanied by an irresistible feeling of self satisfaction and personal gain. For example, most of these steps add new instructions to the program. Hence, personal productivity, as measured by lines of code generated per day, is boosted.

Imagine two teams of equally talented programmers each given the same large IT system to design and develop. After one month, the A team has sheaves of paper plans and designs to show for their efforts, but not a single program instruction. The B team has ten thousand programmed instructions – some chunks of which execute and deliver elements of the desired IT-system behaviour. Which team has made the better progress? Probably team A.

The hidden law of IT-system development that supports this counterintuitive analysis is: the sooner you start programming, the longer it takes to finish.[2] Why? Because thorough design of the proposed system from general capabilities down to specific behaviours offers the best hope for maintaining control of the emerging IT system for as long as possible. Yet the production of programmed chunks, especially ones that cause the computer to do some of what is required, is so much more persuasive of real progress than diagrams on paper.

All but the most self-restrained programmer yields to the elation that large-scale success (i.e., the emergence of a desired new form of program behaviour) tends to generate; he thus succumbs to the temptation to focus down on the fine-grained, local detail which, he knows, ultimately holds the key to the desired morale-boosting final outcome. The text-book programmer, by way of contrast, although he also knows that changes in the fine detail of individual instructions will be necessary, homes in on the necessary changes more slowly and from a global perspective of successive refinements of the system-design documents. The counsel of perfection is for the program detail to be generated (one could almost say "to emerge") as a result of a step-by-step process of focusing down from the general design of the program. However, the enticement of the possibility of a quick fix is always hard to resist. This is true in all walks of life. But in IT-system development a 'patch up' of an emergent problem is both easily hidden (it just blends in with the surrounding masses of fine detail as program instructions do not betray their age) and cheap to re-do should it prove to be inadequate immediately. Add to this mix the further enticement that no one will know of the failed attempted fixes – except the computer, and it is a totally reliable confidant.

Our pathological example, the happy hacker, may dive deep right from the outset unconcerned by the threat of overwhelming complexity (or perhaps eager to meet and grapple with the monster), but all except the most cautious programmer will soon be working at similar depths, struggling to survive right alongside the lovestruck coder. Whether the descent to the edges of chaos is quick, direct, and arrived at in a state of blissful ignorance, or extended over a long period, resisted manfully, and finally arrived at with horror, the result is the same – an unmanageable software product has been generated.

The unmanageability is due to complexity, and the basis of the complexity that I refer to will be familiar to the reader who has struggled through the earlier chapters jammed full of programming detail. For the reader who failed to traverse these detail-packed chapters at the proper depth (sink or skim catches the two extremes of inadequate traversal here), all is not lost. However, much must now be taken purely on trust.

The complexity I allude to is founded on the dependence of overall program behaviour on the myriad, detailed dependencies between components of individual program instructions; it is soon compounded to unmanageable proportions by two further factors: large programs and poorly-structured (i.e., *spaghetti-code*) programs.

There are many principles and guidelines for *well-structured programs* – i.e. programs whose detailed workings are maximally transparent to the human eye-brain combination, the converse of complexity. Earlier our view was restricted to *modularity*. In reality, this is but one, very general, characteristic of the *well-structured* program. A considerable proportion of the efforts of computer scientists during the last decades has concentrated on the problem of characterizing what makes a program *well-structured*: what are the organizational features that minimize program complexity? How do we design programs such that these features are exploited to the full?

As I've said, we now know a lot about how to answer both of these questions, but no one would claim that the last word on this issue has been spoken. Although there is general agreement that divide and conquer is the way to minimize program complexity, there are many varieties and differences of emphasis to be found in the detailed answers to the questions of perspicuous program structure. There are also a few radically different general approaches; a popular one goes by the unenlightening name: "object-oriented design" strategy, which has, for some decades, been viewed widely as the 'path of light'.[3]

Suffice it to say that, although the notion of a *well-structured* program is not rigorously defined, the overall goal of all schemes for 'structuring' programs is to reduce the effective complexity of the software product for the humans who must understand it: the presence of 'good structure' in a program makes the program more easily conceptually manageable.

Recall (from Chapter 10) that a *well-structured* program is like Rheims cathedral, while a chaotically structured one is more like a Heath Robinson contraption – it may function satisfactorily but the internal mechanisms are neither obvious nor self consistent. Each sub-mechanism is an individual and non-obvious creation.

Good structure and hence conceptual manageability is necessary for a number of different reasons. The finished product must be checked for correct behaviour, and then the operational system must be _maintained_: errors that do subsequently come to light (malfunctions known euphemistically as "*bugs*") must be tracked down and removed or at least disabled; and the inevitable requests to change or extend system functionality (i.e., change or add new program behaviour) must be satisfied. Ease of *maintenance* is predicated upon a thorough understanding of current system behaviour.

Notice the meaning of the word "malfunction": to function imperfectly or badly. "Imperfectly" is closest to the meaning for IT systems, and "badly" is the more usual meaning for engineered artefacts. Yet "imperfectly" isn't quite right for IT systems, because, with the notion of problematic software, the implication is not that the computer malfunctions (i.e., fails to process a program instruction in the correct manner). The usual assumption is also that the program, as written, is functioning perfectly correctly as well. The malfunctioning of software (if that's what we're going to call it) refers to the discrepancy between what the program actually instructs the computer to do and what the human users (which may include the programmers themselves) believe that the program instructs the computer to do (or how well the IT system does it). Indeed, a malfunctioning IT system may exhibit all desired behaviours, but do so too slowly or too awkwardly. Even such a performance failing might be viewed as due to a *bug* in the system.

A parallel line of attack on this problem of comprehending exactly how a program is doing what it is observed to be doing has been developed through the use of other programs: *software tools*. One subfield of the software-tools movement is called program visualization where the goal is to provide a more readily comprehensible (than the bare program) representation of what the program is doing. We can, for example, display dynamic images of chosen boxes in the computation, then as the program *executes* we can see the numbers in the boxes changing by means of, say, a bar chart on a screen. With one bar for each box we will see the individual bars going up and down as the program is computing and changing the numbers in the individual boxes.

A common manifestation of this type of aid to ease system comprehension is the graphical displays now routinely found in modern cars. Engine temperature, current fuel consumption, predicted mileage of fuel remaining, etcetera, are displayed as bars of colour (where the colour itself may be indicative of, say, efficient or inefficient driving) in the context of other indicators, such as average consumption. A well-designed display of this graphical nature can be far more comprehensible than bare numbers.

This sort of view of a *software tool* can also give considerable insight into the workings of an IT system. I merely mention this possibility now in order to make you aware that this fundamental problem of program comprehension can (and must) be approached through more than just staring at the bare program, the list of instructions, however well-organized they may be. The notion of programmer support from the computer itself, by means of *software tools* such as program visualization, is taken up later in this book (Chapter 21) when we come to consider what we might do to alleviate the worst problems posed by this technology. First, though, we must continue to expose the nature of the problems themselves.

The size factor that contributes to the complexity problem is relatively simple. In a nutshell: larger programs are more complex (all other things being equal), and very large programs are always complex. The vast majority of changes to programs result in the addition of instructions, i.e., making programs larger.

Given the majority of large IT-system programming is *maintenance* of existing systems rather than clean starts from scratch (i.e. greenfield programming), an important aside here concerns so-called 'dead code'. I might point out that even when the contemplated system change results in the apparent loss of instructions (i.e., some hitherto necessary instructions are no longer used in the new version), it is not uncommon to leave these apparently redundant instructions, the *dead code*, in place. Why would the programmer leave this clutter? Just in case they are in fact still used by some unrealized (perhaps quite uncommon and peculiar and hard to spot) computation that the program will one day need to perform.

When the program is less-than-completely understood (i.e., always with non-trivial programs), err on the side of caution and don't remove any instructions unless you absolutely have to – this might be a guiding principle of the cautious (but somewhat unprofessional) programmer when making changes to a large and working program.

An apocryphal tale from the folklore world of large-scale, long-used software is illustrative of the *dead-code* phenomenon. One of the more ambitious early endeavours of computer programmers was to construct programs that could translate from one language into another, say from Russian to English. The golden age of Machine Translation or MT, as it is known, was roughly the decade from the mid-1950s to the mid-1960s. MT was thus a part of the vanguard of the new computer technology. It was also one of its early failures, at least it the sense of failing to live up to what turned out to be overambitious expectations.

Just think about it: in the mid-1950s a new sort of machine was emerging, it was both incredibly fast and accurate in comparison with humans. Why not store within it a dictionary of Russian, a dictionary of English and a set of grammar rules for each together with how they relate to each other. This surely constitutes most of what will be needed to obtain automatic translation from English to Russian?

The machine will first sort out the words in the original English sentences (via the English grammar rules and dictionary), look them up in its Russian dictionary, and finally use the Russian grammar rules (and the inter-grammar relationships) to compose the translated sentence in Russian. A reversal of this process should translate Russian to English. No one expected the output, of say English to Russian, to be free of mistranslation, nor to be a model of stylistic Russian. But most expected that such a scheme would soon produce crude but fairly useful translations, especially if a few special subprograms were added – e.g. to translate idiomatic expressions. This field is fertile ground for amusing mistranslations, some of which may have a basis in truth. One popular example is the English expression "The spirit is willing but the flesh is weak" which was automatically translated into Russian and back to English again to appear as "The vodka is good but the meat stinks."

The big surprise was finding out just how little of even crude translation could be produced by a dictionary look-up and a word substitution mechanism (even when mediated by the inter-grammar relationships). However, some useful systems were produced in those halcyon days of MT, systems that have been repeatedly reused throughout the intervening decades; SYSTRAN[4] is one such MT system whose descendants are still being used.[5] As is normal in the formative, prehistoric era of a technology the written record is non-existent or fragmentary at best. So it is with SYSTRAN, but this much is known for sure: the SYSTRAN program is essentially the core of the Russian-English system developed at Georgetown University in the USA and repeatedly augmented as the years rolled by in order to adapt it to other language pairs. As my source makes clear,[4]

Very little is available describing SYSTRAN, and much of what follows is informed speculation. What is not speculation is its commercial success and the fact that it has passed so
many tests by disinterested observers.

What is of particular interest to us is the way that SYSTRAN has been adapted to
translate different language pairs. It has all been done by layering new program
patches on the old core program of SYSTRAN together with the development
(through a manual error feedback mechanism) of extensive dictionaries of not just
words but words and semi-sentences – i.e. large chunks of sentences that the system
fails to deal with by analysis and composition at the word-by-word level.

From the evidence available, and the known impossibility of editing the central routines
[i.e. original core *subprograms*] of the system, one may speculate that those routines, and
the passes through the text associated with them, in fact do very little to achieve the final
translation. The work is nearly all done by the long dictionary idioms and the routines [i.e.
subprograms] that apply them, for they express layer upon layer of actual errors made by
the system in its initial functioning. The skill lies in minimising the degree to which these
patches interfere with one another and cancel out each others benefits ... All this has something of the feel of a natural process ... of tree growth, of expanding bands of life, about a
centre (the core routines) that may be effectively dead.

So what does the SYSTRAN program look like? Figure 13.1 is a representative
chunk of SYSTRAN. Quite unremarkably, it is a sequence of instructions not

Fig. 13.1 A representative chunk of SYSTRAN

noticeably different from our well-structured large program (Fig. 10.1 – the good) or from our *spaghetti-code* nightmare (Fig. 10.5 – the bad).With the good and the bad programs already given due consideration, we are left with SYSTRAN (Fig. 13.1) as, not the verified but quite accurately, the ugly. As a quick glance at these three figures (or even three glances at any one of them) will confirm, the beauty of a program, far from being skin deep, is, in fact, totally subcutaneous.

As we now know, programs, unlike cathedrals and cobbled together contraptions, do not reveal their quality to the casual observer. Figure 13.2 makes explicit the *flow structure* of SYSTRAN, and its full awfulness is displayed – including its dead heart. As can be seen, the consequence of long-term evolutionary development, organic growth in an artefact, makes a Heath Robinson contraption look somewhat organized by comparison (as indeed it is).

The *dead-code* problem is, in fact, much worse than this. Figure 13.2 illustrates a view that only an all-knowing intelligence could construct as a certainty. Mere mortals, a phrase which scoops up most programmers (however highly they rate themselves), will only suspect that certain parts of the program are *dead code*, at best. For clearly, within these sublists of allegedly lifeless instructions, there is *flow*

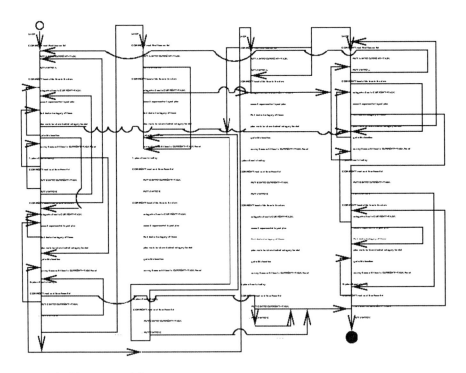

Fig. 13.2   Old tree growth in a program

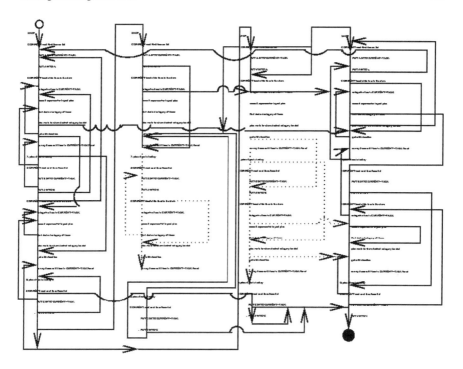

Fig. 13.3 Ghostly *flow paths* in a large program

structure; Fig. 13.3 illustrates it. (A very small, but explicitly detailed, example of *dead code* is given in note 1, Chapter 11.)

The crucial question then is: Is there any *flow path* from the beginning of the program that leads into any of these believed-dead sublists of instructions? Given the chaos of their context, i.e. super-*spaghetti code*, any answers will be highly tentative at best. It is easy for an experienced programmer to determine that a given program is a mess, but he can never be sure just precisely how much of a mess it really is.

The commercial software world is becoming increasingly populated with such dinosaurs of programs. SYSTRAN itself, is still going strong: it is stated to be the basis current state-of-the-art machine-translation in the form of Babelfish.[5] Programs that are coaxed along, propped up with new *subprograms* when necessary, and made to deliver a useful service although large chunks of the system are a total mystery to everyone concerned. There is much believed-*dead code*: unused and many suspected-unusable instruction sequences. But no one is sure what is dead and what isn't. So nothing is removed.[6]

The investment in a substantial IT system will have been high, and thus it is more economic to keep a quirky, but known and therefore fairly predictable, system limping along than to set about redeveloping the system from scratch. The prevalence and ubiquity of this ancient, but still used, software and the problems that it causes is such that it warrants a special name: *legacy software*.

In reality, the situation is little better for the programmer who does have the luxury of developing a complete IT system from the very beginning: my terminology of "lure" and "seduction" suggests that the programmer can unwittingly and even reluctantly end up generating large and ill-structured programs. How can you inadvertently concoct a large and poorly-organized program? The short and cynical answer is: just one small instruction at a time[7]– a succession of increments each reinforced by a behavioural success.

Surely lack of attention to overall design and development will soon become evident in a non-working or erroneous product? The engineer who tries to concoct, say a washing machine, is just not going to meet with any long-term success (and probably precious little short-term success either – for the piecemeal, small component by small component, agglomeration of seemingly useful bits and bobs is hardly likely to yield a working machine at all). The crucial point of difference is, however, that washing machines, and most (all?) other artefacts, are: firstly, functionally much simpler than programs, and secondly, much more expensive to tinker with. Let's deal with the economics issue first.

Programs, especially in the modern era, are composed of a wonderfully pliant substance – strings of symbols. Given also that these symbol strings that are programs are stored electronically for the most part, they are shamefully easy to alter using any one of a wide variety of readily available *software tools* known as *editors*.

Even the weak cost constraint hitherto imposed by the need to record program changes on either punched cards or paper tape has gone by the board. Electronic copies, whether on hard discs, floppy discs or data pens, can be continually reused. Program changes are recorded by simply overwriting the previous version. The scope for virtually cost-free tinkering has to be enjoyed to be believed. The immediate cost of tinkering with possibly useful variants of a given program (by adding, deleting, or substituting symbols) is little more than the tinkerer's, I mean programmer's, time.

Tinkering with the innards of a poorly concocted washing machine, by way of contrast, is likely to be more difficult, more time consuming and more expensive. The penalties for lack of systematic design in conventional engineering are sufficiently severe that the natural human propensity to try it and see is largely eliminated in conventional engineering. Clearly, the programmer is not subject to these natural constraints on production of his artefacts. We can then add to this freedom to speculate, the observation that a major success is recorded just as soon as the computer will accept a program and more desirable behaviour emerges.

Now what about the claimed functional complexity of programs in comparison to washing machines – to continue with this artefact as the random example of a conventional system? There are two aspects to the functional complexity that I allude to: functionality in the mathematical sense of input-output behaviour of the system (i.e. what it needs to be given in order to do its job, and what it delivers up when its job is done), and functionality in the more everyday sense of the internal mechanisms that support the behavioural functionality – i.e. how the machine works to achieve its correct behaviours. Let's call them external and internal functionality, respectively.

The special nature of program complexity is found within both sorts of functionality. To some extent they are both topics for a following chapter because they provide part of the account of why programs tend to run out of control despite our best efforts to prevent this happening. So this general point of functional complexity will resurface later, but let me set out the claims here for they also help account for the fact that program development always gets out of hand. All that good program design does is stave off the excessive complexity for a while, but in any significant program, it gets you in the end.

Internal functionality is the less debatable case. The mechanisms that are necessary for a washing machine to behave appropriately are both less tightly constrained and more modular than mechanisms typically found in programs. This is not, I hasten to add, because of programmer incompetence; it is in part because physical – i.e. mechanical or electronic – components and the abstract components of software are fundamentally different. For without implying that the young discipline of software design and development cannot be improved (I'm sure it can, and will be), I do think that the elaborate demands placed on software systems necessarily leads to more complex internal functionality. These demands are satisfiable because of the absence of physical constraints. When engineering with wires, electronic components, springs, switches, etc., the options are severely limited by obvious and unavoidable constraints (such as physical size of individual components). But when engineering with symbol strings these limitations are entirely absent, and the ones that replace them are nothing like as obvious.

In a washing machine there is need for a motor, for example, and the functional constraints on the motor are quite straightforward and explicit: it must be capable of delivering a certain torque to the drum, achieve certain spinning speeds for a sustained period of time, whilst accepting the usual household power source and fitting into the cabinet space reserved for it.

The door of the washing machine, to take a further functional component example, must open to allow the insertion and removal of washing, it must lock closed when the machine is in operation, and the fitting must be watertight. Now both of these parts of the internal functionality of the washing machine are non-trivial in themselves, but they are not dependent upon each other: these internal mechanisms are modular — each washing-machine component is an "island" pretty much "entire of itself" (as John Donne might have observed).

A successful design for the door, for example, will require some consideration of the drum housing to which it attaches, and so on. The point is not that the mechanisms necessary for successful washing-machine behaviour are totally unrelated to each other, but that they are relatively unrelated by comparison to the constituent mechanisms of a software system. The components of our washing machine are not functionally independent, but they are only loosely coupled together. Furthermore, most functional coupling within a washing machine is explicit: you can see by inspection that the door design must mesh with the drum housing design. Both loose coupling and explicit coupling make for conceptual simplicity of the overall system. Figures 13.4 and 13.5 illustrate these worlds of difference.

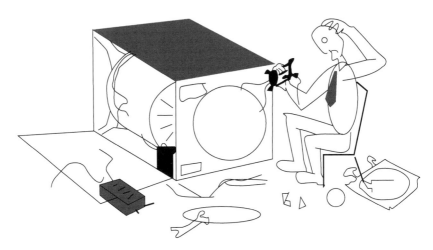

Fig. 13.4 A frazzled engineer sitting amid a heap of wires and components; he cannot help but know he's in trouble

Fig. 13.5 A cool programmer admiring <u>his</u> <u>view</u> of his latest fix within the murky context of the total IT system; he can easily believe that he's done a great job

The tight-constraints difference refers to the fact that considerable leeway in the functionality of system components is usually acceptable in the washing machine. The door will function appropriately as a door throughout a wide range of variation in almost all of its properties. Notice also that as these properties vary, say size or watertight-ness, it doesn't suddenly cease to be a usable washing machine. A dripping door is no more than a nuisance; it tends to become gradually less useful as the leakage increases – classic analogue-system behaviour.

The mechanisms within programs, by way of contrast, tend to be tightly constrained. When a component mechanism strays beyond the narrow but probably not explicit constraints, the program suddenly either grinds to a halt or computes totally spurious values (which may or may not obviously be faulty) – typical discrete-system behaviour.

To construct an example from our own program: it consisted of a *main* program which repeatedly used a *subprogram* named **READ&FIND**. A tight, but implicit, constraint on the internal functionality that we devised concerns the use of this *subprogram*. It was designed to determine and locate a shopping-list item. The particular item that it is supposed to find whenever the computer is directed to *execute* it (as a result of the **DO** READ&FIND instruction in our *main* **SHOP** program) is determined by the value in box NEXT-ITEM at the time when the *subprogram* is used. Our *main* program, quite properly, ensures that the label NEXT-ITEM is appropriately aliased with the next shopping-list item just prior to each use of this *subprogram* (it's done with the **WITH** part of the **DO** instruction).

Hence all goes well, but it will only go well when this implicit constraint is satisfied. If this *subprogram* is used when the label NEXT-ITEM is not properly aliased with a shopping-list item, then an unexpected halt in the computation or spurious computation will undoubtedly result. We'll have either a robot wondering endlessly what to do while it blocks the shopping aisle, or else a robot that gathers together a trolley full of surprises.

If the washing machine is misbehaving it soon becomes quite obvious: the washing comes out dirty, or soapy, or shredded, etc. And because of the modular simplicity of the internal mechanisms, most problems with the washing will tend to point to the culprit component(s) within the machine. If the washing comes out clean, rinsed, and spun dry, then not much can be going wrong with the machine.

With programs it is typically not so easy to decide in this way whether there's a problem, and then why there's a problem, which takes us on to external functionality, i.e., system behaviour. Washing machines don't really do much: they accept dirty clothes, washing powder, water and electricity, and they deliver dirty, soapy water and clean, dry clothes. That's simple external functionality. A program typically has a much more elaborate external functionality. Our earlier effort didn't it's true, but the bank's central computer certainly will, and so will most IT systems.

So this is my point about the complex functionality of programs: they tend to surpass the functional complexity of conventional artefacts in several ways and sometimes by several orders of magnitude – whatever reasonable measure of complexity we adopt. As I said earlier, this point is taken up again in the next chapter.

Having read the earlier chapters we now know a computer will disinterestedly follow any sequence of valid instructions for as long as it possibly can. Hence large, ill-structured programs are, in fact, disgracefully easy to concoct. But how come anybody other than the inventor will ever use such ramshackle concoctions? How come people don't immediately point out: "sure it's working, but it's not working right."

Consider the task of designing and building a garden swing: something like:

what the customer needed

The first system constructed soon fails to meet some of its acceptance tests – a *bug* is discovered: the seat doesn't swing to and fro properly. Here is this first version:

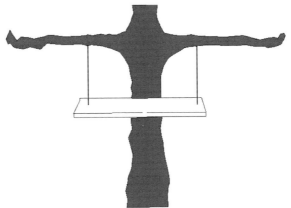

system as built fails some tests and needs modification

The *bug* (to stay with IT parlance) has been identified: the seat does not swing freely enough. The system engineer's first attempt to fix the *bug* is to remove the middle section of the seat, the bit that keeps banging into the tree trunk. This eliminates the original *bug* of lack of to-and-fro swinging, but introduces a new one: the two remaining pieces of seat no longer function correctly to support a sitting person.

The *debugging* continues: the two pieces of seat are rejoined, and the obstructing section of tree trunk is removed. This introduces another new *bug*: a lack-of-support problem which is easily fixed with two external supporting poles. Thus the final system works as required.

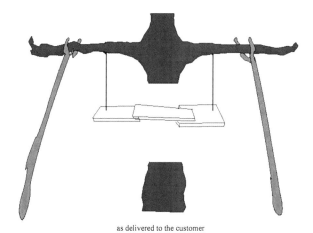

as delivered to the customer

This system design story is absurd for garden swings yet quite plausible for an IT system. Why? Because the functionality of an IT system is much more complex than that of a swing, but, putting this difference aside, a swing is also perceptually transparent with respect to its crucial functionalities, whereas software is not. IT systems are effectively black boxes to almost everyone, and even for those persons with time, motivation and know-how to probe the workings of a large program many of the details of how the program does what it is observed to do will remain a mystery – not a total mystery but certainly more in the realm of hunches rather than certified facts. Finally, you will recall how difficult (or impossible) it is to determine what a large program will and will not do in general.

Figure 13.5 is expanded into Fig. 13.6 which makes clear that even for the *spaghetti-code* system illustrated, the technical expert may be pleased with his neat 'fix' and the project manager may be pleased with the complete system. The former has done a very nice job (of eliminating an error or adding an extra behaviour), but it sits amid a mysterious mass of the rest of the IT system. The project manager on the other hand, who either does not have the technical competence or just no time to apply it, sees thousands of lines of instructions that can be shown to exhibit most of the desired IT-system behaviour.

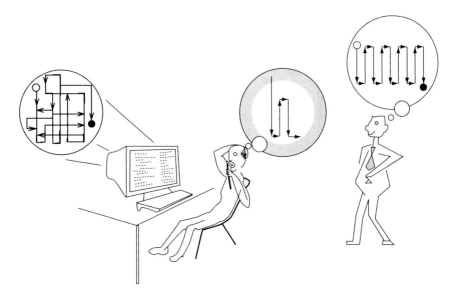

Fig. 13.6 Multiple views of the same IT system

A software purchaser will never be able to tie down with precision (and without unmanageable complexity) exactly what a large program should and should not be expected to do in all circumstances.

The IT-system vendor typically takes full advantage of this by leaving much unsaid, partly because the vendor does not (and cannot) know exactly what the program will and will not do under all conceivable patterns of usage, and partly because there is no pressure to provide a more comprehensive and explicitly detailed description of the product. In addition, any future remedial work demanded by the buyer can only ever be more programming – no chance that will involve the vendor in expensive redesign and retooling, or product recalls.[8]

Why is there no such pressure for a comprehensive guarantee of IT system functionalities? Apart from any questions of lack of competitive pressure, there is the simple fact that any attempt at an explicit, detailed functional description would (like so many other aspects of modern computer technology) quickly exceed all bounds of conceptual manageability.

Complexity, from a variety of sources, is then a major reason why traditional market forces don't suffice to ensure that reliable, high-quality software dominates the commercial marketplace. Added to the complexities of the products there is the problem of short-term evaluation: partly because of the complexity of what you, the software purchaser, are buying, thorough evaluation of the product is a long-term, in-use process.

To be really effective market forces need clear quick feedback on product quality. In the IT-system business both of these criteria are often lacking. Quite strangely I am reminded of another, and totally different, market that seems to have similar characteristics: the educational one. Within a free and competitive educational market it might be expected that the better schools, colleges and universities will attract students at the expense of their competitors that provide a lower quality education.

However, a good education, even considered with respect to quite narrow goals, is going to be a highly complex quality to assess. It is probably impossible to assess quality immediately because one of the prime indicators is surely the long-term 'success' (whatever that is judged to be) of the educated person.

Within this market there is, however, a seductively tempting solution – examination results. Perhaps, the software world is in luck: there is no similarly easy, yet potentially erroneous, measure of quality available, although formal proofs of program correctness might fill this role at some future date. Quality control for software systems is thus a known and recognized problem. We know that there are no quick and easy ways to assess the quality of an IT system.

So the marketing of concocted or cobbled-together software is not too difficult, primarily because we are dealing with an intangible artefact (the name 'software' brings out this point) of great complexity. Complexity that is founded upon a large number of interdependent finely-structured formal elements – the program instructions and the labelled boxes to which they refer.

Why are so many persons prepared to build or cobble together such disreputable software systems? Does programming just attract a bad type of person? Is there some international grand conspiracy?

No, the answer (at one level) is relatively simple: they are lured into it, they are seduced by the computer. In sum: the complex functionality of software products means that questions of program quality quickly become mired in disputes about program detail which few have a firm grip on, and even fewer are prepared to debate about. Code patching (as opposed to well-considered and designed-in changes) is an activity that gathers momentum from many directions and encounters no immediate checks or brakes: the chances of detection are low, the cost of trying is small, and the promise of an immediate 'high' (a behavioural success) is always present.

Program patches are seldom indisputably just quick and dirty fixes. One can always tell oneself, as well as anybody else who might enquire, that what you've just done to the program is in fact the best solution to the problem for any one of a variety of reasons which mesh with the overall complexity of the situation and thus cannot be clearly challenged.

If much of the foregoing seems implausible to you, then consider the long-running saga of the European Airbus, a plane that is largely controlled by computer software – even to the extent that the computer will override certain commands from the human pilot.[9]

This plane has now crashed a few times, and each time there have been charges that the computer system (by which they mean the software or IT system inside it) has made critical mistakes. Believers in the view that what is constructed by a technical boffin can be thoroughly checked out by similar experts in the technology, should be asking themselves "how come this flight-control program has not been either cleared or corrected by now?" There is clearly no practical reason why not – the money, the time, and the human expertise must all be available for the investigation. Why is it that we still don't know if the controlling IT system is at fault or not?

The cynic might answer that both the political and financial implications of finding such a fault have probably hampered, or distorted any technical investigation. They might have point, but then all significant programs that are helping to run aspects of modern society are likely to be subject to similar non-technical constraints. The main reason why we are all still wondering about the quality of this program is that a totally comprehensive check, one that will guarantee to find the errors or certify that none are present, is just not possible. It is not a question of resources, nor one of commitment. We just don't have the know-how to master the technological complexity that we can so easily construct.

There is an absurd story about leaving a troop of monkeys to bang around on typewriters and eventually they will produce the complete works of Shakespeare. If this strange claim has any validity to it, then the monkeys will also generate many useful computer programs, which are after all just strings of symbols like The Bard's best efforts.[10]

The majority of the world's programmers populate the span between these random-key-tapping monkeys and the thoroughly disciplined programmer: the person who only ever generates program instructions as dictated by the outcome of a competent and complete, step-by-well-considered-step process of systematic refinement of a general design document which itself is based on a well-defined specification of the particular problem at hand. The average programmer is simply a victim of the seductive nature of the technology, a technology that society is rushing to embrace comforted by the quite false belief that the computer technologists are the masters of all they program.

We now know why this belief is false, and what else do we know:

- The compulsive nature of programming has long been recognized.
- It is not, however, the addicts that are the problem; it is the less extreme manifestations in virtually all programmers that undermine proper IT system design and development.
- The majority of these afflicted persons are not building IT systems from scratch; they are *maintaining* existent systems – a distinction that severely aggravates all the existing difficulties.
- Effective *maintenance* is based on *program understanding* and this is facilitated by *well-structured* systems, and support from *software tools*, such as *editors*.
- One of the reasons for the prevalence of *maintenance* is that IT systems represent too big a commitment to organizational infrastructure to abandon, so they are *maintained* well beyond their proper life span.
- These long-used IT systems, termed *legacy systems*, introduce further difficulties, such as (apparently) *dead code*.
- Even with a large IT system to be constructed from scratch, the model programmer will eventually be drawn into grappling with an unmanageable system.

- The essential difference between the happy hacker and the sober and well-disciplined programmer is the speed with which an IT system becomes unmanageable, and the extent of the chaos generated (which is often manifest in an excessive need for testing and *debugging*).

The technology always runs away with the programmer, and the resultant programs can run away all by themselves. This is the topic of the next 'real' chapter.

Endnotes

1. In his widely read book, *Computer Power and Human Reason* (Freeman: San Francisco, 1976), Weizenbaum argues for the dangers of a rush to embrace computer technology and its dehumanising effects. He devotes one chapter to *Science and the compulsive programmer* in order to demonstrate that computers do "have the power to sustain megalomaniac fantasies" (p. 130). Weizenbaum's characterization of the activities of the compulsive programmer is supported by Shotton's empirical study (see note 1, previous chapter). She also confirmed that even when the addicts embarked on a programming exercise, it was usually seat-of-the-pants style, live performance at the keyboard rather than a process of careful deliberation and design followed by programming.

   This sort of software system development can never produce really large systems, so there's a built-in safeguard against the extreme hacker, but he can be used to patch and fix, or extend, (i.e. *maintain*) a large IT system which means that society is by no means safe from the worst case scenario.

2. Henry F. Ledgard's amusing collection entitled *"Programming proverbs"* (published in 1975 by Hayden Books, New Jersey, USA) gives that actual proverb as: "Think First – Program Later" (p. 10), and he stresses, "think means think – do not program".

3. In the 1980s, "object-oriented programming" was something of a new way to design IT systems. It was thought by some to be the "way of the 90s" replacing the "structured programming" paradigm that came to dominate the preceding decades. See *BYTE Magazine*, October 1990, for several readable articles promoting a very positive view of the object-oriented (O-O) approach to software systems, but see Halpern's *Binding Time* (Ablex: NJ, 1990) for a more downbeat assessment of what's really new.

   In this new millennium, the object-oriented style has survived the test of time and is used as the basis for many IT systems. In a nutshell: the idea is to structure an IT system as communication between "objects," which enforces *modularization*. An "object" is essentially a *module* of programming-language instructions.

   For example, a payroll IT system for a small business might be built around the "objects" (modules of program code configured in accordance with O-O strictures): *manager, accountant, employee*, together with more abstract "objects" such as, *bank account* and *Inland Revenue*. The payroll IT system would then be constructed in terms of the *accountant* "object" taking each *employee* "object" in turn and authorising a transfer from the *bank-account* "object" to each *employee* "object" and to the *Inland-Revenue* "object" on behalf of each *employee* "object".

   In addition, the computational details that dictate how, say, the *bank-account* "object" works – i.e., it accepts money; adds it to an account total; etc. – is naturally *encapsulated* within the *bank-account* "object". So the *scope* of *storage-box* labels necessary for this object to do its computations, for example, can be restricted to this "object", and O-O programming languages permit the programmer to guarantee such restrictions.

I have not attempted to use this design philosophy in my examples because there would by significant 'start up' costs. If I had done so the *program modules* and *encapsulation*, etc. would have been different (and arguably, perhaps better), but not so as to change any point of the argument presented – complexity will get you sooner or later, and with O-O system-development methodology just maybe a little later.

4. The SYSTRAN example is from a report by Yorick Wilks, a leading researcher in work on Machine Translation. The source is "Machine Translation and Artificial Intelligence: Issues and their Histories" Memoranda in Cognitive Science, MCCS-85-29, Computing Research Laboratory, New Mexico State University, Las Cruces, NM 88003, USA. More accessible and up-to-date material can be found in Wilks' book "Machine Translation: its scope and limits," published in New York by Springer in 2009.

5. Babel Fish is a popular and readily accessible IT system for translating between many different languages, and amazingly on their website we find:

   "The translation technology for Babel Fish is provided by *SYSTRAN*, whose technology also powers a number of other sites and portals. It translates among English, Simplified Chinese, Traditional Chinese, Dutch, French, German, Greek, Italian, Japanese, Korean, Portuguese, Russian, Swedish, and Spanish.

   The service makes no claim to produce a perfect translation, and it is considered just a minor help in modern language industry. A number of humour sites have sprung up that use the Babel Fish service to translate back and forth between one or more languages (a so-called round-trip translation)." (http://babelfish.yahoo.com/ – accessed 2-12-09).

6. This *dead* code appears to have a parallel in the complex systems that evolution has produced: it is widely accepted that large portions of an organisms DNA are "junk code" – strings of bases that do not appear to contribute anything to the overall message. But just as there is debate over whether these apparently dead message strings really do have nothing to contribute and actually are junk, so in IT systems there is debate as to whether the *dead code* really is dead; as a result it is left in place. This intriguing parallel between *legacy* IT systems and the genome are explored the following Hooptedoodle chapter.

7. This 'explanation' for how the most disciplined programmer ends up with an unmanageable program was offered by Fred Brooks in his entertaining tour of the development of one of the first really large software systems. He managed this software development project and wrote up his experiences in *The Mythical Man-Month* (Addison – Wesley, 1975; new edition 1995) – one of the very few 'good reads' in the world of IT-system books.

8. Just one example (p. 21) from a collection of similarly non-encouraging statements to be found in David Lubar's *It's Not a Bug, It's a Feature* (Addison-Wesley, 1995).

9. The Airbus first crashed at the Paris air show when piloted by the very best of pilots. Questions were immediately raised about the flight-control software. The next crash was an India Airways plane, and then a French one. A report in *The Observer*, Sunday September 30, 1990, discusses the apparent cover-up, by the French authorities and states that a Channel 4 Equinox programme "challenges claims by the four-nation Airbus consortium that the fly-by-wire technology used on the A320 – the world's first fully computerised civil aircraft – is almost infallible."

   Letters in *The Independent*, Friday 24 January 1992, about the Airbus crashes raise the question of "ultra-sophisticated aircraft controls" and one concludes by wondering "whether it is pilot error, computer error or *computer-encouraged pilot error*" (my emphasis).

   In 1996, *Computer Weekly* (4 Jan.) published a demand for "tighter software procedures" for A320 after a pilot reported an "uncommanded roll" of 30° without warning on a final approach to Washington DC's National Airport. "The computerized 'fly-by-wire' airliner touched down safely at the second attempt."

   On June 1st, 2009, Air France flight 447, an Airbus 330, crashed into the ocean off Brazil with the deaths of all 228 people aboard. According to *The Times* report (Thursday June 18, 2009, p. 42), headed "Airbus computer bug is main suspect", remarks made by the chief of the French accident investigation bureau "strengthened suspicion among analysts that a bug in the computerised flight system of the Airbus could be the key to the disaster."

10. A poem, just like a computer program, is exactly the right words, in exactly the right order. So poems and programs, we might guess, will be rarer outcomes from random tapping than prose. Yet a number of computer generated poems (using random processes) have been accepted as interesting good poems (often only when the judges did not know about the computer in the background), but no interesting good programs have been so generated. One of the reasons is that the two uses of "exactly" in the first sentence are much more tightly constrained in programming than in poetry. In addition, the first stage of judgement for a program (*grammatical correctness*) is exercised by a very inflexible, totally objective machine.

Chapter 14
Hooptedoodle 3: The Seductive Gene

Scientists crack 'entire genetic code' of cancer

(BBC News, Wednesday 16 December 2009 [1])

"Scientists in China have deciphered the DNA of the Giant Panda" ... it is hoped that this will lead to an understanding of the reluctance of male pandas to engage in sexual behaviour.

(BBC News, 13 December 2009)

Genomics is a hot scientific topic. Some years ago a first draft of the human genome (as well as those of many other organisms) was completed: most of the exact sequence of the four chemical bases that constitute human DNA was recorded.[2] This 'program' for constructing a human body (and mind too, I guess) has been written out. The next step is to 'understand' how this program instructs cells to multiply and diversify in just the rights ways to deliver a human being from a fertilized egg.

So, the grand challenge has been met; the book of life has been written in the sense of transcribed. Now we just have to learn to <u>read</u> it, and that is a far greater challenge, because 'reading' means 'understanding' not simply voicing the sequence of bases encountered in a DNA string. *Pace* the BBC News, scientists have <u>NOT</u> "deciphered" the pandas' DNA, nor have they "cracked" the genetic code of cancer; they have just (!) written both out – more or less.[2] Even the president of the Royal Society, Martin Rees, in his 2010 Reith Lecture[3] talked of "read-out" of genomes.

Surprisingly, this 'reading' task is also the central problem of computer science, and the main focus of this book which presents it as insoluble in practice for useful software systems. Hence the IT-system crisis.

Given that the computer-science analogue is orders of magnitude less complex in every dimension, and open to any further simplification that human ingenuity can devise (such as uncoupling functional interdependencies), the problems of computer scientists must give biologists (not to mention the journalists) pause for thought.

Unmanageable complexities, even in their successively simplified and precise symbolic domain, have forced computer scientists to abandon early hopes of hard

D. Partridge, *The Seductive Computer: Why IT Systems Always Fail*,
DOI 10.1007/978-1-84996-498-2_14, © Springer-Verlag London Limited 2011

proof-based program understanding. We have settled for a probabilistic explanation based on testing which is fraught with problems (and always will be in the context of a discrete or particulate functional basis – just like the genome?). But in a more positive vein, details of the program-understanding struggle of the last 50 years should provide some elements of guidance for biologists – what lines of attack may be productive and which ones will not; what sort of understanding can be expected and what cannot.

Reading the human genome (which subsections cause what operations to occur and how) is in many ways closely analogous to the task of determining exactly what a given computer program will cause a computer to do. The analogies between the DNA-cell system and IT systems are many and varied, with one important difference: all of the computational analogues appear to be far less complex.

Indeed, the history of computer science has been one of simplification in order to assist the core task of *program understanding* (largely because the early history of computer science was one of failure to recognize the enormity of the *program-understanding* task). The computer scientist has the luxury of creating his programming languages, both structures and meanings, as well as the machines that do the interpretation. But accurate readings of programs (predicting exactly what a given program will, and will not, cause the computer to do) remains an elusive goal for all but the most trivial constructions. What does this tell us about learning to read the book of life?

An accurate reading of genomes is expected to lead to undreamt-of advances in medical science, some (such as the correction of debilitating genetic disorders) every sane person will welcome, and some (such as a governmental eugenics policy that requires abortion of 'non-conforming' foetuses) may need to be rigorously outlawed. Many of the promised opportunities fall into the middle ground where their value and ethical status are both hotly debated.

In July 2009, for example, it was announced that British Scientists had created human sperm cells from non-sperm cells.[4] The media latched on to the implication that men were about to be made redundant – perhaps. The truth is that earlier experiments using similarly created mouse sperm did result in the birth of mice, but all were short-lived because the DNA in the sperm was faulty. In IT-system terms: the program contained some *bugs* that only became apparent as the original DNA program played out. So, before this laboratory-created human sperm is launched on the world, the scientists will have to be sure that all the *bugs* have been found and fixed – and we know that this is impossible even for vastly simpler IT systems.

The reader who has read most of the foregoing chapters (and is not just skipping through the Hooptedoodles) will be only too aware of the possible difficulties (in practice, impossibilities) that *program understanding* presents. This will also be true of gene sequences and the operations that they direct, if they are as complex as those we've encountered in IT systems. Well – they are not; they are much more complex in every aspect.

Let's lay out the elements of this analogy in order to see why the IT-systems nightmare presents a good case for the impossible difficulty of the gene-sequence interpretation task.

The analogies		
1.	Program-computer	DNA-cell
2.	String of instructions	String of bases
3.	Discrete token basis	Discrete base basis
4.	Non-local effects	Tertiary structure
5.	Dead (?) code	Junk (?) DNA
6.	Referential transparency	Gene autonomy[5]
7.	Legacy software	The evolutionary history of the genome

Many would challenge my mapping of analogies. However, the challenges would all be along the lines of the IT-systems analogues being gross oversimplifications of their genomic-system mappings. Such objections only reinforce my argument.

A computer program is a linear sequence of discrete symbols that get interpreted by a 'system' (a computer) to determine a sequence of operations, and the genome is viewed similarly. The big issue is what is the 'system' for genome interpretation? It is not simply the cell, as suggested above. My genomic analogue is (perhaps vastly) oversimplified, but this just means that the reality for genome-function interpretation will be even more complex than I am suggesting.[6]

Let's consider a couple of my mappings. The fourth listed analogous relationship refers to the complexity introduced into program understanding by the fact that a small change anywhere in a program can have multiple repercussions anywhere else within thousands of lines of instructions. It may be recalled that the principle of *scope* localization (Chapter 5) was introduced just to mitigate this aspect of program complexity. Within the DNA-cell system, as with any chemical system, proximity of reactants is necessary for reactions to occur; so non-local effects would seem to be a non-starter. But the DNA sequence, the genome, is not laid out linearly in the cell like the instruction sequence of a computer program. The DNA program is elaborately folded in on itself. This means that non-local subsequences (ones far apart in terms of the simple linear view) can be adjacent (and thus co-contribute to chemical reactions) in the chemical soup within a cell. Hence the complexity of non-local effects in the genomic mechanisms, and in addition, the three-dimensional folding of the DNA (and its reactants) is dynamic and changeable; it depends upon the fine details (such as temperature and concentrations) of the mix of reactants that the DNA sequence finds itself in. In some (impractical) sense this is well-defined, but the definitional basis (resting on the ill-understood dynamics of the other reactants) is far more complex than the static and well-defined basis that determines the non-local interactions within an IT system – yet, even these result in unmanageable complexity.

Dead code (introduced in the previous chapter) is another interesting point of analogy. It is best tackled via analogy 7: if the Wallace-Darwin theory of long-term local modification of organisms is broadly correct then modern DNA is a classic *legacy system* (see previous chapter) – it is the good-enough outcome of a long process of successive and localized modifications accepted to address the unignorable problems that have arisen over long-term application. In the absence of a total redesign from scratch (the counsel of perfection when faced with a sufficient accumulation of changed requirements), the emergence of unused subsets of instructions is to be expected. Whether base sequences in DNA or program-instruction sequences in an IT system, the smart strategy is to leave them in place for a variety of reasons.

Why? Because if size (of either IT system or genome) is not a pressing issue, then leave well enough alone in a complex system that is working. For the IT-system maintainer, this *dead code* may in fact have some unrecognized role – i.e., dormant rather than actually dead. And similarly within the genome, the so-called 'junk code' may have a direct but unrecognized role in some operations, and very likely an indirect role in non-local effects because removal will be liable to change the folding behaviour of the resulting DNA sequence.[7]

So *dead code* in IT systems and junk code in the genome have arisen in similar ways, and may not be dead or junk, respectively, and for much the same reasons.[8] As with IT systems we will snip out the junk subsequence of DNA at our peril.

The experience of computer scientists, contrasting the ease of constructing useful software and the impossibility of obtaining a reliable understanding of the systems constructed, is a signal that reading the genome is a task whose full enormity has not been properly acknowledged.[9] It is also, perhaps, a comfort to those with reservations about the implications for humanity that a highly-precise understanding of genomic functions might entail.

If computer science is a guide, then the extreme complexities of reading the genome with anything more precise than partial and probabilistic implication will mean that the profound choices now conjectured will never become a reality. The male Giant Panda, for example, can rest easy in the near certainty that his sexual proclivities will never be read from his DNA, and so become public knowledge.

IT systems can be, and regularly are, commissioned in the full knowledge that the system has many *bugs* – i.e., that various aspects of the system's behaviour are not understood. Genetic interventions cannot be entered into quite so cavalierly, nothing like so cavalierly one hopes. So while our ignorance of all IT-system intricacies is not a bar to the application of such systems, similar uncertainty with respect to gene function should preclude many potential applications.[10]

More immediately, and prosaically, it is a warning to use all software – both software models and software tools in bioinformatics[11] – with great care because no one knows for certain exactly why the programs do everything that they are observed to do.

Endnotes

1. **"Scientists crack 'entire genetic code' of cancer**
   By Michelle Roberts
   Health reporter, BBC News Wednesday 16th December 2009

Scientists have unlocked the entire genetic code of two of the most common cancers – skin and lung – a move they say could revolutionise cancer care. Not only will the cancer maps pave the way for blood tests to spot tumours far earlier, they will also yield new drug targets, says the Wellcome Trust team. Scientists around the globe are now working to catalogue all the genes that go wrong in many types of human cancer."

As usual "unlock the entire genetic code" should be read as "written out the entire genetic code," and that is almost certainly an overstatement (see note 2). This major news story of the day then continued to say: "The lung cancer DNA code had more than 23,000 errors largely triggered by cigarette smoke exposure."

So, in the much simpler programming terms: the scientists now just have to determine which of the 23,000 identified errors, or combination of some subset of the 23,000, causes the undesired system behaviour. There are more candidate subsets than atoms in the Universe (even if we assume the simplification that the temporal order of occurrence of the accumulated errors is not a significant factor). In addition, we note that this is the DNA of one individual, and therefore there is no general problem (such as which errors, in general, trigger lung cancer) until many more lung-cancerous genomes have been sequenced and the common errors among the 23,000 have been identified. This strategy for homing in on the likely suspects further assumes that there is a <u>general</u> lung-cancer disease whose genetic causes are being sought. Each example may be individual, or any intermediate option between totally general and totally individual. If this is not daunting enough, we might also note that significant causal factors may be external to the genome itself.

2. L. D. Stein's *Nature* article (see note 9, below) begins by explaining the 'unfinished' nature of the human genome sequence work.

3. Broadcast on Radio 4, 1 June 2010: Martin Rees' use of the term "read-out" is perhaps strictly true, but it implies an understanding that the alternative term "write-out" correctly avoids.

4. "British scientists tout human sperm creation", July 8, 2009, The Associated Press. LONDON – British scientists claimed Wednesday to have created human sperm from embryonic stem cells for the first time, an accomplishment they say may someday help infertile men father children. The technique could in 10 years allow researchers to use the basic knowledge of how sperm develop to design treatments to enable infertile men the chance to have biological children, said lead researcher Karim Nayernia, of Newcastle University, whose team earlier produced baby mice from sperm derived in a similar way.

The research, published in the *Journal Stem Cells and Development*, was conducted by scientists at Newcastle University and the North East England Stem Cell Institute.

5. N. Dillon, *Nature* 425, 2 Oct. 2003, p. 457.

6. Chris Fields (personal communication, July–November 2009) notes:

The information coded into the body of the computer can with reasonable assumptions be ignored, and is easy to discover at any rate. We know, after all, what wires are. But the information encoded by the body of an organism can NEVER be ignored, there's a lot more of it than there is information encoded by the genome, and we have very little idea how to specify any of it. We can't predict protein folding. We can't model metabolism. In any really interesting case, we can't even measure a metabolic state, at least not without perturbing it so badly we have no idea what the next state would have been. We do not know, and cannot find out, the biochemical history of any given organism, so there is no sense in which we can predict the current biochemical state of any organism's body, or even any one its cells, from some hypothetical initial state. So even if the genome was TRIVIAL, we'd still be totally in the soup.

7. The issue of 'junk' DNA is constantly under review. In 2004, M. Peplow (*Nature*, 21 October, p. 923) stated that "More than one-third of the human genome, previously thought to be non-functional [i.e., junk], may in fact help to regulate gene expression …".

8. D. Bentley writing in *Nature* in 2004 (27 May, p. 440) suggests that it was perhaps "premature to write noncoding DNA off as 'junk', and so it has proved" for among other things, "it maintains short-range and long-range spatial organization of sequences".

9. In his article "The End of the Beginning" (*Nature*, 21 October, 2004, pp. 915–916) L. D. Stein begins to acknowledge the enormity of the new task of decoding the genome; he wrote:

   In sequencing the human genome, researchers have already climbed mountains and travelled a long and winding road. But we are only at the end of the beginning: ahead lies another mountain range that we will need to map out and explore as we seek to understand how all the parts revealed by the genome sequence work together to make life.

   This recognition of the new difficulties might be summarised as (borrowing from Dawkins in order to stick with Stein's alpine metaphor) Climbing Mount Improbable. However, the inescapable implication from IT-systems experience is that Climbing Mount Impossible is a more accurate description if getting to the top means possession of a full and guaranteed understanding of the functions coded in a genomic sequence. Accomplishing the improbable is hard, but so much easier than scaling the truly impossible.

10. In the genome-cell-organism system there is the further danger (in, for example, the sperm-creation project mentioned above) that ill-understood innovations, once introduced will spread out into the organisms gene pool for all time. Dangerous IT-systems can be trashed, and that's the end of the story, but for some genome applications it will be the beginning of a never-ending problem. The IT-system analogue, 'runaway' programs (the subject of the next chapter), will seem benign by comparison.

11. S. Bottomly, Bioinformatics: smartest software is just a tool, Correspondence, *Nature* 429, 20 May 2004, p. 241.

Chapter 15
Runaway Programs: Dr Frankenstein's Predicament

> *"Remember that I have power; you believe yourself miserable, but I can make you so wretched that the light of day will be hateful to you. You are my creator, but I am your master; – obey!"*

words of advice for Dr Frankenstein. (Mary Shelley, 1817)[1]

In the previous chapters we've seen how easy, indeed, inevitable it is that large IT systems will be unmanageable. It is not because irredeemable hackers work on the systems. With the best intentions in the world, the incautious or highly-pressured programmer will also produce unmanageable software systems. In the long run even the paragon of programming probity working an appropriately appointed Nirvana will generate excessively complex artefacts, simply because there is no known alternative. Large IT systems are machines for generating endless emergent behaviours, each determined by a myriad of detailed interactions; humankind is not capable of comprehending and hence controlling such systems.

But once we've struggled to produce a usable IT system, things can only get better, right? Wrong. But surely, as each residual error is found and eliminated, and the user becomes familiar with the system's idiosyncrasies, confidence will justifiably grow that the IT system is working correctly?

Successful system use is a positive, but IT-system *maintenance*, which must involve making changes, is fraught with danger (as Chapter 13 made clear). So IT systems tend to <u>*runaway*</u> from the initial (but already limited) user understanding and control due to long-term *maintenance* activity. They may drift away quietly or suddenly leap flamboyantly through a black hole in our understanding. In either case, away they go as a result of collateral damage associated with targeted *maintenance* changes.

In 1985 Lehman and Belady gave us[2] three laws of program evolution, the first two declare, in effect, the inevitability of *runaway* behaviour; they are:

I The Law of Continuing Change

"A[n IT] system that is used undergoes continuing change until it is judged more cost effective to freeze and recreate it."

D. Partridge, *The Seductive Computer: Why IT Systems Always Fail*,
DOI 10.1007/978-1-84996-498-2_15, © Springer-Verlag London Limited 2011

II The Law of Increasing Entropy

"The entropy of a[n IT] system (its unstructuredness) increases with time, unless specific work is executed to maintain or reduce it."

As the opening quotation makes clear, fear of the human capacity to create the unmanageable is not a new worry. Dr Frankenstein's creation was fictional (and likely to remain so for the foreseeable future). The programmer is unlikely to be confronted in this way by the products of his programming efforts, however ill-conceived. That's the good news; the bad news is that the problem may be worse, in some ways – if it's possible for something worse than a malevolent creation that kills ones wife, father, brother, and best friend!

The biggest problem is the unrecognized drifter that begins to wreak havoc left, right and centre without the creator, or users, or anyone else, being aware of the destruction quietly being wrought. This is perhaps quite unlikely for such a visible object as Dr Frankenstein's monster, but the average computer program may beaver away, merrily out of control – deleting files, corrupting other programs and databases, etc. – for long periods of time before anyone notices that they have a problem, as many virus victims have found to their cost. It is, perhaps, these covert *runaways* that are the real menace, but we'll tackle the general *runaway* phenomenon first whether overt or covert.

Having seen the specific nature of the technological complexity that defies human comprehension on the IT-system scale, we are now in a position to explore the deeper principles in an effort to get to the bottom of the problems. These fundamental peculiarities are common to all conventional computer technology (both nature and usage), and lead inexorably to the undesirable aspects of the resultant systems.

We need to get past the possibility that I simply chose a rather poor programming language, and that was why I could illustrate such difficulties in our small program. The problems are much deeper than choice of programming language[3] or system-design strategy, as the illegible programs in Chapter 13 were designed to demonstrate; it is time to delve deeper.

Let me establish two general principles. These principles encapsulate as succinct generalizations much of the discussion in the previous chapters. They provide general reasons why programs can so easily elude the control of their programmers irrespective of programming language or design methodology used. These reasons are particularly important because they constitute yet more special pleading: they are founded, it is claimed, on phenomena that are unique to modern computer technology.

I do believe that there are important special characteristics of computer technology contained in these two claims, but I'm not so certain that they are truly unique to it. Nor do I believe that they are necessary characteristics of all possible computer technology (as will be revealed in later chapters).

One of the world's leading computer scientists, and one who was permanently appalled by the cavalier attitude of most programmers, claimed that computer technology confronts us with what he termed "two radical novelties." Edsger Dijkstra (a Dutchman who worked for the last decades of his life in the USA) is the scientist I refer to, and his radical novelties are: the excessive conceptual span of the technology, and the behavioural unpredictability of large-scale discrete systems.[4]

I'll give you my version of these unfortunate peculiarities of (supposedly) all computer technology. Their affects are tightly coupled.

radical novelty 1. the need for elasticised brains
radical novelty 2. small changes can produce big effects

Computer technology is a mind stretcher, and the importance of paying full attention right across the complete range of structures (from individual characters to large *subprograms*) is in no small part due to the fact that every component structure is potentially crucial.

By "mind stretcher" I am not referring here to the deep logical, philosophical and technical problems that abound in this meshing of mathematics and engineering. What I want to bring to your attention, to make explicit within your fresh appreciation of what it means to program a computer, is that the programmer's mind is stretched in an almost literal sense. The attention of a programmer must (if it is to maintain or obtain a mental grasp of the program) stretch its grip from the details of individual instructions through all intervening levels of structuring up to inter-module interactions dictated by high-level design – from the *scope* of a particular *storage-box* label to how exactly the 'projectile identification' module shares information with 'the laser-gun aiming' module in the *Star Wars* system, for example. In Dijkstra's words: "He [the programmer] has to be able to think in terms of conceptual hierarchies that are much deeper than a single mind ever needed to face before."[4]

This vast gulf, from micro elements of the program instructions to behaviours of the major sub-systems, must be closely managed by the programmer because these two levels (and all intervening ones) will contain hidden, but tight couplings – i.e., small changes in one level will directly generate large changes at another level.

> "There are no small errors in IT systems."[5]

The bank's IT system may be running faultlessly for years, yet change the label on one *storage box* and the whole system will come crashing down causing untold financial chaos on the way. Another way to describe this unfortunate characteristic of computer systems is that micro changes can have macro repercussions.

These changes may be alterations to the IT system itself, which was Dijkstra's concern. However, changes to the system's usage – anything from direct changes to inputs to indirect changes in the context of its use are also capable of suddenly wrecking a system that has worked (apparently) faultlessly for years. Remember (Chapter 7) how a more powerful motor on the satellite launch rocket, Ariane 5, stalled its on-board IT system and wrecked the mission. Or more down-to-Earth, a move to the latest must-have version of Windows is entertained lightly at your peril.

Such vulnerability to change in complex systems is unusual. More typically, small changes in diverse types of systems (from human bodies to battleships) have small and quite predictable effects or no macro-effect at all, as we shall see.[6] If, for example, the load on a bridge is continually increased, the bridge will gradually start to sag to an increasing extent, and finally it will bend down to the ground or collapse. If we increase the size of the main supporting spans we will, most likely, have a correspondingly stronger (and thus less saggy) bridge. This analogue relationship between the undesirable system behaviour and its cause is fairly straightforward, and so is the remedy.

If a violinist misplaces a finger, a slightly wrong note will be generated. In the context of an orchestral performance hardly anyone will notice, and for those that do it will be merely a minor irritation; it is not likely to bring the whole symphony to a halt. This continuity between finger placement and veracity of note produced is an analogue relationship. And furthermore, this small inaccuracy will have a similarly small effect on the quality of performance of the overall system, the Orchestra.

These analogue relationships, which typify naturally complex systems, also often exhibit the further simplicity of change in one direction only: for example, as heavier loads are placed on the bridge it sags a bit more; at no point does it start getting straighter instead of sagging more. If both changes (i.e. loading and sagging) are continually in one direction only then the relationship is called _monotonic_.[7]

In IT systems this sort of smooth relationship between system features is not common. Dijkstra attributes the discontinuity of behaviour in IT systems to the fact that programs are _discrete_[8] systems rather than _analogue_ ones. In discrete systems the smallest possible change, say one letter in a _storage-box_ label, can have the most drastic consequences; make this small change and the program may then compute a totally different function, or cease computing altogether. In an analogue system a small change of a system component will generally result in a similarly small change in the function computed.

Discrete systems are not rare outside the world of computers, but complex, totally-discrete systems are. In order to make this important point quite clear, let's look at an everyday example. The typewriter of yesteryear is a system with both discrete and analogue aspects. The key stroking mechanism is discrete. Either you hit the right key and get the right character (note: not always a digit) on your paper, or you don't. Should an ill-aimed fingertip fall somewhere between the key for "T" and the key for "Y", you do not get an intermediate letter printed – you get a "T" or a "Y" or neither, such is the nature of discrete systems.

The printing ribbon is a part of the system whose main functionality is analogue. When the ribbon is new, the printed characters are dark. As the ribbon becomes more used the printing steadily fades in intensity of colour – a classic _monotonic_ analogue relationship. A ribbon anywhere in between brand new and nearly exhausted will most assuredly deliver an intermediate print colour. If it is quite new, then the print will likely look as good as new, but if it has seen considerable use then faded print will be discernable. Ribbon usage is predictable from print intensity, and vice versa.

This is the general nature of analogue systems, and most of the complex systems that populate this world are substantially analogue. It should be a source of comfort to us that most of our dealings are with analogue systems, for the analogue property makes prediction of system behaviour easier and more reliable.

If there is any truth in my claim "that the unpredictability of the world makes intelligence necessary and the predictability makes it possible",[9] then the fact that analogue systems dominate the world of intelligent beings is not simply a happy coincidence. Analogue systems are fundamentally predictable, whereas discrete ones are not. This is one of the points that undermine the validity of testing IT systems to determine correctness.

Now we are at the level of esoteric speculation, notice that dice are discrete systems (and usually viewed as digital): the outcome is just one of the six sides, nothing in-between is possible. Even God could not throw 5.134, the die system gives Him either a 5 or a 6. Such musings give a whole new interpretation to Einstein's famous throwaway comment professing disbelief in the possibility that God plays with dice. For in order to give us a sporting chance of getting to grips with His world, God must have transformed the discrete-system outcomes into largely analogue mechanisms, for it is overwhelmingly these more-predictable systems that humanity has had to grapple with.[10] However, the new but quickly growing exception is IT systems.

Once again it is the fundamental nature of conventional IT technology that gives us these systems of discrete complexity; their discrete nature appears a several forms:

1. Continuous phenomena, such as the *real numbers*, must be represented with a sequence of discrete values (a problem discussed in Chapter 7, 'Going to Ground with Symbols').
2. Formal logic is the basis for decision making in IT systems (fundamentally the *branch conditions* such as the one controlling the REPEAT-UNTIL loop in our SHOP program in Chapter 3). Logic specifies that the only alternative to a *branch condition* being 'true' is that it is 'false.' Notions such as 'almost-true', or 'nearly-true' are difficult to represent, so 'nearly-true' and 'totally-false', for example, both collapse in the IT-system decision structure to 'false.'[11]
3. These two aspects of IT-system discreteness conspire to make IT-system simulation of smooth analogue relationships unreliable.

According to Dijkstra, who also maintained that "digital" systems of great complexity are unique to <u>all</u> computer technology,[12] the implication of this peculiar property of computer systems is that we cannot rely on our customary practice of inducing accurate predictions from observation of specific behaviours – i.e., testing for correctness. In addition, wholesale changes in system behaviour can be triggered by a change in just one character of a *branch condition*, primarily because of point (2) above.

The disastrous effects of the decision-logic framework of IT systems can be clearly seen when the IT system is represented as a 'tree' of logic, a <u>*decision-logic tree*</u>; Fig. 15.1 is a (grossly simplified) representation of such a tree, it illustrates the possible *flow paths*, the *flow structure*, of an IT system. Any specific execution – i.e., a computation from input values to output result – of the IT system will thread a specific *flow path* through *branch points* in the tree as determined by the input values used, a path up from the root (labelled **a**) to one of the eight a top-level, final, 'leaf' nodes (labelled **h** through **m**) – the IT system outputs.

The main point to note is that there are seven *branch points* that will each send the computation towards certain outputs (and thus exclude others) if the specified *branch condition* is 'true', and towards the others if 'false', or 'nearly-true', or 'almost-true', etc. Irrevocable decisions are made at every *branch point* on the basis

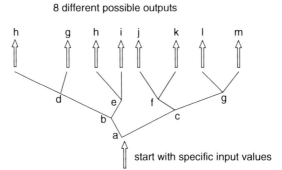

Fig. 15.1 The essential discrete nature of IT systems, a tree of decision logic

of these easy-to-get-wrong *branch conditions*. Thus once the decision at, say, *branch point* **a**, has been made to branch towards **b**, then possible outputs **j** through **m** have been excluded.

It is, of course, possible (and usual) to introduce cross links, from say **e** to **f** (as, say, **e'** just after **e** if we are to maintain only two-way splits), and so reintroduce the possibility of outputs **j** or **k** from **e**. But then the *flow path* to, for example, output **j** (assuming left branch is the 'true' decision) would be either 'true **a**, not-true **b**, and not-true **e**, not-true **e'**, true **f**, or it might have been 'not-true **a**, true **c** and true **f**. The only similarity between these two *flow paths* to the same output is the final true-**f** condition, and if any one of these brittle (and thus easy-to-get-wrong) decisions is not correct then an entirely different output will be produced.

Scale these considerations up to thousands (if not millions) of *branch conditions* (with just as many cross links) and the difficulty of understanding IT-system behaviour is obvious: every general property of the IT system's behaviour amounts to a diverse collection of these very long *flow paths*. If just one character in a *branch condition* is changed, say, $X = 3$ to $X < 3$, then any number of *flow paths* (components of entirely different system behaviours) will have been diverted to totally different outputs. However, if it happens that the value of *storage box* **X** is always 4 or greater in the system tests, then no change in behaviour will be observed. The IT system has not exactly *runaway* but it's poised in the starting blocks to take off and surprise its users just as soon as the value of **X** should ever become 3 or less. This is why "there are no small errors in IT systems."

We might speculate further: if the nature of computer-system complexity really is new and peculiar, a system characteristic that has no parallel in the natural world, then our evolutionary history is unlikely to have equipped us to reason effectively with such systems. Our genetic programs may be totally lacking in mechanisms that can deal effectively with discrete complexity.

Much closer at hand, traditional science similarly has not evolved techniques for the conceptual management of high-level complexity of this type. Discrete complexity, which exists only as a dominant feature of human artefacts (notably IT systems), may elude the otherwise spectacularly effective grip of modern science.

Yet, curiously, its discrete logical basis presents us with the false promise of exactly the opposite.

In their book *Collapse of Chaos*,[13] Cohen and Stewart mount a sophisticated argument to explain the human ability to manage the complexity of natural systems effectively by using "a system of rules [that] can engender simple features", which are "simplified general concepts." Large-scale discrete systems, such as IT systems, do not appear to be amenable to accurate reasoning through such "large-scale simplicities." Given that "instances are just particular aspects of the natural world ... the bits of nature that our brains can grasp as simple wholes", we can use one of their examples to point up the problem in binary decision-logic based reasoning. The planet "Mars is an instance of the feature 'nearly spherical body'." To the scientist this simplification means that it will always be sensible to consider reasoning about Mars as a spherical body; in IT-system decision logic, however, it means 'Mars is a sphere' is false, and so it is likely that all further reasoning based on the 'spherical body' feature will be eliminated – i.e., exactly the opposite of the intended initial simplification to facilitate reasoning about complex systems. What Cohen and Stewart justifiably call the "Reductionist Nightmare" may be precisely what IT-system understanding entails confronting full on, because discrete complexity it not obviously amenable to the scientist's simplifications that they describe.

As an example of this important analogue quality of complex systems, consider the elastic metaphor which fits the span-of-levels peculiarity quite well, but not the problem of lack of continuity in system behaviour. A piece of elastic is a classic analogue system: tug at it gently and it stretches a bit, pull a good deal harder and it stretches a good deal more. Given several observations of this sort of behaviour, we can then predict fairly accurately what the length of our elastic 'system' will be when a previously untried pull is applied to it, especially if the predicted elongation is a result of a pull that lies between the ones already tried. It is not going to surprise us by shrinking when subjected to certain intermediate-force pulls, it is not going to change colour nor will it explode. This is an example of the sense in which analogue systems do exhibit ready predictability.

However, should we pull at our elastic really hard, it may well surprise us by snapping instead of stretching. Continuous systems can also exhibit discontinuities of behaviour. It is precisely this discontinuity of behavioural response, although exceptional and typically a limiting condition, that can badly undermine our ability to predict system behaviour (e.g., when a bridge will collapse instead of just bending a bit more, or when a dog will attack instead of continuing to retreat from a threatening situation). There is an important subfield of system science that addresses it; the subfield enjoys the evocative name of "Catastrophe Theory".[14]

A catastrophe, in terms of this special usage, occurs when, as one feature of a system is slowly varying (e.g., gradually increasing the strength of the pull on our elastic), there is a sudden snap change in the value of some other previously steadily varying feature (i.e., from a situation of steadily increasing length the elastic suddenly shortens drastically – a snap change if ever there was one!).

To return to our radical novelty in computer technology: catastrophic behaviour in computer systems is more the norm than the exception. Although this is meant to be a use of the limited technical meaning of "catastrophic behaviour," the implication (when coupled with all the attendant problems of the technology) is inescapably that the everyday meaning of this phrase will also hold good on many occasions. Consider, for example, what this new revelation does to our flawed, but essential, process of IT-system testing: test results on two values of an important quantity may well tell us absolutely nothing about system behaviour, even on the intermediate values.

So there are two major aspects to the complexity of computer programming due to over-stretching: a need to maintain a conceptual grasp across a vast spectrum of levels of phenomena, and a need to maintain a tight conceptual grasp on the elements at each level because they interact as well. A minor change at one level can wreak havoc at any other, or on the system as a whole. No human being possesses the requisite conceptual capacity, perhaps because large-scale discrete systems are not features of the natural world. Human minds don't stretch that far, and they stretch even less far whenever finely detailed appreciation is required. Here we can now see the origin of much of the challenge in the programming game. It is far too complex to ever hope for mastery, but there's always potential for improvement if your brain is sharp enough.

We can also see why IT systems can *runaway* unnoticed so easily. They are inevitably monitored somewhat superficially, because that is the best we can do. Proper attention to all of the vast quantity of fine detail is not humanly possible. Flying the system on a wing and a prayer is the best that can be done, until the system itself throws out an obvious malfunction that catches the operator's attention, and so initiates an investigation into the details of the system's innards. In the absence of obvious malfunctions (remembering that computer systems can spend virtually all of their time shuffling electrons around electronic wizardry) all is bound to seem well with the world.

The allure of chess is somewhat similar to that of programming. Chess is a game whose complete mastery (i.e., being always able to see the long-term possibilities in the alternative moves) is beyond the power of the human mind, although totally well-defined. However, persons steeped in the game (and possessing the requisite type of brain) are constantly exploring, uncovering and mastering new features of the game which increases their conceptual grasp of what is, in the final analysis, ungraspable in its entirety.

As a leading computer scientist has put it: the only problems that we can deal with in a satisfactory manner are "nicely-factored" ones[15] – i.e. problems in which the overall complexity can be broken down into a collection of fairly independent, less-complex subproblems – a collection of "islands". A not insignificant portion of computer science is devoted to this issue: how to best break up large and complex problems, and indeed we saw the positive benefits of *modularity* and *encapsulation* earlier. The component complexities of chess can be teased apart quite successfully, which does not make chess an easy problem but it does make it much more manageable than it would otherwise be.

It turns out that some problems can be "nicely factored" to a dramatic extent. These are typically mathematical and abstract problems; they are also typically the exemplars in the more formal computer science text books.

Sadly, many real-world problems (as opposed to formal abstractions – e.g. real aircraft control rather than abstract aerodynamics and hydraulics calculations[16]) don't seem to factor nicely at all. Or nice factorisation can only be bought at the cost of an unwelcome increase in size, because independence of system components is achieved by carrying their context with them; this leads to much repetition that would be otherwise avoided by setting the essential contribution of each component within the context of a subsystem. And this, of course, leads to a proliferation of tight couplings. A contextual framework can be a valuable aid to human comprehension of a complex system, an aid that is lost when each system component is (virtually) context free. (For a concrete example, see Self-Explaining Systems, the first chapter in Part III.)

In addition, there is the related problem of abstraction – i.e. making problems more manageable by neglecting specific details, many of which are no more than minor perturbations that the real world introduces. This is a powerful strategy provided that either the neglected phenomena are really minor, or that their effects can be accurately 'added' back in at a later stage. Chess is a problem that can be treated as an abstraction with very little degradation of the problem, but aircraft flight control is not.

So, although chess is often a neat example of a complex problem, it can be misleading. In some crucial respects it's rather too simple and straightforward. Beware of leaps into abstractions. This technique embodies great power, but it can also lead to the poverty trap – i.e. the manageable abstraction is so impoverished that it is not possible to get back to the original problem by any simple process of adding small features of reality back into the neat abstract solution.

At this point, the reader who is not a programmer has every right to be wondering how it is that large programs ever function decently. Given the inordinate span of levels that the programmer must wrestle with and the fact that the smallest error at the lowest level can propagate through the system to produce totally unforeseen behaviour, the obvious question might be: how on earth do these people manage to construct large and useful programs at all?

Part of the answer we've seen earlier: firstly, a useful program does not have to be a guaranteed correct program (in fact it never is); and secondly, disciplined programming (i.e., following the precepts of good program development) does minimize the impact of the adverse characteristics inherent in the technology. But there is yet another facet in the complete answer to this question, and it pertains to the radical novelties discussed above.

Complex systems do not necessarily compound or even propagate the characteristics of low-level behaviour up to the higher levels. Even in the case of IT systems a single mistake with say a *storage-box* label might not get multiplied up through the layers of the system to become a significant behavioural error in the overall system – there is no necessary compounding of error up through the levels of the system. Further than this, the single low-level error may not filter up through the intervening levels to become a behavioural error in the overall software system at all – higher levels may act as a filter, and effectively remove low-level error. By such means errors can lie quietly in an IT system until some modification kicks them into life (recall the earlier one-character change to the *branch condition* $X = 3$).

This blocking and filtering of micro-changes, whether they are errors or not, is not just a desirable but rare event, like say winning a national lottery. In some types of system it is more the norm than the exception.

As an example in a programmed system, consider the **SHOP** program (see note 17 for a copy to refer to) that we constructed earlier: within the SUBPROGRAM **READ&FIND**, if we change all three occurrences of the box label "CURRENT-TASK" to any other label (apart from the label "NEXT-ITEM"), no change in the program's behaviour will occur. If however we change as much as one character of the box label "NEXT-ITEM" (even if we change both occurrences in precisely the same way), the system will go haywire. The exact nature of the resultant problems is not determined because the program was not completed in full detail. They may be immediately obvious – as a rampant Dalek in Sainsbury's is likely to be. Or it may runaway unobtrusively – by, say, not retrieving one specified item on every tenth shopping expedition.

The point is that the macro result of seemingly similar micro changes can vary between no effect to total disaster in overall system behaviour. Why is it, for example, that changing both occurrences of the box label "NEXT-ITEM" to any other label will wreak havoc in the program, but a change of all three occurrences of "CURRENT-TASK" to any of the other label (apart from "NEXT-ITEM") will have no macro-effect? The answer is not obvious; it lies buried in program detail[17]. In addition, do not lose sight of the fact that our example program is an utterly simple object in the real world of IT systems.

So, on some occasions certainly, even a computer program will exhibit this micro-error-filter behaviour, but within organic systems it is much more the norm than the exception. There is, I believe, an important lesson here for the computer technologist if only he will acknowledge it.

Many good examples of the micro-error-filter property are to be found within us all. DNA replication, for example, is a continual, low-level activity within our bodies; it is also an imperfect mechanism. Mistakes occur quite frequently in the process of copying strands of DNA. Luckily most of these low-level errors do not propagate through to become overall system malfunctions. Some do, of course, but most don't. They are blocked.

There may be a general law of complex systems behaviour which embraces this phenomenon as well as many others. Here is this possible law.

the Law of Nonconservation of Indeterminacy

Low-level indeterminacy does not necessarily produce high-level indeterminacy.

Or less pretentiously, *reliable wholes may result from dodgy parts*; and with respect to IT-system construction:

Predictable systems can be built from unpredictable components.

This is one of the lesser known, non-conservation laws, I admit, but it covers the case of micro-fluctuations failing to generate macro-effects. This law can be startlingly illustrated again and again from within organic systems.

For example, we (like all life forms) are the products of cell division coupled with specialization. We start out as a single fertilized cell that quickly multiplies up by successive divisions (only about 48, apparently!) to eventually present the waiting world with you, or me, and by exactly the same process all of our friends and enemies.

In concert with this process of successive doublings there must be one of cell specialization – otherwise we would end up as just a heap of jelly, an unsightly pile of fertilized-egg cells. The essential process is specialization: at various points in the doubling process certain cells take rather different routes – some become bone cells, others muscle cells, etc. Now this is obviously a very good thing, but the point of this digression is to remind you that the high-level, or macro effects are fairly predictable – i.e., we mostly tend to end up with two legs, and two arms, just one head but two eyes etc. Moreover, the relative positions of these products of cell specialization and division are similarly predictable (but not guaranteed) – e.g., feet at one end and eyes toward the other.

There is the high-level, or macro, determinacy of the system. But quite amazingly which actual cell will opt for which particular specialization is apparently quite undetermined in the very early stages of the process. If cells of a growing embryo are moved from one place to another, then cells that would have led to say a leg if left in their original position do in fact lead to say an arm if their new location is one that would normally give rise to an arm. So, at the micro-level, the level of individual cells, the future of each individual cell is not predetermined, at least not within the individual cells themselves. This is the microindeterminacy.

Yet fertilized human egg cells tend almost invariably to end up as a very large conglomerate of cells that look just like their mother, or father, or the postman – there is sometimes a difference of opinion on the closest resemblance question, but all candidates for the best lookalike have a very large number of undisputed mutual similarities.

Further examples can be found at levels below that of single cells which are, after all, extremely complex systems in their own right. There is, for example, the Heisenberg Uncertainty Principle way down at the subatomic level. Yet the chemical properties of atoms are wholly predictable. The microindeterminacy is not propagated up to the macro level. To some this very property of overall stability of a complex, despite the lack of predictability of individual system components, is the hallmark of a system. Paul Weiss, a distinguished biologist, used this property to define the notion of a system[18]:

A System

Let us focus on any particular fractional part, A, of a complex suspected of having systematic properties, and measure all possible excursions and other fluctuations about the mean in the physical and chemical parameters of that fraction over a given period of time. Let us designate the cumulative record of those deviations as the variance, $v\{a\}$, of part A. ... [similarly we obtain] $v\{b\}$, $v\{c\}$, $v\{d\}$, ..., $v\{n\}$. Let us similarly measure as many features of the total complex, S, as we can identify and determine their variance, $V\{S\}$.

Then the complex is a system if the variance of the features of the whole collective is significantly less than the sum of the variances of its constituents; or, written in a formula:
$V\{S\} \ll \Sigma(v\{a\}, v\{b\}, v\{c\}, ..., v\{n\})$

This is a formalist's way of saying that a system's behaviour is surprisingly stable (and in that sense, predictable) given the instability of many of its components. The whole is more stable than some (perhaps all) of the parts.

In short, invariance, or stability (or homeostasis), is the basic characteristic of a system; it is what makes a conglomerate of variable constituents a system. This definition excludes complexes such as IT systems. Computer programs are notorious for being unstable (i.e. grinding to an abrupt halt or careering wildly off course) on the basis of just a single micro-level change. In fact, computer programs seem to epitomize almost the opposite of a system in the Weissian sense: they tend to be unstable despite the totally fixed and predictable nature of their component elements – the whole is unknowable yet the detailed elements are all known precisely.

We know that programs are machines (as a previous chapter demonstrated), but are they systems (as they are commonly labelled)? According to Weiss they cannot be.

To sum up, a major aspect of a system is that while the state and pattern of the whole can be unequivocally defined as known, the detailed states and pathways of the components not only are so erratic as to defy definition, but, even if a Laplacean spirit could trace them, would prove to be so unique and nonrecurrent that they would be devoid of scientific interest. This is exactly the opposite of a machine, in which the structure of the product depends crucially on strictly predefined operations of the parts. In the system, the structure of the whole determines the operation of the parts; in the machine, the operation of the parts determines the outcome. (Weiss 1970, p. 55)[18]

Does this mean that programs, and IT systems, are not really systems at all? And hence that software behaviour is predictable from the operation of its parts (say individual instructions) in a way that the behaviour of say, tree growth, is not?

Clearly, there may be several orders of magnitude in complexity difference between even a very large program and a tree, a difference that is going to make prediction of the precise growth pattern of the tree more difficult than prediction of the behaviour of the program. But is there a difference in principle? Weiss seems to be affirming that there is. I'm not so sure (remember the SYSTRAN story, in an earlier chapter?). IT systems are in principle predictable machines, but in practice they are unpredictable systems. Maybe organic-system stability could be gained by systematic and comprehensive programmed redundancy?

Experience, though, shows that programmed systems are in general much more sensitive to micro-error than other classes of system, living systems as well as man-made ones such as bridges, buildings and steam engines. So either there is something of a unique radical novelty inherent in the very nature of IT systems, or else software system designers have yet to recognize and exploit some essential features of these other types of system.

I think that there is a measure of truth in both of these possibilities. We've already seen the argument for the unique radical novelties of computer technology. Now let's examine possible reasons why much current program-design technology leads to *runaway* programs. In general: it fails to recognize and compensate for the unique qualities of the technology. It has refused to come to terms with the unavoidable imperfections which must occur in every technology; it has tried to pretend that computing can be, at some fundamental level, a perfect technology.

If you build an unsinkable ship, then the case for providing lifeboats is seriously undermined – known as the Titanic approach. Why go to the cost, time and trouble needed to obtain them, and why provide the space and necessary mechanisms on the ship itself? Now, although you might quickly begin to conjure up reasons such as fire, pestilence, etc. why lifeboats might still be a good idea for our ship, consider how this philosophy leaps in credibility when applied to programs. Programs cannot be holed by icebergs, nor are they at risk of fire in the very driest of summers. Their total immunity to the adverse effects of natural disasters should be the envy of every Lloyd's underwriter.

A program is a well-defined, formal object. We know precisely what each instruction means – i.e. will cause the computer to do. Moreover, we can give a pretty good guarantee (as good, if not better than most others in this world) that the computer itself will not malfunction. So, if we can formally prove that our program instructs the computer as it's supposed to, there is no need for safety nets – i.e. checks, error traps and redundancy in general, no system brakes on *runaway* programs. This philosophy relegates the word "redundancy" to the category of undesirable qualities.

This peculiar philosophy can be traced to the 'mathematical' lobby in computer science. There is no need for redundancy in the relevant mathematics: one thread of correct reasoning is sufficient to prove a theorem, multiple threads would be superfluous. Similarly, if the required program behaviour is correctly based on a sequence of programmed instructions, further instructions are superfluous (as well as inelegant). They would waste time and space, eat up more of the budget, and add unnecessary clutter to the program, thereby increasing its complexity. After outlining a few useful techniques for "over engineering" IT systems, Hoare[19] warns us that "it is not unknown for catastrophes to be caused by the very measures that are introduced to avoid them."

I've exaggerated a bit, but the point that I want to make is no less forceful simply because everyone doesn't proclaim it absolutely. My caricature of the Titanic effect in computer science is not so far out of kilter with reality: this is the underlying, prevailing mindset.

> Build programs correctly the first time, and most of our worries about software reliability will vanish.

How could we think otherwise? Well, we might try for macro-predictability through a consensus of individually non-guaranteed micro-structures – software systems built like organic systems. We'll speculate on several possible ways to realise such a goal in later chapters. For now I just want to establish that the general philosophy of building guaranteed programs from a single, but guaranteed, thread of individually guaranteed micro-elements is not above reproach. In fact, if you stand back a bit and view it dispassionately, it looks decidedly suspect.

I like the metaphor of the weight of a conventional computation being held by a single, indestructible thread, i.e., the program is the device from which the computation hangs. What I have called the mathematician's approach is to hold the computation with a single, unbreakable steel fibre, and as it's not going to break (by definition) any more than one is an unnecessary waste of resources, and inelegant to boot. A major alternative might be termed the arachnoid approach in which a multitude of mutually reinforcing threads, none of which can be guaranteed, but none of which is crucial to a successful computation, all contribute to the task. Figure 15.2 illustrates these two strategies.

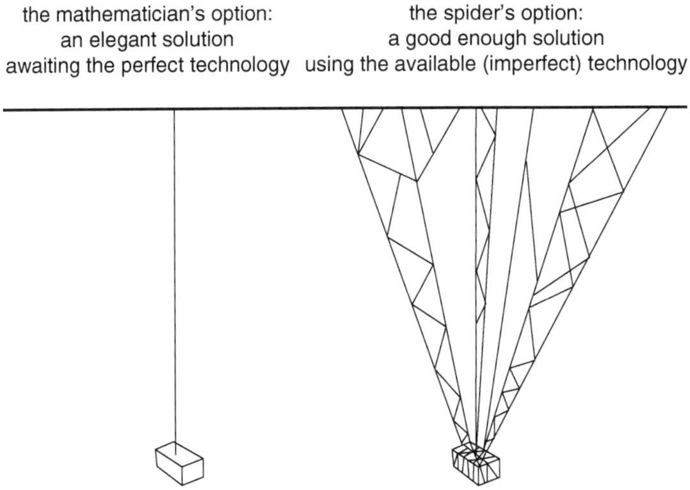

the mathematician's option: the spider's option:
an elegant solution   a good enough solution
awaiting the perfect technology   using the available (imperfect) technology

Fig. 15.2 Two ways of holding up a computational weight

This alien proposal is not just a vague and suspiciously impractical notion. It is a current reality, albeit limited, in, for example, certain so-called neural-network computational systems (see Chapter 22 for a concrete example).

The spider's choice becomes more compelling when we become aware of one of the major failings of this metaphor: physical threads (steel fibres or not) tend to be analogue systems with respect to tensile behaviour, not discrete ones. If too much weight is put on a steel fibre it tends to stretch, and not just break. Within programs, as we have seen, the computational pathways don't stretch at all, they simply perform as expected or they break – a classic discrete behaviour. This is a crucial characteristic of discrete systems.

Added to this bimodal, work-right-or-fail-completely feature of discrete systems is the unhelpful existence of tight, hidden couplings between subsystems. The reason for this tight-coupling of internal functions is founded on our inability to break-down completely the complexity of the overall problem when we first design our program. This inability to generate a "nicely-factored" problem (a string of "islands" – to persist with John Donne's take on complex systems) may stem from either programmer incompetence, sheer problem complexity, or both. Whatever the root causes, the result is the same: one small error can result in a cascade of unpredicted behaviours from the program – it runs away from us.

IT systems, unlike trucks, can *runaway* quite steadily, and for long periods, and yet nobody notices. Much worse than this: the runaway activity can be very short-lived and sporadic, and then it may be almost impossible to correct before some real damage is done. Imagine the family car with this sort of potential for effectively random malfunction – it wouldn't last long as a commercial artefact.

The "Millennium Bug" episode nicely illustrates the lack of transparency in IT systems. This was a concern for IT-system behaviour as the date changed from 31 December 1999 to January 1, 2000. The suspicion was that some IT systems had been designed, constructed and tested under the assumption that dates would always be 19-something. On the first January morning of the new millennium, this assumption would suddenly no longer be valid – the context will have changed for all IT systems. What would happen?

Perhaps new dates would be generated as the year 1900 (because the first two digits were automatically generated); perhaps some use of the number 19 would suddenly be replaced by 20 because a tricky programmer had long-ago saved some time or space by using the first two digits of the date calculation as the constant "19"; perhaps the IT system would go haywire for any number of reasons based on a misplaced reliance on the permanence of the twentieth century as an immutable fixture.

The simplest possible malfunction is based on the erroneous year calculation – i.e. 1900 rather than 2000. Even this problem can vary from relatively innocuous and obvious – e.g., the company's reports etcetera are printed out with this wrong year – to highly damaging and well hidden – e.g. the latest transactions are treated as much earlier transactions (a ridiculous century earlier, but an IT system will not be alerted by any such commonsense observation). If so, all computations based on this erroneous sequencing will be wrong, perhaps not immediately obviously so.

As far as we know, nothing much went wrong. Does this example undermine my case for the inevitable fragility of IT systems? No, it strengthens it.

Prior to the momentous date change, virtually all businesses hired expensive IT consultants to check out their IT systems. Millions of pounds were invested in trying to ensure that the date change would not have an adverse effect. It was money wisely spent one might think, and perhaps it was. The date change should be a small, localized and a very focused problem, and so the IT specialists could determine whether it would cause problems in each IT system, and implement remedial action where necessary.

The point, however, was that even with this seemingly trivial and well-focused problem, the IT consultants did not, and could not, issue guarantees that the IT systems they checked out would not have a date-change problem. On the night in question no airliners fell from the sky, and no major IT-systems catastrophes were reported. However, no one could be sure of this until the new millennium had actually arrived. At which point, nervous observers could 'see' (to some degree) whether their IT system had actually been told to do what they believed it had been told (and they had paid handsomely for it) to do. When no major malfunctions were observed everyone breathed a sigh of relief. In addition, they fervently hoped that none of these IT systems was either sneaking away surreptitiously or poised to deliver unpleasant surprises in response to some future new conjunction of events.

Now we have some general principles of IT-system technology, and general system characteristics to underpin our earlier knowledge of the detailed complexity of modern programs. What are the foundations that we've added?

- During long-term use every IT system needs to be *maintained* by making changes that will inexorably undermine good structure and understanding; in this sense they will always _runaway_.
- In general, IT systems defy human comprehension because:
  1. Full understanding demands mastery of an excessive span of detail.
  2. Small misunderstandings can have large repercussions.
- IT systems pose wholly new challenges to human understanding because they are complex *discrete systems*, quite unlike both natural systems and other engineered complex systems.
- The discreteness of IT systems is manifest in several ways; it is primarily the single-threaded _decision-logic_ _tree_ basis of IT systems that causes difficulties.
- Small, "nicely-factored" *discrete systems* are readily amenable to formal analysis (possibly even proof of correctness); large *discrete systems* with tight internal couplings (such as most IT systems) are not.
- Small, "nicely-factored" systems are also readily comprehensible; large ones (made even larger by the avoidance of the succinct power of inter-couplings) are not – they present as a conglomerate of individual components, which, of course, they are if all inter-couplings are eliminated.
- Complex natural systems achieve stability through redundancy, and predictability through _monotonic_ analogue (rather than discrete) basics.
- 'System science' has failed to encompass systems of discrete complexity.
- The mathematical basis from which much of programming practice has been developed has severely undervalued redundancy as a system feature.
- *Discrete systems* tend to be unpredictable – hence the extreme weakness of IT-system testing as a validation procedure.

It is IT system technology itself that delivers discrete complexity, and that is at the root of the problem. So changing programming language or system-design strategy is not going to solve the basic problems with IT systems.

As if this technological opacity and fragility were not enough, it is not the end of the problem. The runaway phenomenon derives from the basic nature of the technology and our inability to master it – both when we construct large IT systems, and, in particular, when we attempt to maintain their useful functionality over time. The only alternative is to eschew *maintenance* – work around the system's undesired behaviours, and hope that the operating context does not change too much.

But even this somewhat impractical solution does not ensure that your IT system will remain no worse than new. Previously stable, useful IT systems can suddenly go native or drift unobtrusively away because they have been altered either maliciously or by mistake. These worrisome beasts are the subject of the next chapter.

Endnotes

1. The quotation is, of course, from Mary Shelley's classic horror story *Frankenstein, or the Modern Prometheus*, first published in 1817. At this early date, programming did not, and could not figure in the construction of Dr Frankenstein's android. Programming hadn't been invented, although Mary Shelley was contemporary with Babbage, and was the aunt of Miss Byron who is sometimes called the first programmer, see Chapter 3. The misguided doctor was himself seduced by the fascinations of science, but built his creation as an approximate facsimile of the biological version, both internally and externally. The tendency nowadays would be to simulate, or indeed bypass, many of the biological internals using sophisticated electronics and certainly a substantial programming effort. A later chapter in this book compares and contrasts classical programming (derived from mathematics, particularly logic) with a new style that begins to mimic (in some small ways) properties of complex, biological systems.

2. M. M. Lehman and L. A. Belady published *Program Evolution* (Academic Press: 1985), a study of the processes of software change. Even at this early date it was acknowledged that "software systems are rarely completed on time, contain a seemingly inexhaustible stock of faults and are excessively costly to create and maintain" (Preface, p. xi). Among many other studies, they propound three Laws of Program Evolution, and the first two, the ones given, support (although on the more optimistic side) our view here.

   The third law is:

   III The Law of Statistically Smooth Growth: (I will paraphrase as) despite erratic small scale changes, IT-system growth tends to follow a predictable route (size, complexity, etc.) (pp. 169–170).

   In 1992 ("The Risks of Software" in *Scientific American,* vol. 267, no. 5), Littlewood and Strigini imply that there is nothing stronger than wishful thinking to lead one to conclude that these laws have been undermined by progress in software engineering.

3. The programming world is stuffed full of a variety of programming languages. My choice of programming language instructions in the earlier chapters was entirely fictional and simplistic, but not at odds with the wealth of popular procedural languages. If I had to pick out a different sort of programming language, I would choose PROLOG as the radically new language of recent decades. PROLOG (largely a British invention first developed in France in the early 1970s) permitted programming in logic – almost (and the "almost" means that it wasn't a language of formal logic; the claim is akin to being almost pregnant). PROLOG did expose some intriguing new insights on programming, but all the old problems (as well as some new ones) arose. In particular, we might note that a large conglomerate of "nicely-factored" (see note 15, below, and text to which it refers) PROLOG instruction-groups detracts from, rather than enhances, overall system comprehension. The PROLOG bubble has now burst, and it remains as no more than an interesting oddity.

4. E.W. Dijkstra, "On the cruelty of really teaching computing Science" *Communications of the ACM*, vol. 32, no. 12, December 1989, pp. 1397–1414. Edsger Dijkstra, who was arguably the pre-eminent formal computer scientist of all time, uses his claims about the "radical novelties" of computer technology as a basis for the argument that programming must be a correctness-preserving exercise, i.e., if we are to have reliable programs then programming must be a formal process of deriving correct implementations from accepted problem specifications. Anything less is a recipe for disaster. Needless to say, his somewhat extreme views do not go unchallenged, and the cited article is followed by commentaries from other respected computer scientists who variously support or attempt to refute most of the points that he

makes. Modesty almost makes me omit to mention that I too chimed in: D. Partridge, "On the difficulty of really considering a radical novelty," *Minds and Machines*, vol. 5, no. 3, pp. 391–410, 1995.

5. The text box is a terminologically updated (i.e., "IT system" substituted for "data processing") 1983 quotation from software guru Joseph Weintraub. It is to be found on page 201 of David Lubar's compendium *It's Not a Bug; It's a Feature* (Addison-Wesley, 1995).

6. Changes to the context of an analogue system are similarly unlikely to wreck, or fundamentally disrupt, the overall system behaviour. This is because the external change will impact on some element(s) of the system, and it is precisely the stability of analogue-system behaviour with respect to internal change that discrete systems do not exhibit.

7. *Monotonicity*, the technical term for the simplest types of analogue relationships, appears to be almost universal in natural systems. This may be more a function of human perception than an objective reality – i.e. the predictive difficulties that non-monotonic relationships can introduce may not be readily apprehended because historically they have not been useful for human survival. One (of the very few) non-*monotonic* relationships that springs to mind is that between the temperature and density of water: liquid water gets steadily more dense as its temperature is decreased. This *monotonic* relationship continues only until the water temperature is 4°C. At this temperature the density stops increasing and starts to decrease so that when the water freezes at 0°C the ice floats on the denser cold water around it. If this peculiar non-*monotonic* relationship did not exist, maybe we wouldn't either. It seems like a good example for those of the Creative Design persuasion.

8. "Digital" systems (Dijkstra's and most people's preferred term for computer-related systems) are a special case of "discrete" systems: the case in which the discrete components are digits. So we are really contrasting discrete systems with analogue ones, thus we will tend to use the more general term except where it rings too oddly, e.g., 'discrete computer'.

   Curiously, modern computers are not really digital systems: the basis for most modern computers is two discrete states (usually magnetic charge in two distinct directions or electric pulses at two distinct levels) which we represent at this basic level in terms of binary numbers "0" and "1", which are digits. But they are merely a convenient digital representation of the discrete binary electro-magnetic basis of computers.

9. Just one of the pearls plucked from my *New Guide to Artificial Intelligence*; it alludes to the fact that an important element of human intelligence is accurate prediction of the immediate future on the basis of incomplete information. Uncertainty about the future would not exist if we had all necessary information (and the time to process it); a 'mechanical' reasoning procedure could do the job, and 'intelligence' would not be required. But this is not the case, and we must predict as best we can in the time, and on the information, available. The prevalence of analogue systems supports the possibility of a good measure of predictive success in less than ideal circumstances, and we call the outcome 'intelligence.'

10. In a discrete-system world brute force and ignorance may have characterised the dominant species, or perhaps a different sort of intelligence would have evolved, one that endowed its possessors with a much better capability to develop and manage large IT systems.

11. This long-recognized weakness has been addressed by the many attempts to devise 'probabilistic' logics, 'fuzzy' logics, three-valued logics (true, false and maybe) and so on. Whilst a number of these new formal systems work quite nicely within themselves, what they all fail to do is to plausibly replicate human reasoning with uncertainty (a challenge made all the more difficult by our tendency to irrational behaviour when faced with uncertainty). A further big problem is that the human concepts, such 'generally true', 'almost true', 'most probably false', etc. must all be transformed into precise value systems (such as the *real numbers*) for use in a formal system, and there is no known sound basis for the required transformations. A 2010 contribution to the vagueness-and-precision debate is the 300-page book, *Not Exactly: in praise of vagueness* by Kees van Deemter (Oxford University Press). A chapter discusses theories of degrees of truth. The cost of such theories, he observes, is "expulsion from Boole's two-valued paradise" although the programmer struggling with an IT system might well say: "two-valued hell."

12. In the mid-1990s I sent Dijkstra a pre-publication draft of my attempted refutation of the universality of his "radical novelties" (see note 4, above). He very kindly read my argument and wrote me a letter (he prided himself on hand-written letters penned with his Mont Blanc using his personal mix of ink) that pointed out in detail why he disagreed. So we agreed to differ.

13. *Collapse of Chaos* by Jack Cohen and Ian Stewart was published by Penguin Books in 1995. All of the quotations used are drawn from Chapter 13, pp. 408–411.

14. A short article on catastrophe theory with the wonderful title of "Experiments in catastrophe" was published in Nature, vol 254, no 5,499, pp. 392–395, in 1975 by J.M.T. Thompson. A general exposition of the notion can be found in the small book Catastrophe Theory by Alexander Woodcock and Monte Davis, first published in 1978 and now in Penguin.

15. It is C. A. R. Hoare, Professor of Computer Science at Oxford University, who advocates this ultra-conservative view of what sort of problems the computer programmer should (and, more importantly, should not) be tackling. Hoare is only too well aware of the sorts of problems that I am emphasising in this book, and his response is two-pronged:

    1. Limit computer technology to manageable problems, i.e., problems that are "nicely factored" (i.e., can be broken up into more-or-less independent chunks), and
    2. Work on developing the proper mathematical basis for programming such that we will be able to <u>prove</u> that our programs do what we want, and what we expect.

    The view taken in this book is that such a stringent limitation on the types of problems to which computer technology should be applied is impractical (no-one will stick to it), and probably undesirable as well. This urge to (what I see as) excessive restriction on application of computer technology is considerably undermined if the second part of Hoare's response is, in fact, fundamentally flawed.

    Ever the optimist, Hoare's 1996 paper "How did software get so reliable without proof" (Springer LNCS 1051/1996, FME'96) states in the abstract: "By surveying current software engineering practice, this paper reveals that the techniques employed to achieve reliability are little different from those which have proved effective in all other branches of modern engineering: rigorous management of procedures for design inspection and review; quality assurance based on a wide range of targeted tests; continuous evolution by removal of errors from products already in widespread use; and defensive programming, among other forms of deliberate over-engineering. Formal methods and proof play a small direct role in large scale programming; but they do provide a conceptual framework and basic understanding to promote the best of current practice, and point directions for future improvement." Littlewood and Strigini's hard-nosed assessment of software reliability (in *Scientific American*, vol. 267, no. 5, 1992) denies that there is any significant evidence for a number of Hoare's claims, e.g., they say that *bugs* can be simply corrected is "an unsubstantiated assumption", and that the value of "mandating the use of 'best practice' " is similarly unknown.

16. As Bob Malcolm has pointed out to me (among many other things), supposedly scientifically-based disciplines, such as aeronautics, arrive at many of their 'laws' by ad hoc, heuristic routes. *What Engineers Know and How They Know it: Analytical Studies from Aeronautical History* (Johns Hopkins University Press, 1990) by W. G. Vincenti backs this view with many case studies. A short article in *The New Scientist* (11/05/1996), entitled "Article of faith fails aero engineers," states that "a key equation used in the design of aircraft for the past sixty years is wrong … [and] may have caused the tiles on the space shuttle to fall off."

17. Here is the program that we need to scrutinize. The main program:

SHOP
SET alpha-letter **AS** A
REPEAT
    COMMENT read next item on list & locate this item in the store
      DO <u>READ&FIND</u> **WITH** alpha-letter **AS** NEXT-ITEM

3. place item in trolley
    SET-NEXT alpha-letter
UNTIL list is empty

SUBPROGRAM <u>READ&FIND</u>
COMMENT read next item from list
    PUT NEXT-ITEM **INTO** CURRENT-TASK
    PUT 0 **INTO** NEXT-ITEM
COMMENT locate this item in the store
    categorize item in CURRENT-TASK
    consult supermarket layout plan
    find desired category of items
    plan route to where desired category located
    go to this location
    survey items until item in CURRENT-TASK found

The big difference between the two explicit box labels used within the SUBPROGRAM is that one, "CURRENT-TASK", is *local* to the SUBPROGRAM (i.e. it only occurs within the SUBPROGRAM) and the other box label, "NEXT-ITEM", is not (i.e. it also occurs in the *main* program, **SHOP**).

Thus any change of the three occurrences of "CURRENT-TASK" is, in fact, a consistent change of <u>all</u> occurrences, and so has no overall effect. But to change the two occurrences of "NEXT-ITEM" within the SUBPROGRAM is to fail to take into account the use of this box label within the main program (the inter-module link), and so a malfunctioning system will result.

18. This definition is given in his 1970 article (referenced below). Such considerations lead us into the reductionist-holist debate in science, which is not a place that we want to spend a great deal of time. It is, however, by no means irrelevant to the question of the manageability of software systems. An anti-reductionist argument for the biologist is given by Paul A Weiss, "Life, Order, and Understanding", The Graduate Journal, University of Texas, vol. VIII, supplement, 1970. Cohen and Stewart (see note 13, above) present another with respect to science in general.

19. C.A.R, Hoare's invited paper whose title – How Did Software Get So Reliable Without Proof? – implies that in 1996 at least he did not accept many of my basic assumptions. But as the selected quotation (from p. 11) suggests there is actually a good deal of agreement as well. The paper is in Springer's LNCS FME'96, pp. 1–17.

Chapter 16
Sneakaway Programs: Everybody's Predicament

Crimewatch USA

Sunday 4th January, 1987: I could see the hacker going fishing on Milnet [a network of computers in the USA]. One by one, he tried fifteen Air Force computers ... no luck ...until he tried the Air Force Systems Command, Space Division [after two failed attempts, he tried to gain entry with]

name: *Field*
password: *Service*

WELCOME TO THE AIR FORCE SYSTEM COMMAND - SPACE DIVISION

Shazam: the door had swung wide open. He'd logged in as Field Service. Not just an ordinary user. A completely privileged account [including] the ability to read, write or erase any file on the system. He was even authorized to run security audits on the Air Force computer ... Somewhere in Southern California, in El Segundo, a big Vax computer was being invaded by a hacker half-way around the world.
    His next moves weren't surprising: ... he disabled the auditing for his jobs. This way, he left no footprints behind; at least he thought not. How could he know that I was watching from Berkeley?[1]

The preceding chapters have explained why an initial understanding (albeit necessarily incomplete and erroneous) of an IT system is always in danger of deteriorating over time – it runs away from those whose job it is to administer the system. IT system understanding can also deteriorate more subtly and insidiously; it can *sneakaway* from those responsible due to both inadvertent erroneous changes and changes introduced by malicious design, two activities outside official maintenance procedures.

The complexity of computer systems, combined with the high speed of operation, together with the human inability to follow the fine detail on a system-wide scale, all conspire to make invisible runaways far from rare when the creations in question are IT systems. The solution to IT-system *sneakaways* is to control access strictly – the problems stem from system changes, so strict control of who is allowed to change what, is vital; this is *access control*.

D. Partridge, *The Seductive Computer: Why IT Systems Always Fail*,
DOI 10.1007/978-1-84996-498-2_16, © Springer-Verlag London Limited 2011

The spectrum of potential system changes ranges from inadvertent introduction of problems as part of regular maintenance changes to malicious introduction of problems by unauthorized 'hackers' (reverting to modern parlance). All IT systems will, from time to time, need *maintenance* changes, but none need hacker-introduced changes. Sophisticated *access control* is the accepted way to deal with this problem.

The previous chapters should have made clear why it is impossible to determine that each and every character in your program is indeed correct with respect to its intended behaviours. It is then devastatingly easy to appreciate the enormity of the task of recognizing the presence of a disguised minor corruption introduced by a malevolent hacker, or a clumsy maintenance man.

There are standard ways to protect important and widely used IT systems. They can be set up to allow *read only* access, for example. This means that the program can be inspected – e.g. displayed on a screen – and used but not changed.

This is all well and good, but consider: someone must have the authority to set and remove software locks such as *read only* access. There must be privileged users, persons with the authority to change any part of a large and complex system. No IT system can exist for long without some *maintenance* activity. Great power resides in such authority, and so it must be given out cautiously. Such global *change-control* access (more usually called *read-write* access) is typically vested in only a few trusted and competent individuals. Like many forms of power it must be used sparingly, if it is to be used to full effect. This stipulation that the power of a privileged user must be wielded sparingly is not, I hasten to add, driven by concern for the corrupting quality commonly associated with power (although I suspect that so-called 'super-user' power is not special in this respect).

This apparently simple and easy IT-system protection strategy is, of course, neither easy nor simple in large IT systems (even if we have for the moment neglected the unauthorized entry of the hackers). A further measure of protection can be gained if the system 'logs' all accesses with details of who accessed the system, when, and what they then did. Failed attempts to access the system should also be logged with perhaps a lock-out from the system after several failed attempts to gain access.

These log files can then be inspected manually and even monitored by another program that looks for 'suspicious' activity – but then 'suspicious' has to be precisely defined if we are going to program it. If the definition programmed in is too broad then the deluge of false alarms will cause the monitoring system to be ignored; if the definition is too narrow, then accesses that should have been investigated will be missed. And as with all 'programmed' checks, once the hackers determine how the checks have been programmed, they can work around them. Email spam filters are a well-known example of this phenomenon.

Highly limited *read-only access* can also lead to seemingly absurd situations. A case in point was presented on BBC Radio 4 in 2008; it concerned the Immigration Control IT system used in the USA. Within this system biometric details, such as fingerprints and retina scans, are stored together with name and full passport details of all foreigners entering the USA. So on first entry, the visitor is required to press his or her fingers on a special pad and to look into a camera. The immigration officer on duty then enters this biometric data into the IT system associated, of course, with the person's passport details.

On one such occasion a husband and wife were entering together and the immigration official inadvertently entered the husband's biometric data with the wife's passport details, and vice versa. No problem was noted.

A week or two later as the couple were leaving the USA and their biometric characteristics together with their passports were checked out, alarms sounded and they were abruptly hustled away and down to a holding room where they spent several uncomfortable hours as suspected terrorists before the mess was sorted out.

The sorting out, however, only extended to the officials acknowledging the mix-up in their system, and apologizing to the unfortunate tourists. It specifically did not extend to correcting the IT-system entries for this couple. Indeed, they were warned that their problem would reoccur every time they attempted to visit the USA. This seems absurd, but we know why it is not.

Why did one of these officials not correct the IT-system entries? The answer is that none of them had the power to do it. In this super-secure IT system, the officials had only *first-entry access* (i.e. the biometric data could be entered, but then it was fixed and unchangeable) coupled with the usual *read-only access*.

If the IT system is to be totally secure then *read-write* access can only be given to very few persons, because otherwise the system would be too vulnerable to illegal access and modification. Restricted access is controlled by 'keys' (typically passwords for an IT system), and the more keys that exist (or the more copies of the same key), the higher the probability that a determined intruder will gain *change*-access rights. Once this happens, the essential integrity of this IT system has been irreversibly compromised; the only way to avoid this disaster is to limit *change*-access rights very severely.[2]

There is an unavoidable tension between IT-system security and *change*-access rights. This difficulty, although fuelled by concerns for malicious IT-system changes, is not limited to pressures from illegal activity. Even for IT systems that do not demand ultra-high levels of integrity (like the US Immigration System), it is good practice to limit *change*-access rights, minimize the number of 'privileged' users; the complexity and fragility of IT systems makes this obvious, I hope.

Even an authorised privileged user should be reluctant to invoke his system-change privileges simply because the less authority[3] he wields within the IT system, which may contain thousands of programs, the less likely he is to do inadvertent damage – a misplaced keystroke can erase a whole program, or, less obviously, compromise a complete system; a slightly misunderstood system command may have unforeseen, and potentially disastrous, side-effects in the system, etc. The rule then is for the privileged user to invoke no more of his privileges than are necessary to get the job done. A good system administrator (typically the most-privileged user) 'treads very lightly' when he is working within an operational IT system. An element of this careful approach is for the privileged user to grant himself the minimum change authority necessary to get his current job done (e.g. authority to change some components of the system but not others).

The inadvertent and non-malicious corruption of IT systems is always a possibility, but more worrying is the truly malicious IT-system intruder: the 'hacker' in modern parlance.

How does the hacker gain illegal access to an IT system? He either finds the 'keys' that authorize entry or he finds an unrecognized (and thus unguarded) entry point.

Dealing with what we might term a simulated authorized entry first: stealing and copying the 'keys' will not typically involve pressed-wax moulds and subsequent metal work. It will be finding the character strings that the IT system accepts as proof of authorization, and there are many ways to do this. These character-string keys are, of course, known as passwords (which should <u>not</u> be proper words) – all those supposedly unimaginable character strings that we must memorize (and keep distinct) if we wish to use a range of IT-system technology.

All computer-system users, from gamers, email users and Internet surfers to professional software engineers, are familiar with password guarded access to their personal systems. Large-scale sensitive IT systems may have much more elaborate key structuring (such as dynamic personal access-code generation devices that provide the authorized user with the access code of the moment), but the underlying principles are the same: the IT system will give access whenever it gets the anticipated codes.

The next generation of *access-control* procedures combines the password strategy with biometric data, such as fingerprint or voiceprints. Once inside the system, this biometric data is, of course, just a character string (e.g. a coded retina-scan image), but probably a more difficult one to get hold of than the average password. The expense of installation, and the new difficulties introduced by the need to manage such an authorization strategy mean that they are not widely in use. In addition, the sometimes handy flexibility of authorizing access by loaning your password (which should, of course, be immediately reset, but never is) is not the same simple convenience when biometric data is used.

The degree of IT-system access that a person can garner is determined by that person's 'name' (in general, a personal identification label) and more importantly by knowledge of certain passwords. Access to a large IT system is gained by first typing in your 'user name' – the scare quotes indicate that it doesn't have to be your real name (for how could the computer check anyway, unless it had access to appropriate biometric information). The name just has to be one that the particular IT system will accept as a valid 'user name', but with that acceptance comes the expectation of one or more passwords. It is these passwords that have to be provided correctly, on demand, in order to gain entry to the computer. These passwords are also used to determine how much authority a person can command in the system: the user name for a System Administrator may have several associated passwords, and the one used will determine the authority associated with that particular entry to the system – anything from *read-only* access to total freedom to modify any aspect of the system, and all the intervening levels of authority.

It is passwords that are the heart of security in large IT systems, and so they must be guarded and protected. Clearly, the IT system itself must know all the valid passwords in order to be able to recognize them as such when a potential user tries to gain entry. But does this mean that all of the valid passwords occupy boxes within the computer memory? If this were the case then any programmer on the system (with sufficient authority gained by legitimate means or not) could read, record, change, etc. all of the locks on the system.

In order to thwart this possibility, passwords are encrypted – i.e. transformed by an encryption program into a seemingly random sequence of characters. The computer actually stores the encryptions of the passwords. The encryption process is specially chosen to be one that is easy to do from password to encryption, but (practically) impossible to reverse, from encrypted character string back to password, even if you have a copy of the encryption program (which, of course, must also be inside the computer). There is an elaborate science of encryption techniques, many of which are designed to have just this property. But we do not need to go into them, we need only know that they exist, and know that they are hard to circumvent, but not perfect.

Any reader who indulges in more than the absolute minimum of computer usage will be familiar with the problem of personal password management. In a nutshell: your data (such as credit-card details and bank accounts) will be more vulnerable to unauthorized access if you use one password for all system accesses, but the task of remembering a multiplicity of different passwords each for a different IT system is onerous. The temptation is to use one easy-to-remember password for your access to many different systems, and, like so many tempting things in life, this one too is a recipe for disaster.

The point of going into all this password stuff is that, because it is central to the restriction of access to computer systems, it is usually the prime target of hackers trying to gain illegal access. How do they go about it?

There are a number of techniques. The opening (true) story illustrates illegal access by the simple expedient of guessing likely passwords. As other stories in the same book make clear, people tend to display a startling lack of imagination when called upon to dream up a password for themselves. So one popular route to illegal access is to spend time simply trying 'likely' passwords. Or better (as our potential intruder is a programmer, remember), is to write a program that generates and tries passwords. Provided the system will let it, such a program can generate and try millions of passwords in a very short time.

A second technique is to gain a first access (maybe through a loophole in the system, or having guessed the password of a minimal-authority user), and then install a *Trojan Horse* program. This beast, as the name suggests, looks like an innocuous program (all programs look the same, remember) but is in fact designed to result in total control of the system by the hacker. Such a program may be set to pre-empt and duplicate the behaviour of the normal program that requests and checks passwords, except that it does no checking. It simply stores a copy of each password it receives, tells the user that he or she made a mistake (e.g. a typing error), and hands over to the official password checker for everything to continue as normal when the user tries again. This *Trojan-Horse* program will soon collect the passwords of all the regular users of the system, and no one (except the hacker) will realize that trouble is imminent.

A third technique uses programming again, but this time the password encryption program is applied to a dictionary of words, and each encrypted word is compared (by the program) to all the encrypted passwords. Whenever a match is found then the hacker has found a system password. The way to defeat this sort of attack is not to use dictionary words as passwords, but to use some jumble of letters and digits say. But, of course, a password to be effective must be readily memorable, and proper words are much easier to remember then random jumbles of characters. In addition, the 'dictionary' of potential passwords need not be a real dictionary; it may be a list of character strings constructed at random or from likely combinations of names and numbers (such as birthdays).

In addition to all these ways of gaining unauthorized entry to a computer, there is the added complexity caused by global networking of tele-communications: in a phrase, the Internet. The developed world is now enmeshed by a network of computers, and this greatly facilitates global communication.

Sadly, _viruses_ and _worms_ (i.e. programs that are designed to sneak into your computer system) are part and parcel of everyday life for the Internet and email user. This is not the book to dig deep into this murky world of intricate _sneakaway_ threats. We just note their existence and move on to a specific example that reveals some of the depths of the problem.

This worldwide networking of computers is great for quick, cheap and easy communication for a wide variety of persons, organizations and companies. Unfortunately, it is similarly great for the hacker. In addition to sending messages through these networks, it is possible to use them to access computers across the world, and then to use these remote machines as if they are under your desk, or on your lap.

So, when not simply programming the hacker can exercise his talents roaming many of the world's computer systems. Whether this roaming has a sinister basis or not, it has the potential to inflict a fatal change (just one single character change will do, remember) on the IT systems in any computer that is reached.

The intruder being observed in the opening story of this chapter was first detected when a system manager noticed that someone, who he knew was away and had no access, seemed to be working on the system. The system manager became curious because a valid, but unexpected, user name was active on the computer. When studied more closely, it became clear that a 'professional' hacker possessing passwords for many interconnected computers was at work inspecting and copying files back to his base.

But where was his base? It could have been someone in the room at another terminal, someone down the hall in another office, or someone almost anywhere else in the world.

It took months of tracing back every time the hacker appeared on the computers that were being closely watched. Even the surveillance had to be carefully set up (once officialdom had accepted that the problem was potentially serious): a new computer was attached to the network; it was blocked against external entry; and it was disguised as an innocuous (but impenetrable) machine in the network.

Such seemingly extreme precautions had to be taken because the hacker was a very cautious professional. Before exploring a new computer (to which he had gained entry), the hacker would use his skills to determine who else was currently active on the system (modern computers typically service the needs of several dozen humans at the same time). He would withdraw immediately if he detected that any system managers or other highly competent (and thus potentially dangerous) users were also active on the computer system.

The tracing effort required help from other system managers, the telephone company, international communications experts and the German Bundespost. The variety of diverse communications options exploited by one wily intruder are illustrated in Fig. 16.1.

This intriguing case, loosely illustrated in the figure, is known as "The 75 cent Fraud". A major spying activity was going on in the form of illegal access to supposedly secure, and secret, information held in a computer system; the spy was detected as a result of a fortuitous decision to track down the source of a 75 cent discrepancy in the computer system's accounting – i.e. the only external sign that the system was being periodically misused was a very small discrepancy in the accounting information computed.[4]

This story illustrates an important sense in which nobody notices that something untoward is happening within the computer, but one this is largely outside the remit of this book, concerns computer fraud – i.e. when the program is subtly altered or when someone surreptitiously misuses access to a program, both for illegal purposes.

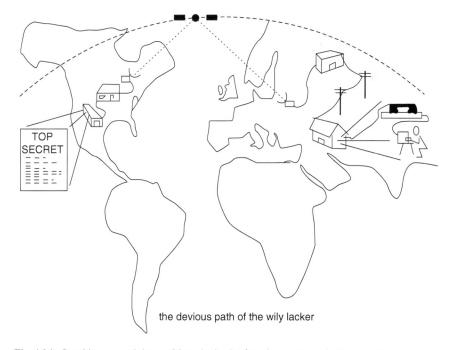

the devious path of the wily lacker

Fig. 16.1 Sneaking around the world on the back of modern communications technology

The potential criticality of every character and our inability to monitor computer systems at this required level of detail, coupled with the vast throughput of information that the speed of these machines makes possible, has opened up a whole new world for the fraudster. To further aggravate the legal issues, most of what is illegally accessed, copied, or stolen is intangible symbol structures, and these prove to be slippery property for traditional legal systems to grasp and deal with appropriately.

For example, because my computer is networked to the world, I can (and do) send vast amounts of information – programs, documents, data – all over the world. No organization appears to be monitoring the wealth of information that is criss-crossing the globe at the speed of light, day and night. In truth, how could they?[5]

One of my ex-students who became an IBM man in the late 1970s told me of his experience with customs control and high-tech: he worked in the USA but was regularly required to work in one of IBM's Canadian offices, and he needed to take his data back and forth. In those days data was stored on large reels of magnetic tape, impressively big objects – briefcase size. The border officials always hassled him over what was on these tapes, and insisted that he got official clearance for exporting and importing the data on them. But then the forerunner of the Internet emerged, and he sent his data electronically back and forth. No more hassles. The source of difficulty had disappeared from official view.

Added to the problems of designing and constructing well-understood IT systems, once they are released and go operational, fresh new problems appear, problems that are founded on the old and (by now, I hope) familiar ones of over-whelming complexity and extreme fragility.

In summary:

- In-use IT-system confidence becomes suspect every time an IT system is exposed to <u>potential</u> changes.
- The elements of IT-system *access control* are introduced and discussed.
- Inadvertent change, due to clumsiness, or covert malicious change causes IT systems to *sneakaway*.
- All IT systems must be open to change; usually managed through passwords.
- Biometric access control, such as fingerprint matching, is a growing alternative to passwords. These avoid the memorisation task of many passwords but:
  1. Successful duplication or simulation will open <u>all</u> doors (whereas use of multiple passwords can protect against this).
  2. We lose the convenience of giving (perhaps temporary) access to someone else.
  3. Matching to approve access becomes complicated (and thus error prone).
- Beyond the privacy concerns of *read-only access*, access to change IT systems must be closely controlled and monitored.
- This control is at odds with ease of access for essential system changes, e.g. just adding new information, or making corrections.
- *Change-access* (or *read-write* access) control for an IT system may be a complex, multi-level procedure, i.e., different users require access to different system-modification possibilities.

- Further complication to the ever-present threat of malicious system access and modification is introduced through the convenience of computer networking, such as made possible by the Internet.

In sum, the mix of human curiosity (not to mention malevolence), the extreme fragility of programs, and the speed and complexity of the Internet constitute a serious threat to the stability of every IT system. The potential for unnoticed change must be contemplated for any IT system that is not rigorously guarded, used only on isolated machines, never copied, etc. – even then you can never be sure.

Endnotes

1. This extract is taken from *The Cuckoo's Egg* by Clifford Stoll (Pan Books: 1989). The author recounts, in a very entertaining way, how his task of tracking down a trivial accounting error in a California computer led him to uncover military espionage based in Germany.

   In the first decades of the twenty-first century this is till happening as a consequence of very poor IT-system management. The USA is attempting to extradite Gary McKinnon, a UK citizen who infiltrated a number of 'secure' US IT systems. McKinnon, who claims that he was merely looking for evidence of the existence of UFOs, maintains that many break-ins were unbelievably easy. He just tried the obvious passwords (like "Field" and "Service" in the opening story), and supposedly secure and sensitive IT systems let him in.

   Computer Weekly (www.computerweekly.com posted 13-6-08, accessed 11-11-09) reported: "It was child's play to get into US military systems, McKinnon said. Many were running Netbios over TCP/IP with blank or default passwords, which allowed him to access-administrator privileges.

   He admitted writing scripts to harvest passwords, and to using password crackers to get into more protected systems. Gaining secret access was clearly seductive. McKinnon speaks of 'megalomaniacal' feelings when he was deep inside systems. But he was not alone, he said. By querying who else was connected and investigating IP addresses, he found Chinese, European and other nationals visiting the same computer systems. 'At first I thought they might be offsite contract workers, but that was not the case,' he said.

   Once he was inside a network, especially a military network, McKinnon found that other computer systems considered him a trusted user. This was how he was able to get into the Pentagon's network. 'It was really by accident,' he says." And notice that he also described the experience as "seductive."

2. The happy ending to this story is that the BBC contacted the US Department of Homeland Security (the blighted couple had already done so, but got no response). This department, which is responsible for the IT system in question, then made the necessary switch of biometric data and passport details. Because this system is 'ultra-secure', authority to change the data must be 'ultra-protected' which, in practice, means that changing the data will be a big hassle (as it should be). Change-access authority is fundamentally at odds with IT-system reliability, and yet it must be possible. The proposed UK system for ID cards, which is presented as an ultra-reliable system for identity proof, must grapple with exactly this conundrum, further complicated by the difficulties that will accompany the necessarily approximate matching of biometric data. Password matching is simple – exact match, or no match; biometric data is never exactly the same on two different occasions, so the decision becomes – near–enough match, or not-near-enough match.

3. The coarse distinction between read-only-access and read-write-access rights is the simplest case. All manner of intermediate access rights are possible in a complex IT system. It may

well be the case that various system users are given limited rights to change (or simply enter data), and the limitations may be different for different classes of user. The guiding principle should be that each class of user is given the minimum necessary access rights, and that all accesses are automatically logged.

This problem is one (but by no means the only one) that is bedevilling the UK Government's attempts to produce a comprehensive IT system to support the National Health Service. In this case the problems are compounded by a further incompatibility between widening valid access to personal medical data records for those who have a right and a need to know the details, and maintaining the strict privacy of the same data by excluding access to everyone else who has no right to read it (let alone change it).

4. The complete story is in Clifford Stoll's book (see note 1 above). For further details: K. Fitzgerald, "The quest for intruder-proof computer systems" *IEEE Spectrum*, vol 24, no. 8, pp. 22–26, 1989.

5. Since 9-11, the US authorities, in particular, have put much time and money into monitoring global communications in an effort to automatically filter out the 'suspicious' ones. This task is made virtually impossible by:
   1. The ease with which messages can be disguised once the perpetrators have some idea what the programmed system's 'keys' for 'suspicion' are.
   2. Messages can be easily encoded to eliminate all potentially obvious keys.
   3. The real decisions, which must be based on human understanding, are overwhelmed by the sheer volume of data, even after filtering.

   In April 2009 the UK Government announced that it was dropping plans to similarly monitor email communications. The good reason was erosion of civil liberties; the real reasons suggested were cost (in a time of national budget crunch) and likely ineffectiveness due to the very poor quality of natural-language understanding systems.

Chapter 17
Hooptedoodle 4: Bases for Data Security

> *Of the 46 UK Government databases surveyed, one quarter was "fundamentally flawed and almost certainly illegal."*
>
> (Research commissioned by the Joseph Rowntree Reform Trust, 2009[1])

More and more information about us is finding its way into IT systems. Sometimes we would wish it so – as with medical records held in the local hospital; sometimes we might wonder if we like the idea – as with supermarkets logging our shopping habits; and sometimes we may fight against it tooth and nail – as with personal lifestyle information amassed by the government.

The UK, like much of the western world, is in the forefront of the movement to store information on computers systems. To judge from media stories, the UK is a world leader in its propensity to lose copies of this information.

In 2007, the Home Secretary announced to the British parliament that details of 25 million recipients of child benefit had been lost. Subsequently, we heard that a CD containing the details of all Britain's prisoners has been lost. USB memory sticks similarly go missing while holding large amounts of sensitive data. A laptop containing the account details for a large number of bank customers was stolen from a parked car.

The outcry and indignation that typically follows these revelations usually centres on whether the correct procedures had been in place, and whether staff had followed those procedures. Whereas, if the procedures had been properly put in place, the staff would have had no alternative but to abide by them. If the procedures had been programmed into the IT system that stored the information, then foolish behaviour is no longer an easy option.

Information, be it medical records or shopping habits, is known as *data*, and is stored in a computer as a *database*. Databases may be standalone objects that are accessed by a variety of IT systems – such as personal medical records accessed by your GP and by any hospital's A&E department – or they may an integral part of a large IT system – such as your shopping habits in the supermarket's promotional mailing system.

D. Partridge, *The Seductive Computer: Why IT Systems Always Fail*,
DOI 10.1007/978-1-84996-498-2_17, © Springer-Verlag London Limited 2011

In all cases, it is possible to have a program that interfaces between the data and any accesses to it. This system can, and should, control all access to the database along the lines discussed in the previous chapter.

For every database, procedures have to be agreed for access[2]: who has *read-only* access to what data, who has *change* (aka *read-write*) access, and who has *copy-out* access (and under what conditions – e.g., copy-out may only be permitted with encryption, or with anonymization of a crucial key, such as name). Then these procedures should be programmed into the interface system. With this in place, employees (or anyone else) have no option but to access the database records through the specified procedures.

As with IT systems in general, accesses, both successful and unsuccessful (especially these latter), should be logged by the interface program: who accessed the database; what they did after gaining entry; and when they did it. This logged information will provide an audit trail for the system administrators, and so permit them to report and track data breaches. In order not to minimize loss of possible nuggets in mountains of log data, decisions will, in general, need to be made about what to log, and what not to log. In addition, 'crawler' programs can be written to rummage through large log files looking for 'suspicious' activity (but see later caveat associated with the pensions-credit scam).

Copying portions (if not the whole database) must be closely managed, and so should only be permitted in strictly controlled ways once clear authority has been given. For example, certain 'keys' (such as passwords) may permit copying, and the key used for each copy-access is logged (with the implication that the key owner has authorized the copy operation, and so bears the responsibility for it).

Copying data appears to be the major source of lost information. Copying onto a personal storage device – such as a CD, memory stick or laptop – is a great convenience for necessary work on the database information; it is also a major vulnerability that can be drastically lessened if the copied information is encrypted (and the decryption program, or its key, is not stored on the same device!). Quite apart from the convenience of working out of the office, copying out information to work on may be necessary if the database is 'live' – i.e. it is in use. Management of database integrity (e.g., no conflicting information) is always troublesome when changes are being made to a live system, but these issues are largely outside of our current remit, except to note that copying may be a legitimate and necessary activity.

The proposed access-control program described above is, of course, an IT system (or part of one), and so it is subject to all of the problems (such as correctness) that this book has been elaborating. However, it can be a small and nicely-factored program – all access requests can be composed from the independent operations of *read-access*, *write-access*, *delete-access*, *copy-access*, etc. Hence, it should be possible to avoid the worst problems that plague large and complex IT systems. Nevertheless, the access-control program will not be exempt from all worries.

The claim that the necessary access-control program will be small and nicely-factored is an expectation based upon the essential nature of the task: it must accept access requests; log all the details; decide if authorized; if not, refuse access, and if authorized, execute the request. Executing the request is potentially the most complex element here (if we anticipate a wide variety of different types of requests), but this element must exist anyway. All that our new program does is decide whether to execute the request or refuse it.

A further feature that can undermine the nicely-factored simplicity of our proposed access-control program will be the complexity of the control procedures that the database owner requires: in general, the more complex the procedures, the less nicely-factored the program can be. This observation raises another important aspect of this whole issue: programming of proposed procedures soon makes it crystal clear how well-thought-out and self-consistent the proposed procedures are. The act of programming requires detailed, formal specification of the procedures, and this can be a surprisingly enlightening exercise in itself.

So why is this relatively simple way to control database security so often neglected? Ignorance and incompetence certainly play their parts, but there is also an unavoidable conflict between keeping a database secure and keeping it up to date. For the former: get it set up and checked thoroughly, and then prohibit all but read-only access – databases can sneakaway and runaway just as readily as other IT systems; for the latter: give write and copy access to all the people with new information to add. These two standpoints are incompatible, so every database system must operate at some point of compromise. But it may well be that for many current databases the chosen operating point is too far towards easy update rather than security.

Privacy of data is another worry that comes to the fore as databases proliferate. In March 2009, news reports surfaced in the UK of the discovery of an illegal database detailing 'undesirable' characteristics (e.g., "Don't touch this man.") of thousands of workers in the construction industry. The database had been innocently (!) bought by many of the leading construction companies.

In general, we do not hear as much about privacy violations as about lost data, but that may be just because privacy violations, by their very nature, are much more likely to stay private. It is to be expected that data privacy concerns have added a lot of unwanted complexity to further bedevil the UK government's NHS IT system, Connecting for Health. The complexity caused by privacy concerns centres on the difficulty of making ones medical records quickly and easily available for any legitimate access (e.g., an A&E doctor who receives your injured body at any UK hospital), and yet unavailable to (almost) everyone else (from a bored cleaner in the A&E, to a nosy neighbour working as a secretary in your local GP practice).

This proposed system will contain 100s of millions of health records. And once again sheer size raises its own problems: in this case data validity. Since January 22, 2009, The Information Commissioner's Office in the UK has new powers to enforce the correctness of information in databases. Moves are afoot to ensure that part of the responsibility of a database owner is to ensure the accuracy of the data it holds.

The British Computer Society, the main professional body in the UK associated with all matters of programming technology, has stated that 1–5% of all database entries are erroneous. Given 100 million data items, then at only the minimum 1%

level, one million of them will be erroneous. Mistakes in a database, like so much else associated with IT systems, can vary from mildly aggravating to life threatening. It all depends on the nature of the mistake and the usage of the database.

In general, the repercussions of a database error will be directly related to the (supposed) security of the data: if the data is deemed to be highly accurate and totally secure, then the powers that use it, will feel free to implement drastic measures whenever the database suggests that they are necessary. We already have (in the preceding chapter) a horror story of innocent tourists flagged as potential terrorists by a simple data mix-up in the USA's database for Homeland Security.

The UK's proposed National Identity Card scheme threatens to repeat such overblown (and very hard to rectify) official reactions to errors in its database, or accesses to that database. The Foundation for Information Policy Research cautions against the likely abuses of so much personal information, so widely available, and accessible through a single key – the National Identity Number.[1] Curiously, exactly this concern was voiced and thoroughly investigated in the USA many decades ago.

It has long been the practice in the USA for citizens to memorize their Social Security Number (SSN), and to give it out as part of almost any transaction – from supermarket cheque guarantee, driving-licence application, application for a bank loan, or registration at a University. In the early 1970s, it was recognized that there might be significant unwanted repercussions of this ubiquitous use of a simple and supposedly unique personal number as databases began to proliferate, and so a study was commissioned.

The result in 1973 was a report[3] from the "Advisory Committee on Automated Personal Data Systems" to the then Secretary of State, Casper Weinberger, which recommended that individuals should, for their own protection, cease to casually give out their SSN. They were obliged to give it to the military and the taxation authorities, but that was all. The recommendations also said that computer databases should not be constructed with SSNs as the search keys.

The Committee concluded that "under current law, a person's privacy is poorly protected against arbitrary or abusive record-keeping practices." One wonders what the implications are for the UK's National Identity Numbers as the key to better governance.

We've had decades of progress in database technology (many more databases; hopefully, more awareness of security issues; but more sophisticated unauthorized accessing). We've also witnessed the personal privacy 'relaxations' due to the "War on Terror."

One final observation reflects back to the blind obedience of IT systems, and one example demonstrates this danger.

A multi-million pound pensions-credit scam was uncovered by an IT-system administrator who attention was caught by the fact that the system was paying out hundreds of different claims into just one bank account. The IT system itself didn't miss a beat; it 'happily' paid claims from a variety of different people into exactly the same bank account.

Another example of the truism that computers do just what you tell them to do. If you don't tell the IT system to watch out for this particular suspicious behaviour, it doesn't do it. But should one wish to try to fix this weakness, there would be a very long (probably endless) list of dodgy behaviours to program in as system alerts.

Databases, just like IT systems in general, are an ever growing feature of our lives, but with databases action can be taken to lessen the chances of our data getting into the wrong hands; it's a pity that no such (relatively) quick fix is known for IT systems as a whole.

Endnotes

1. This highly negative report issued in March 2009 can be found at http://news.zdnet.co.uk/ security/ (accessed 24/03/2009).
2. These terms have been explained earlier, but are repeated here: *read-access* allows the user to read information but not alter or copy it; *read-write-access* allows reading and writing to the database; *delete-access* allows the user to delete data from the database; and *copy-access* allows copying out of the data (to say a personal laptop), and so on. The precise interpretation of each access function (and what the full set of access functions is) is tailored to the needs and restrictions associated with individual databases.
3. This comprehensive 346 page report by the Secretary's Advisory Committee on Automated Personal Data Systems entitled *Records, Computers, and the Rights of Citizens* was published in July 1973 by the US Department of Health, Education & Welfare, DHEW publication number (OS)73-97.

Chapter 18
The Roles of Software in Society

Old programs never die, they just get invisibly patched up.

possible bumper sticker

Of course, IT-systems aren't always failures, certainly not spectacular public ones. Many, very many, large IT systems are out and about in the real world and they are doing difficult tasks amazingly well: tasks that would be totally impossible in a computer-less world. Why is this? The answer is founded on recognition that the sensitivity of application domains varies widely as does the degree to which such systems are pampered (and, of course, some IT systems are developed more responsibly than others). User pampering – the extent to which the local users will go out of their way to work around the less-than-perfect aspects of the IT system – is important because it can transform a near disaster into a good-enough system. So, there are two quite different facets to the roles of software in society:

1. The first concerns how computer technology is applied to social problems
2. The second concerns the way that the software is treated during its useful life

There is, of course, a variety of human responses in society to IT systems that display the imperfections of the technology. If the bank's computer mistakenly fails to accept that your plastic card and code number is valid, you may well get annoyed. If it erroneously debits money from your account, you should get very annoyed. But if the local (and even not so local) nuclear power plant starts boiling over as a result of unreliability in the IT system that controls it, your reaction is quite justified in exceeding the limits on any scale of annoyance.

To take the first class of role: how is software used in society? As a correct cog in the overall machine, or an inherently suspect component whose behaviour must be closely watched?

Classical science is fundamentally analytic: the scientist observes, ponders and probes the world by means of experiments in order to devise a law that captures some aspect of the way the world works. The Computer Scientist's activities are fundamentally synthetic: the overall goal is to construct systems that exhibit a desired set of behaviours, and the subfields of programming-language development and system-design principles are just two of the contributing areas of research.

D. Partridge, *The Seductive Computer: Why IT Systems Always Fail*,
DOI 10.1007/978-1-84996-498-2_18, © Springer-Verlag London Limited 2011

Stated too grandiosely: the classical scientist tries to further our understanding of God's work while the computer scientist is trying to extend it (without the handy, if not essential, attributes of omnipotence and omniscience). It is a small wonder that IT systems often fail.

The classical scientist must be content with best-guess theories, proof is not an option. The computer scientist wants to do better. He or she doesn't want to tinker with a program until it seems to be okay – i.e. until no more errors can be found. The aim is to prove that it is correct, and hence to deliver a guaranteed cog. Absolute correctness is the preserve of abstract mathematics, not of classical scientists.[1] Hence many computer scientists see themselves as mathematicians, mathematicians with very powerful adding machines at their disposal – to put it crudely, but not so as to introduce major distortion. And an adding machine really should be guaranteed to get its sums right if it is properly programmed.

This is particularly true if the IT system is used to, say, control an aircraft or monitor a nuclear power plant. A failure in these systems could result in a major disaster. With such _safety-critical_ IT systems failures cannot be glossed over, worked around. It is with these extreme applications that we might expect to find similar extremes of human effort to prove that an IT system is correct. Even here, however, formal proof of correctness is not on the agenda. The requirement is not even to make them failure free – the goal is to minimize and to (formally) quantify the uncertainty concerning system reliability.

Even this is not possible because the statistics required must rest on assumptions whose validity is open to question: for example, finding and fixing a _bug_ improves system reliability. Does it? Sometimes, is the honest answer, and that is no basis upon which to build formal guarantees.

Tacitly admitting the impossibility of formal guarantees, Government legislation tends to mandate 'best practice'[2] in system design and development. "How good is such assurance?" Littlewood and Strigini[3] ask, and answer: "Arguably, not very good."

More generally, they argue "that our ability to measure it [i.e. software reliability] falls far short of the levels that are sometimes required." Consequently, "the appropriate level of safety will be guaranteed only if the role of the software is limited." Even this may be erring on the over-optimistic side with respect to the robustness of the guarantees given.

Programs running on actual computers are complex artefacts that are in some ways more like bridges, buildings and internal-combustion engines than like the formal theorems of the mathematician. From this viewpoint, programs are the products of an engineering discipline. The move from mathematics to engineering is a big move: it's a jump from the certainty of formal abstract worlds to the uncertainty of the real world. The symbol structures must eventually be _grounded_, and as we've seen, every such landing necessarily causes some potential buckling of the original structures.

IT systems appear to straddle this divide: a program is a formal abstract object, yet it is also a concrete artefact interacting with a very real world. This divergence of roles accounts in no small way, I believe, for the general absence of consensus on what the problems with computer technology really are, as well as how we might best try to solve them. This schizoid reality within which IT systems operate certainly spills over from the realms of the academic computer scientist and into the everyday world of us all. It is manifest in the way that we use IT systems which is in turn somewhat dependent upon the presumptions under which the system has been constructed.

A second and rather different, but not unrelated, aspect of the roles of IT systems in society concerns what is called the *software life-cycle* – the sequence of events in the life of an IT system. We have already begun to look at this aspect of IT systems when we switched attention from the problems of system design and development to the problems of system *maintenance*. A typical IT system life-cycle is:

SPECIFY-DESIGN-PROGRAM-TEST-USE-FIX-FIX-FIX-...

So commercial IT systems are not just constructed, sold, used by the purchaser, and then thrown away. In fact, they are almost never thrown away but are reworked and extended, and reused continually (recall the SYSTRAN translation program described at length in an earlier chapter). The long tail of FIX-FIX-FIX... is, of course, the system *maintenance* that I have made much of already in this book.

Most commercial artefacts, say a bottling machine at the baby-food factory, are also made to serve a useful function for as long as possible (and the possibilities are usually tightly constrained by economics). If the bottle design is changed, then every effort will be made to modify the existing machine to accommodate the new bottle shape. So, in this general sense there is a similar life-cycle associated with conventional commercial artefacts as well, but this is where the similarity ends. Again software represents a special case. Why?

It is primarily because of the malleability of the software medium together with the (almost) limitless possibilities for what a program might do. With a computer program anything is possible, and it's cheap and easy (not to mention great fun) to explore the prospects for achieving the desired functionality by trying changes and seeing what happens. Then like so much else in this domain, the switch from small problems to large systems transforms "cheap and easy" to "very expensive and impossible."

This point takes us right back, full circle, to the happy hacker and the programming game. Have pity on the software engineer: the boss dumps a multi-thousand instruction program on his desk (by means of an innocent little email) with the information that this program does X,Y and Z and to please alter it to do X-plus, Y and not Z but A.

You should now be well-placed to appreciate what the enormity of this task might be: first, the development of a detailed understanding of how the current program does indeed do X, Y and Z (and it usually doesn't, at least not in the simplistic way described by the boss); and second, the design of modifications that will introduce the new functionality requested without destroying any of the old, and still required, functions of the system (most of which will need to be painstakingly discovered before their continued existence stands a sporting chance of being preserved).

Programmers prefer to construct and rework their own creations rather than someone else's, but the vast majority find themselves doing the latter. The fact that some 80% of commercial programmers are doing this sort of *maintenance* work rather than developing programs from specifications speaks loudly for the quantity of residual errors that lurks within the software world, and the longevity of IT systems. Unless, of course, these maintenance programmers are primarily engaged in system enhancements – but let me assure you, they're not.

This life-cycle view of IT systems – i.e., that they are continually probed and modified, in a word maintained, during years of use – contrasts with the notion of greenfield programming described in the first part of this book. Most programmers are not constructing a new program from scratch.

In this second part, we have shown how much worse all of the programming problems are if the programmer is not working on his or her own brainchild – well-structured, and exhaustively and accurately documented. Imagine having to get to grips with someone else's tangled heap of instructions totally devoid of supporting *documentation*, or worse, littered with out-of-date misleading *documentation*. Worst of all, suppose the object of attention is an ancient program that bears the innumerable (but superficially invisible) scars of many earlier *maintenance* operations that it has undergone at the hands of a multitude of different programmers none of whom left any explanatory *documentation* and all of whom are now untraceable!

This new, and more accurate, view of the role of programs and programming activity in society does not undermine the earlier arguments about the difficulties presented by this technology. Quite the contrary, it gives them more force. All of the problems discussed in the earlier chapters still exist. The only change is that they've increased in severity.

To return to the swing system: Fig. 18.1 illustrates a number of alternative maintenance actions to fix the *bug*: seat not level. Again we have to consider why this is so absurd for a swing, yet commonplace when dealing with large IT systems. A major point of difference is that the essential functions of a swing are relatively simple, and the degree to which any particular swing will exhibit these functions is, to a good approximation, quite evident from a superficial visual inspection – with programs this is definitely not the case. Recall the good, the bad and the ugly – they all look disconcertingly similar. They are all just long lists of correct programming-language instructions.

Even with a new product, the software vendor is free to rush it out with known imperfections, and then issue fixes and patches free of charge. Although there are limits as has been cynically observed:

> Even Microsoft couldn't build a successful marketing campaign around the slogan: *Unlike the 50 million copies we've already sold you, this version actually works*.[4]

We know that changes tend to increase the complexity of an IT-system, and that changes designed to remove an error are possibly going to introduce an equally bad or worse one.[5] So there comes a point in the life of every large software system when those in the know advise: "leave well enough alone." Instead of trying to remove the known errors, you just steer clear of them when using the software or

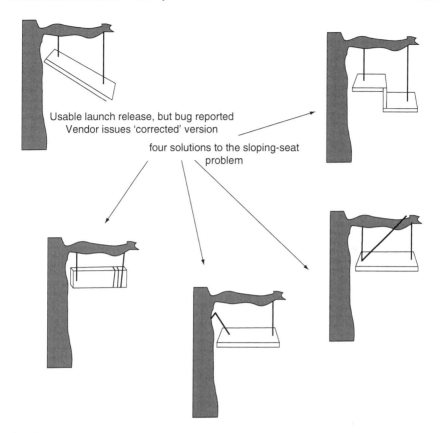

Usable launch release, but bug reported
Vendor issues 'corrected' version

four solutions to the sloping-seat
problem

Fig. 18.1 Creative maintenance on the swing system

ignore their results when they cannot be avoided. A known error, you may remember, is typically not the real villain in this story.

"A fundamental problem with program *maintenance* is that fixing a defect has a substantial (20–50 percent) chance of introducing another. So the whole process is two steps forward and one step back."[6] This doesn't seem too disastrous. It is still a process of overall improvement. But successive changes to large software systems tend to steadily increase the complexity of the system. Before long "the fixing ceases to gain any ground. Each forward step is matched by a backward one."[6]

Much of the foregoing might be interpreted as laying the blame for the current lamentable state of IT systems on the youth and exuberance of the technology itself. It is moving fast, and so it is inevitable that it is out of step with many of the more ponderous aspects of society. It will settle, then societal infrastructure (such as law, education, attendant technologies, etc.) lumbering along will eventually catch up, and all will be right with the world. Or will it?

Take education: most human adults, which includes the captains of industry and their senior managers, did not grow up within a computer culture. So how can they be expected to properly choose, specify, accept and reject the myriad IT systems that now impinge on their professional activities? Surprisingly few of the ever-growing army of software system developers, software engineers, etc. has been properly trained in their craft. Most have adopted it in recent years; many are ex-whiz-kids who have been forced into gainful employment. What reason have we got for expecting the highest levels of craftsmanship in their software creations? Many of the trainers are simply passing on practical knowledge that they have picked up on the fly. Even the professional educationalists have seen what they teach change beyond all recognition in the last few decades.

So we are right to expect that as the technology settles and ceases to keep rushing forward with its current unseemly haste, certain problems will disappear or certainly lessen in severity. But it is hard to see the fundamental problems altering very much.

The nature of education is necessarily not much like the real world experience. Small programs (the examples used for educational purposes) and very large programs (the ancient conglomerations of coded instructions that litter the real world) are not just different in size. They are entirely different sorts of objects. Educational programmes are necessarily limited to one sort, and the world is packed with the other. Yet again, the gulf between small and large is all too apparent (and not easily bridged).

Should we let IT systems constrain our lives? Sometimes it's part of the price we pay for the general benefit of living within a modern technological society. We make all sorts of sacrifices and accept all manner of constraints. We have no choice. It's either knuckle under or opt out, and this latter option is becoming increasingly less possible.

The ultimate question then, one that merits our full consideration, is: what role should we permit computer technology to assume in our society? Not passive acceptance of whatever we're told that's for sure. But what can a non-specialist do in the face of the programmed *fait accompli*? "I'm sorry, but the computer won't accept/permit that."

Again we face a range of possibilities: from the *Star Wars* initiative of Ronald Reagan, which caused leading software experts to protest that an IT system could never be trusted with what was being proposed, to IT systems that unnecessarily impose minor aggravations on our daily lives.

As I confessed right at the outset: I can tell you a great deal more about the problems that arise with modern computer technology than about the solutions to these problems. The problems have now had full exposure, and we must now ask "what's being done about it?" Although no complete and comprehensive solutions are yet available, we are not entirely clueless.

The next section explores a variety of potential technical solutions. The question of what we might call social solutions – i.e. solutions founded on changes in social response to this technology – is not only more tricky, but also heavily dependent upon prerequisite changes in the technology itself.

For example, if we can push the mathematician's dream through to completion then we shall be dealing with software systems that can and should be verified correct. In which case all understanding and acceptance can be focused on the *specification* of the problem, because the program will be a guaranteed correct implementation of it. If, on the other hand, the mathematician's challenge peters out, trampled perhaps by the heavy-duty boots of the practising software engineer, the labourer at the code face, as it were, then attention is likely to be fixed on the working system, the engineered artefact and its success in fulfilling the day-to-day demands on its services irrespective of what the original specification might have stipulated.

However, given the excessively sluggish nature of movement to new IT systems – reluctance based on well-founded fear and solid economic arguments – we cannot realistically expect any significant changes in the foreseeable future.

So, where are we?

- IT systems have a *life-cycle* in which *maintenance* is the dominant activity.
- *Maintaining* (i.e. extending and debugging) an IT system that you did not develop exacerbates all of the IT-system problems, and _is_ the major programming effort.
- At a certain point in IT-system complexity, further *debugging* is a self-defeating exercise.
- We all live within a mesh of IT systems: some offer conveniences that we can either accept or reject, others do not give us a choice.
- The outputs of an IT system may be viewed as a useful guide to be accepted cautiously, or as the ultimate truth to be accepted blindly; the reality of all IT systems will lie somewhere in between these two extremes.
- IT systems are not extended or amended lightly, because change is so dangerous; hence, we tend to 'work around' their failings.
- Many IT systems improve our lives.
- Some IT systems have negative impacts, all the way from minor aggravation to life threatening.
- There are no easy answers (as far as we know). So for IT systems in *safety-critical* roles where failures have the potential to cause deaths and/or disasters, the best advice is too lessen the criticality of their roles and to limit expectation of what they can deliver.

There are, however, some radically novel possibilities. In truth, nothing that promises wholesale replacement of the brittle, yet so easily mutable, technology we currently use, but possible options to be used on certain components of IT systems. It's plasters and patches at best.

Endnotes

1. Even this is to overstate the scope of proof in its technical sense: theorems are the certificates of mathematical proof, and yet many a theorem has been, and always will be, shown to be invalid after years of acceptance as a proof. So even this strongest manifestation of the notion of proof is ultimately a matter of faith: faith that a proof is valid because many other mathematicians accept that it is; or faith that every step in the theorem is a valid one as claimed.

2. See next note for full details of article which states that the basic message in "The widely used document of the Radio Technical Commission for Aeronautics, RTCA/DO-178A ... is that designers must take a disciplined approach to software ... That is, the best assurance of reliability is to verify that utmost care was used in the design" (p. 66).

3. Bev Littlewood and Lorenzo Strigini, leading researchers in the quest for formal assessment of IT-system reliability at London's City University, published these views in their article "The Risks of Software" in *Scientific American* (vol. 267, no. 5, pp. 62–75, November 1992). They present a comprehensive, yet accessible, guide to the challenge and the problems of quantifying software-failure risks. Their answer for safety-critical IT systems is to make the role of such software "not too critical" or "to accept the current limitations of software and live with more modest overall system safety."

4. Another quotation provided by David Lubar on page 48 of his compendium *It's Not a Bug: It's a Feature* (Addison–Wesley, 1995). He is quoting "Paul Bonner, reviewing Windows 4.0, or Chicago, or Windows 95, or whatever it's called this week, 1994."

5. This phenomenon, as we have seen earlier, appears to be a universal of programming; recall the Second Law of Program Evolution:

   The entropy of a system increases with time unless specific work is executed in order to maintain or reduce it.

which can be paraphrased as:

   IT systems become more chaotic every time they are changed unless the changes are introduced with great care and wisdom.

   Given that it is an empirical fact that IT systems always become less maintainable over time, we must assume that either this law is too optimistic, or there is never enough care and wisdom put into the changes. Most likely, Murphy wasn't the only law-making optimist. Our knowledge of the fragile technology and the excessive demands for detailed understanding occasioned by a large IT system, both further exacerbated in the maintenance context (rather than initial development), give weight to the view that this Law needs toughening.

   The source is M.M. Lehman and L.A. Belady in a book entitled *Program Evolution* (Academic Press, 1985). This information is clearly not new, but perhaps still the best we have. The difficulty of collecting empirical evidence about IT systems is that the IT systems themselves have to be realistically large ones, and the number surveyed must also be large enough to give the results some validity. In depth analysis of the long-term behaviour of a large number of large IT systems is a very demanding exercise.

6. Once more, the quotation is from an entertaining series of essays on large-scale software development, entitled *The Mythical Man-Month* (Addison–Wesley, 1975, with valuable additions, 1995) by F.P. Brooks, the project manager working for IBM on one of the largest software systems constructed at the time.

Part III
Pieces of Resistance

I've now spent long enough explaining both the origins and the manifestations of the problems that must be faced when dealing with modern computer technology. We've seen all the special pleading to support my claims that this technology is something quite new and different from anything that has preceded it. It therefore presents us with problems that science, technology and society as a whole have never had to face previously – the primary one being that it carries us effortlessly and inexorably into realms of unmanageable complexity and tempts us with a promise of perfection that cannot be kept.

We the technologists know far more about the nature of these problems (although there is a lack of fundamental agreement about their exact nature, as I'm sure you now realise) than we do about the solutions. This introduction is meant to be an early warning that I cannot provide solutions in anything like the depth in which I presented the problems. On reflection, however, I wonder if this apologia is necessary: for how could it be otherwise? If we knew the solutions then we wouldn't have the problems, would we? Problems cease to be problems when solutions are found.

What I shall do in this section of the book is to outline and explain a number of different routes to what may eventually prove to be solutions, or partial solutions, or maybe just patches for the major problems posed by computer technology. I shall start out with a selection of enhancements to the conventional technology. I shall then indulge in a speculative tour of a couple of possible solutions that lie outside conventional technology. These far-flung possibilities deny pride of place to the (seemingly) fundamental notion of discrete programming – the rock upon which the conventional technology is built (or founders – as I've argued). So, from tinkering with the status quo, we shall travel to new and perhaps fertile ground for the future development of computer technology, although the cynic might retort that I am simply swapping one set of problems for another – only time will tell.

Chapter 19
Help from Within

if only computers could tell you their troubles

*On 28th March 1979, just after 4 pm, an alarm went off in the
nuclear power station at Three Mile Island, Pennsylvania in
the USA. This was no real cause for concern. There are so
many checks and consequent alarms built into such a system
that minor faults trigger alarms regularly. However, this time it
soon became apparent that this was not a minor fault. A relief
valve to facilitate extra cooling of the uranium core had stuck.
Almost immediately the core began to overheat threatening a
nuclear explosion.*

*After days of frantic activity a nuclear catastrophe was
averted – just. But why did a problem almost become a
disaster? "The major factor that turned this incident into a
serious accident was inappropriate operator action" which
was, as President Carter's Commission further reported, due to
one thing "confusion."*

*An operator reported: "I noticed that we had every alarm,
just about every alarm, on panel 15."*

*Another said: "alarms were going off; pumps were being
started and stopped; valves were being cycled ... I was
thoroughly not able to follow what was going on."*

*An investigative committee subsequently reported: "the
operator was bombarded with displays, warning lights, print-
outs and so on to the point where detection of any error condition
and the assessment of the right action to correct the condition
was impossible."[1]*

This retrospective on the near nuclear disaster at Three Mile Island does not blame
unprepared or untrained operators, nor technical inadequacies of the power station,
nor a lack of checks and safety measures built into the system. The problem, roughly
put, was <u>too</u> <u>many</u> checks and consequent alarms. More precisely, the problem was
that the organization of alarms and warnings was poorly human-engineered.

If every safety check imaginable is built in and associated with a warning light
or an alarm, this will provide a valuable early warning for every minor fault as it
occurs. But once the system runs into a real problem situation every alarm and
warning light is triggered to report its own particular little part of the problem. The

D. Partridge, *The Seductive Computer: Why IT Systems Always Fail*,
DOI 10.1007/978-1-84996-498-2_19, © Springer-Verlag London Limited 2011

operator is then faced with an uncoordinated cacophony of light and sound – and the wood is totally lost among the trees – a veritable *son et lumière* to accompany the impending disaster.

What is needed is a summary explanation of what the problem really is, and ideally an explanation from the computer system automatically generated by the computer. A computer that can tell you what is wrong with itself is not pure science fiction. After all, many complex machines nowadays will do this. The modern car will tell you that "the door is ajar" when you've not closed it properly, or that "your seat belt is unfastened" if you are resistant to buckling up.

If we take a less literal interpretation of "tell", then indicator and warning lights are commonplace. In this sense all cars will tell you when they' rerunning out of fuel, etc. So can we alleviate some of the problems that arise in modern computer technology by getting the computer to monitor its own functioning and tell us about any problems it finds? The short answer is "we can, and we do", but the best answer is not this simple.

If you cast your mind back to the beginnings of this book, you might recall that one of the crucial attractions of programming was its open-endedness – everything is possible, well almost. So while we can clearly build checks into a computer program and trigger warning messages when problems are detected (just like the red, warning lights on most car dashboards), the smart programmer should be able to do more than this. And indeed he can.

The rise of so-called *expert systems* or *knowledge-based systems* in the closing decades of the last millennium has, as one of the many side effects, spun off a neat and powerful mechanism for self-explanation in computer software. As I stated earlier, in this book I'm trying hard to avoid dragging in that subfield of modern computer technology known evocatively as Artificial Intelligence, or AI. I am studiously avoiding this body of work, not because it is worthless or unimportant, but simply because it is unnecessary and will cloud the essential issues. However, at this point there is no alternative but to dip into it briefly. This I shall do with a minimum of fuss.

Put simply, _expert-system technology (EST)_ endeavours to build computer systems that mimic, and hence reproduce, the abilities of human experts – e.g., the expertise behind diagnosing tumours from X-ray plates and other patient data. EST is founded on a couple of easy-to-grasp insights. The ones that are of immediate concern to us involve the basic mechanism for reproducing human expertise within a computer system. A so-called _knowledge-based_ system is a program that separates the factual information from the control mechanism that uses it to derive diagnoses, predictions, analyses, etc. What does this mean?

Consider a program for diagnosing faults in a car engine. The factual component, the *knowledge base*, is a collection of facts and rules that are valid for car-engine fault diagnosis. For example, we might have the following *rules*:

Rule 1: IF the engine turns over slowly AND the lights are dim
          THEN the battery is flat
Rule 2: IF the battery is flat AND the battery is >3 years old
          THEN have a battery check

*Rule 3: IF the battery is flat AND the battery is not >3 years old
            THEN check charging circuit*

These rules are the beginnings of a *knowledge base* that captures the factual information needed to support a mechanism of car-engine fault diagnosis.

The addition of some specific simple *facts* about a particular engine, such as:

Fact 1: The car won't start.
Fact 2: The engine turns over slowly.

will permit our embryonic car-engine-fault-diagnosis expert system to begin reasoning about the particular car that provided our two simple facts.

Fact 1 tells the system that there is a fault to be diagnosed. Then as Fact 2 is part of the condition (i.e. the IF-part) of Rule 1, it will begin reasoning from this rule. However, before it can draw a conclusion using Rule 1, it must find out if the other part of the condition is also true – i.e. it must determine if the lights are dim. As there is no fact in the knowledge base pertaining to the dimness of the lights, it generates the following question for the system user:

Are the lights dim?

Let's suppose that the user (perhaps mechanic or concerned owner) checks the car's lights and finds that they are indeed lacking in brightness. So he (or she) answers the question positively. The user has thus provided a useful fact:

Fact 3: The lights are dim.

At this point the expert system knows that the complete condition to Rule 1 is true, hence it can determine that the conclusion (the THEN-part) is also true. So the system has reasoned that the car's battery is flat. This new, derived fact (Fact 4, say) happens to be part of the condition for both Rule 2 and Rule 3. So focusing on Rule 2 (as it happens to be encountered first in the knowledge base), it will attempt to complete its knowledge of the condition by asking:

Is the battery more than 3 years old?

Let's assume that the answer is again positive (and the system stores this as Fact 5). The system will then be able to conclude that the battery ought to be checked (Fact 6). This diagnosis can be presented to the fretting owner or the nonplussed mechanic, as the case may be.

At this juncture in the automated reasoning process, the computer has increased its initial list of two facts to six, they are:

Fact 1: The car won't start. (given initially)
Fact 2: The engine turns over slowly. (given initially)
Fact 3: The lights are dim. (user provided)
Fact 4: The battery is flat. (deduced)
Fact 5: The battery is greater than 3 years old. (user provided)
Fact 6: The battery should be checked. (deduced)

Following each fact listed, I've noted its provenance, which, as you will soon see, is also a useful thing for the computer to do. It facilitates the automatic generation of informative explanations.

The important point for us is that the system could reason with facts and rules to obtain new facts and finally to generate a diagnosis of the problem.

So that's the *knowledge base*: a collection of relevant information composed of *rules* and *facts*. So where's the separate control mechanism that I mentioned earlier? It was buried in my narrative leading you through from rules and facts to conclusions. Laid bare, the control mechanism combines rules and facts to generate further facts which can then be combined with other rules, and so it can go on. This is a mechanism of *logical inference* (see examples and discussion in Chapter 8); it permits the system to <u>infer</u> new facts from known facts and rules. Hence this separate control mechanism is sometimes called an <u>*inference engine*</u>.

After that whistle-stop tour of expert systems technology we are sufficiently grounded in this emergent technology to appreciate why it has opened up a window on the possibility of software systems explaining their own actions.

Suppose that during the course of the above-described reasoning sequence, the user, being awkward, declines to answer the system's question about the age of the car battery. Instead of responding simply "yes" or "no", the user asks "Why do you want to know this?"

On reaching this situation a traditional software system is likely to either crash, or give up gracefully, or re-ask its original question having issued a sharp rebuke to the user along the lines of "pay attention and answer only 'yes' or 'no'". An expert system is admirably placed to deal intelligently and sympathetically with such quizzical specimens of humanity. The system can display the rule that it is currently focused on together what it already knows about the condition part, and easily frame a well-constructed explanation of why it asked that particular question at that particular point in the diagnosis. Such an explanation might be:

Given the rule, Rule 2, that:
      IF the battery is flat
      AND the battery is >3 years old
      THEN have a battery check
together with the known fact, Fact 4, that:
      the battery is flat
if it can also be determined that:
      the battery is more than 3 years old
then it will be possible to conclude that:
      the battery ought to be checked

This is, I think, a reasonable explanation of why the system asked the question that it did ask. However, if our recalcitrant user is not satisfied with this explanation, the following further question to the system might be forthcoming:

"How do you know Fact 4 is true?"

Once more the well-engineered expert system can field this query with ease, and generate an explanation of its reasoning. In this particular case it might respond:

Given the rule, Rule 1, that:
>   IF the engine turns over slowly
>   AND the lights are dim
>   THEN the battery is flat

together with the known fact, Fact 2, that:
>   the engine turns over slowly (a given initial fact)

and the known fact, Fact 3, that:
>   the lights are dim (you told me this)

it was concluded, Fact 4, that:
>   the battery is flat

And so it can go on. The user can ask any number of "how" and "why" queries and a competent expert system can automatically generate detailed answers, in effect, good explanations of how it inferred some fact and why it is asking a particular question.

There is, of course, more to the general notion of explanation than this, but this is a good start. It is one of the strengths of *expert systems technology* that it can so easily support this sort of self-explanatory behaviour. The necessary underlying mechanism – *knowledge base* and *inference engine* – can be applied to thoroughly conventional software systems. There is no necessity that we have an AI problem before we can use this handy means of problem solution.

In a book called *The Creative Computer* the authors' argument occasionally parallels some of the main lines of discussion in this book – e.g. that technological progress has led to a state of unmanageable complexity, and that the major problem facing technologists is not extending their technology but making its products comprehensible. I mention this book here because, as you will see, the authors use EST as the major platform for their proposed "escape from complexity pollution."[2]

In *The Creative Computer*, Michie and Johnston take an unusual tack on the impacts of computer technology on society. They sketch out a worrying picture of ever increasing technological complexity, peppering the landscape with salient cameos of chaotic incidents: the Three Mile Island accident, a succession of spurious nuclear attack alerts, etc. All induced, according to them, by a failure to manage the complexities of technological advances. "The moral of these stories is the same:" they write, "that as technological systems get more complicated, they become more and more difficult to understand and therefore to control. This applies especially to computing systems, which have to be complex even to do the simplest things. As we strive to give them power to handle substantial tasks from the real world, we increase their complexity to a level outside the ability of a human or even teams of humans fully to grasp" (p. 60).

Clearly, on reading this you could be forgiven for imagining that I have been flogging the very same horse that these authors rode to death some years previously. But I'm not, although there is definitely a similar general motivation behind their ideas and mine. I have presented a novel and detailed portrayal of the precise nature of this complexity problem. My belief is that a general appreciation at a level of fine detail is a necessary prerequisite for understanding the *IT-system crisis*; and a necessary prelude to combating its worst manifestations. I also maintain that

Michie's and Johnston's proposed solution is nothing like a complete solution, but it just might be some help.

Why does EST fail to provide the solution to the *IT-system crisis*? Firstly, it contains some unadvertised glitches which may or may not scupper it, in the long term. Secondly, there are a number of other equally encouraging possible routes to easing the *IT-system crisis*, and I shall lay them before you. But back to the current possibility: programs that can explain themselves.

Michie and Johnston make the point that technological advances tend to be accompanied by increases in inscrutability of the systems that result. Hitherto the prime goals of the technologist have been maximum power and efficiency at minimum cost. A reassessment of the goals is needed to bring human comprehensibility (of the desired system) up to a position of much higher importance than it is customarily accorded. Such a re-prioritization of design constraints should lead to the products of technological advance operating in "the human window" (to use Michie's and Johnston's term). The human window is that region of technological possibilities where processing capability and the memory demands used are similar to those possessed by humans. It contrasts with both fast, intensive processing computation, and computation founded on perfect retrieval of information from a vast store. There is a region of balance between these two extremes, which are often complementary alternatives, that humans can manage conceptually, and so can understand; this is the human window.

Automation that is aimed at the human window they call "soft automation", and this is increasingly needed, they claim. "The greatest social urgency attaches not to extending automatic processes but to *humanising* them" (p. 72, authors' emphasis).

The last point of theirs that I want to mention ties *EST* in with this aim for soft automation. "Rule-based expert systems ... are specifically designed to operate with human concepts, both accepting them from the domain specialist and displaying them to the user as explanations. These provide a start, but much research still needs to be done on the technology of the conceptual interface" (p. 72). In this chapter, we have seen exactly how this technology can support a general self-explanation capability, i.e., not one based on situation-specific pre-coded (and therefore, foreseen) explanations.

So what are the problems with this neat idea? To begin with, there is more to explaining the workings of a complex system than trotting out IF-THEN rules together with associated facts. Just like programs themselves, which look deceptively easy in the small, a few IT-THEN rules can look like a good explanation. But once faced by a large collection of IF-THEN rules explanatory force evaporates. Complex phenomena become even more complex when re-written in terms of simple independent elements, such as IF-THEN rules – more complex structure is required within the explanation mechanism or else the 'explanation' gets buried (and effectively lost) in an unstructured mass of detail.

What constitutes a good explanation will depend upon many contextual factors, such as: who wants the explanation; what they already know about the system; and what it is they now want to know. There is scope for tailoring the expert-system self-explanation facility to generate explanations that are sensitive to these contextual constraints (remember everything is possible for the programmer). Indeed, some crude examples of customized self-explanation do exist: different explanations for users who are classified as novices rather than experts with respect to the system that's doing the explaining, for example. But any attempt to produce sophisticated and detailed customizing will launch this self-help project deep into the uncharted wastes of AI. We will not follow it there, but we will note, as we draw back from the brink, that all of the conventional problems of complexity and incomprehensible programs exist in the twilight zone of AI, only there they tend to be worse.

This observation brings me on to what I consider to be the major stumbling block for self-explanation as a means for improving human comprehension of programs: the self-explanation facility is just another piece of program. It is thus subject to exactly the same problems as any other program: do we really know how any given explanation is being generated? Can we really be sure that there is no hidden error in the explanation-generation instructions? And so on. An automatically generated explanation is simply a piece of program output, just like the output it's purportedly explaining. Why should we be any more confident of our ability to correctly program explanation generation than of our aptitude to get other activities of a program working just right? The short answer is: we shouldn't.

It is true that a simple logic-based explanation generator might be a simpler system than the one it is purporting to explain, and so it is reasonable to assume that we ought to be able to build high confidence in its correctness (maybe even formally verify correctness). Set against this positive case, we might note that:

1. A mechanism founded only on pure formal logic is unlikely to be satisfactory (e.g. how to accommodate certainties that fall short of absolute truth – i.e., most, if not all, empirical facts).
2. A large set of simple explanatory elements soon loses its explanatory power.

So what are the salient points of this chapter?

- A general mechanism for self-explanation was a spin-off of _Expert Systems Technology (EST)_ which attempted to mechanise human expertise using IT systems composed of a _knowledge base_ (a _database_ of _rules_ and _facts_) and an _inference engine_ (that deduces further information from user input and the _knowledge base_).
- It is persuasive in the small, but fails in the large.
- Just as with programs, the clarity of small context-free elements (program instructions or IF-THEN rules) is quickly lost when the system, or the purported explanation of the system, grows to be a large collection of these elements.
- The simplest explanation of a complex system may be complex (although hopefully less complex).

- Comprehensibility of complex explanations is probably best achieved (insofar as it can be achieved at all) through a combination of sophisticated structure and simple elements; it cannot be achieved through an unstructured mass of simple elements.
- A putative solution that is programmed, like self-explanation, is subject to all the same difficulties as the IT system it claims to explain.

Endnotes

1. This small example is taken from Michie's and Johnston's book (see next note) which provides far more detail on this near-disaster together with a further selection of cautionary real-life tales all aimed at emphasizing the information-management problem engendered by modern computer technology.
2. *The Creative Computer* (Penguin, 1984) by Donald Michie and Rory Johnston (the first pioneer of British AI, and a science journalist, respectively) is an interesting and readable, upbeat account of the possibilities for advances in Artificial Intelligence (AI) rescuing humanity from the unmanageable complexity of the products of technological progress – e.g. nuclear power stations. Their concluding remarks tell us that, contrary to popular opinion, AI is not about making "super-clever Daleks, unfathomable to man", its aim is "making machines *more* fathomable and *more* under the control of human beings, not less" (p. 214, authors' emphasis).

    I argue for much the same general dangers in modern computer technology (although not for precisely the same reasons). The current chapter echoes Michie's and Johnston's proposed response, but with much less enthusiasm for computer-generated explanations being a panacea.

Chapter 20
A Moderately Stupid Assistant

Dialogue with a thoroughly stupid assistant[1]

Human:	*Give me the balance of my current account please.*
Computer:	*THE BALANCE IS £120*
Human:	*What about my other account?*
Computer:	*I'M SORRY, I DON'T UNDERSTAND THE WORD "ABOUT"*
Human:	*Sorry, I didn't phrase it well.*
Computer:	*I'M SORRY, I DON'T UNDERSTAND THE WORD "SORRY"*

Beware of computers masquerading as humans. The apparent understanding may be illusory, although some small steps in this direction can be beneficial. Even if we can't be sure that a computer will reliably explain its actions, perhaps it can be induced to help out in other less dramatic ways.

Management of complexity is the essence of the challenge facing the computer programmer, and we know that the simplest of programs can generate more complexity than even the best of us can manage. We also know that, while the happy hacker may be generating complexity at a prodigious rate, good programming practice can slow the inexorable growth of complexity.

One of the strictures of programming science is: avoid complexity rather than try to manage it. While this is a laudable goal, it does seem to be denying the point that non-trivial programs working in real-world applications will be very complex objects however well they are designed and constructed. By all means exploit the science to the full in order to minimize complexity. However, ultimately there is nothing else for it but to tackle the problem of complexity management.

One obvious source of help is immediately to hand – the computer. Why not set up the computer to function as an assistant, an assistant that will reduce the effective complexity of the programming task? For reasons that will become apparent soon, what we might aim for here, to use Winograd's phrase, is the computer as "a moderately stupid assistant".[2]

A large part of the overwhelming complexity of programming hinges on the requirement to keep in mind the precise details of many objects, e.g. the *storage-box* labels used and what exactly you used each one for. This is exactly what

D. Partridge, *The Seductive Computer: Why IT Systems Always Fail*,
DOI 10.1007/978-1-84996-498-2_20, © Springer-Verlag London Limited 2011

computers are very good at, and people are not. We may well have the edge on computers as far as intelligent reasoning goes, but we can't come near their ability to store and recall precise details of vast amounts of information. Clearly, the computer is just what's wanted for managing some of the complexity of the programming task.

Recall our earlier principles underpinning *well-structured* programs: *modularisation*, *encapsulation* and *scope* localization. Consequently, in large programs there is a demand for large numbers of *storage-box* labels and *subprogram* names. You may also recall that one way to reduce overall complexity when breaking a large computation up into many small *subprogram* modules is to restrict the *scope* of each *storage-box* label as far as possible – e.g., the value held in a given box labelled, say, "NUM" is only changed by a minimum of *subprogram*s. This is a good idea because if the box labelled "NUM" appears to be holding a wrong value this restrictive practice limits the number of places in the program where we need search for the instruction that is causing the trouble. However, such a box must also be accessible to any *subprogram* that may need to change its value. So in general, a *storage box* is accessible to some subset of all the *subprogram*s that constitute the complete program.

This range of accessibility, you might recall (when the *scope* principle was first introduced in Chapter 5), is known as the *scope* of a *storage-box* label. If something is amiss with this *storage box*, or if we wish to modify its use within the program, then we need only concern ourselves with the *subprogram*s in its *scope* – this is a strategy for reducing the complexity of the final program.

It is easy to appreciate that with many labels and many variations in their individual *scopes* there is a lot of detailed, but quite straightforward, information in just this aspect of a large program. It is also precisely the sort of information that the computer could automatically store away each time the programmer makes a decision about the *scope* of a box label. Subsequently, when the programmer is racking his brain trying to remember if, say, box labelled "XY" can be changed by any *subprogram*s other than SUBPROGRAM ABC, all that need be done is to ask the computer this simple question. It will flash back the list of relevant *subprogram*s, and so focus the programmer's attention quickly and accurately, and yet relieve him of this memory burden.

This sort of help may seem like a pretty trivial addition to the programmer's arsenal of helpful tools, hardly an enhancement at all. It turns out, however, that very many such simple answers are needed whenever the programmer is attempting to alter or just understand a non-trivial program.

Many of the errors in both alteration and understanding of IT systems can be traced to the non-realization, or simple forgetting, of just one such tiny feature of a program. Some such errors are quickly picked up and put right, others may lay dormant for years until an unusual combination of input information (or change in the context) triggers a major system crash, much to everyone's surprise. Even the former, less insidious errors cause considerable frustration and a significant decrease in programmer productivity. By freeing the programmer from the need to remember a myriad of such trivial detail, he can concentrate on the non-computer-manageable aspects of programming. The resultant program will be better, and it will be produced more quickly.

One question that might be agitating for recognition at the back of the reader's mind is: what actually does this information storage and retrieval? The answer is: it is another program that is resident within the computer and is set up to monitor the programmer's program-writing activity. It runs unobtrusively in the background while the programmer gets on with the task of programming in the foreground, as it were. The details of how the computer can cope with several different programs at once need not concern us, but rest assured it can, and quite easily too.

'What *subprogram*s can change the value in *storage box* "F6"?', we might ask when contemplating changing the use of this box in the program, or when trying to track down an error that might be associated with a surprising value found in this box. Our moderately stupid assistant can flash back the correct list of *subprogram*s instantaneously. Without such assistance the programmer has no alternative but wrack his brains in an attempt to dredge up this once-known mote of information, or to trawl through the list of 10,000 instructions looking for occurrences of the box label "F6" – neither strategy is likely to yield a precisely correct answer. This sort of assistance can be called the 'super-secretary' role, although this is to over-glorify it considerably or, conversely, to undervalue the functions of a good secretary.

Far from being a moderately stupid assistant, what I have been portraying so far looks more like a pretty dumb assistant: ask simple questions and a simple answer is forthcoming. There is clearly more to the story. There are more ambitious tasks that the computerized assistant might undertake. In addition, potentially useful information might be volunteered to the programmer, rather than simply supplied on request. At this point we begin to move into possible future worlds instead of sticking with automated assistance than is, or can be, readily available today.

Once we contemplate more sophisticated help from the computer we are in largely unknown territory. If we want to be able to ask, 'What *subprogram*s are likely to put very large values in box F6?', then a good answer can only be based on what I might term an 'understanding' of the nature of the individual computations that generate values to be stored in box F6. We are asking for 'best guess' information which could be very useful but cannot be computed by means of a simple, and totally reliable, storage-and-retrieval process. This doesn't mean that we can never expect this level of assistance. It just means that it will not be available soon.

The idea of volunteered information also takes us into the realms of the somewhat unknown, or at least an area where what exactly we should aim for is highly debatable. Imagine the programmer merrily typing in instructions and the computer suddenly flashes up a message: ERROR IN LAST INSTRUCTION. This could be a very handy interruption (particularly if the warning includes specific information about the source of the error). The programmer can then correct the erroneous instruction and return to his programming comforted by the knowledge that the computer, which has a faultless appreciation of the instructions it will accept, is keeping its eagle eye on his every instruction-entering act.

This is all well and good; any interruption of this nature is probably to be welcomed. But what if the interruption is not pointing out a clear-cut error? Suppose the computer is offering the programmer a warning about something dubious (rather than downright wrong) that has just been entered? Well, like most warnings it might be important, timely and thus most welcome, but it might be misconceived by the computer in which case the programmer has every right to be annoyed. Repeated non-useful interruptions will quickly transform the helpful assistant into an unhelpful nuisance. So the tendency is not to aim too high – the simpler the information the more easily it can be guaranteed to be correct and appropriate – and to prefer 'on demand' help rather than spontaneously offered assistance.

Hence 'moderately stupid', rather than 'intelligent' is used to characterize the type of computer assistance to be expected. Intelligence is the role of the programmer, and in the absence of anything approaching real intelligence in computers it is advisable to steer clear of anything aimed above moderate stupidity. A poor attempt to be smart is worse than no attempt at all. A little AI can be a dangerous thing, especially in an IT system.

There is a further role that a supportive computer system can fill. It is that of a filter – the computer can monitor and filter out bad practice. The performance of such a role by the computer may again be manifest in interruptions, warnings and suggestions to the busy programmer.

A collection of such assistance sub-systems built into a computer system is sometimes called a _programming support environment_. A well-engineered environment can transform the productivity of the human programmer in terms of both quality and quantity of his IT-system development.

"Power tools for programmers" has long been a slogan of supporters of this initiative.[3] This support environment is a toolbox of programs that the IT-system developer (or maintainer) can choose to use to help him with his task.

Consider the analogy of constructing programs with, say, constructing car bodies: at one end of the spectrum of possibilities the competent engineer may have nuts, bolts, a drill, saw, a spanner set, and a lot of sheet metal at his disposal, but at the other end (in a commercial production-line environment) he will have an array of complex support machinery such as metal cutters and presses, and sophisticated machining tools. What are the trade-offs here?

Clearly, the engineer with the bare, primitive tool set will take much longer to make a car body than his counterpart working within a production-line support environment. On the other hand, it will take much more time and money to set up the production line than to collect a basic tool set, but the payback is expected when a large number of car bodies must be produced rather than just one. In addition, the cottage-industry approach will produce a series of unique car bodies, while the production line will turn out clone after clone.

Returning to the problems of IT-system construction, much the same observations apply. The big difference is that a _programming support environment_ is composed not of hulking great machines but of other programs all of which will be packed unobtrusively within the computer. So, to the untrained eye there will be little difference between the most primitive cottage-industry IT-system production (the hacker with the bare minimum: a _programming language_ and an _editor_), and the most sophisticated *programming support environment* (the disciplined programmer working with an array of high-tech programming-support facilities).

The casual observer will see both persons simply sitting in front of a visual-display screen and tapping away at the keyboard. But just as the production-line work has little in common with the hand-crafted artefact, so the two programmers are in reality functioning in totally different worlds, and their products will reflect this difference.

One further difference between our two car-body engineers, and one that is often seen as supportive of the cottage-industry approach, resides in an appreciation of the unique. A world full of identical objects does seem to be less attractive than one packed with individualized variety. To my mind, this argument certainly has some merit when applied to cars, houses, furniture, etc., but not when applied to computer software. Computer programs are never built for aesthetic appreciation, after all there's nothing much to see.[4] They just cause computers do things.

So one further, somewhat special, and very important, advantage of *programming support environments* is that they can be used to <u>impose</u> <u>constraints</u> on the programmer. Any environment will do this. The sophisticated machinery on a car-body production line makes all sorts of operations quick and easy, but it also makes a lot of conceivable operations quite impossible without abandoning the machinery and reverting back to more primitive tools. And so it is also with *programming support environments*.

The beauty of this is that the programming support tools can be designed to minimize bad practice. The well-designed *support environment* will force the programmer to work according to the accepted standards of good program design and development; it will enforce a discipline of programming, and so permit only the production of *well-structured* programs. The happy hacker should find his natural inclinations leading him nowhere; it's either shape up or ship out.

For example, a *programming support environment* designed to thwart the foolhardy programmer could refuse to accept speculative changes in the IT system under development. It could, for example, insist on accompanying, or prior, justification – e.g. it will accept instruction changes only if they are derived from changes in some abstract design structure that is also stored within the computer. But notice that even this little idea has jumped once more from the easily doable into the realms of *hopeware*.[5]

A less contentious function of the *support environment* might be to enforce COMMENTing as described in the early programming chapters – say one COMMENT with every three program instructions. Such a restriction is easy to enforce: the support environment software can easily count COMMENTs and non-COMMENTs. However, the wily programmer, who cannot be fagged to keep COMMENTing his code, will just throw in meaningless COMMENTs whenever a COMMENT is demanded by the support environment (or even program a patch that generates random COMMENTs in the ratio demanded). So, to properly implement even this restriction, the environment will have to 'understand' both the COMMENT and the meaning of the code being COMMENTed – we are into the realms of *hopeware* once more.

But why then, you must be asking, are simple yet comprehensive support environments not commonplace in the software-engineering world? First, note that economies of scale are the main justification for mass-production manufacturing. However, once we have a useful IT system, mass production is trivial and almost costless: we simply make copies. So there is no economy-of-scale justification for software factories. Second, there will be considerable start-up costs associated with adopting a sophisticated support environment for a new IT development project, and there will be inevitable constraints on the software engineer's freedom to program (e.g. choice of version of programming language might be fixed). So accepting the useful help that such an environment can give must be set against the constraints it imposes and the effort needed to learn the system.

Nevertheless, there have been, and still are, companies and organizations that wanted to cash in on some degree of 'factory' production of software. Towards the end of the 1980s the Europeans initiated their software-factory idea.[6] Similarly, projects were launched in the USA and Japan, but did not survive beyond the 1990s in terms of the grand vision. Today there are a number of companies and organizations that offer some sort of software-factory service (i.e. quickly produced, reliable and reasonable priced IT systems) usually for certain niche applications.

In conclusion, we can see that the computer may assist in complexity management in two rather different ways:

1. It may be used to reduce the effective complexity of the programming task.
2. It may be used to impose good programming practice on the programmer.

Notice, however, that we've necessarily moved away from the relatively simple decision that precedes every programming exercise – i.e. what programming language to use. In the current context the decision is more one of what *programming support environment* to use. The actual programming language chosen may be a relatively insignificant part of the selection process. It may be that the type and sophistication of the available 'help' systems that constitute the support environment are the really important decisions to be made. Programming has ceased to be merely a question of which *programming language* to use.

A good analogy here is the modern warplane. The way that the cockpit of a high-performance jet plane is equipped with instruments and displays is crucial to the effective use of this sophisticated machine. There are many support facilities that can be given to the pilot to reduce the complexity of high-speed, low-level flight. But a good flight environment (i.e. the fully-equipped cockpit) is not just a collection of everything available. It is a well-integrated, carefully selected and appropriately presented set of 'help' facilities, and so is a good *programming support environment.*

To push this analogy just a little further: a modern jet fighter is quite unflyable without the IT system that works in the background, filtering input signals, generating displays and automatically coupling instrument signals to flight control actions. Just so the future of high-performance *programming support environments* will similarly be dependent upon a myriad of support programs running on the computer in the background and largely unperceived by the programmer while all is going well. The production of high-performance, highly reliable programs may, in turn, be crucially dependent upon the existence of a well-engineered moderately stupid assistant. However, the threat of death and destruction, which eliminates the possibility of unsupported joy-stick-and-throttle jet fighters, is largely absent in the IT world, and so the effort of building and using support environments can be postponed. And it usually is.

What do we now know about eliciting the computer's help?

- IT-system development complexity can be lessened by the use of other programs that monitor the programming and provide information about program structure to the programmer.
- An integrated suite of such helpful programs is a _programming support environment_.
- Simple, factual support is easily provided.
- More sophisticated support quickly extends into AI research areas, and is not easily provided.
- Accurate simple support is preferable to sophisticated support of dubious quality.
- 'Moderately stupid assistance' is the level of help to expect.
- Automated support may be either pro-active or on-demand only, or some combination.
- Constant interruptions with worthless, or erroneous, 'help' are worse than no help at all.
- Substantial support only comes at a price, and there must be tangible incentives to pay it.

Endnotes

1. This dialogue, which is not totally fictitious, is recycled from page 324 of my _New Guide to AI_. It models the dialogue system called SRDLU (Terry Winograd's PhD work, see next note) which is often credited with being the most cited AI system. The actual dialogue given is also by no means absurd, at least not for a computer system – and that is precisely the point. Computers can, and often are, programmed to communicate with words and phrases that are totally devoid of meaning for the computer system that is using them. The average human, naturally, tends to find this odd which, of course, it isn't for a computer.
2. It was Terry Winograd at MIT who coined this phrase as long ago as 1975. He was one of the golden boys in the golden age of Artificial Intelligence, an era of unprecedented hype and oversell; he is still a significant figure in the field. But subsequently, he campaigned vigorously for a more measured view of what Artificial Intelligence has really achieved, and for a more cautious approach to 'intelligent' software systems. His most readily accessible work in this vein can be found in the paperback book co-authored with Fernando Flores (an ex-Minister of Economics and of Finance in Chile!) _Understanding Computers and Cognition_ (Addison–Wesley, 1988). More recently, with John Bennett, Laura De Young, and Bradley Hartfield (eds.), he published _Bringing Design to Software_ (Addison Wesley, 1996) a collection of essays offering a variety of opinions on this difficult problem.
3. B. Sheil in 1983 entitled his article "Power tools for programmers" (published in _Datamation_, Feb. issue, pp. 131–144). In 1992 I reviewed, cautiously I thought, the state of the art of

sophisticated (i.e. the *hopeware* margins of) software support environments, but I was way overoptimistic (see D. Partridge, Chapter 9 in *Engineering AI Software*, Intellect: 1992).

4. Some Computer Scientists, e.g. those in the Dijkstra tradition, would deny that computer programs are never built for aesthetic reasons. They might say that their main goal is to produce correct and beautiful programs, and moreover that these two qualities are likely to go hand in hand as beauty involves simplicity and elegance, qualities that should make for more readily comprehensible programs.

5. *Hopeware* is the name given to AI 'breakthroughs': a first small sample of some wondrous AI development is presented (e.g. communication in English) and the substantive development remains to be done. It is hoped that this small step is the first in a sequence leading eventually to full achievement of the intelligent behaviour desired. 'Like climbing a tree as the first step towards getting to the Moon,' as one early AI critic put it, which suggests that a better name might be 'no-hope-ware.'

6. The Eureka Software Factory project (ESF) was set up by a Group of European partners in 1987. Its objective was broadly to improve the large-scale software production process by introducing an industrialised approach to have The Software Factory challenge social, organisational and technical aspects. The project was set up under the pan-European Eureka programme, and it was funded by the partners together with their national governments.

Chapter 21
Watching Programs Work

A program may make certain admissions by its static form but it fully confesses only in its changes.

after Thomas Hardy

Just in case it hasn't become apparent to you yet, I should point out that in our efforts towards furthering *program understanding*, for purposes of both prediction of the future and reassurance of the validity of past performance, we have been looking at one thing and drawing conclusions about another. We've been focusing on the program, a static abstraction, in order to understand the dynamics of the program-computer combination. We have learned to appreciate the *flow structure* as more important than the program as a list of instructions, but the *flow structure* too is a static abstraction. This limited viewpoint accounts for some of the difficulty, although not all by any means. Some appreciable element of difficulty, however, is introduced by this process of looking at one kind of representation and trying to draw implications about another.

Clearly, our illustrations of programs with *flow structure* superimposed, as a way to see what quality and complexity of program we have, is a device that implicitly concedes the poverty of the bare list of instructions. It makes explicit the order that the computer must follow, executing one instruction, then the next, then the next, etc.

However, just about the last thing we want is the obvious visualization of seeing each instruction as the computer *executes* it. This is entirely possible: it can, for example, be arranged that batches of instructions, say individual *subprogram*s, are highlighted in some way (e.g. coloured green) whenever the computer is *executing* the instructions within that *subprogram*.

One drawback of this simple-minded visualization is speed. The computer moves from one instruction to the next so fast that any real-time visualization would be no more than a rapidly changing blur. To counter this, the visual display could be slowed down drastically. The programmer would then be able to watch his program in slow motion in order to learn more about it. But then there are also more imaginative, and useful, ways to 'picture' a computation rather than the program itself. It is an old cliché that a picture is worth a thousand words; a well-designed one may well be worth at least 10,000 program instructions.

D. Partridge, *The Seductive Computer: Why IT Systems Always Fail*,
DOI 10.1007/978-1-84996-498-2_21, © Springer-Verlag London Limited 2011

The question that this chapter addresses is: can we avoid the necessity for this conceptual leap from a fixed list of instructions to an ever-wriggling live computation? Is there some way that we can look at the running program itself at the time when we are endeavouring to understand its actions?

The answer to this question is, 'yes', but not simply, 'yes'. We must ask ourselves what we really mean by 'look at the running program'. If, for example, at the races you want to look at the horses in order to better appreciate their individual qualities and therefore, hopefully, predict the winner in a race, there are many ways to do this. You might want to watch them racing, or physically examine each horse, or look them up in the form book, etc. There are many ways to look at the horses with a view to understand them better.

Similarly, there are just as many ways to look at a running program, and then there are more. Programs and horses are very different sorts of objects (I trust that this point can be agreed without supporting argument). One of the results of this difference is that we have almost unlimited freedom to view our running program. With horses this open-endedness does not exist in the same way: it is true that there is an infinite number of possible camera angles recording horses, and there is an infinite amount of possibly relevant data that could go into the form book, but the different types of visualization possible are few and fixed by comparison to the programmer's wealth of options.

I have written of a running program as being in control of a computer – i.e. the computer has no option but to compute exactly what the program specifies. This is true, but it is not the whole story. Most programs do not have the computer entirely to themselves for a variety of reasons (you might recall, for example, the 'help' programs which should be running in the background). A running program is usually under the control of a master program – _the operating system_, if you would like a new piece of jargon. This master program is itself only a program, and, for the person who wants to look at his program running, this master program can provide him with a route to almost limitless possibilities.

By augmenting this master program a vast range of alternative program visualizations seems to be possible, and the computer scientists have long been exploring them. A running program can be probed (e.g. values in specific storage boxes can be sampled), monitored (e.g. the number of times that the computer executes a given instruction can be recorded), and even interfered with (e.g. by the introduction of new instructions) by suitable additions to the master program. Thus the master program can obtain from a running program any information that we wish it to have.

The second part of this visualization possibility concerns the presentation of this information to the programmer. In the old days this information was collected in a log file and when the running program had terminated, this log file could be inspected as an aid to understanding. In this day and age it is quite possible to present the programmer with information about his running program at the same time as the program is running.

The computer's monitor screen can be set up to display any number of 'windows' of information at the same time. These windows may be side by side, or partially overlapping, or even completely overlapping. This latter option may seem a little perverse because if you put a new window of information slap bang on top of a previous window, then the earlier information will be totally obscured. However, we also have the facility to 'peel off' and discard, or just move to one side the new window thereby making the earlier information clearly visible once more.

So what do we use this windowing capability for? In short, we can use it to display, in any combination of simultaneous or sequential presentations, multiple views of our program. Views of what the program is computing (the conventional view), of what values are being placed in specific boxes, of how many times each *storage box* is given a new value, of the history of re-*execution* of particular *subprograms*, etc.

Figure 21.1 shows a screen displaying multiple windows each presenting a different view of the **SHOP** program. In addition to the windows, in the lower right corner of the display screen are two 'controls' for the visualization process. One is to allow the viewer to adjust the speed at which the computer processes instructions (e.g., slow it down an awful lot). The other is to allow the viewer to switch between going forwards through the program and going backwards in order that any earlier part of the computation can be re-inspected whenever desired.

Just as the human viewer can move, expand, contract, open or close-up windows by simply 'touching' pre-specified places on the screen (either touching directly, or indirectly using a mouse, or other pointer device), so the viewer can similarly adjust the slider on the "speed" scale or flip the "switch" between forwards and back to an earlier point in the computation.

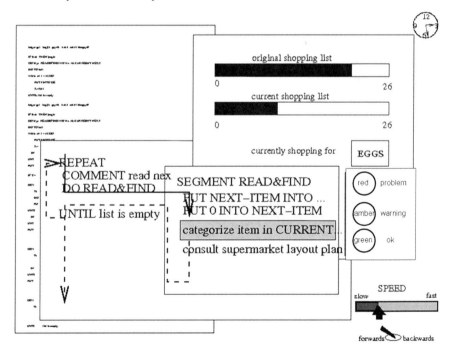

Fig. 21.1 A variety of windows on the **SHOP** program

The possibilities for what we might 'view' are virtually endless. Not only are there no end of types of information to display, but there are also endless different ways to actually present this information visually (not to mention other modalities such as audio).

For example, the monitoring of a specific box used by the program does not have to just display the numeric value in the box, and change the number displayed each time the value is changed by the running program. Given the high speed of computation we are dealing with, this sort of naïve display option is likely to result in a variety of different numbers flashing by the programmer at a speed that makes them simply a blur. A more useful display might be as, say, a thermometer: we represent the numeric value as a bar of red colour on a numeric scale. Then the value changes will be seen as a growing and shrinking bar of red colour which is visually easier to appreciate. To further aid visualization, we can slow the computer down. We can, for example, make it step slowly through the program's instructions. We can allow the enquiring human to view the results of each instruction before the computer is permitted to proceed to the next instruction. In this way we can get the benefit of hand execution avoiding much of the pain and with none of the scope for human error.

The monitoring and display mechanisms are simply programs, and, at the risk of being repetitive, because the limitations of programs are usually no more than the limitations of the programmer, anything is possible.

An analogy from a more everyday domain might help convey this idea. Consider the repairing of complex engineered artefacts, such as a modern car engine, or a television set. What does the repairman do when faced with a broken or malfunctioning artefact? One thing he tends not to do is to spread out the blueprints, circuit designs, etc. and pore over them for hours. This is the programmer staring at the list of instructions and design documents that comprise a malfunctioning program.

The repairman takes out his test equipment, attaches it to specific points on the malfunctioning object, and reads off measurements from dials, gauges, an oscilloscope screen, etc. In other words the repairman uses one set of equipment to explore the problems in another. So it can be with computer software. We can design test-equipment software to aid in the interpretation of our IT systems. This aid can be during the development of the applications program as well as during analysis of malfunction.

A natural extension of the notion of program visualization as an aid to program understanding is the idea of _visual programming_ – i.e., designing and constructing programs with the aid of visual techniques such as _flow-structure_ diagrams. This is a radical approach to the programming task, and one that represents yet another leap into _hopeware_.

As with the moderately-stupid-assistant idea of the previous chapter (and the two are, of course, quite closely coupled), the idea of program visualization has not been developed to the full by any means. With both notions the sky is the limit and it may take a very long time to realize some of the more ambitious possibilities, but many more-mundane, although startlingly innovative, advances can be expected. Program visualization, like automated assistance, is not an all-or-nothing strategy;

any initial developments along the endless road to the most marvellous manifestations are likely to be useful.

Finally, although the human capacity for visual communication is vast and varied, it is not the only channel available. Why not exploit others? Some minimal use is now made of audio communication.[1] Most computers will beep at you when you give them a wrong command. Much more use could probably be made of audio communication, and the tactile possibilities have been virtually ignored. Virtual reality systems that do make some considerable use of this variety of communication channels for human-computer interaction do exist, but not for IT-system management. These systems are found in training systems, like aircraft flight simulators, and they are beginning to emerge as the next generation of computer games, but serious use in the battle for control of the basic technology is probably confined to a few research laboratories. Why? Probably because the payoff is larger, more immediate, and guaranteed in the gaming world; also because application to improve our understanding and control of software systems is both not assured and not obviously necessary. Thousands of large IT systems are being constructed, sold and used every year so clearly it can be done without such fancy assistance. But could it be done much better with it? Probably. But at what cost, and for what improvement? No one knows.

Before we move on to something completely different, here are the summary points:

- IT systems are fundamentally dynamic objects, yet we try to understand them via static representations.
- Computer systems are quite capable of generating dynamic representations of ongoing computations.
- Every IT system *executes* in the context of an *operating system* which can execute other programs at the same time.
- The power of the human visual system can be exploited to aid IT-system understanding via dynamic system-visualization techniques.[2]
- The related idea of *visual programming* was introduced.

Endnotes

1. Computer gaming and IT systems such as Flight Simulators have seen the most development of audio and tactile communication with computer systems, but it has not contributed significantly to development or maintenance of IT systems.
2. In the 1995 addition to his 1975 classic, *The Mythical Man-Month* (Addison-Wesley), Brooks dips briefly into the possibility of improving the efficiency of software production through visualization. He maintains that programs are "inherently unvisualizable"(p. 186) because they are "not inherently embedded in space" and hence have "no ready representation in the same way that land has maps, silicon chips have diagrams" etc. (p. 185).

   This argument does not seem unchallengeable: visualization will not suddenly reveal all desired aspects of program structure, but surely a well-crafted visualization can reveal some useful aspects?

Chapter 22
Classical Reconditioning:
Doing What Happens Naturally

What a piece of work is man

– a miracle of rare design?

As I have indicated here and there throughout the book, there are other ways to compute – new species (to maintain the biological ambience) of computer technology. The discrete, sequential, dynamic-*flow-path* programming that we have explored in all the earlier chapters is the model for virtually all IT systems. It is time to at least open the box (which hopefully was not once Pandora's) and take a look at other possibilities.

This chapter will begin to probe the possibilities for building reliable systems from collections of individually non-guaranteed building blocks (as was mentioned earlier when we compared IT systems to the general notion of a system – Chapter 15).

The world that we happen to find ourselves in appears to be the product of an evolutionary process – classical reconditioning. Without attempting to enter the fray on just how evolution works, we can agree that it is not a process of redesign from scratch to produce new organisms. It is a process of reconditioning existent organisms to more aptly fit the ecological niches available at the time. At least this is the result, the actual process is not so goal directed: it appears to be more a process of continual hacking (to transport a metaphor) from which occasional products fortuitously constitute improvements that therefore thrive and multiply.[1]

The important point for us is that the organisms that populate the world have been cobbled together by evolution rather than each properly designed from scratch in accordance with a full specification for what they should and should not do. The absence of a General Omniscient Designer behind the products of the natural world is clearly seen, for example, in the opposable thumb of the giant panda (see Fig. 22.1).

What at first appears to be a sixth digit, this opposable thumb, is in fact a reconditioned wrist bone that evolution has pressganged into service with the opposable functionality which the panda requires to strip bamboo leaves (its primary food) from their stalks efficiently. Any self-respecting system designer would have redesigned the panda's hand from scratch.

In computer programming terminology the panda's thumb is a patch job, a *kludge* – a contraption not a lovely contrivance, as one biologist has put it.[2] So, although I'm about to lead you along a line of argument which implies that biology may have

D. Partridge, *The Seductive Computer: Why IT Systems Always Fail*,
DOI 10.1007/978-1-84996-498-2_22, © Springer-Verlag London Limited 2011

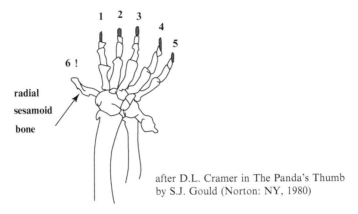

after D.L. Cramer in The Panda's Thumb
by S.J. Gould (Norton: NY, 1980)

Fig. 22.1 Beware of pandering to evolution

something to teach the computer technologists, we must also treat the biological solution with some caution – beware of classical reconditioning, but don't ignore it.

Whatever the mechanistic details, for most readers a casual glance around (or even into the mirror) will serve to confirm the suspicion that highly complex, reliable systems are possible. Most, perhaps all, organic systems have significant complexity characteristics similar to those of IT systems, and they have more complexity in every common characteristic.

An example here is the interdependence of functional modules in the human body – the liver is separate from the kidneys. The two organs are separate functional modules, yet they are interdependent in many ways. To a certain extent the blood and circulatory system constitute another functional module. But it would be fatal (perhaps literally!) for the physician to consider these modules totally independently, to neglect their interdependencies.[3]

This observation should be such as to provide some comfort to the embattled software designer locked in an endless struggle with a very large computer program – some comfort, but probably not much. For, although the products of evolution tend to display tightly-coupled functionality which gives rise to amazing macro behaviour (like, say, speaking, listening to, and understanding English) as a result of chemical interactions between molecules, the macro behaviours are quite reliable but, significantly, they are not guaranteed.

By 'reliable' I don't mean that organic systems can be counted on to do what they are told or what they promise to do. This is an entirely different aspect of reliability, and not one that need concern us for the purposes of this book. I refer to system reliability with respect to what the system was 'designed' to do – primarily to continue to survive and reproduce successfully in order to maximize the occurrence of its genetic material in future generations.[4]

Even given this clarification of what I mean by reliability, some of the results of evolution's best efforts, i.e. you and your friends, might want to contest my assertion about the reliability of these systems. You might point out that many people appear to inhabit quite unreliable systems – they are always ill, many die young, etc. Even those that do make it through to maturity some not insignificant proportion still fail to send any of their genetic makeup on the long voyage to eternity; it all dies with them, because of infertility, or a foolhardy attempt to cross a busy road at an inopportune moment, or a failure to find a compatible partner as the bisexual reproductive scheme demands. The possible reasons really are legion, but we need no more than a sample.

So, let me quickly acknowledge the truth of all this and grant that the reliability of organic artefacts, even in the limited sense we are using this word, is not total. As I said earlier, there are no guarantees (apart from death and taxes, and I'm not so sure about the taxes). But the reliability of organic systems is pretty remarkable, nevertheless, especially when compared to the computer programmer's best efforts which are also far less ambitious in what they aspire to do reliably.

Can the programmer learn from this existence proof of complex reliable systems? Evolution, requiring it seems aeons of system development time, offers no comfort as a mechanism for generating reliable computer software in accordance with the shorter-term planning periods that commerce insists on. Can our programmer learn anything by studying the resultant structure of these products of evolution? Can he capitalise on all the 'man-hours' that evolution has invested in discovering a structure for reliable, complex systems? Can't the programmer just study the internal workings and copy them?

These are open questions, much more open than they should be, I feel. Why is this? Notice that there is no obvious, plausible scenario that can correlate a regime of proof and verification with organic systems, neither with their development nor with the internal workings of the finished product.

Computer science grew out of mathematics, and it has yet to shake off the domination of its ancestry. The benefits of its rigorous parentage are undeniable, but development of the full potential of the offspring usually requires some rejection, or at least re-prioritisation, of the older generation's best and thoroughly well-intentioned advice – times change and better ideas will emerge.

It is, I believe, time for computer scientists to cast about more widely for potential paradigms to guide the design and development of reliable computer systems. It's just possible that the biological answer embraces a few usable secrets for the open-minded IT-system designer.

Even though biological systems have not yet been thoroughly explored as harbourers of a possible pattern for the programmer, I would not want to try to pretend that they have been completely ignored. There have been many attempts by computer technologists to glean and subsequently use information from the realms of biology.

Neural Computing or NC, quite apart from application in IT systems, it is already a substantial and fast-growing area that bases computation on a network of primitive, interacting processors working in parallel.[5] The analogy here is obviously with the structure of the brain, but in truth the biological underpinnings implied by the term, neural networks, are far stronger than the reality. The analogy with brain structure and function is highly tenuous at best, as any neural-network specialist will quickly admit. At least part of this admission is forced by the sad fact that we really know very little about how the brain actually works,[6] and therefore about which aspects of the structure and observed functioning are crucial and which are merely circumstantial, or even detrimental to the qualities that we wish to reproduce. If the brain as a 'symbol-manipulation machine' is so little understood, then we can hardly be expected to extract details for the design of a computing 'engine' from our knowledge of it at the moment.

So, given that our understanding of how biological systems work is far from perfect, we might be better advised to start with what little is known about the major differences between the structure and functioning of conventional computer programs and of biological systems. We can then consider reducing these differences by programming differently, and subsequently assess the impact, particularly with respect to system reliability, of our new programming style.

At a general level we can contrast typical programs with biological systems. We began to expose one seemingly salient point of difference in an earlier chapter. Now is the time to take a closer and longer look.

Reliable systems built with unreliable components, as you should realize by now, is definitely not what conventional computer technology strives to achieve.[7] The accepted goal of conventional computing technology is to build reliable (if not guaranteed) systems from guaranteed components – and to build by means of a totally precise process of selection and composition in order to get the resultant system precisely right, and so allow the building-block guarantees to be inherited by the total system.

This, the traditional way to construct a computer program, might be termed 'micro-engineering': we piece together tiny bricks (the individual *programming language* instructions) in order to build a vast edifice (the IT system) which is as strong as its weakest brick.

In addition, each of the bricks has a precise and well-defined function – i.e. each programming language instruction will cause the computer to do something quite specific. In a well-defined programming language the specific action of each instruction is guaranteed (to the extent that anything can be guaranteed in the real world). The underlying philosophy is roughly that with a complete and sufficient set of guaranteed bricks we really ought to be able to produce guaranteed buildings, if only we do the building properly.

It is then quite understandable why much of the effort and energy of computer scientists is directed towards discovering this 'right way'. It is generally assumed that it must be founded on the notion of logical proof – the mechanism that can give guaranteed results when operating from a well-founded platform such as a properly defined programming language can provide.

Now a logical proof is a series of guaranteed steps that leads to a guaranteed conclusion (given certain provisos about the initial assumptions). It is a lean and elegant way to certify the validity of new knowledge. I say it's a "lean" way because every step is individually guaranteed, so none of them need any alternative support.

There is no need for extra argument. It would be redundant, unnecessary clutter around the clean, crisp proof.

The emphasis on program structure and function reflects this notion of proof. The goal is a lean and elegant program composed of series of guaranteed steps. If you just concentrate on getting what you do right, then there is no need to further bolster the system with error-correcting mechanisms, or alternative computational pathways; they would just be superfluous, computational blubber.

A metaphor was introduced in Chapter 15 of a program as a means to hold up a computational weight. This view is illustrated in Fig. 15.2. We can now ground "the spider's option" in a computational technology.

A traditional computation ("the mathematician's option" in Fig. 15.2) is visualized as a single thread of unbreakable steel bearing the weight of individual computations; it is clean, lean and elegant glinting in the sunlight. Furthermore, we can be assured that it will hold the weight of the computation because it is, as we've agreed, unbreakable.

In addition to the effects of Murphy's Law (i.e., when the unbreakable breaks), a further point of weakness, which this metaphor accurately reflects, concerns the anchoring of this cable. However strong it might be, if it is not securely fixed at one end then it can fail to hold the weight put on it. Logic is guaranteed, but only if a few quite demanding basic requirements are met: a logical argument must be anchored by a set of assumptions that are both consistent and complete. Assurance that these basic requirements are met is not always possible in practice. In fact, it is more usual for the assurance to be that these two requirements have not both been met, in which case the logic-based guarantees are not just suspect: they are totally null and void.

Such a state of inherent instability suggests a metaphor reversal: a computation is a guaranteed tower of individually guaranteed bricks that holds up a weight. It is, however, built on a house of cards. Figure 22.2 illustrates this viewpoint and emphasizes the foundational weakness.

Way back in Chapter 6 we sketched out a proof that the **SHOP** program does indeed process all possible shopping lists correctly (within the constraints of the chosen shopping-list structure): it starts with the first item on the shopping list, works successively through the list, and terminates immediately after all items have been shopped for. The validity of this proof rests upon (among other things) the assumption that the initial shopping list is correctly structured, i.e., that n items are given in the first n *storage boxes*, and $n \leq 26$.

How does this compare with biological systems? Firstly, tiny building blocks, call them molecules or cells or atoms, whatever level you choose as the basic bricks, they are not guaranteed. At best their behaviour can be described probabilistically.

I don't want to get bogged down in a discussion of exactly what is not guaranteed and why it is the case. I just need to make the point that the absolute guarantees that come with a well-defined programming language, and with logical proofs are just not applicable to the basic building blocks in the organic world.

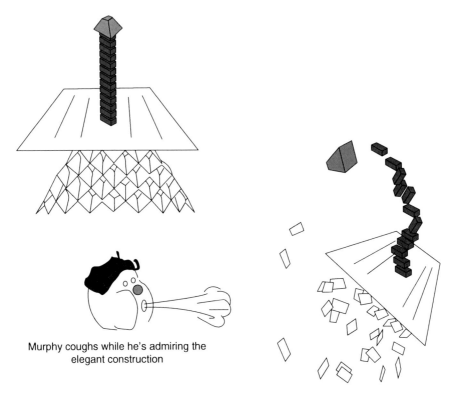

Murphy coughs while he's admiring the
elegant construction

Fig. 22.2 A foundational problem in conventional computing: invalidate, alter or forget an axiom
and Murphy will surely cough

This observation immediately rules out the possibility of system reliability founded on an elegant thread of logical proof. So, for biological systems, the first-choice paradigm of computer science is just not applicable. Evolution seems to have spotted this early on in the game and thus opted for a strategy of alternative and additional support at every step – redundancy on a grand scale.

Instead of the single steel thread gleaming in the sunlight we find in biological systems a matted web of alternative pathways and redundant processing. The weight of the computation (if I can use this term for the output of a biological system) is borne by an untidy mass of individually weak threads. No one thread can be trusted with the weight, but it doesn't have to be because it's duplicated many times at every position – in Fig. 15.2 this was illustrated as "the spider's option".

This vision translated back into the computer world is expected to engender profound distaste:

'Replace our structure, stripped of superfluous clutter, composed only of clean and elegant logical steps, with a sprawling intertangled web of unpredictable processing elements. This would be a disastrous step backwards into the heyday of cobbled together software.'

There's some validity to this objection, but I think that it is not irredeemably damning; salvation can still be attained. Let me sketch out a few scenarios for exploiting the biological model in computer programming.

The field of *neural computing* (NC), or *connectionism*, or *parallel distributed processing* (PDP) – it has many names and many different manifestations[8] – has shed some light on the possibilities for effective use of the biological metaphor. It is a computational technology that provides a grounding for "the spider's option".

It is perhaps no more than a metaphor given our lamentable state of understanding in biology (I refer to our understanding of the 'big picture' in terms of neurons functioning as elements of a computational system – it's a daunting problem).[6]

I shall lump together the various manifestations of NC under the name *Network Programming* (NP)[5]: we have no need to probe the points of distinction; and this name steers clear of the persuasive, but misleading, idea that we are simulating the mechanisms of the human brain.

The first point to note about NP is that unlike conventional programming it is not a micro-engineering activity. This fundamental difference is in fact required. Constructing the single threads of correct computation as normally demanded of the programmer is difficult enough to do. Imagine what it would be like to try to micro-engineer an interlocking mesh of such threads for each computation path in the desired program – this option doesn't bear much thinking about. Our exemplars, the organic systems, weren't micro-engineered as a whole, in one big step, but gradually produced in ever-more-suitable versions. This process is driven by feedback from the environment, so we must anticipate a similar feedback-mediated process to produce network programs. (I'm stretching the evolutionary metaphor a bit here, but it bears this interpretation in that some versions of the new system survive to propagate themselves – positive feedback – and others don't; their genetic material fails to reach the next generation – negative feedback.) In NP, rigorous training regimes have been devised for the generation of network programs, misleadingly called neural networks.[9]

Loosely put, NP amounts to setting up an initial network and then training it with a set of examples of the desired functionality. Let's jump to an example of NP in order to dispel some of the mystery that must be creeping into this book at this point.

One famous example of network programming was a system called NETtalk which learned to pronounce English.[10]

In English, letters in words can be pronounced quite differently in different contexts. For example, the letter "G" in "GUN" and in "ROUGHLY" has totally different sounds. Phoneticians, the scientists of pronunciation, have singled out some 26 basic sounds that we make with our voice when speaking English words. Any letter (or syllable) pronunciation is some combination of these basic sounds.

So what the NETtalk network computed was a selection from the 26 basic sounds. The input to this program was a letter in the context of various words (the network actually used up to three letters either side to provide the necessary context for deciding on the right pronunciation). The idea being that that the collection of basic sounds output by the network should be a correct pronunciation of the letter input, in the context of the word, or words, comprising the 7 letters

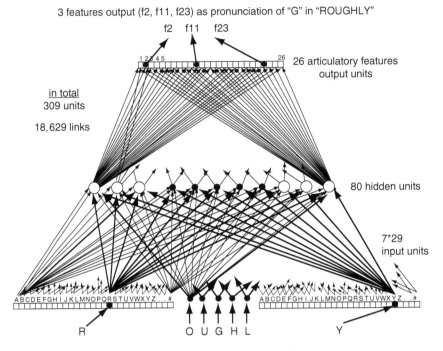

Fig. 22.3 The NETtalk network (many links and nodes omitted)

input. The NETtalk network was set up to compute with a 7-letter sequence as illustrated in Fig. 22.3.

The circles and squares are _nodes_ or processing _units,_ and the lines between them are _links_ each of which has an associated number, called its _weight_ (typically a decimal number, such as 2.719). Notice that NETtalk is composed of three layers of _units_: 7 × 29 _input units_ (1 block of 29 units for each network input which is either 1 of 26 letters, or 1 of 2 punctuation symbols, or a word 'space'), 80 _internal units_ (or _hidden units_), and 26 output _units_ (to display the computed pronunciation). It is a three-layer network, containing just one hidden layer. Initially each _unit_ has outgoing _links_ to all _units_ in the next layer – i.e. input to hidden, and hidden to output. Network training is started with all _link weights_ set as random decimal numbers.

How does this network compute? Each hidden unit is a small processor, and they all process in exactly the same way. They receive input values (decimal numbers called _activity_ values) from their incoming _links_ (the ones pointing into them); they sum the total input they receive from their incoming _links_; they then 'squash' this total to become an output _activity_ value between zero and one (the bigger the total, the closer to one, and the smaller the total, the closer to zero)[11]; they each send the resultant output _activity_ value along all their outgoing _links_. The _links_ themselves transfer any _activity_ that they are given after multiplying it by their _weight_ value. And that's all there is to it, except to say that _activity_ is transferred, in parallel, through the network from input _units_, through hidden layers (only one in this case), to output units.

All this must appear decidedly mysterious and quite *ad hoc*; it is perhaps the former but it's not the latter. Many of these NC regimes, including this one (which glories under the name of _multilayer perceptron_ or *MLP*), are formally well-founded (we will touch upon what this means shortly).

First, let's talk through a computation with NETtalk. We choose input data – a string of 7 letters. How about the English word "ROUGHLY"? Each of the 7 input units groups shoots an *activity* value of 1.0 along their outgoing *links* and into the hidden-layer *units* according to which letter they each receive: from the first input *unit* group of 29 *units*, it is *unit* 18 (the "R" *unit*) that sends *activity* into the network; of the second group, only *unit* 15 (the "O" *unit*) sends activity into the network, and so on for the other five input *unit* groups. In this way the letters "R", "O", "U", "G", "H", "L" and "Y" are input to the network.

For each hidden unit, the resultant incoming *activity*, multiplied by the *weight* on each incoming *link*, is summed, squashed, and passed to each of its outgoing *links*. These outgoing *links* pass any received *activity*, again multiplied by their *weights*, to the output *units*. So *activity* values arrive, and are also summed and squashed, at each output *unit* which then compares its final input *activity* with a threshold value. If the final input *activity* computed exceeds the threshold then that output *unit* is _activated_, i.e., the basic sound represented by that output unit becomes part of the pronunciation computed. If an output unit is not *activated* then it makes no contribution to the pronunciation output.

So, from a word input to the network, it computes a pronunciation (in the form of a collection of activated output *units*, each of which represents a basic sound). In sum, for each input string of seven letters (or punctuation marks and word spaces) we get a pronunciation output. So it's just like a conventional program in that sense, but the way it computes internally is totally different – there are no programming language instructions and no storage boxes involved (at least not in the conventional way that we programmed earlier in this book).

How well does this network compute pronunciations? It's awful! What could you expect when there were no thoughtful decisions about which *units* to link to which (each *unit* was simply linked to all *units* in the next layer) nor about what *weights* to put on each link, etc.?

If in the earlier part of this book I endeavoured to convince you of the excessive complexity demanded by conventional programming, now imagine the enormity of the task for the network programmer: he must decide on which *units* to *link* to which, and worse he must decide on all the *weight* values (the NETtalk network contains more than 18,000 *weights*). How would the poor programmer begin to find the correct value for a *link weight*? Because of the nature of the network computation, it is impossible to reason about the value of any *link weight* in isolation. It is like trying to identify the essential contribution of any one worker bee to the functioning of a hive. Nevertheless, it and all similar bees undoubtedly account for the operations of the colony.

There is no 'correct value' for a *weight* in isolation; it is the population of all *weight* values that collectively determine the quality of the output – in the NETtalk case, how good a pronunciation is generated. Equally good network programs can be composed of different combinations of *link weights*. No single *weight* value is crucial to a good computation. Indeed, just like any worker bee in a colony, any *link* (and hence its *weight*) may be removed from a network program without a noticeable effect of the overall computation. This is, of course, the opposite of the potential criticality of the smallest elements of a conventional program. Notice also that the *flow paths* of NETtalk are not a *decision-logic tree*. All paths are *executed* in every computation. What makes one computation different from another is the quantity of activity that flows along each path. It is the balance of *activity* in the 'wave front' of *activity* values that distinguishes one computation from another. So, with a network program, we have something different, but how do we get it?[12]

I've only told you half of the story: such networks cannot be hand-programmed; they must be *trained* to compute the desired function – e.g., in the case of NETtalk to pronounce English correctly. The initial untrained network just produces random babble.

Training is achieved by modifying the *link weights* as a result of the measured errors observed on a *set of training samples*, i.e. a set of words each paired with its correct pronunciation. In the particular computation described above, the network will produce some (almost certainly) wrong pronunciation for the "G" in "ROUGHLY", because the network had random *link weights*. But we know what the correct pronunciation is (or the phoneticians do), and the difference between the set of basic sounds the network actually computed and the correct set for this particular input gives us an error signal. This error signal can be used to compute a change in all the network *link weights* such that if we try this same input again it will be guaranteed to compute a more accurate output (more precisely, the guarantee is that it will become no worse). By using a long series of these compute, feedback error signal to alter the *weight* values, and re-compute we can eventually train the network to compute the correct pronunciation. An important point here is that the *weight*-change computation is done with an algorithm (i.e., the computer does it automatically) that has formal guarantees attached – i.e. we can be assured that no change will be for the worse, and usually it is for the better. This sort of thing is nice to know; it is the basis for the earlier claim that this type of NC is formally well-founded.[13]

In NETtalk, output was classed as "perfect" when exactly the right set of basic sounds was computed for specific input letters, and as a "best guess" when the correct set was closest to the actual set, although not identical. NETtalk learned to pronounce over half of English "perfectly" after 50,000 words of training, and at this point nearly all its computations (95%) were at least "best guesses".

The tape recording of NETtalk's progress through training is impressive. By feeding the activated pronunciation units into a speech synthesizer, actual pronunciations can be generated and broadcast through a loudspeaker.

The initial untrained (randomized *weights*) network starts off with random babbling, of course. As the automatic training progresses something more structured (although not clearly English) is heard. Then quite suddenly a strange but discernibly English pronunciation emerges, and soon it becomes quite good English.

On each input of a training sample, a small change is automatically made to the values of all the network *weights*. Presentation of all of the training samples may be repeated thousands of times in order to change all the weights from their initial random values to their optimal values.

This sort of computation is all the more remarkable because English pronunciation is generally acknowledged to require about 300 rules to characterize it – i.e. to specify what combination of basic sounds should be generated for each letter in all the contexts in which that letter occurs in the English language. No such rules were considered in the construction of NETtalk, yet the trained network computes as if it were obeying these rules. Conventional programming of this pronunciation task would involve a study of the rules and their translation into sequences of programming language instructions, i.e., extensive microengineering – a long, tedious, and error-prone activity.[14]

This is where the breathless excitement of bottom-up emergent self-adaptivity becomes manifest as the next great revolution in software development.[15] Sadly, it doesn't. The reality is more prosaic (isn't it always?).

Undeniably, program design and construction is totally different when we are network programming. But what about reliability, that was, after all, the main impetus for this foray into biology as a source of inspiration?

As it happens these networks are very reliable in a similar way to their biological counterparts – as the bee colony analogy has been used to suggest. If we randomly change link *weights*, or remove complete *links* from a trained network, it seldom wrecks the computation. Typically, we observe that some computations are not quite as good as they were. In general, the more we destroy or distort the trained network the more that the quality of the answers degrades – in NETtalk, perfect pronunciations become best guesses, and best guesses get worse.

This type of reliability is called graceful degradation; it can be contrasted with that of conventional programs which tend to just crash, either to a halt or by generating totally spurious results. So network programming does seem to offer the promise of a solution for certain sorts of computational problem. Notice also that this characteristic of network programs is a direct contradiction of what we earlier considered as a fundamental problem with all computer technology, viz. **radical novelty 2**: small changes produce big effects (see Chapter 15).

In some applications, totally accurate answers are the only usable ones (e.g. computing your bank balance), best guesses are no better than totally incorrect computations. Graceful degradation in these circumstances is not much use, but there are many applications where absolute precision is not required, is perhaps not even a sensible option (e.g., when to send customers a letter offering them a new financial service). For these sorts of problems there could well be a role for network programming.

So, while I don't want a neural-net computing my bank balance because it will not get it precisely correct, it will not get it wildly wrong either. The guarantee of approximate correctness is swapped for the instability of 'dead right or thoroughly wrong'. Notice that there is no *correct* pronunciation for English, certainly not in the sense that there is for my bank balance. If the goal is pronunciation of English, there is merely an (ill-defined) range of acceptable pronunciations – a 'good enough' computed result.

In addition, the automatic nature of network training (the analogue of manual, solution design in conventional programming) changes the economics of software development such that multiple versions of network programs can be developed far more cheaply than a single version of a conventional program.

Once we realize that the set of network versions can all be different (e.g. different initial networks, different random initialisation, different training sets) a completely new door to software reliability opens: use of sophisticated voting procedures to select a correct answer from a set of different versions all computing the same problem.[16]

However, as you might have guessed network programming is not all sweetness and light. Far from sweeping through the software-development world, network programs are few and far between as elements of IT systems. This is because there are a number of problems associated with this programming paradigm.

The problems are: how best to set up the initial network that is efficiently trainable, and how to best train it such that the training is reasonably fast and yet produces a network that generalizes – i.e. is accurate on more than just the training set of examples. After all the whole point of training is to produce a system that will work well on new inputs, ones that are not in the training set of samples. There are also problems with modifying a trained network in order to obtain a slightly different or extended behaviour from the program – e.g. we might want NETtalk trained on BBC English to switch to a Scottish accent.

The first problem is akin to program design in conventional programming except that we don't have to design the network to compute the desired function merely to be able to be trained to compute this function. The network programmer's initial design decisions are: how many layers of units to use, and how many units to have in each layer. The problem of initial link connections and weights is not so critical because with randomized weights and total connectivity the non-useful links soon become apparent because their weights are modified towards zero during training. The initial design of optimal networks is by no means a solved problem, but the point is that it is nothing like the high-precision microengineering required to construct an initial versions of a conventional program.

The subsequent training is a bit like the testing of a conventional program: in both cases a selection of specific input-output pairs are tried on a program, and when it gets them correct we assume that it will also function correctly on the untried ones. But this similarity may be quite superficial: the way that the two sorts of program generalize between the tested points may be quite different. For it is not at all clear that a network program is a digital system in quite the same way that a conventional program is[12] (it may be useful to recall, or even reread, the earlier discussion of this "radical novelty" of modern computer technology, Chapter 15). In fact, a good deal of the promise in network programs rides on the assumption that these programs do not exhibit this unhelpful characteristic – or at least exhibit it only to a minor extent.

The task that in conventional programming is euphemistically called *maintenance* – i.e. the fixing of errors and the adding of enhancements to the program – similarly becomes a very different task for the network programmer, and here we may be uncovering some of the bad news for the network programmer.

One of the big surprises that NETtalk sprung upon the programming community was the seeming contradiction between the fact that it behaved (after training) as if it embodied the 300 rules of English pronunciation. Yet all attempts to locate the rules (or any internal structure that might vaguely represent individual rules) within the trained network program have failed quite dismally. Casually, you might think that as the program pronounces English well, it must have learned the pronunciation rules. In which case you have every right to expect that suitable delving into the innards of the network (aided perhaps by some program visualization tools) would eventually reveal that certain parts of the network account for certain pronunciation behaviours – but this is not the case.

You should recall that every computation involves the successive transfer of *activity* values from all *units* in one layer to all *units* in the next (i.e., all *flow paths* are used in every *execution*). So, for each and every pronunciation computation, a wave of activity, successively encompassing all the *units* in each layer, is seen to flow through the network. You might expect that within this wave there would be one (or just a few) high-*activity* path(s) – i.e. from one *unit* to another, layer to layer – within a generally weak wave, but this does not seem to be the case. Contrast this functioning with a conventional program in which there is one (and only one) 'activity path' (by which I mean the sequence of instructions that the computer actually follows) through the program for any particular computation. This is one *flow path* through the *decision-logic tree* (which actual one is determined by the choices computed at each *branch point*), one *flow path* through the maze of possible paths illustrated in our earlier *flow-structure* diagrams (and in Fig. 15.1).

On further reflection you will see that this situation is not so strange. It turns out that any specific pronunciation computed by NETtalk is a cooperative computation – i.e. each processing *unit* (and hence every *weight*) contributes something to produce the overall behaviour every time the program is run. We say that the computation is *distributed*, hence the name *Parallel Distributed Processing* (PDP). It is this distributed nature that is expected to provide the reliability that we seek – any small, non-critical contribution to an overall behaviour can be removed without much observable effect (like a single worker bee from the colony).

This type of processing, although quite at odds with conventional computation, is not at all strange. It is commonly found in complex human communities, especially ones with well-defined goals: consider a car-manufacturing plant. To the outside observer steel, glass, plastics, etc. are input; one combination results in Model Xs being generated, and other results in Model Ys. The plant is a car-manufacturing 'program' in which the internal processing units are people.

But which people are the Model-X makers, and which make the Model Ys? Who is the Model-X radiator maker? Most probably, the workforce doesn't divide up neatly in this way. They all contribute something, in differing degrees, to all the cars made in the plant. The Model-X radiator is probably produced by the cooperation of a number of persons who each also contribute to all sorts of other car-making activities. The component functions of car manufacture are distributed throughout the workforce. When one person is on holiday production doesn't grind to a halt.

This is because that person's functions are all partially duplicated by other workers, and these others can compensate for a holiday absence fairly easily. Production may slow down, and the product may be slightly inferior (as the speciality functioning of the holidaymaker is taken over as a side-line by his or her workmates), but production can continue. The system doesn't crash because one worker is absent.

Notice that no sane person would expect to design and construct a complex manufacturing plant, to the level of precise activities of every worker, in one go. From a general, and small-scale, initial setup, an efficient and effective system is evolved and developed over time; they are not created *ab initio*. Interpreted broadly, evolution, as a mechanism for complex system development, also appears to be an element of the biological metaphor with some considerable validity for IT systems development.

To return to *network programs*: notice also that the static network (i.e. just *units* and *weighted links*), which corresponds to the list of instructions of a conventional program, is likely to tell us nothing at all about how the network computes what it is observed to compute. Instead of a list of instructions like: **IF** X = 0 **THEN PUT 1 IN** NUM, which is readily interpretable (even if only a very small contribution to a total *program understanding*), we are faced with just *units* and *links* with *weight* values as well as the simple summation and squashing operations. None of these structural elements of the network (and there are no others) are likely to be easily interpretable in terms of the network's general behaviour – e.g. in NETtalk focusing attention on *units* and *link weights* contributes precious little to an understanding of how the network is computing the correct pronunciations.

How do we then gain an understanding of the functioning of a trained network? How can we develop an understanding of how the network computes what we observe it to compute? The answer is: I don't know, and neither does anyone else. If it's difficult, or impossible, to gain a full understanding of the workings of a conventional program, it seems to be almost as hard to gain <u>any</u> similar understanding of a *network program*.

There are positive arguments to weigh against this wholly unwelcome revelation. First, it's early days yet, and progress, perhaps substantial progress, may be made with this problem. Network visualization tools, for example, tools that transform *unit*-and-*link* clusters into something more readily comprehensible are expected to be useful, and are a largely untapped resource. After all, a complex piece of electronics is an incomprehensible morass of electron shuffle and jump, if we look at too low a level. But appropriate test equipment feeding into, say, an oscilloscope transforms these low-level actualities into voltage fluctuations, etc. that permit a trained human to see what's going on in the system. This suggestion takes us back to the topic of the previous chapter – program visualization – only now we are interested in visualizing *network programs*.

Second, so much is different about *network programs* in comparison to conventional programs that perhaps an understanding of the mechanistic details of a network is not as important as it is for a standard program. Because they are automatically trained rather than laboriously microengineered, and because they must be retrained rather than hand-modified in order to change their behaviour, the demand for an understanding of exactly how they work does not seem to be so great. It is quite conceivable that *network programs* can be built and can function entirely satisfactorily as black-box software – i.e. software for which a desired behaviour can be obtained and tested for reliability, but whose detailed workings are, in some real sense, a mystery.

Third, the analogue nature of *network programs* promises predictability. Hence system reliability from the observation of macro characteristics becomes a likely possibility which it is not for the discrete systems that are conventional IT systems. Test probes too should offer more reliable information when applied to analogue properties of the network-programmed system.

These ideas go completely against the grain of current computer technology, but that doesn't mean that they're worthless. The quest for "a full understanding," which has preoccupied us for most of this book, presupposes an important need to conceptually master the detailed innards of the system. This need may be a figment of the nature of conventional programming, although it does appear to be intrinsic to the notion of science itself. Can we then abandon the task of coming to grips with the fine detail? Perhaps we can because our problem is not so much one of science, but of engineering: building systems to serve societal needs.

Notice that this suggestion will allow us (in fact *network programs* seem to force us) to avoid the first radical novelty of computing – **radical novelty 1**: the need for elasticated brains (in Chapter 15). Quite curiously, *network programming* might offer a radical solution to this radical novelty: the inherent impossibility of comprehending the fine details of a network program precludes any possibility of mastering them!

As you now can see, I hope, the biological metaphor does seem to offer a new way to program computers. In fact, I hesitate to use the term "program" in this new context, for networks are constructed so differently from conventional programs. Networks as programs present us with a whole new mindset (perhaps a scientific revolution), and because of their radical nature the conventional touchstones of good practice cannot be relied upon for guidance. I've been at pains to point out some of the radical changes that network programming introduces, others might be that statistics and geometry replace logic as the appropriate mathematical foundation, and that redundancy is no longer a negative term. This last point, sometimes called the Titanic effect (i.e. if the ship is unsinkable then the provision of lifeboats is a waste of space and money – mentioned earlier) is important irrespective of whether we adopt this new way to program or whether we stick with the conventional approach.

One final observation is that there is also a middle ground, and some have already begun to stake it out. The problem of the non-interpretability of *units* and *weighted links* is circumvented by replacing them with modules of conventional programming language instructions. So instead of the simple *units* of our neural network we construct our network using more complex *units*, a bit like the *subprograms* in our earlier programs. These new *units*, sometimes called *agents*, will then be used to compute cooperatively – i.e. each will contribute to many computations, and none will be able to compute anything useful on its own, but each will represent some comprehensible activity on its own.[17]

This style of programming, which is even less well-understood than *network programming*, is often described in terms of emergent behaviour – the overall behaviour of the program emerges from the cooperative interaction of a community of autonomous agents.[18]

As a matter of fact, the earlier example of the car manufacturing plant is more closely akin to this emergent-behaviour notion, than it is to the networks which I used it to illustrate. Clearly, the processing elements in the car plant are people and people function as autonomous agents – i.e. a person can typically carry out his or her assigned task independent (to some degree) of everybody else in the factory doing what they are supposed to be doing. A study of any one person will most likely reveal a number of small but quite understandable functions that are performed at different times, but it still might be difficult to relate the specific actions of one particular agent to the overall production of cars (and remember, it would be cheating to ask either the agent or anyone else to explain, because the program will contain no such sentient beings just waiting to explain things to you).

A further extension of this analogy suggests that managers are unnecessary. In this community of co-operating agents (as in the networks) there is typically no single locus of control – i.e. no overall manager who directs operations. So the analogy better fits the human notion of a commune than it does the typical factory. Complex human organizations do seem to function better with some concentration of decision-making power (i.e. some managers). If this is due more to the nature of humans than to the nature of complex systems, then the computational analogues may succeed with their totally distributed philosophy. But, if not, then some element of conventional programming will be needed to 'oversee' the processes at various levels.

It may be that this approach to computation exploits the best of both worlds: the reliability of distributed processing and the ready comprehensibility of clear instructions. Alternatively, it may be shackled by the problems of the two extreme approaches: the fragility of instruction *subprograms*, and the incomprehensibility of distributed processing. Which way the balance will eventually tilt, or how to ensure that it embraces only the positives, are both totally open questions.

There is no clear answer to the question of whether biology provides the inspiration (if not the firm basis) for a new and useful way to compute. Each new suggestion solves some problems but generates or exacerbates others. The point is that there may be usable radical alternatives, and we should be more active in exploring them, rather than keep on banging proof and logic together in the hope that the resultant sparks will eventually light up the answers.

To summarize:

- The organic world is full of stable, reliable complex systems.
- IT systems' technologists may therefore find some useful structures and processes in the world of biology.
- Evolution, crudely viewed as a process involving time, random changes and selection, has found application in complex optimization.
- Neural computing (originally inspired by the impressive computational properties of brains) has been developed in a number different ways.
- So-called *neural networks* as computational devices embrace a wealth of special terms – *units, weights, activity* values –and introduce *distributed computation*.

- *Network programs*, hence <u>*network programming*</u>, appear to circumvent some fundamental weaknesses of conventional programs.
- But *network programming* has its own weaknesses and cannot, as yet, be used for large-scale, multifunctional IT systems, although network programs could be elements of such systems.
- *Network programming* may offer the software engineer a new paradigm and so require fundamental shifts in thinking about applications and management of computational technology.

Endnotes

1. Not surprisingly perhaps, attempts have been made to simulate biological evolution as a method of developing intelligent programs. Although denied the possibility of letting their 'evolutionary' systems evolve for millions of years, the enthusiasts hoped that the very high speed of computers might permit them to show progress over much shorter periods of time. In terms of evolving useful IT systems, or even useful elements of IT systems, the results have never been encouraging.

   The next step was a further possible speed-up by circumventing the seemingly very wasteful step of random changes by trying to restrict the randomness to 'possibly useful' changes. What has emerged is a vigorous subfield clustered around the strategies of *Genetic Algorithms* and *Simulated Evolution*: program development based on 'possibly useful' changes that are assessed and either discarded or kept for subsequent modification in a population (i.e. a collection of similar copies of the software under development) of samples. This evolution-like approach to program development has not come close to producing good IT systems but it has found valuable application in optimisation technology – i.e. given a program that performs some unitary task adequately, we can usually 'evolve' it to get a better performance.

2. The American palaeontologist, Stephen Jay Gould, provided this example. Full details can be found in *The Panda's Thumb* (Norton, 1980), a collection of his fascinating and informative essays.

3. It was a lack of appreciation for such biological-system interdependencies that scuppered the more ambitious applications of Expert Systems Technology (a Chapter 19 topic) in the last decades of the last millennium. A mass of simple rules and facts can reproduce the human expertise needed to decide on credit-card applications, but it falls dismally short when used in an attempt to replicate the diagnostic expertise of a medical practitioner.

4. I am assuming here that Richard Dawkins is right. But for those readers who are perplexed by the notion that the propagation of genetic material and not organisms is the driving force behind evolution, I recommend that you peruse Dawkins' compelling and eminently readable book, *The Selfish Gene* (Oxford University Press, 1976). And for those who are not bothered either way, but like short, well-written, informative books touching on the secrets of life this is also the book for you.

5. I originally introduced this idea as Non-Programmed Computation in an article of that name published in 2000 in the online version of the leading US Computer Science journal called *Communications of the ACM*, vol. 43, issue 11es.

6. Of course, various specialists know an awful lot about how the brain works. For example, neural pulses are quite well understood in terms of molecules and atoms. The image processing capabilities of single neurons in the optic tract (an extension of the brain) are well understood. The behaviour of neurons *en masse*, via EEG recordings, is also somewhat understood. However, none of this specialist knowledge is the sort of knowledge that is needed to model brain activity as a computational process, and hence not the sort of knowledge that is needed

in order to build 'real' neural computers – i.e. machines that compute in 'much the same way' as the brain does. We ran into this problem some years ago: see V. S. Johnston, D. Partridge and P. D. Lopez, "A neural theory of cognitive development", *Journal of Theoretical Biology*, vol. 100, pp. 485–509, 1983.

7. There are significant exceptions: for example, in some systems engineering, such as reliable data transmission over an unreliable channel, designed-in redundancy can be the norm.

8. There is now a wealth of introductions to this blossoming subfield of computer technology. Under the simple banner of say, connectionism, there are very many, fundamentally different schemes. Once again, my *New Guide to AI* (Intellect, 1991) springs to mind as an introduction that is comprehensive yet not unduly burdened with unavoidable technicalities.

9. One final time I'd like to note that I'm trying to avoid the misleading labelling that dominates this area: 'training' (a straightforward feedback procedure for function optimization) is often called 'learning' which then licenses extravagant leaps into the complexities of human learning. 'Neural networks' similarly seem to induce unwarranted speculation based on the computational wonders of real neural networks, i.e. our brains. In reference to 'training' procedures, Johnson's *Emergence*, for example, states that in "A few decades from now [2001]" development of this technology will "begin to convincingly simulate the human capacity for open-ended learning" (p. 208). Classic *hopeware*, based on a failure to appreciate the yawning gulf between our knowledge of how to optimize functions automatically and our ignorance of the mechanisms underlying "the human capacity for open-ended learning" (if that is indeed what we possess). Incidentally, "a few decades" have already passed since one of the most powerful of these optimization technologies (the Multilayer Perceptrons) has been in wide use (see note 8), and no development towards open-ended learning has appeared.

10. The NETtalk system was devised by Terry Sejnowski and Charles Rosenberg at Johns Hopkins University in the USA in 1986. Details of the system have been reprinted in many books, including the one referenced in note 8.

11. There are many possible 'squash' functions; the S-curve is commonly used. It is sketched out below.

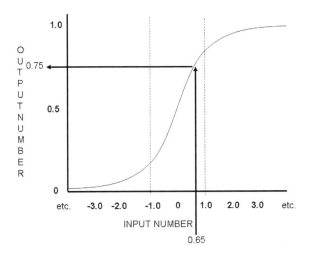

Any number input to this curve (via the horizontal axis, the input value 0.65 is illustrated) will be 'squashed' to an output value between 0 and 1 (via the vertical axis, where the output value of 0.75 is illustrated for the input value of 0.65). Notice that the horizontal, the input, axis can take all decimal values from minus infinity to plus infinity (although only −3.0 to 3.0 are illustrated). The vertical, the output, axis is illustrated in full – the minimum output is 0 and the maximum output is 1.0. Only inputs between about −1.0 and 1.0 will give outputs that are not close to 0 or 1.0. All other input values, however large or however small (large negative), will generate output values close to 1.0 or 0, respectively.

12. There is an obvious objection to my claim that NETtalk exemplifies a fundamental change in programming technology. Neural network systems are, after all, constructed using conventional programming languages and are executed on conventional digital computers. But in just the same way all natural systems are built from the discrete units we call atoms, and yet they can be analogue systems. It is a question of levels: in both cases (computational neural networks and natural analogue systems) the individual discrete components have no readily interpretable meaning at the system level.

13. For this particular type of network, a Multilayer Perceptron (or MLP, by far the most widely used NC technology), the training algorithm is (some version of) the Backpropagation of Error (the BP, or backprop) algorithm.

14. Computer Scientists might object that building programs by piecing together tiny elements of instruction is exactly the problem: the proper way to generate programs is top-down in the sense that individual instructions are refined, in functionally modular clumps, out of elements derived from a formal specification, via design abstractions. They do have a point, programming by selecting instructions and fitting them together one by one is a poor general strategy for the construction (or fixing) of reliable programs. Ultimately, of course, all such tasks will boil down to microengineering the final outcome. So the temptation is to bypass the foreplay with plans and design modules, and get straight to the instructions details where all solutions reside.

Unsurprisingly then, the majority of programmer time is spent working on programs in this way rather than by eliciting the fine detail from high-level abstractions – i.e., the bulk of IT-systems work is microengineering them. Adding to the problem, top-down program-development schemes (especially the thoroughly formal ones) only work to a certain degree and in certain situations. I'm sure that there could, and should be more top-down programming, but I'm not at all sure that it is realistic to expect it ever to usurp the majority role from microengineering – especially when we recognize that most commercial programming activity is the fixing and altering of other people's large, undocumented (poorly or misleadingly documented, it makes little difference) piles of instructions, i.e. grappling with *legacy software* systems whose only guaranteed 'description' is the program instructions themselves.

15. Steven Jonhson's *Emergence* (Penguin, 2001), although addressing many interesting phenomena, is guilty in this respect when referring to general software development. "In the short term, though, emergent software promises to transform the way we think about creating code" (p. 173) In which case Johnson asks: "Who is driving here, human or machine? Programmer or user?" (p. 174). The answer, as we know, is neither; it's the program that drives the behaviour irrespective of what the user and, perhaps more pertinently, the programmer believes about the programmed components he constructed. The 'promise' may well be realized for game playing and for human-computer interaction phenomena, but not for IT systems that must exhibit pre-specified, complex behaviours. This single-function optimization technology, such as the MLP example in the chapter, has been well-understood for decades, and this understanding includes all the attendant technical problems and limitations.

16. Use of multiple systems, on the principle that a variety of answers (one from each system) can deliver (e.g. by simple majority vote) a more reliable result than any single system, has developed into the active subfield of Multi-Classifier Systems (MCS) with its own annual conference and numerous books, published by Springer.

17. There is blossoming subfield of 'autonomous intelligent agent technology' but (like so many of the good ideas that trespass into *hopeware*), all of the proposed systems are largely future events.

18. One readable, but fanciful, exposition of this notion is *The Society of Mind* (Simon & Shuster, 1986) by a pioneer of AI, Marvin Minsky. For his PhD work, Jonathon Rowe attempted to transform *The Society of Mind* philosophy into a concrete IT system, one that displayed creativity in the context of game playing. His project clearly revealed both the strengths and the weaknesses of this general idea. The full project together with a survey of the notion of creativity in IT systems can be found in a small book – *Computers and Creativity* by D. Partridge and J. Rowe published by Ablex, NY and then Intellect, Bristol in 1994.

In general, forays into the possibilities for so-called emergent-behaviour programming were inaccessible to the non-specialist until Steven Johnson's *Emergence* was published in 2001, but it does use a somewhat fragile definition of the term: "The movement from low-level rules to higher-level sophistication is what we call emergence."(p. 18) Johnson's explanations of this rather open 'definition' oscillate between the obvious (new behaviours emerge from an interaction of primitive ones) and the fanciful ("systems built with a conscious understanding of what emergence is" p. 21). There is much mention of "laws of emergence" but, curiously, no laws are explicitly given.

My view is that with all programs we are grappling with emergent behaviours which are no small part of the reason why large IT systems will always grow beyond comprehensibility. If one wishes to impose a more restrictive view of emergence, then one has to draw necessarily arbitrary boundaries within the multidimensional continuum of the universe of programs. I can see no justification for this.

Chapter 23
A Computer That Knows When It's Wrong

There's lies; damned lies; and statistics.

On the morning of July 7, 2005 in London, the first medics to arrive at each scene of terrorist carnage had life-critical decisions to make concerning where to apply their skills for maximum effectiveness – i.e. who of the injured was likely to survive if treated quickly, and who was not. Given general information about an injured person, such as approximate age, as well as details of their injury and current state, such as eye-response to light, can likelihood of survival be accurately predicted? In some cases, yes, but in others the best prediction will be equivocal. This problem has been studied using computer systems in order to optimize predictive accuracy as well as to identify salient survival indicators.

Beyond awkward medical decision making, computers are now routinely used when the results cannot always be deemed to be clearly correct or incorrect. As we have seen, IT-system technology is not readily adaptable to the production of systems whose results are, at best, sometimes equivocal. Even for IT systems whose results are simply correct or incorrect, a computational technique that automatically incorporates an assessment of the reliability of its computed results would be valuable.

Our bank-balance IT system, for example, would be able to report the confidence that it had in each specific balance it generated. In the high-confidence cases (presumably the vast majority) no further action need be taken. But if a low-confidence rating occurs with a specific computation, then a warning could be issued with the dubious result.

Typically, results outside the options of correct or incorrect are dealt with on a problem by problem basis, or worse, go unrecognized as equivocal. How much better if unavoidable equivocation can be indicated, by the system, as it arises <u>as an integral system feature</u>, rather than as an add-on calculation? Usually this latter approach is implemented as an associated probability estimate computed together with the result for which a measure of equivocation is desired. Thus, a meteorological IT system might compute that there is a 80% chance of rain tomorrow. Such a result is likely to have been computed by combining discrete probability estimates associated with each of the major elements of the 'rain' result.

D. Partridge, *The Seductive Computer: Why IT Systems Always Fail,*
DOI 10.1007/978-1-84996-498-2_23, © Springer-Verlag London Limited 2011

How else could this probabilistic result have been computed? In detail, of course, there are many different ways to do this computation. But how could it have been fundamentally different from conventionally discrete programming? The computation could have been based upon systematic combination of the probability distributions of the major elements rather than on discrete values and associated probabilities. It must be time for an example.

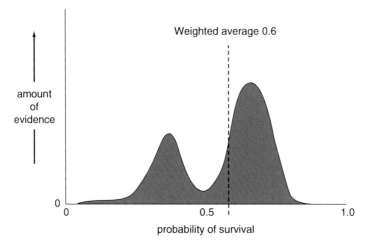

Fig. 23.1 A probability distribution for the survival of a trauma patient

Figure 23.1 is an example of the output of, say, an IT system that computes the likelihood of survival of a traumatically injured patient. This computation is based upon input such as the person's age, weight, sex, type of injury, etc. This probability distribution result indicates that there is evidence (derived from the input values) for a probability of survival of about 0.4, and even more evidence for a probability of survival of about 0.65. A weighted average of the result might yield the discrete overall probability of survival of 0.6.

The novel aspect of the fundamentally probabilistic computation is that the discrete result (0.6 probability of survival), if desired, is derived from a probability distribution, and the distribution can provide information on the 'quality' of the discrete summary. In general, a distribution that is tightly clustered around the average signals indicates that the average is trustworthy, and a widely dispersed distribution indicates that the simple average must be treated with caution. It is the shape and spread of the probability distribution that enables the computer to know when the discrete result derived is secure or not – i.e., it can know when a discrete summary is likely to be misleading.

To take a more straightforward classification task: suppose that we built an IT system to distinguish between apples and oranges, but we only input two features of each fruit sample as a basis for this classification. If the two features are, say, 'colour' and 'roundness', then 'orange' coloured and 'very-round' fruit will almost certainly be correctly classified as oranges, while 'green' and 'not-very-round' are likely to be apples. But, in general, these two features, colour and roundness, will not be sufficient information to classify all unknown fruit samples correctly as either an apple or an orange. Some classifications will be equivocal.

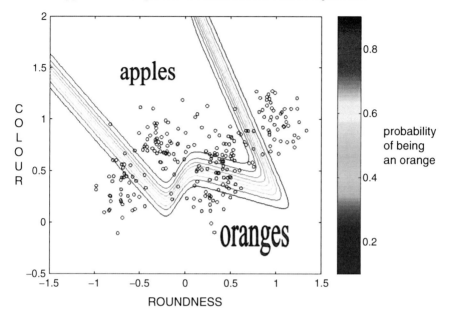

Fig. 23.2 A probabilistic separation of apples from oranges

In Fig. 23.2 a large number of fruit samples (all apples or oranges) have been plotted according to their 'colour' and 'roundness' values. If perfectly correct classification was possible using only 'colour' and 'roundness' then the two sets of plotted points would not be intermixed as they are in Fig. 23.2. As it is, no single, smooth line can be drawn that will separate all apples from all oranges.

The probability distribution computed for each sample – the probability that it is an orange – has been colour coded into the circle that represents each fruit sample. To aid visualization of the probability field that separates these two classes, lines of equal probability have been added – the probability that a sample falling on that line will be an orange. (Note: for a two-class problem, such as this one, the probability of being in one class must be one minus the probability of being in the other class.)

The series of lines in Fig. 23.2 provide a variety of possible discrete separations of our two classes of fruit. The IT system user, who requires simple discrete results, could then choose one of these lines (or any other equal-probability line) as the dividing line between apples and oranges. The choice would be based on the decision as to what probability value maximizes correct orange (or apple) classifications in the context of the specific application of the classifier system envisaged. Alternatively, this IT system can use the probability space to equivocate with precision – i.e., specific and detailed interpretations of the probability distribution it generates.

Figure 23.3 shows the probability distributions for three fruit samples selected as 'indisputably apple', 'indisputably orange' and an equivocal sample 'maybe-apple

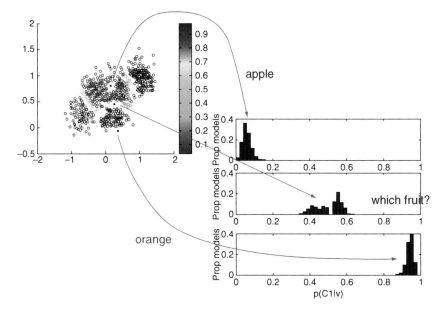

Fig. 23.3 The probability distributions for 3 fruit samples

or maybe-orange.' The probability distributions for these three fruit samples are shown in the three boxes in the lower right of the picture. The third sample is classified by the bottom distribution. It shows that the evidence for classification of this sample is all clustered about the probability of 0.9 of being an orange. Given this probability distribution, we may decide to say that this fruit is an orange with a 0.9 probability. But this latter statement is a discrete interpretation of our fundamentally approximate computation – a summary, if you like. Many other summaries are possible but whichever we choose, the point is that much information within the computed result will have been discarded, e.g., the 0.9 (presumably) average probability can derive from an infinite number of different distributions around the 0.9 value. I've casually called this sample, 'indisputably orange,' and it is mirrored by the top distribution for the other extreme, apple.

Look at the middle distribution: it comes from a fruit sample that falls in the boundary area and so we would not expect it to be centred close to 1.0 (the orange class) nor close to 0.0 (the apple class, because probability of apple is: 1.0 minus the probability of orange). The distribution we find is squarely in the middle, but it is not simply clustered around 0.5, as we might expect. It is split into two clear distributions, one just below 0.5 and one just above. The average might well be 0.5 but our split probability distribution should be able to tell us more than this simple, and perhaps misleading, average.

This split distribution presents the full equivocation details of the classification computed. This distribution is what is computed as the classification result. How it is best interpreted, and how it can (as well as whether it should) be converted to a simple discrete result are complicated questions that we will not get into. The point is simply that probability distributions, as examples of precise approximations, can be computed systematically as an alternative to conventional discrete results.

An IT system for separating apples and oranges is unlikely to find widespread use, but within the world of medical health there are countless niches where an IT system, using precise approximation computation, would be valuable.

Regular screening for breast cancer, for example, is achieved by recording mammograms that a specialist doctor must examine to determine if there is any evidence of a tumour. The specialist diagnostician is confronted, on a daily basis, with large numbers of mammograms to examine, the majority of which are quickly dismissed as 'clear.' A few will be identified as potentially indicative of a tumour, and so further examination and tests can be focused on just those few woman who might benefit. A daily review of large numbers of mammograms most of which will be clear will inevitably lead to mistakes. The particular mistake that we want to avoid is a mammogram classified as clear when it is not; it should have been classified as 'problematic.'

Unfortunately, humans will always make mistakes, but the number can be minimized by reducing the doctor's classification task: the fewer mammograms that need to be reviewed, the fewer miss-classification errors are likely.

So why not use an IT system to remove the indisputably 'clear' mammograms from the original set? In fact, why not design an IT system to do the doctor's classification job? The IT system will not suffer from fatigue; it will analyze every mammogram with exactly the same thoroughness. It will also be able to perform this classification task 24 hours a day, and no end of copies of the IT system can be made in order to scan as many mammograms as desired.

Sounds like a great solution, and it would be if we could indeed design such an IT system, but mammogram classification is too ill-understood (and too fundamentally equivocal) to be programmed into a conventional IT system. This is an example of the sort of problem that deflated much of the *Expert Systems* euphoria of a few decades ago (the topic of Chapter 19): certain human experts can perform the classification task with a high degree of accuracy, but they cannot articulate the basis for their skill in terms of the discrete rules needed to convert it into a computer program.[1]

A much less demanding sub-task, however, is to classify the set of mammograms into those that are 'indisputably clear' and those that are not. Someone would still have to draw the line between these two classes: what exactly is an 'indisputably clear' classification? Which probability contour and what shape of distribution signals 'indisputably clear'?

Suppose we could compute, from each mammogram, an accurate distribution of the likelihood that it is in the 'clear' subset, then human-expert judgements on the same set of mammograms could be used to determine exactly what features of the computed probability distributions should be used to identify the 'indisputably clear' ones. Figure 23.4 illustrates the sort of probability distribution that might be interpreted as 'indisputably clear.'

In Fig. 23.4 we can see that all the evidence from a given mammogram is clustered around 0.0 for the 'probability of a tumour.' In the right-hand panel we show the other way to present these results, because (just like the orange-or-apple problem)

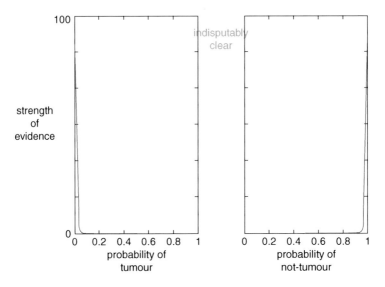

Fig. 23.4 Precise approximations for mammogram screening

this is a two-class task, so one option is one minus the other option. The panels are mirror images of each other.

We use the fundamental uncertainties of a problem to generate a well-defined context of probability specific to each result. The system can then report its level of uncertainty on a computation-by-computation basis – the computer 'knows' which of its computed results are generated with confidence, and which are more equivocal. Recognition of this uncertainty, with respect to each computation, can mitigate the adverse effects of the inevitable unreliability associated with IT systems.

The key idea is that repeated computation of every result, based on systematic variation of the procedure used, will give a probabilistic distribution of all reasonable answers. It follows that <u>disagreement</u> amongst the set of results (i.e., a broad distribution) implies uncertainty, while <u>agreement</u> (i.e., a narrow distribution) implies certainty. This is the basis for the computer's assessment of reliability. This idea is made practical by: first, low cost of computer power which permits massive recomputation, and second, associated developments in statistical computation which provide a sound theoretical basis for the recomputation strategies.

State-of-the-art statistical methods[2] are used to perform this 'analogue' computation; we can call this style of computing with continua, _Precise Approximation Computation (PAC)_.

One demonstration of PAC uses data collected by the Helicopter Emergency Medical Service of the Royal London Hospital – the problem of predicting likelihood of survival after serious injury. Our systems performed as well as the NHS systems developed specifically for the problem, but in addition our system can automatically provide the doctor with precise uncertainty assessments for focusing her/his judgement.[3]

Agreement between all reasonable alternative recomputations is a sound basis for certainty in the answer, but in fact do all have to agree? This seems an excessive demand, but then where is a threshold to be placed? Also, our probability distributions contain more information than the binary distinction we are currently using, but what finer calculations of certainty can be deduced, and how?

What does "all reasonable alternative recomputations" mean? State-of-the-art statistics and probability technology provide a scientific basis for the automatic generation of "all reasonable alternatives", but only for a prespecified classification procedure[4] – of which there are many to choose from. If our chosen procedure is unable to model the data well, then there will be an excess of equivocal classifications (such a system is reliable, but hardly useful), or worse, the occurrence of confident but actually incorrect results.

Such unsatisfactory results may signal corrupted or unrepresentative data, or they may signal a poor choice of classification procedure. The first two causes must be addressed through data analysis, but the last is due to a limitation of the chosen classification procedure. Why do we have to make this choice a priori? Why not set up the statistical framework to select the best variants of the best procedures? The necessary statistical theory exists, but is currently unusable because the functions demanded for implementation appear impossible to construct, and the demand escalates exponentially with each new procedure added. The challenge therefore is to further develop this approach to PAC by devising a computationally feasible route through this statistical theory.

A final example of PAC, and one that has been applied to an operational IT system, is the work at The University of Exeter, in the UK, on the STCA system of the National Air-Traffic Services (NATS).[5] STCA, the acronym for Short-Term Conflict Alert, is an IT system that runs at Heathrow (and many other airports) to monitor all pairs of aircraft within the managed airspace in order to alert air-traffic controllers if any pair of aircraft appears to be in danger of breeching proximity restrictions (i.e., issue an alert if a conflict may occur). It predicts possible conflicts by projecting the flight path of each aircraft forwards in time in order to determine if a conflict appears likely. The STCA system uses only radar tracking data and aircraft size information; it does not have access to the communication between pilots and air-traffic controllers, so it cannot take any intended changes of course into consideration. It can only respond to what it 'sees'. This is done so that the STCA system provides in extra element of security because it is independent of the other monitoring systems; the downside of this restriction is that the STCA system generates false alarms.

Periodically, all STCA systems are manually tuned: employees dedicated to this IT system alter some of the fixed values (such as, maximum horizontal closing velocity) that the system uses to compute an alert or not. The objective of this tuning of the system is to minimize the false alert rate whilst also maximizing the true alert rate.

The STCA IT system contains more than 1,500 fixed *storage-box* values, called *parameters*, which it uses to compute alerts and non-alerts. Each different setting of these parameter values gives a slightly different version of the system each with

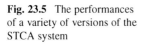

Fig. 23.5 The performances
of a variety of versions of the
STCA system

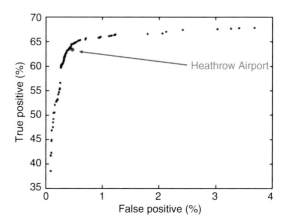

its own false alert and true alert rates. This variety of STCA system options can be displayed as shown in Fig. 23.5.

In Fig. 23.5 there is one dot for each version of the system evaluated, and it is plotted according to its performance in terms of false alerts and true alerts. In such a diagram better operating performances are to the top left: minimum "false positives" (i.e. false alerts) and maximum "true positives" (i.e. true alerts).

This set of STCA systems (each a result of different *parameter* settings) were generated automatically, and, as can be seen it the figure, some them appear to slightly outperform the actual STCA system (manually optimised) in operation at Heathrow Airport. However, the performance recorded for each of these versions of the STCA system is their performance on a test set of examples, and we know the dangers of putting too much faith in test-set outcomes.

The set of test cases is selected as a representative sample from actual operational data, but necessarily from past operation of the system. The concern is that (as Stock Markets have made worrying clear) past performance is not always a reliable guide to the future.

It may be that the test set used 'favoured' the automatically generated systems, so the actual Heathrow version will perform the best in the real operating environment. Because of the potential discontinuities of system performance associated with a range of test-case values in discrete computations, we would like to be assured that our optimally performing systems are 'stable' – i.e., their performance level does not plummet with a slightly different set of test cases.

Again, PAC can address this problem by switching from discrete system evaluations to continuous probabilistic ones. In Fig. 23.5 we see a discrete curve (or we would if we filled in the gaps with more system evaluations) of optimal STCA systems in a space (either side of the curve) about which we know nothing. How does the performance of these 'optimal' system versions change as we vary the test data? Do they improve or deteriorate badly? Are they stable, with respect to performance, or not?

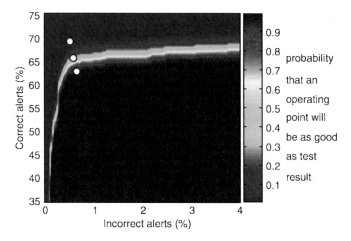

Fig. 23.6 A probability field for the STCA system

If Fig. 23.5 was a field of probability with respect to system performance, we would have a guide to this important question of STCA-system operating stability. Figure 23.6 illustrates this desirable state of affairs.

How is this figure to be interpreted? Pick any point on it; the colour of that point is an estimate of the probability that the STCA system with the *parameter* settings represented by this point will perform as well as the test performance.

For example, the three points indicated by white circles in Fig. 23.6 indicate three possible versions of the STCA system. The top system sits at about 0.1 in the probability field which means that although it may perform better than either of the other two selected systems (because it is closest to the top-left corner, the optimum) the probability that its operational performance will be this good is only 0.1.

The lowest of the three systems may be the poorest performer (of the three) but there is a high probability (approx. 0.9) that it will perform at least this well when operational. The middle system is at a 0.5 probability point which means that this system has a 50:50 chance of operating better (or worse) than the test performance.

As with probability distribution results for classifier systems, the fundamental result is a continuous distribution, which may or may not need to be transformed into a discrete result. In this case the choice of a specific version of the STCA system. And similarly, there are awkward questions about how to make this choice, and how any discrete choice is to be interpreted.

Figure 23.7 illustrates one potentially useful, simplifying discretisation in which points of equal probability have been connected to give contours of equal probability.

In addition, both of the examples of PAC are still research topics rather than tried and tested technologies. In both strategies there are issues of the validity and

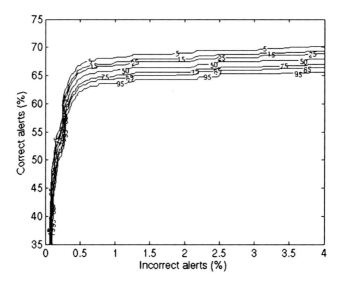

Fig. 23.7 Contours of equal probability in the STCA-system space

applicability of the underlying statistical theory, although both are based on sound and systematic statistical procedures, not on ad hoc probability calculations.

In summary:

- Useful IT systems may operate in domains in which results are fundamentally equivocal, and this is at odds with the correct-or-incorrect basis of computing technology.
- In reality, all IT system results are to some degree equivocal, and, instead of retrofitting conventional discrete technology to accommodate this feature, we might compute in terms of well-founded continua – *precise approximation computation* (PAC).
- An IT system with PAC-based components can determine (from the manner in which the computation proceeds) whether a computed result is suspect or not, and valuable use could be made of this 'knowledge'.
- *Precise approximation computing*, in several manifestations, appears to offer the possibility of providing the necessary 'self-knowledge'.
- Like neural-computing technology, the precise approximations technologies are currently limited in scope and would apply to specialist components of IT systems rather than to IT systems as a whole.
- The move to continuous probability distributions or spaces does circumvent some of the problems associated with discrete computation, but it also introduces issues of discrete interpretation, or summaries, of the continuities computed.
- Although the precise approximation strategies illustrated are based on sound statistical principles, fundamental assumptions are involved, and these need to be thoroughly researched before full weight can put on the probabilistic continua computed.

Endnotes

1. It may be that the disappointing performance of many so-called *Expert Systems* was due to the discrete computational technology used in their construction – they were based on collections of discrete IF-THEN rules you may recall from the earlier chapter on this topic. With the emergence of the new computational technologies, such as precise approximation computing, it may be valuable to revisit some of these desirable but hitherto unattainable Expert-System applications. However, as this chapter, and the previous one, make clear, these novel technologies are still, at the moment, severely limited in scope.

   This *Expert-system's* disappointment is an uncanny parallel of a major plank of the argument running through this book: the irresistible success of small-scale discrete (IF-THEN...) explanations lured the technologists into the incomprehensible complexities of such explanations on a large scale.

2. These fancy statistical tools (known as Reversible-Jump Markov Chain Monte Carlo, or RJMCMC, methods together with Bayes' Rule) provide us with a sound theoretical basis for the probability distributions computed, but they are, of course, not without their own problems; they are thus the subject of ongoing research. Full details can be found in: W.J. Krzanowski, J.E. Fieldsend, T.C. Bailey, R.M. Everson, D. Partridge, V. Schetinin, Confidence in classification: a Bayesian approach, *Journal of Classification*, vol. **23**, pp. 199–220, 2006.

   These examples of PAC, presented to promote the merits of computing with probability continua, are programmed conventionally – i.e., the continuous probability distributions are constructed from large numbers (tens of thousands) of discrete computations. 'Continuous versus discrete' is a complex issue, and as much an issue of representational level as of intrinsic difference – starting with particle versus wave theory of matter. Notice that the analogue systems that populate the natural world are all constructed from discrete atoms and molecules.

3. T.C. Bailey, R.M. Everson, J.E. Fieldsend, W.J. Krzanowski, D. Partridge and V. Schetinin. Representing classifier confidence in the safety critical domain – an illustration from mortality prediction in trauma cases, *Neural Computing and Applications,* vol. 16, 2007, pp. 1–10.

4. There are many different procedures (different algorithms based on different mathematical models) that can be used for data classification. On a given data classification task some procedures will give better results than others. We call this the 'fit' of the model to the data, and the best-fit procedure is not easily determined.

5. R.M. Everson and J.E. Fieldsend. Multi-Objective Optimisation of Safety Related Systems: An Application to Short Term Conflict Alert, *IEEE Transactions on Evolutionary Computation*, vol. **10**, no. 2, pp. 187–198, 2006.

Part IV
The End of the Affair

I'll wrap up this polemic with a list of the main elements of my argument, each associated with a pointer to where exactly it is justified in the preceding chapters. The final conclusion is a similar point-by-point summary of: where we are with IT systems; what we might best do now to improve the situation; and where hope for significant change in the future might come from.

The mess that we are in with respect to the development of large IT systems derives from a basis of many inter-related issues, but two rather different aspects of unhelpful allure can be identified. The two major sources of seduction are:

1. The challenge of the programming game – tightly constrained yet promising anything that the human brain is smart enough to devise.
2. The possibility of formal program verification – given a technological basis that is discrete, abstract and well-defined.

The sad reality is a struggle to contain an emergent chaos by means of the wholly inadequate process of testing to see what our IT system will, and will not, do on each particular test case.

Chapter 24
Analysis and Counselling

Let's see how this unencouraging analysis has been developed. Alternatively, if you're starting out here, you can see what the sequence of conclusions through the general argument has been, and the chapter in which each was presented. Special usage of language is italicised and underlined as well if defined in that chapter.

Chapter 1 provided a general introduction to the nature and consequent difficulties of IT-system production.

- IT systems are everywhere, and will continue to infiltrate the lives of all of us.
- We cannot easily check that an IT system is computing correctly.
- IT systems all fail: sometimes immediately and spectacularly, sometimes unobtrusively just once in a while, and sometimes in any combination of these two extremes.
- IT-system failures vary from production of blatantly incorrect results to failure to produce a desired result.
- The interplay of a variety of causes means that all large IT systems are unmanageably complex.
- IT-system complexity is discrete complexity rather than complexity based on continua.
- If, by chance (combined with exemplary practice and much effort), an IT system is constructed with no possibility of failure behaviour, we can never know this.

In the confessional Chapter 2 every effort is made to convey the seductive allure of the programming 'game': it is an open-ended (and private) game, promising powerful achievements once the gamer proves himself smart enough to thread his program through the mesh of constraints imposed.

- To some, programming is an alluring man-machine tussle that ultimately promises to put great power in the hands of the man.
- The first challenge (the easy one) is that a program must be _grammatically correct_ before a computer will accept it.
- But the (much) bigger challenge is getting an accepted program to cause the computer to behave in precisely the way you want it to behave; it is _behavioural correctness_ that is the really big problem.

D. Partridge, *The Seductive Computer: Why IT Systems Always Fail*,
DOI 10.1007/978-1-84996-498-2_24, © Springer-Verlag London Limited 2011

Chapter 3 employed the simplistic device of a 'squirrel computer' to take us on the first steps on the path to understanding this technology.

What knowledge (and necessary jargon) did it impart?

- We know the basics of programming technology: a _computer program_ is a list of instructions, each selected from a _programming language_, that tell the _processor_ to manipulate symbols (in our case, to add and multiply numbers) and what _storage boxes_ of the _memory_ to put the results in.
- Once your program is accepted as _grammatically correct_, the computer will _execute_ it, and the behaviour it specifies will emerge; a behaviour that depends on the precise order of the instructions. Programming thus demands a high proficiency in all-round trivia management (from instruction order to _storage-box_ naming).
- The instruction sequence dictates a _flow path_ through the program, i.e., the order in which the computer will _execute_ each instruction.
- The resultant emergent behaviour may be correct, i.e., what you intended, or incorrect, not what you intended.
- But even when the snippets of observed behaviour look to be correct, the full details of the causal links between correct behaviour and your intentions are hard to verify. So, general correctness of IT-system behaviour will remain a faith-based property.

In Chapter 4 the rudimentary knowledge of what programming involves is further developed by switching to a shopping robot as the example IT system. It reinforces the basic characteristics of programming, and adds:

- All programs are simply a list of instructions that the computer will follow mindlessly.
- The instruction list may be reduced in length by making repeated segments into a single instance of a _subprogram_ which is _executed_ repeatedly from the _main_ program.
- Other repeated instruction segments may be included in a _loop_ structure that directs the computer to repeatedly _execute_ the instructions included within it.
- Use of a _loop_ structure introduces a _branch point_ where the _execution_ sequence may either go around the _loop_ or not.
- This list of instructions, the program, then determines a complex _flow structure_ (as the collection of all potential _flow paths_), but makes no effort to expose it.
- It is the _flow structure_ (in conjunction with _branch conditions_ and specific _storage-box_ values) that directly determines the program behaviour that emerges.
- _Stepwise refinement_ from _program plan_ to programming language instructions is introduced and contrasted with _ad hoc_ concoction of programs.
- Some _program style_ guidelines (just **COMMENT**s and indentation as a layout feature) were introduced as an aid to human comprehension.
- _Subprograms_ and _loops_ reduce program size but increase _flow structure_ complexity.

- Consequently, the programmer attempting to eliminate an error, or otherwise modify the emergent behaviour, can only work by rearranging the list of instructions but must think in terms of the *flow structure* repercussions.

This is all of the programming competence we need in order to fully appreciate the essential technology of IT-system development. From this basis, we can begin to see important implications.

In Chapter 5 our robot-shopper program is used as a source of examples to give more substance to the claim that the programmer is required to conceptually manage excessive detail. The notion of stylistic aids is further developed, but with the caution that poor style (another seductively easy outcome) may be worse than no style.

- Programming demands mastery, on a massive scale, of fine grained complexity springing from a network of constraints: some logical, some stylistic and some an ill-defined combination.
- Principles of *program style* and *structured programming* – such as, *modularity*, *encapsulation*, and localization of *scope* – minimize complexity and so facilitate *program understanding* through *flow-structure visualization*.
- Principles of *program style*, naturally developed through *stepwise refinement*, are made manifest through layout conventions, and can significantly facilitate understanding of the all-important *flow structure*.
- Poor, incomplete and outdated stylistic aids, a natural consequence of the Happy Hacker Syndrome, can seriously misdirect *program understanding*.
- IT-system *documentation*, such as design diagrams and notes, can similarly assist *program understanding*, or misdirect it.
- Programming in the small is totally different from large IT system development – size really does matter.
- Whiz-kid hackers are the worst IT-system developers.
- IT-system *maintenance* is first introduced as a further aggravation in our quest for high-quality IT systems.
- A lot of IT-system *maintenance* is *debugging*, i.e., finding and fixing errors.

Chapter 6 is a tough chapter. It examined the hope for formal proof of what an IT system will, and will not, do. This is the route to guaranteeing IT-system behaviour, and an anticipated pay-off for using a discrete technology. It showed us why we might think that IT systems can be proven correct, and why, in fact, they cannot.

- An IT-system *specification* is a complete, precise and unambiguous statement of what the desired IT system should do.
- A *correct* IT system is one whose behaviour is exactly as *specified*.
- Testing can never deliver a guarantee of IT-system *correctness*.
- Programs are, however, well-defined symbol structures just like mathematical formulae, and thus hold the promise of being *proven correct*.
- Mathematical proof, the time-honoured mechanism for demonstrating the correctness of well-defined symbol structures, has its strengths and weaknesses especially in relation to IT systems.

- IT systems, by virtue of sheer complexity, have significantly muddied even this neat mathematical idea.
- Both proofs and *specifications* of IT systems will be large and complicated 'objects' just like the programs.
- There are some fundamental problems with IT system *specification*, and a major source of difficulty is explained in the next chapter.

Chapter 7 explored one of the inherent weaknesses of a mathematical proof for an IT system: in essence, an IT system cannot remain as a purely abstract object, a symbol structure, so symbol *grounding* is examined.

- *Grounding* is an interpretation of a symbol structure in terms of some real-world phenomena – e.g. the decimal number that appears next to "Final Balance" on my bank statement is taken to be the amount in pounds that I had in the bank on the date given (another symbol structure to be *grounded*).
- If an IT system is to be used to impact on the real world, the symbol structures of the program, just like those in mathematical formulae, must be interpreted in terms of real-world phenomena – parts of the program must be *grounded*.
- *Grounding* is not rule-governed; it is a matter of choice and so shatters certainty of abstract behaviour.
- Formal verification of programs (or parts of programs) is a potentially useful tool for grappling with IT-system correctness, but it can never be a complete answer.

Chapter 8 is the first diversionary chapter and it tries to dispel the common myth that scientists prove things about the world.

Chapter 9 further developed the grounding problem: in particular, it demonstrates the arbitrariness of the hardware-software distinction by means of a non-restrictive approach to the notion of a machine.

- There is no valid reason to limit the notion of a machine to hard components.
- A computer program is a machine, a *soft machine*.
- An IT system is composed of a hard machine (usually electronic components) and a *soft machine*, a computer program.
- In principle, the relative mix of hard and soft components in an IT system is entirely arbitrary.
- In practice, IT systems are primarily *soft machines*.
- The *soft machine* becomes *grounded* within the hard components of an IT system (the computer hardware), and the IT system as a whole is then *grounded* by the context in which it is used, and its inputs and outputs are interpreted.
- Even this initial *grounding*, which cannot be avoided for a *soft machine*, wrecks the scope for formal proofs of IT system correctness.

Computers are our mindless slaves; so if they do unwanted things, it is our fault for telling them to so. Chapter 10 contested this viewpoint.

- Computers most assuredly do only what we tell them to do.
- What we've told a computer to do must be distinguished from what we believe we've told it to do.

- Knowing what you've told a computer to do is impossible to establish with certainty.
- A program *module* has only one flow-path in and one flow-path out.
- *Well-structured* (i.e. modular) IT systems can be contrasted with *spaghetti-code* systems, and the former considerably assist the task of knowing what you've told the computer to do.
- Modern IT-system design and development still suffers from the puzzle solving-and-setting practices that were important in the early days of programming, such as the *one liner*. This remains a detrimental element of the allure of programming.

The diversionary Chapter 11 introduces and explains the powerful computational notion of recursion. It demonstrates how the logical simplicity of recursive procedures is at odds with its mechanical complexity for human reasoning. Experiments with the comprehension of English sentences seem to show that the human brain lacks the mechanisms to process recursive procedures.

The aim of Part I of this book was to instruct the novice in the rudiments of the craft of programming. The goal was *not* to transform every reader into a programmer, but to make clear the basic nature of the task:

- The nature of its complexity in sufficient detail.
- The unsolved problems concerning good, bad, correct and erroneous programs.
- The majors ways that these problems are being addressed.
- And the controversy about how they should be addressed.

You now know why there is no easy answer to the question: "Is this program correct?" You now have sound reasons to be thoroughly suspicious of anyone who is prepared to answer "yes".

In Part II, with the necessary technical detail digested (or at least thoroughly appreciated), we stepped back to look at several aspects of the repercussions of this technology in the wider context.

Chapter 12 is a one-off, but justified by the puzzle that is intriguing, and may be at the heart of our problems with IT systems: the programming game is a man thing. A fundamental argument in this book is that men (almost exclusively) get transported into an unhealthily close relationship with their programs – some worse than others but the allure is seldom totally resisted successfully (and always spills over to the detriment of IT systems). This chapter examined our understanding of human close relationships to see if they shed any light on this strange phenomenon.

What might we extract from this dip into human psychology that could shed light on why programming is compulsive, but almost exclusively for males?

- Male-female close relationships are not symmetrical.
- The tireless, non-judgemental and (apparently) endless novel responses of a computer supply the interdependence required for a stable close relationship.
- An entity capable of endless and inexhaustible giving may be more attractive to males than females.
- For a sustained relationship, the creative genius needs interaction with the ever-ready and lightning-fast machine – but why primarily males?

- Males (more than females) tend to perceive, and resent, under-benefit in a relationship; this never happens when the partner is a computer.
- The intimacy, based on total guaranteed privacy, can be expected to encourage a close relationship – all faults are accepted without rebuke.
- The non-competitive computer never challenges self-image – another primarily male weakness when developing a close relationship.
- The happy hacker has found a partner that:
  - Understands him
  - Values his talent
  - Cares for him
  - Needs to be cared for (perhaps led rather than mothered)
- What more could a man want? Or a woman? But perhaps she too readily sees through this perception whereas a socially isolated male does not?
- Perhaps it's a male-male bond not a male-female one; the drive is to scale new heights with his amazing partner, not to isolate themselves in a bond of mutual admiration?

Chapter 13 argued that the irredeemable addicts may be few and far between, but precious few programmers (perhaps none) are totally immune, and it is these mostly-responsible programmers that are the real problem, not the addicts. For they slip through the coarse filters that can only catch the extreme cases. The average programmer is simply a victim of the seductive nature of the technology, a technology that society is rushing to embrace comforted by the quite false belief that the computer technologists are the masters of all they program.

We now know why this belief is false, and what else do we know:

- The compulsive nature of programming has long been recognized.
- It is not, however, the addicts that are the problem; it is the less extreme manifestations in virtually all programmers that undermine proper IT-system design and development.
- The majority of these afflicted persons are not building IT systems from scratch; they are *maintaining* existent systems – a distinction that severely aggravates all the existing difficulties.
- Effective *maintenance* is based on *program understanding* and this is facilitated by *well-structured* systems, and support from *software tools*, such as *editors*.
- One of the reasons for the prevalence of *maintenance* is that IT systems represent too big a commitment to organizational infrastructure to abandon, so they are *maintained* well beyond their proper life span.
- These long-used IT systems, termed *legacy systems*, introduce further difficulties, such as (apparently) *dead code*.
- Even with a large IT system to be constructed from scratch, the model programmer will eventually be drawn into grappling with an unmanageable system.
- The essential difference between the happy hacker and the sober and well-disciplined programmer is the speed with which an IT system becomes unmanageable, and the extent of the chaos generated (which is often manifest in an excessive need for testing and *debugging*).

In the third diversionary chapter, Chapter 14, we look at the hype that surrounds current Genome work. We see that the problem facing those who wish to understand the behaviour of the base sequences revealed is analogous to the very difficult (ultimately impossible) problem of *program understanding*. The big difference is that the genomic analogue is much more complex in every respect.

Now we have some general principles of IT-system technology, and general system characteristics to underpin our earlier knowledge of the detailed complexity of modern programs. What are the foundations that Chapter 15 has added?

- During long-term use every IT system needs to be *maintained* by making changes that will inexorably undermine good structure and understanding; in this sense they will always *runaway*.
- In general, IT systems defy human comprehension because:
  - Full understanding demands mastery of an excessive span of detail.
  - Small misunderstandings can have large repercussions.
- IT systems pose wholly new challenges to human understanding because they are complex *discrete systems*, quite unlike both natural systems and other engineered complex systems.
- The discreteness of IT systems is manifest in several ways; it is primarily the single-threaded *decision-logic tree* basis of IT systems that causes difficulties.
- Small, "nicely-factored" *discrete systems* are readily amenable to formal analysis (possibly even proof of correctness); large *discrete systems* with tight internal couplings (such as most IT systems) are not.
- Small, "nicely-factored" systems are also readily comprehensible; large ones (made even larger by the avoidance of the succinct power of inter-couplings) are not – they present as a conglomerate of individual components, which, of course, they are if all inter-couplings are eliminated.
- Complex natural systems achieve stability through redundancy, and predictability through *monotonic* analogue (rather than discrete) basics.
- 'System science' has failed to encompass systems of discrete complexity.
- The mathematical basis from which much of programming practice has been developed has severely undervalued redundancy as a system feature.
- *Discrete systems* tend to be unpredictable – hence the extreme weakness of IT-system testing as a validation procedure.

Chapter 16 added further to the problems of designing and constructing well-understood IT systems: once these systems are released and go operational, fresh new problems appear, problems that are founded on the old and (by now, I hope) familiar ones of overwhelming complexity and extreme fragility.

- In-use IT system confidence becomes suspect every time an IT system is exposed to potential changes.
- The elements of IT-system *access control* are introduced and discussed.
- Inadvertent change, due to clumsiness, or covert malicious change causes IT systems to *sneakaway*.
- All IT systems must be open to change; usually managed through passwords.

- Biometric access control, such as fingerprint matching, is a growing alternative to passwords. These avoid the memorisation task of many passwords but:
  - Successful duplication or simulation will open all doors (whereas use of multiple passwords can protect against this).
  - We lose the convenience of giving (perhaps temporary) access to someone else.
  - Matching to approve access becomes complicated (and thus error prone).
- Beyond the privacy concerns of *read-only access*, access to change IT systems must be closely controlled and monitored.
- This control is at odds with ease of access for essential system changes, e.g. just adding new information, or making corrections.
- *Change-access* (or *read-write* access) control for an IT system may be a complex, multi-level procedure, i.e., different users require access to different system-modification possibilities.
- Further complication to the ever-present threat of malicious system access and modification is introduced through the convenience of computer networking, such as made possible by the Internet.

In sum, the mix of human curiosity (not to mention malevolence), the extreme fragility of programs, and the speed and complexity of the Internet constitute a serious threat to the stability of every IT system. The potential for unnoticed change must be contemplated for any IT system that is not rigorously guarded, used only on isolated machines, never copied, etc. – even then you can never be sure.

In Chapter 17, the final diversionary one, we examine the issues surrounding lost data from the many databases that now exist. We challenge the popular excuse that the proper procedures were not followed by suggesting that an appropriate IT system would give the users no choice but to follow the procedures implemented. We also acknowledge, however, the tension between necessary accessibility (to add or change data) and the security and integrity of the data – a strong echo of a major issue with all IT systems.

In Chapter 18, we surveyed the current reality of IT systems impacting on our lives. Given the excessively sluggish nature of movement to new IT systems – reluctance based on well-founded fear and solid economic arguments – we cannot realistically expect any significant changes in the foreseeable future.

- IT systems have a *life-cycle* in which *maintenance* is the dominant activity.
- *Maintaining* (i.e. extending and debugging) an IT system that you did not develop exacerbates all of the IT-system problems, and is the major programming effort.
- At a certain point in IT-system complexity, further *debugging* is a self-defeating exercise.
- We all live within a mesh of IT systems: some offer conveniences that we can either accept or reject, others do not give us a choice.
- The outputs of an IT system may be viewed as a useful guide to be accepted cautiously, or as the ultimate truth to be accepted blindly; the reality of all IT systems will lie somewhere in between these two extremes.
- IT systems are not extended or amended lightly, because change is so dangerous; hence, we tend to 'work around' their failings.

- Many IT systems improve our lives.
- Some IT systems have negative impacts, all the way from minor aggravation to life threatening.
- There are no easy answers (as far as we know). So for IT systems in _safety-critical_ roles where failures have the potential to cause deaths and/or disasters, the best advice is too lessen the criticality of their roles and to limit expectation of what they can deliver.

In Part III some _hopeware_ were offered in the form of innovative technologies that may provide a means to change and perhaps lessen (if not solve) the fundamental problems of IT-system development and long-term management. The ideas and technologies presented varied from minor assistance to radical overhaul, but the best that many can offer is little more than future promise.

We began in Chapter 19 with some classic _hopeware_ developed during the Expert Systems boom towards the end of the last millennium – self-explaining systems. An automatically generated explanation is simply a piece of program output, just like the output it's purportedly explaining. Why should we be any more confident of our ability to correctly program explanation generation than of our aptitude to get other activities of a program working just right? The short answer is: we shouldn't.

So what were the salient points of this chapter?

- A general mechanism for self-explanation was a spin-off of _Expert Systems Technology (EST)_ which attempted to mechanise human expertise using IT systems composed of a _knowledge base_ (a _database_ of _rules_ and _facts_) and an _inference engine_ (that deduces further information from user input and the _knowledge base_).
- It is persuasive in the small, but fails in the large.
- Just as with programs, the clarity of small context-free elements (program instructions or IF-THEN rules) is quickly lost when the system, or the purported explanation of the system, grows to be a large collection of these elements.
- The simplest explanation of a complex system may be complex (although hopefully less complex).
- Comprehensibility of complex explanations is probably best achieved (insofar as it can be achieved at all) through a combination of sophisticated structure and simple elements; it cannot be achieved through an unstructured mass of simple elements.
- A putative solution that is programmed, like self-explanation, is subject to all the same difficulties as the IT system it claims to explain.

More promise, perhaps, is in Chapter 20: The production of high-performance, highly reliable programs may, in turn, be crucially dependent upon the existence of a well-engineered moderately stupid assistant.

- IT-system development complexity can be lessened by the use of other programs that monitor the programming and provide information about program structure to the programmer.
- An integrated suite of such helpful programs is a _programming support environment_.

- Simple, factual support is easily provided.
- More sophisticated support quickly extends into AI research areas, and is not easily provided.
- Accurate simple support is preferable to sophisticated support of dubious quality.
- 'Moderately stupid assistance' is the level of help to expect.
- Automated support may be either pro-active or on-demand only, or some combination.
- Constant interruptions with worthless, or erroneous, 'help' are worse than no help at all.
- Substantial support only comes at a price, and there must be tangible incentives to pay it.

Chapter 21 examined program-visualization technology; a strategy for automated assistance to program understanding that has been realized, and can probably be developed a good deal further. Here are the general points to take forward:

- IT systems are fundamentally dynamic objects, yet we try to understand them via static representations.
- Computer systems are quite capable of generating dynamic representations of ongoing computations.
- Every IT system *executes* in the context of an *operating system* which can execute other programs at the same time.
- The power of the human visual system can be exploited to aid IT system understanding via dynamic system-visualization techniques.
- The related idea of *visual programming* was introduced.

Chapters 22 and 23 presented two radical new technologies: one attempting to capitalize on the distributed stability of biological systems, and the other on the information-rich computation with continua rather than discrete summaries.

There is no clear answer to the question of whether biology provides the inspiration (if not the firm basis) for a new and useful way to compute. Each new suggestion solves some problems but generates or exacerbates others. The point is that there may be usable radical alternatives, and we should be more active in exploring them, rather than keep on banging proof and logic together in the hope that the resultant sparks will eventually light up some neat, formal answers.

- The organic world is full of stable, reliable complex systems.
- IT systems' technologists may therefore find some useful structures and processes in the world of biology.
- Evolution, crudely viewed as a process involving time, random changes and selection, has found application in complex optimization.
- Neural computing (originally inspired by the impressive computational properties of brains) has been developed in a number different ways.
- So-called *neural networks* as computational devices embrace a wealth of special terms – *units*, *weights*, *activity* values –and introduce *distributed computation*.

- *Network programs*, hence _network programming_, appear to circumvent some fundamental weaknesses of conventional programs.
- But *network programming* has its own weaknesses and cannot, as yet, be used for large-scale, multifunctional IT systems, although network programs could be elements of such systems.
- *Network programming* may offer the software engineer a new paradigm and so require fundamental shifts in thinking about applications and management of computational technology.

Chapter 23 demonstrates possibilities for computing with probability distributions that can be reduced to a discrete result when required, but because of its provenance the IT system will know how much confidence to put into every discrete summary it generates. Even for our bank-balance IT system, it would be a valuable advance if the IT system knew when its calculations were sound, and when they were suspect so that a warning (or further internal checks) could be activated automatically.

- Useful IT systems may operate in domains in which results are fundamentally equivocal, and this is at odds with the correct-or-incorrect basis of computing technology.
- In reality, all IT system results are to some degree equivocal, and, instead of retrofitting conventional discrete technology to accommodate this feature, we might compute in terms of well-founded continua – _precise approximation computation_ (PAC).
- An IT system with PAC-based components can determine (from the manner in which the computation proceeds) whether a computed result is suspect or not, and valuable use could be made of this 'knowledge'.
- *Precise approximation computing*, in several manifestations, appears to offer the possibility of providing the necessary 'self-knowledge'.
- Like neural-computing technology, the precise approximations technologies are currently limited in scope and would apply to specialist components of IT systems rather than to IT systems as a whole.
- The move to continuous probability distributions or spaces does circumvent some of the problems associated with discrete computation, but it also introduces issues of discrete interpretation, or summaries, of the continuities computed.
- Although the precise approximation strategies illustrated are based on sound statistical principles, fundamental assumptions are involved, and these need to be thoroughly researched before full weight can put on the probabilistic continua computed.

Let me now try and reduce all of the foregoing to one (fairly) short list, a super-summary:

- Programming aspires to be the science of designing and developing systems with specific emergent behaviours, and (almost) any desired behaviour is possible.
- Programmers are readily seduced into abandoning best practice.
- The principles of good IT-system construction (to aid human comprehension) are:

- − Hard to enforce
- − A drag for the programmer
- − Detrimental when sloppily applied
- The conventional technology of IT-system construction is:
  - − Excessively fragile
  - − Too readily malleable
  - − Impossibly intricate

Thus:

- Large IT-system development is the art and science of fighting a losing battle against emergent chaos.
- The fragility of large IT systems, which cannot be developed according to formal principles, is exacerbated when built from a standpoint of 'do it right; prove it's right.' − redundancy is undervalued.
- Large IT systems defy human comprehension (whether single programmers or teams) at the level of detail necessary for prediction of all the behaviours that will emerge.
- Testing for IT-system correctness is a time-consuming and fundamentally inadequate procedure.
- Testing is the basis for **all** IT-system checking.
- IT-system maintenance (an economic and technical necessity) always further degrades a system over time.
- In addition to intentional and supposedly benign IT-system changes, IT systems are vulnerable to malicious tampering.

Chapter 25
The Epilogic

*But returning to the arguments, I would repeat that I fear none
of the existing machines; what I fear is the extraordinary rapidity
with which they are becoming something very different to what
they are at present.*

(Samuel Butler, *Erewhon* 1872)

The case has been made for the fundamental role of discrete (or digital, if you prefer) computer-programming technology as the central villain in IT-system failures. This case, however, is not a simple cause and effect phenomenon. Unmanageable IT-system complexity is the outcome that leads directly to unexpected and unfixable system failures, but the route to this situation of emergent chaos is as rich as it is irresistible.

The flow from IT-system conception and commissioning through development to usage and maintenance is a meld of many factors woven into the basic technology:

1. A technology that offers high-precision, but hides the demand for an impossible level of attention to detail.
2. A technology that (falsely) promises a route to the stars for those that are creative enough to devise it.
3. A technology that makes no attempt to reveal the essential dynamics of the routes to its emergent behaviours.
4. A technology that invites 'try it and see' (as a seemingly costless and intensely private strategy) – a sure route to eventual chaos.
5. A technology that, like so many drugs, initially delivers easy 'highs' (of working programs), but quickly reduces to no more than a never-ending struggle for progressively more-elusive minor successes.
6. A technology that includes no requirement for ease of human comprehension, neither in the mechanisms of its products nor in the patterns of their behaviour.
7. A technology that allows, but offers no inducements, to human-engineer programs.
8. A technology that imposes no sanctions on wholly misleading (stylistic) human-engineering of programs.

D. Partridge, *The Seductive Computer: Why IT Systems Always Fail*,
DOI 10.1007/978-1-84996-498-2_25, © Springer-Verlag London Limited 2011

9. A technology that holds out the promise of formal guarantees for system behaviour, but not seriously.
10. A technology that results in IT systems that can only be <u>tested</u> for validity: a process that is often (nearly) information-less and thus effectively endless.
11. A technology that gives rise to products that no one fully understands.
12. A technology that is amenable to small demonstrations that deny all of the above-listed difficulties.

There is also a little more to the issue of size: large IT systems compound all the problems, but few useful systems are small enough and well-structured enough for exactly all of the desired emergent behaviours to be anticipated with confidence. In practice, we hardly need to bother with the qualification 'large' (and mostly, I do not). The important distinction is between large-enough to be useful and very-small, nicely-factorable examples that do not stray beyond discrete value sets, such as the integers.

These 12 factors, although technology based, draw in all parties to collude in the fiction that a substantial IT system can be specified, designed and developed according to estimated time and budget constraints. Once we admit that the process will be one of struggling to gain sufficient control of the emergent chaos then we know why many IT-system project estimations are pretty worthless.

The technology is not wholly to blame. In fact, one might say that it is not the technology but its misuse by the human factions associated with IT-systems: the users who don't really know what they want and don't want; the system commissioners who decide what others really want; the system designers and programmers who get lost in the necessary intricacies and never fail to rise to the temptation to master them on a piece-meal basis that results in delivery of some particular wants as a good-enough approximation to the original goals; the users of the delivered system who are prepared to make the best of it (or not in some cases); and the software technicians who continue the fight to make the system behave acceptably using (by this time perhaps necessary) local fixes. But it is, however, the nature of the technology that exploits the various human weaknesses, and so delivers, with amazing consistency, very expensive IT-system failures. This technology is not an immutable feature of the world; it is a human creation from start to finish. Surely this is not the best mankind can do?

In many cases project management can be improved, as the British Computer Society[1] and the National Audit Office[2] both maintain in the UK. IT systems can be designed using a more "human-centered" approach, as Norman, in the USA, advocates.[3] But ultimately, as Brooks has forcefully argued,[4] "there is no silver bullet" to slay the werewolf of IT-system failure.

In an area full of different 'potential' fixes to the problems of software engineering, the single coalescence of agreement is that large IT systems with estimated development times of more than, say, 2 years are doomed. Large IT systems can only be developed incrementally. As long ago as 1971 in the USA, Harlan Mills (an early star of the software-development world) proposed that IT systems should be grown by incremental development.[5] Also in the USA, Brooks runs with this idea in his essentially negative 20-year re-assessment of the likelihood that the cost and schedule overruns associated with IT-system development will be significantly reduced. In the UK, Aaron Sloman's analysis[6] of the problems associated with the UK Government's National Health Service IT system (a 10-year project!) makes exactly this point:

Large IT systems must be grown, not built.

What can be done, apart from develop the patches suggested in the closing chapters, or go and live on a desert island (without a solar-powered laptop)?

Do not commission one-shot long-term large IT-system development projects, such as the UK government's NHS Programme for IT.[7] Instead, use a model of organic growth, add new functions once the basic ones are working satisfactorily. This allows for the changing world over time:

1. It also allows for re-design as a result of experience with basic system behaviours (a well-known, but often ignored, strategy of rapid prototyping[8]).
2. It will avoid the massive IT-system disasters.
3. It may provide a natural curb on excessive (and thus totally unmanageable) complexity, leaving users with a basic, but good, IT system.

BUT

1. It may result it one-step-forward and two-steps-back development (which always happens anyway, and under this model should provide useable systems along the way).
2. It may result in 'spaghetti' systems (but not *spaghetti code* necessarily) if modularity principles not rigorously enforced.
3. It will result in the difficulties of (outline) designing for the unknown additions (but current one-shot large-scale design is often designing for some fictional target that is changed beyond recognition once system development finally gets there).

   • Design and develop the system using belt-and-braces principles[9] – 'if it can go wrong; it will go wrong' must be the slogan, rather than 'if I do it right; it will be correct.'
   • Use formal methods, even formal verification, in the system components where this is possible, but recognize their severe limitations.
   • In addition to formally verified system components where possible, the new and innovative technologies should also be employed for suitable system components.
   • We must be a lot more cautious about what we will expect our IT systems to do, and the reliance we put upon the belief that they will always do it correctly.

Because of the basic fragility and detailed complexity of the fundamental technology (which is not going to be superseded by an equally powerful and less troublesome alternative in the foreseeable future), large-scale IT systems will always be expensive to produce, and somewhat unpredictable in behaviour. Current practice can be improved, perhaps significantly improved, as a result of a more realistic understanding by both managers and software developers of the inherent weaknesses in the technology – weakness as a system technology as well as weakness with respect to its seductive effects on those at the code face.

IT-system development, however, will not be transformed into a neat and formal exercise that produces well-understood systems. Society must accept this whilst continuing to exploit the many undoubted benefits of IT systems. But acceptance together with a full and measured exploitation must rest on an equally full acknowledgement of the weaknesses. The knowledge of inherent frailty and limitations is needed to replace the current mystery and consequent over-exuberance that all too often is the mindset behind the leap to acquire, or impose, a new IT system.

Large IT systems will always fail to some extent – i.e., they will contain errors and they will not always deliver the desired behaviours – but they need not fail to the extent that we commonly witness. An aim of this book has been to provide sufficient technological detail to show why this is so. IT-system failure need not be total, and can be reduced in frequency right across the board from life-threatening failures to life-style aggravations. A second goal has been to provide pointers to the changes necessary to minimize failure: from the recruitment and management of programmers, through best-practice system design and development, to opportunities for novel technologies.

It is a change in human attitudes to IT systems, rather than technological changes, that holds most promise for reducing IT-system failure. Better awareness through education (as it so often is) is the key to progress: awareness of the scope and limitations of the technology for those who commission IT systems; a similar awareness but with a more knowledge of technological detail for those who manage and control the design and the development of the commissioned systems; awareness of the seductive allure of the technological details and the potentially detrimental consequences for global system integrity and long-term system usage for those who write the program code; and awareness of potential IT-system weaknesses for those who will make use of the IT-system behaviours.

From this long argument some short slogans might be extracted:

IT-system behaviour is an emergent phenomenon.
A variety of characteristics conspire to produce inevitable unmanageability.
Small-scale examples are a poor guide to large-scale consequences.
IT-system technology is well-defined in principle, but ill-defined in practice.
From development to maintenance IT system personnel are grappling with incipient chaos.
The technicians are seduced by the detailed challenge of the technology.
The scientists are seduced by the promises of their technology.
The managers and users are seduced by the mysteries of the technology.
No IT system is fully understood, so surprising behaviours will always emerge.

In summary, IT systems will always fail, but remember: difficulties with the technology and the immediate management of workers at the code face are just one (important) part of the reason why IT system commissioning, development and operational use are all so problematic; this is, however, the only part that this book addresses.

Endnotes

1. "Why Are Complex IT Projects Different?" a summary of the BCS Thought Leadership Debate, 16 March, 2005, www.bcs.org (accessed 09/03/2009).
2. Stated in the BBC's News item, "Offender IT failure 'avoidable'" see news.bbc.co.uk (accessed 13/03/2009).
3. In his book *The Invisible Computer* (MIT Press, 1998), Donald Norman, a psychologist, focuses on reducing the unnecessary complexity of personal computers for the average human user. Although it is not his major concern, Norman is only too aware of the complexities of large-scale programming. He notes: "The wonder is that large software programs get written at all." (p. 94) For Norman the (possibly tongue in cheek) solution to large IT is: "Simply say no." (p. 95).
4. Fred Brooks' essay entitled "No silver bullet" was originally published in the proceedings of an academic conference in 1986, but was reprinted (with a wealth of his replies to supposed ripostes) as part of the additional material in the 1995 re-publication of his classic, *The Mythical Man-Month* (Addison-Wesley). He divides the problem of IT-system development into "essential tasks" – the mental crafting of the conceptual construct – and "accidental tasks" – representing the conceptual design in programming-language instructions. He views many suggested fixes as improving his accidental tasks, but for major improvements, he says, we must address the essential ones, and he still didn't see that happening in 1995. There is absolutely no reason to think that he would be any more positive one decade into the new millennium.

    I would claim that a major element of the excessive complexity of programs is the tight couplings that stretch right across the system. Thus, detailed programming-language level decisions can have repercussions in the conceptual design, and vice versa. To my way of thinking, Brooks' division is far from clear-cut or clean (and to be fair, he does admit some interaction). Remember Dijkstra's "radical novelties" of computer technology, in particular, his "radical novelty 1: the excessive span of the technology" (Chapter 15) which is, to some significant extent, a denial of Brooks' separation of concerns.
5. Harlan D. Mills, "Top-down programming in large systems", in *Debugging Techniques in Large Systems*, edited by R. Rustin (Prentice-Hall, 1971) is the book chapter quoted with approval and reiterated by Brooks in his 1995 update to his *Mythical Man-Month* (Addison-Wesley, originally 1975).
6. Aaron Sloman's case for this is in his article *The iSoft Affair* at www.cs.bham.ac.uk.
7. In December 2009, the UK Chancellor, Alistair Darling, announced that this (suddenly) "non-essential project," which had by then eaten up some £4bn of taxpayers' money, was not going ahead – a big saving for Government and a way out of a big IT mess (two birds with but one stone?).
8. Rapid prototyping – essentially mocking-up the basic input-output behaviour of the proposed system in order to get user feedback before more irreversible commitments to internal mechanisms are made – is also one of the main strategies advocated by Brooks (see note 4).
9. In the closing decades of the last millennium a movement known as "defensive programming" gained considerable momentum. Much of our earlier discussion of *well-structured* programs and *programming style* are elements of a defensive programming philosophy. Extensive and

explicit guidelines for defensive programming were developed to provide principles for the IT-system developer, and particularly the programmer, to apply and so produce less buggy and more comprehensible programs. The strictures developed are effective but to realize their benefits the technicians need to work with discipline (a related movement was called "disciplined programming"), and they also have to have been educated in the use of this programming strategy – neither requirement is typically found in the whiz-kid programmer.

Glossary

(Italicised words in the Glossary explanations indicate that these words are also Glossary items.)

access control
: refers to the principles and procedures in place to allow only legitimate access to an IT system, and to allow only legitimate operations for each type of approved user (see *read-only access, change access, first-entry access, copy-out access, read-write access, passwords* and *biometric keys*).

activated unit
: is a component of a *neural network*, a *unit*, that has accumulated a total *activity value*, from its incoming *links*, greater than some preset value called a threshold (an example of an *IT-system parameter*); *units* whose total *activity value* falls below this threshold remain unactivated.

activity values
: is the name given to the numerical values that are computed and passed along *links*, from *unit* to *unit*, in a *neural network*.

adaptive hill climbing
: is a technique for automated improvement of one aspect of the behaviour of a computational system: changes (by a variety of means from random to manually directed) are introduced and the new system is reassessed to see if it is has improved (with respect to the chosen behaviour). If an improvement has occurred this version is kept and further changes are explored (the system has taken a step up the hill towards optimal performance); if its behaviour is worse then the latest changes are reversed and new ones are tried (see also *genetic algorithms*).

agent
: in an IT system is a module of *code*, usually designated autonomous and sometimes even 'intelligent', that makes a more or less independent contribution to the operation of the

	total IT system which would normally contain a variety of these agent modules interacting with each other – often classic *hopeware*.
analogue	used to describe systems in which the features of interest and/or their interactions are best represented as continuous and generally *monotonic* (see *discrete*); for example, the distance travelled by a thrown spear and time.
artificial intelligence (AI)	one of the names given to the efforts to construct 'intelligent' *IT systems*; for the purposes of this book, we need to beware of proposed 'solutions' to the *IT-system crisis* that begin to trespass on this domain of *hopeware*.
behavioural correctness	the degree to which an IT system's behaviour is exactly as *specified*, or sought by the system designers, or desired by users (these three behavioural expectations should be identical, but never are).
biometric keys	are unique personal features, such as fingerprints, that are used to give access to IT systems (see also *passwords*).
branch condition	a statement about the values in *storage boxes* that is either true or false, e.g., X=3; it determines which of the two *flow paths* at a *branch point* in the *flow structure* the computer will take when it is *executing* the program.
branch point	a point in program *flow structure* where a *flow path* splits into two, alternative paths (see *branch condition*).
bug	an error in a program/IT system (see *debugging*).
change access	refers to *access control* that gives an IT-system user the power to change the system, change instructions and/or data (usually combined with *read-access* and called *read-write access*).
code	a synonym for 'programming language instructions' which derives from the days when these instructions were largely viewed as alpha-numerical codes.
COMMENT	a programming instruction that is ignored by the computer and is used purely to facilitate *program understanding* by humans in-program *documentation*.
compulsive programmer	see HHS.
computer	is a machine composed of a *processor* and *storage boxes* (its *memory*).

computer program	see *program*.
copy-out access	gives a user the ability to copy portions of a *database* (see *access control*)
data	the values placed in *storage boxes*.
database	an *IT system*, or the part of an *IT system*, that is primarily *data*.
dead code	refers to segments of an *IT system* (i.e. blocks of *program instructions*) that are <u>believed</u> to play no possible part in the emergent behaviour of the system.
debugging	a euphemism for the process of identifying and eliminating *IT-system* errors, usually failures of *behavioural correctness*.
decision-logic tree	the essential discrete nature of IT systems.
digital	used to describe systems primarily represented by digits, i.e., the numbers 0 through 9. Most commonly misused in the description 'digital computer' because it is common practice to represent the two states of the machine with the digits 0 and 1 (see *discrete*).
discrete	used to describe systems primarily composed of separate components which may be digits (hence *digital* systems) and tend to interact erratically (compare *analogue*); IT systems are typically discrete systems.
distributed computation	such as a *neural network* exhibits refers to the fact that all elements of the IT system (e.g., all *units* in a *neural network*) are *executed* in every computation; there is no single *flow path* of *execution* in which some *program instructions* are executed and others are not in each particular computation (as with a conventional *program*).
documentation	of an *IT system* is the charts, text and diagrams that 'explain' the structure of the *IT system*, and how it was designed and implemented to compute the *specified* behaviours (see also **COMMENT** instruction).
editor	is a software editor is a *program* that facilitates the development and *maintenance* of an *IT system*; it is an example of a *software tool*, and a component of a *software support environment*.
emergent behaviour	is all *IT-system* behaviour. Emergence is a much (and variously) used, but seldom clearly defined, term. The usual implication is of a

mysterious, or at least unfathomable, interaction of system components giving rise to the 'emergent' behaviour. IT-system behaviour is completely and precisely defined, but effectively unfathomable in its entirety.

encapsulation
is a principle of program *well-structured*ness in which *IT-system* operations and *storage boxes* are limited to a particular program module (see *modularisation* and *scope*).

execution of program instructions
is the process of the computer's *processor* doing what a program instruction dictates. A program is only *executed* after it is *grammatically correct*.

expert system
is an *IT system* whose goal is to replicate some aspect of human expertise, and usually based on the philosophy of *expert-system technology*.

expert-system technology (EST)
is a computing strategy traditionally based on a *knowledge base* of *rules* and *facts* coupled with an *inference engine* to generate new information from the *knowledge base* in combination with user inputs; a bubble of *AI* expectation (roughly 1970s and '80s) that (mistakenly) predicted that many domains of human expertise could be cheaply reproduced once that expertise was captured as a *knowledge base*.

facts in a knowledge base
are simple statements of truth (either specific to a computation, such as: the patient's temperature is 99.5°F, or general to the domain, such as normal temperature is 98.4°F) that are used by the *inference engine* for its 'reasoning' activity.

first-entry access
gives an IT-system user the ability to enter new *data*, but one time only (i.e., no re-entry to make changes) (see *access control*)

flow path
is the route through a *program* (or a *program*'s *flow structure*) taken by a *processor* when *executing program instructions*.

flow structure
is the complete set of possible *flow paths* defined by a *program* (it is *branch points* in the program that provide alternative *flow paths* through the *flow structure*).

genetic algorithm
is the name given to the wide range of computational methods that endeavour to automatically improve some aspect of IT-system behaviour by maintaining a set, or 'population', of alternative

versions that compete against each other; the best are kept and 'mutated' (more or less random changes are introduced to the fundamental 'chromosomal', i.e., bit-string, representation of each version) and the new population compete among themselves again. It is a class of *adaptive hill climbing*.

grammatical correctness

if each *program instruction* is written out precisely as it is defined then the program is grammatically correct. Programs are first checked by the computer for *grammatical correctness* before they are *executed*.

grounding

is the interpretation of symbol structures in terms of real-world phenomena. In particular, a program as a symbol structure must be grounded in terms of an actual computer, and then the resultant *IT system* must be grounded with respect to its application in the world.

Happy-Hacker
  Syndrome (HHS)

is a generally irresistible tendency to focus down on program detail to the detriment of overall IT-system structure and behaviour (aka compulsive programming).

hopeware

are proposed programs (and even initial small demonstration systems) that appear to exhibit (some aspect of) human reasoning capabilities, and thus promise a major breakthrough 'soon'; for us, almost a synonym for *artificial intelligence*.

indentation

is an element of *programming style* that facilitates *program understanding* by, for example, indenting to the same degree all instructions of a program module (see *modularisation*).

inference engine

is the overly grand name given to that component of an *expert system* which 'infers' the computed results (e.g. diagnoses if a diagnostic medical system) using the system inputs and a *knowledge base*.

IT system

is a (usually) large *computer program* (but see also *database*).

IT-system access

is the strategy for controlling who has what rights to an IT system – to inspect or alter *code* or system *data* (see *access control*).

IT-system crisis

is due to our inability to know whether and to what extent any IT system will fail (see *IT-system failure*). A new name for the long-acknowledged *software crisis*, but a renaming that carries the further implications of the expanded ambitions (and consequent extension of problems) of the modern generation of IT systems.

IT-system failure | is IT-system behaviour that is not in accord with the *specification*, or the developer's/designer's intentions, or the user's (valid) expectations; an absence of *behavioural correctness*.

kludge | is the name given to messy (i.e., unsystematic), and hence likely to be impenetrable, fixes to *IT-system* problems such as *bugs* or a need to extend the system behaviour; the worst approach to *IT-system maintenance*.

knowledge base | is a combination of *rules* and *facts* that explicitly capture some specialist domain of human knowledge, e.g. diagnosis of bacterial meningitis.

legacy system/software | is a long-used IT system that has become effectively a black-box system; it works well enough including behavioural problems that are well-known and worked around.

life-cycle of IT systems | the series of stages that an IT system goes through; the one we used was SPECIFY-DESIGN-PROGRAM-TEST-USE-FIX-FIX-FIX... which in reality is seldom a life-cycle for large IT systems because they are never killed off.

links in neural networks | are explicit connections from one *unit* to another usually associated with a *weight* value; neural networks compute by transferring *activity* values via these links from one unit to another.

machine learning (ML) | encompasses a wide variety of techniques aimed at producing 'better' IT systems automatically, *neural network training* and *adaptive hill climbing* are two examples – the former based on feedback error correction and the latter more open ended. Despite decades of intense research our automatic techniques do not come close to the power of human learning.

main program | refers to that part of the program that has overall control, the core of the computation as opposed to *subprograms* to which it transfers *execution*.

maintenance of IT systems | one of the great euphemisms:
"A program can work properly a thousand times and suddenly fail the next time. It might

thereby give the appearance of having worn out, but what really happened is that an unusual set of circumstances was encountered for the first time. A program doesn't fail because you wear it out; it fails because it didn't work properly to begin with and you finally have occasion to notice that fact."[1]

Maintenance of IT systems is primarily residual error removal (*debugging*), but also includes changing or extending system behaviours to meet new needs.

memory
in a computer is the set of *storage boxes* available to hold computed and preset (see *parameters*) values during a computation.

modularisation
a programming strategy for minimising complexity by breaking programs into a sequence of maximally independent, self-contained segments of program instructions, the modules. (see also *subprogram modularisation* and *well-structured programs*)

monotonic
is the technical term we use to describe the most predictable analogue relationships between system properties; changes in one direction of one property cause continually increasing, or decreasing, changes in the related property.

network computing (NC)/ programming
is a strategy for computation based on many primitive processing *units* passing *weighted* values (*activity* values) through connecting *links* usually with significant parallelism involved; aka neural computing (see *neural networks*).

neural networks
are the structures that are (usually) *trained* to compute certain behaviours in *network computing*; structures so (mis)named because of very superficial resemblances to real neural networks: a large number of simple(?) processing units interconnected by links and functioning with a lot of parallelism.

parameters
are pre-set and fixed *storage-box* values that an IT system uses during its computations.

---

[1] A quotation dated 1985 on page 199 of David Lubar's compendium: *It's Not a Bug; It's a Feature* (Addison-Wesley, 1995).

passwords	are the most common type of 'keys' used to give individuals access to (parts of) IT systems (see also *biometric keys* and *access control*).
precise approximation computation (PAC)	is a strategy for computing with continua rather than a discrete technology; the examples use statistics and probability rather than the traditional logic.
processor	is one of the two (the other is *storage boxes*) fundamental components of a computer. The *processor* performs the actions dictated by each *program instruction*.
program	a *computer program* is a sequence of *program instructions*.
program instruction	is an command from within the set that constitute the chosen *programming language*. It dictates actions that the *processor* will *execute* (but see exception, *COMMENT*).
program layout	techniques of *indentation* and use of blank lines that are intended to make program structure explicit (see *well-structured programs*).
program proof	a demonstration that a program as a symbol structure (i.e., not a *program* actually installed on a real *computer*) will always transform a general class of inputs to a general class of outputs; e.g. that an 'adding' program will always transform any two integers into the sum of these input integers.
program understanding	is a detailed appreciation, and hence explanation, of how the program causes each and every IT-system behaviour; a full and complete *program understanding* is an unachievable goal.
programming language	is a set of different sorts of *program instructions* (e.g. PUT 'a value' INTO 'a storage box', such as PUT 3 INTO X) each of which dictates an action that a *processor* can *execute*. It defines the structure of each *program instruction,* and hence *grammatical correctness*.
programming style	refers to the *program-layout* conventions (such as *indentation*) and use of *COMMENT* instructions whose aim is to make program structure (such as *modularisation*) explicitly visible; it is ignored by the computer.

proof
a logically sound argument that a given symbol structure can be deduced from a set of initial assumptions (see *program proof*).

read-only access
is a restriction on user access to an IT system that allows the inspection of a system but blocks any attempt to make changes to the system (see also *read-write access*).

read-write access
a user that has this access to an IT system (usually determined by a *password* or *biometric key*) is allowed to both inspect and change the system (a variety of change permissions may be in force, i.e., restrictions on exactly what the user can change and what he/she cannot change).

recursive programming
is a style of programming in which elements of system behaviour are constructed in terms of (simpler) versions of themselves: e.g., the length of a shopping list is computed as (1+the length of the list without its first item). NB a hooptedoodle concept only!

rules in a knowledge base
are usually based on simple IF … THEN … inference rules of logic.

scope localisation
is a principle of program *well-structured*ness that limits the use of particular *storage boxes* to as small a segment of the *IT system* as possible (see also *modularisation* and *encapsulation*).

simulated evolution
is the name given to the many varieties of 'learning' technologies that are loosely founded on repeated random changes and selection of the best performing versions, i.e., a crude simulation of the basics of biological evolution (see *genetic algorithms*).

software crisis
is a term used to capture the emergent programming problems and coined as long ago as 1969. The software crisis is the kernel of the current *IT-system crisis*. Over the intervening decades, mitigation due to developments in programming methodology as well as in programming languages has been swamped by the escalation in expectations for what the systems should be able to do.

software tool
is a program that is used to facilitate development, *maintenance* or *understanding* of an *IT system*.

specification	is a complete, precise and unambiguous statement of what an *IT system* should do (an unachievable ideal).
squashed sum	is a fundamental processing element of each *unit* in many neural networks: a numerical value input is reduced to a value between zero and one, the larger the original value the closer to one will be the 'squashed' result, and the smaller it is the closer to zero will be the result.
storage box	is one of the two (the other is the *processor*) fundamental components of a computer. Storage boxes (also called just "boxes") are given names by the programmer and values (numeric or character strings, such as "eggs") are stored in them for possible subsequent use in the computation (see *data*). The set of these boxes constitutes the computer's *memory*.
subprogram	is a single module of programming-language instructions that typically 'replaces' repetitions of this set of instructions within the *IT system*.
subprogram modularisation	reduces overall program size but necessitates an explicit transfer of control to and back from the *subprogram* wherever the original repetitive instruction sets occurred; it thus increases *flow-structure* complexity.
testing	refers to execution of an *IT system* with specific input data to check for *behavioural correctness*.
training of networks	is a process of feedback error correction on a set of sample inputs (whose correct outputs must be known--- called the training set) to automatically modify an initial (partially randomised) network so that it learns to compute the set of behaviours from which the training set was drawn.
understanding	of an IT system is the central problem; an (unavoidable) lack of complete *program understanding* is the basis for the *IT-system crisis*.
units in a neural network	are the fundamental processing elements of neural networks; simple processing (typically summing input values and outputting the *squashed sum*).
verification	is the process of *proving* a program *correct*.

weights of links

are real-valued numbers associated with every *link* in a *neural network*; the *squashed* output value, generated by each unit is (usually) multiplied by the associated weight as it is passed along each link to the connected *units*. It is these weights that are modified in network *training*.

well-structured programs

are programs that exhibit best practice in programming, such as *modularisation*, and in *program layout*, such as *indentation* to make the *modularisation* perceptually obvious. Thus, it is a combination of minimal complexity programming coupled with a presentation (e.g. indented layout and COMMENTs) that facilitates human comprehension of the programming strategies used (see *programming style*).

Index

The Seductive Computer